ROMANTICISM AND MUSIC CULTURE IN BRITAIN, 1770–1840

Music was central to everyday life and expression in late Georgian Britain, and this is the first interdisciplinary study of its impact on Romantic literature. Focussing on the public fascination with virtuoso performance, Gillen D'Arcy Wood documents a struggle between sober "literary" virtue and luxurious, effeminate virtuosity that staged deep anxieties over class, cosmopolitanism, machine technology, and the professionalization of culture. A remarkable synthesis of cultural history and literary criticism, this book opens new perspectives on key Romantic authors – including Burney, Wordsworth, Austen, and Byron – and their relationship to definitive debates of the Georgian age.

GILLEN D'ARCY WOOD is Professor of English at the University of Illinois, Urbana-Champaign.

CAMBRIDGE STUDIES IN ROMANTICISM

Founding Editor
Professor Marilyn Butler, *University of Oxford*

General Editor
Professor James Chandler, *University of Chicago*

Editorial Board
John Barrell, *University of York*
Paul Hamilton, *University of London*
Mary Jacobus, *University of Cambridge*
Claudia Johnson, *Princeton University*
Alan Liu, *University of California, Santa Barbara*
Jerome McGann, *University of Virginia*
Susan Manning, *University of Edinburgh*
David Simpson, *University of California, Davis*

This series aims to foster the best new work in one of the most challenging fields within English literary studies. From the early 1780s to the early 1830s, a formidable array of talented men and women took to literary composition, not just in poetry, which some of them famously transformed, but in many modes of writing. The expansion of publishing created new opportunities for writers, and the political stakes of what they wrote were raised again by what Wordsworth called those "great national events" that were "almost daily taking place": the French Revolution, the Napoleonic and American wars, urbanization, industrialization, religious revival, an expanded empire abroad, and the reform movement at home. This was an enormous ambition, even when it pretended otherwise. The relations between science, philosophy, religion, and literature were reworked in texts such as *Frankenstein* and *Biographia Literaria*; gender relations in *A Vindication of the Rights of Woman* and *Don Juan*; journalism by Cobbett and Hazlitt; poetic form, content, and style by the Lakes School and the Cockney School. Outside Shakespeare studies, probably no body of writing has produced such a wealth of comment or done so much to shape the responses of modern criticism. This indeed is the period that saw the emergence of those notions of "literature" and of literary history, especially national literary history, on which modern scholarship in English has been founded.

The categories produced by Romanticism have also been challenged by recent historicist arguments. The task of the series is to engage both with a challenging corpus of Romantic writings and with the changing field of criticism they have helped to shape. As with other literary series published by Cambridge, this one will represent the work of both younger and more established scholars, on either side of the Atlantic and elsewhere.

For a complete list of titles published, see end of book.

ROMANTICISM AND MUSIC CULTURE IN BRITAIN, 1770–1840

Virtue and Virtuosity

GILLEN D'ARCY WOOD

CAMBRIDGE UNIVERSITY PRESS
Cambridge, New York, Melbourne, Madrid, Cape Town, Singapore,
São Paulo, Delhi, Dubai, Tokyo

Cambridge University Press
The Edinburgh Building, Cambridge CB2 8RU, UK

Published in the United States of America by Cambridge University Press, New York

www.cambridge.org
Information on this title: www.cambridge.org/9780521117333

© Gillen D'Arcy Wood 2010

This publication is in copyright. Subject to statutory exception
and to the provisions of relevant collective licensing agreements,
no reproduction of any part may take place without
the written permission of Cambridge University Press.

First published 2010

Printed in the United Kingdom at the University Press, Cambridge

A catalogue record for this publication is available from the British Library

Library of Congress Cataloging-in-Publication Data
Wood, Gillen D'Arcy.
Romanticism and music culture in Britain, 1770–1840 : virtue and virtuosity / Gillen D'Arcy Wood.
p.   cm. – (Cambridge studies in romanticism)
Includes bibliographical references (p. 222) and index.
ISBN 978-0-521-11733-3 (hardback)
1. Music and literature–Great Britain–History–18th century. 2. Music and literature–Great Britain–History–19th century. 3. Romanticism–Great Britain–History–18th century.
4. Romanticism–Great Britain–History–19th century. I. Title. II. Series.
ML79.W66 2010
780′.082–dc22
                                                                                            2009047744

ISBN 978-0-521-11733-3 Hardback

Cambridge University Press has no responsibility for the persistence or
accuracy of URLs for external or third-party internet websites referred to
in this publication, and does not guarantee that any content on such
websites is, or will remain, accurate or appropriate.

For Nancy, Lucas, and Clara

Contents

Preface	*page* ix
List of illustrations	xi
Introduction: virtuosophobia	1
1 Seward's Handelomania	20
2 The Burney baroque	53
3 Wordsworth castrato	88
4 Cockney Mozart	118
5 Austen's accomplishment	151
6 The Byron of the piano	180
Coda: the mechanical nightingale	215
Select bibliography	222
Notes	233
Index	283

Preface

This is, in many ways, a personal book. Its official brief is to unite the fields of literary Romanticism and musicology, but it also, in its more ineffable margins, answers questions raised by my own experiences in literature and music. In music school in Melbourne in the late 1980s, I labored long days upon digital exercises for the piano, while at the weekly concert I joined in laughing scorn for a fellow pianist who displayed all the technical proficiency I so conspicuously lacked. He employed his technical facility to shallow ends, we all agreed, arpeggiating mindlessly up and down the keyboard. Only much later was I struck by the contradictions in my own relationship to the piano, and moved to investigate the easy consensus that designated the class virtuoso an object of ridicule.

Having belatedly recognized that my deficiencies as a musician were not "merely" technical in nature, I came to the United States in the early 1990s to embark on a graduate program in English. Here I was struck again by the singularities of music culture, this time in comparison with my new literary-scholarly community (or its lack). While in my experience as a musician it was accepted that egotism be put aside for the common purpose of making music, I found no such sociable imperative enlivening graduate studies in literature, which seemed demoralizingly competitive and isolating by comparison. I thus began this study with the object of better understanding, through history, the seemingly insuperable differences separating the cultures of literature and music. As bookwriting happily tends to do, however, it soon forced me to confront the imperfect assumptions of my own premise, and so I made the book about those instead. The result is a kind of sequel or companion volume to my earlier study, *The Shock of the Real: Romanticism and Visual Culture, 1760–1860* (2001). Taken together, the books represent my long-term scholarly interest in the metropolitan culture of Romantic-era Britain – in particular the sometimes rough crossings between Romantic literary aesthetics, Georgian cultural politics, and the rapid commercial expansion of visual and performance media that we associate with industrial modernity.

The sociable structures of literary-academic culture are certainly evident in the generous support of institutions and individuals I have enjoyed while writing this book. Fellowships from the Mellon Foundation and the Illinois Program for Research in the Humanities provided invaluable time for research as well as, in the latter case, a highly productive seminar in which to present work-in-progress. The wonderful libraries at the University of Illinois have been indispensable, and I wish to thank the staff of the Music Library, John Wagstaff and Marlys Scarborough in particular, for their helpfulness and patience. My self-education in musicology owes much to them. Among the broader world of Romantic studies and musicology, I am grateful to Kevin Hart, Peter de Bolla, Christina Bashford, Simon McVeigh, and Tom Mole for their invitations to present my ongoing research. I am indebted likewise to those colleagues who offered their time and expertise to comment upon various portions of the manuscript – Jack Stillinger, Clara Tuite, Marshall Brown, Jed Esty, and Ted Underwood – to Teresa Barnard for so generously sharing her unpublished book manuscript, and to the editors of *Modern Language Quarterly, Studies in Romanticism, English Literary History*, and *The Blackwell Companion to Jane Austen* (2009), all of whom published early versions of various chapters and have graciously consented to their appearance in revised form here.

During my year in Australia, Melissa Bailes was a conscientious and utterly dependable research liaison at Illinois. At the University of Melbourne I enjoyed the support of the School of Culture and Communication (latterly the English Department) to whom my sincere thanks are likewise due. And no mention of Australia must pass without loving mention of my musical family who, in the distant past, first sat me down at our storied Bösendorfer piano, and introduced me to the grand and life-affirming mythologies of music. Through all these peregrinations – intellectual and geographical – my wife, Nancy Castro, and our children Lucas and Clara have been my beloved daily companions. Bookwriting is proverbially tough on families; this one has been no exception, and my debts of unsociability are greatest to them.

Illustrations

1. Edward Francesco Burney, *The Handel Commemoration, 1784*. View of the orchestra. Westminster Abbey. — *page* 21
2. Thomas Gainsborough, *Johann Christian Fischer* (*c.* 1780). The Royal Collection © HM Queen Elizabeth II. — 54
3. Charles Loraine Smith, *A Sunday Concert* (1782). National Portrait Gallery, London. — 61
4. Jacopo Amigoni (1682–1752), *The Singer Farinelli and Friends* (*c.* 1750–2). Oil on canvas. National Gallery of Victoria, Melbourne, Australia. Felton Bequest. — 89
5. Biagio Rebecca, *The Opera House: The Auditorium* (*c.* 1792). The Royal Collection © HM Queen Elizabeth II. — 134
6. John Smart, *Misses Elizabeth and Harriet Binney* (*c.* 1806). Victoria and Albert Museum, London. — 154
7. Josef Danhauser, *Franz Liszt am Flügel* (1840). Nationalgalerie, Staatliche Museen zu Berlin, Germany/Art Resource, NY. — 188

Introduction: virtuosophobia

I

The heroine's introduction to the sights of London in Frances Burney's *Evelina* (1778) includes a visit to Cox's Museum, an exhibition of mechanical wonders staged by James Cox at the Great Room in Spring Gardens in the early 1770s. Burney herself visited the exhibition. She joined thousands of Londoners in marveling at sumptuously gilded musical cabinets and clocks with elaborate chiming mechanisms, including one hidden within "a Griffin seated upon a rock, supporting a Vase ... the pedestal itself being supported by four beautiful Palm Trees." Three times a day, the musical automata sprang into brilliant sound, a mechanical gala concert that featured a "magnificent Asiatic temple ... out of the dome of which gradually rises a Pagoda to the musick of its chimes."[1] The *coup de grâce* of Cox's show was "a pineapple, which, suddenly opening discovered a nest of birds, who immediately began to sing."[2]

The musical pineapple captures the attention of the party in *Evelina*, whose debate on Cox's dazzling automata rehearses a popular eighteenth-century aesthetic discourse: the critique of virtuosity. The vulgar Madame Duval has seen nothing "eleganter," while xenophobic Captain Mirvan derides it as "all *kickshaw* work," and demands to know the "use" of such vanities. Ornamental musical machines were the height of fashion at the time of *Evelina*. Their repertory "combined pretty *galanteries* with ... fast passage-work and elaborate ornamentation that took advantage of the machine's capacity for unlimited virtuosity."[3] Evelina herself finds the exhibition "astonishing" but dismisses it in the same breath as "mere show," a virtuosophobic formulation we will meet with continually throughout this book (77). For the Georgians, virtuosity was a Janus-faced bogey: it produced both anxiety over luxury, historically associated with the aristocracy, and a style of future shock encounter with technological modernity. The established Georgian opposition between luxury and utility thus blends, in the Cox's

Museum episode, with a distinctly modern debate over the union of music with the engineering wonders of the machine. The scene concludes with a performance of a Handel Coronation Anthem played (in fact) by a mechanical band of kettle-drums, trumpets, and organ. The music lovers among Cox's clientele who remembered the exhibition space as a concert hall in the 1760s – for performances by the composer J. C. Bach and the Viennese prodigy Mozart – would have been delighted, or perhaps disquieted, at the ironies of Cox's mechanical concert. But certainly not surprised. The musical history of the Great Room shows an interpenetration of urban-commercial and "high culture" elements rivaled only by the Georgian book trade.

Burney grew up in a family of professional musicians, and the heroine of her novel *The Wanderer* (1814) is a "virtuosa," a modern usage, signifying technical proficiency on a musical instrument, which appears distant from its early modern English definition as a gentleman collector of curios.[4] In the fifteenth century "virtuoso," derived from the Latin *virtus* (virtue), connoted manliness, but by the mid-1600s the opposite signification, effeminacy, had come into use, allowing Henry Stubbe, in a lament for cultural decline that would become a standard of Georgian commentary, to originate the wordplay revived by my book's title: "We are regenerated from the School of Aristotle to that of Epicurus, from all Moral Gallantry and Virtue, to a most impertinent and effeminate virtuosity."[5] As late as 1751 Samuel Johnson continued to define the virtuoso as an amateur devoted to "subjects of study remotely allied to useful knowledge," a gentle summary of a century's worth of attacks on virtuosity as a "useless" and potentially dangerous amusement of the leisured aristocratic class.[6] In Thomas Shadwell's comedy *The Virtuoso* (1676), Sir Nicholas Gimcrack enrages the local peasants with an invention they believe will supplant their labor. His defense is characteristic: "We virtuosos never find out anything of use, 'tis not our way."[7] The statement echoes the doyen of virtuosi, Sir John Evelyn of the Royal Society, who distinguished between "use" for which God had provided and "Curiosity, which is Endless."[8] By the early eighteenth century, however, proto-professional elements within the Royal Society committed to new "scientific" values were exerting increasing pressure on the amateur virtuoso ethos.[9] The consummation of the virtuoso's career, according to the Earl of Shaftesbury, was no more than a useless "cabinet of curiosities," his description of which reads like a negative review of Cox's Museum: "he has erected a Cabinet in due form, and made it the real Pattern of his Mind, replete with the same Trash and Trumpery of correspondent empty notions, and chimerical Conceits."[10]

Textual evidence strongly suggests that Burney studied Cox's *Descriptive Catalogue*, which commends the exhibits as "*usefull* and *philosophical* enough to defend them from the reproach of being only glittering gewgaws" – exactly the debate Burney stages in *Evelina*. Cox points to the very useful business to be made in selling luxury clocks and mechanical toys to China, a voracious market for expensive "Jem cracks," as the skeptical Captain Mirvan terms them. The volume of this eighteenth-century luxury trade, dominated by Britain, amounted to tens of thousands of items.[11] Cox's collection at the Great Room alone was valued at almost £200,000 and "brought half a million [pounds] into the kingdom, [and] for years they furnished employment to hundreds." The Chinese emperor Ch'ien Lung alone owned four thousand mostly English clocks and other bejewelled curiosities for display in his palace. The change of venue for Cox's automata – from emperor's palace to urban showspace – exhibits in miniature the expansion of the luxury goods trade in the eighteenth century from royal courts to the bourgeois marketplace. According to this historical trajectory, Cox's Museum represents a modern, commercialized form of the aristocratic pleasures of collecting, a symbolic transition of virtuosity "from 'natural philosophy' ... to the Industrial Revolution," and from private cabinet to public musical spectacle.[12] In terms of cultural consumption, Cox's exhibit, like the word "virtuoso" itself, tracks the shift in eighteenth-century cultural leadership in Britain from elite circles of connoisseurs, such as the Royal Society, to an urban, commercial market patronized by a mixed metropolitan gentry.

In the same terms as the critique of Cox's automata in *Evelina*, the performance of virtuoso musicians was compulsively attacked through the Georgian period as the "mere show" of technical accomplishment without deeper meaning, the exhibition of an automated body detached from the heart and sensibility. It remains a standard trope of music criticism more than two centuries later when "some critics seem unable to utter the word virtuosity without the appendages 'empty' or 'meretricious.'"[13] The connection between the virtuosity of Cox's Museum and the modern meaning of superlative instrumental technique lies in the substance of Shaftesbury's critique of virtuosic "emptiness." In eighteenth-century London the crazy, useless machines of Sir Nicholas Gimcrack and the luxury wonders of James Cox took human shape. Musicians such as Charles Burney had long struggled against the social stigma of music's association with the artisanal trades, and the relegation of its "professors" to a glorified servant class. With the advent of bravura Italian singing in Britain and its adaptation to the violin and piano, however, public music culture and the wonders of virtuosic musicianship gained greater visibility, while raising, for its critics, the specter of a mechanized humanity driven by (merely) technical accomplishment.

Subsequently, in the early nineteenth century, the improved technologies of piano manufacture in particular seemed to amplify the sonic power of the virtuosic medium beyond natural limits. "The ten fingers of a single man," exulted Franz Liszt, "are sufficient to render the harmonies produced by the combined forces of more than one hundred instruments of the orchestra."[14] The virtuosic feats of these visiting musical celebrities – from Farinelli in the 1730s to Liszt in 1840 – impressed English audiences as a wonder of superhuman discipline but were devoid, it was feared, of any greater aesthetic or moral value, especially if imported to the domestic sphere and opened to women. In Burney's *The Wanderer*, the hero Harleigh's doubts about the gentility of the mysterious heroine are removed by the spectacle of her virtuosity on the piano and harp, but her attempts to commercialize her accomplishments are disastrous. The Georgian critique of virtuosity dwelt on this paradox of luxury and labor, on what the conservative music historian Sir John Hawkins called "the languid effects of misapplied industry."[15] In the emergent industrial and professionalized order of Romantic-era Britain, the virtuoso represented the lure and threat of gratuitous, non-productive labor, a dangerous residue of aristocratic uselessness.

Evelina finds "little pleasure" in Cox's exhibit, but it is important enough to Burney's novel for the question of its "use" value to be revived later, when the hero Lord Orville summarizes the Georgian anti-virtuosic critique:

"The mechanism," answered he, "is wonderfully ingenious: I am sorry it is not turned to better account; but its purport is so frivolous, so very remote from all aim at instruction or utility, that the sight of so fine a shew, only leaves a regret on the mind, that so much work, and so much ingenuity, should not be better bestowed." (111)

Lord Orville's judgment, which Burney grants the honor of the last word, is reminiscent of contemporary critiques of the novel. The critic John Moore remembered the 1780s as a time when "the very words Romance or Novel conveyed the idea of a frivolous or pernicious book."[16] Burney was clearly mindful of the charge. After the publication of *Cecilia* (1796) – at a time when the status of the novel "was at its nadir" – she took care to record in a letter to her sister Mary Delaney's remark that "No Book ... ever was so *useful* as this."[17] In her preface to *The Wanderer* almost two decades later, Burney still felt anxious to defend her fiction on the question of "utility":

> Divest, for a moment, the title of Novel from its stationary standard of insignificance, and say! What is the species of writing that offers fairer opportunities for conveying useful precepts? ... And is not a Novel, permit me, also, to ask, in common with every other literary work, entitled to receive its stamp as useful, mischievous, or nugatory, from its execution? Not necessarily, and in its changeless state, to be branded as a mere vehicle for frivolous, or seductive amusement ... [as] mere entertainment?[18]

By the time of *Evelina*, where this study begins, the music business was coming increasingly to resemble literary culture in its middle-class, commercial character, with an explosion in publishing and a network of distribution modeled on the book trade.[19] A fashionable young woman might receive the latest novel with the most current operatic arrangements for piano in the same mail. We are assured, for example, that Burney's Cecilia, though growing up in the country, had "regularly received from London the works of the best masters."[20] Burney's anxieties for her own novel's place within this new bourgeois luxury economy extend beyond the familiar debate over the novel's role as a virtuous repository of "utility and instruction," to the question of whether the production of fiction might itself be a "frivolous or seductive amusement," a performance of mechanical, specialized labor without deeper significance or use. "The *commercial* fashion of writing gains Ground every day," Hester Thrale remarked pointedly to Burney, soon after the young novelist's admittance to her salon at Streatham.[21] Was Burney no more than a machine-like virtuoso of manners, "a Camera Obscura in a Window of Piccadilly," as Thrale once described her?[22] And were her readers no better than the tourists of Covent Garden, "a multitude of listless idlers" – as Thomas Love Peacock would portray the modern literary consumer – "yawning for amusement, and gaping for novelty?"[23]

II

The anxieties implicit in the Cox's Museum episode in Burney's *Evelina* capture the tense history of literary and music culture in Georgian Britain as I shall describe it in this book, a period in British history when "disputes over music were among the most significant episodes of cultural politics."[24] From the mid-eighteenth century the expanded publishing industries of polite music and literature began to flood the same marketplace, sharing forms of distribution and consumption, as well as cultural capital.

This produced, in reaction, a discursive *cordon sanitaire* designed to separate the luxury, effeminacy, empty sociability, and mechanical display associated with music from the nascent values of interiority, sincerity, and sublimity that would define Romantic literary culture. As it does for Burney in *Evelina*, virtuosity served for Romantic writers as a composite bogey embodying both the aristocratic tradition of the amateur against which their own professionalized practices would be drawn, and the forbidding mechanistic potential of that new order of specialization and mass production. English virtuosophobia, which the early nineteenth century inherited from the Georgians, provided a readymade vocabulary for Romantic self-articulation. Expression, sincerity, and the sublime acquired their power as Romantic tropes to a great extent from their opposition to the virtuosic "world" of fashion, performance, and material luxury, all deeply associated with metropolitan music culture. Though never so elegantly theorized as the sublime and beautiful – that binary beloved of literary and art historians – the "musical" opposition between virtue and virtuosity, in its various coded forms, was one of the rhetorical preconditions of British Romanticism and, no less than the aesthetics of the sublime, represents a founding trope of modernity itself.[25]

The virtuoso is a prominent figure in the work of Lawrence Kramer, Richard Leppert, and Dana Gooley among others, and is synonymous with musicology's recent turn toward cultural historicism. This focus, however, as in traditional music history, is concentrated on continental Europe, in particular the talismanic figure of Liszt, whom I follow to England in my final chapter. The purpose of this book is to extend a material history of virtuosity geographically to Britain and rhetorically to readings in the literary and cultural history of the Romantic period. In writing *Romanticism and Music Culture* I have found the relation between late Georgian literary and music culture to be a history of politicized conflicts about art, fashion, commerce, gender, and nation, with the image of the virtuoso as its perpetual irritant. Accordingly, each chapter exemplifies a significant instance of the Romantic critique of virtuosity.

In chapter 1 I read Cowper's attack on the 1784 Handel Commemoration in *The Task* as a repudiation of the sociable model of culture embodied in the public performance of Handel's oratorios. Cowper perceived, in the ritual apotheosis of Handel, the coercive operations of a monarchical-nationalist consensus, of which his literary rival in the 1780s, Anna Seward, was a celebrated "muse." Seward's "musical" poetics in her popular verse novel *Louisa* (1785)[26] advertised just that sociable, virtuosic lyric voice against which Romantic poets such as Cowper and Wordsworth would come to define their own practice. The high Romantic repudiation of musical sociability is likewise the subject of chapter 2, in which I read the shape of Frances Burney's career as an increasingly dogged assertion of Romantic literary "virtues" against her musician father Charles's "toadyism" – his dependent status in the aristocratic, luxury economy of music – and against the virtuosic musical values of the Italian opera he championed. For Burney, her father's aristocratic style and tastes, identified with music culture, threatened to obscure her trademark literary ethos of "natural" gentility – the defining virtue of both her bourgeois heroines and her own social persona – within the leveling domain of metropolitan fashion. Chapter 3 further explores the theme of literary Romanticism's ambivalent relation to virtuoso culture by examining the tropic conjunction of music, poetry, and effeminacy in one of its core texts. For his attack on the "inane phraseology" of fashionable poetry in the Preface to *Lyrical Ballads*, Wordsworth drew upon an anti-virtuosic language with a long pedigree in Georgian cultural commentary. But placing the masculinist virtuosophobia of the famous 1802 Preface alongside Wordsworth's little-known translations of gender-bending opera lyrics for the *Morning Post* that same year exposes, I will argue, the "effeminate," virtuosic strains of the ballads themselves.

Music was the most cosmopolitan of the Georgian arts and relied upon a steady continental traffic both in performers and printed music. The Napoleonic Wars disrupted this trade to a significant extent. Consequently, the second half of *Romanticism and Music Culture* resumes its history in the 1810s, with the introduction of Mozart and Beethoven to Britain as emblems of avant-garde taste and bourgeois ambitions for cultural leadership. Like Cowper, Leigh Hunt doubted the politics of the traditional noble patrons of London's polite music culture. In chapter 4 I show how the *Examiner's* campaign to bring Mozart's operas to the King's Theatre against the will of its aristocratic leaders politicized both Mozart and the opera house, and converged with Hunt's larger reformist agenda centered on Parliament. The "literary" reform of music culture is the theme also of chapter 5, where Jane Austen's conventional critique of female musical accomplishment as a corrupting mechanical labor in her novels is accompanied, in the hidden figure of Beethoven in *Emma*, by marks of a convergence of interest in Regency literature and music in the construction of a middle-class professional subject through a Romantic poetics of interiority and *Bildung*.

In my final chapter, the figure of the Byronic Liszt revives the eighteenth-century aristocratic vices of effeminacy, spectacle, and ritual power, while evoking, in the display of "mechanical" genius, an anxiety over the modern regime of automation and specialized skill that was the flipside of virtuosophobia. My examination of Liszt's Byronic disillusionment during his 1840 tour of Britain, and of the "virtuosic" poetry of Byron he carried with him as a talisman, offers a summary image of the Georgian history of antagonism between literary and music culture centered on the virtuoso: the transcendent union of musical performance and literary sensibility proposed by the "tone-poet" Liszt meets with a chilly British reception. Liszt's response was to describe the London musical scene as an "aristocracy of mediocrity," a wry articulation, at the beginning of the Victorian era, of an increasingly influential middle-class cultural regime that wished to be purified of virtuosic display.[27] In the brief coda to the book I examine the popularity of the nightingale, and its mechanical nemesis, as a definitive melopoetic figure expressive of this enduring anti-virtuosic agenda. Shadowed by its automaton "other," the ubiquitous nightingale in Georgian poetry and music embodied virtuosity as a mode of social being tainted by both past and future prospects, by the discredited legacy of aristocratic luxury and the looming demands of the technocratic, bourgeois nation state.

Thus, while the focus of this book is on Romantic-era texts, my examination of the conflict of virtuosity with literary idealism spans the entire eighteenth century. It was the business of professional writers, beginning with John Dennis and Joseph Addison, to place a hygienic distance between an emergent metropolitan, middle-class literary industry, centered on the poets and periodicals, and a decadent aristocratic music culture symbolized by the virtuoso foreign singers of the Italian opera: "Nonsense grew pleasing by his Syren arts," lamented Addison, "And stole from Shakespear's self our easie Hearts."[28] The King's Theatre opera house – the most important in Europe outside Italy – embodied a multitude of perceived dangers to the English nation: effeminacy, cosmopolitanism, luxury consumption, the tyranny of fashion, and a thriving aristocratic culture of patronage. Georgian virtuosophobia thus belonged to a larger xenophobic and reform discourse, which viewed bravura musical style as another dangerous continental import, like Parisian dress, absolute monarchy, or Popery. Of virtuosity, the early Victorian music critic John Davison stated, "happily no such thing exists in England ... The 'virtuosi' ... though artistically incontinent, are exclusively continental."[29] Virtuosity existed in Britain, of course, but was not allowed to be native – was greedily consumed but never generated. In his disavowal of virtuosity, Davison, like his Georgian predecessors, policed a fragile boundary between British character and British taste, asserting the integrity of one against the corruptions of the other.

By Davison's time, as the metropolitan middle class came to assume more control of the forums of Britain's musical life, the focus of anti-virtuosic anxiety had shifted from the dangers of luxury and effeminacy to those of mechanization, toward the increasingly professionalized, industrial order of the post-Waterloo state. By "professional," I refer here not only to its technical definition – remunerated labor in a non-manual field requiring specialized skills – but also to its larger sociological sense of self-regulating professional bodies advocating legal status and protections (such as copyright), and managing a discursive presence in the public sphere by which both to represent their claims to cultural leadership and to disguise their connection to industrial labor.[30] The founding of the London Philharmonic Society by a group of professional musicians in 1813, and their promotion of Beethoven as a model of Romantic genius – a history I discuss in chapter 5 – is an exemplary instance. The cultural movement we call Romanticism was coincident with the rise of professionalism in British society because it was the professional classes who required the romanticization of their being and labor. Deep into the nineteenth century, virtuosity remained a diabolical nemesis of that project, of the Romantic consecration of art, individual genius, and the auratic "work." The eighteenth-century virtuoso, whose amateurism had to be surpassed, was consequently demonized on new terms as the incarnation of soulless technical efficiency. Virtuosity was not endemic to professionalism in reality, but its toxic image was used to establish boundaries between Romantic construction of an independent high culture and an increasingly specialized, market-driven society. The virtuoso – a figure of extraordinary ubiquity, pliability, and menace – was thus the *pharmakon* of Georgian cultural discourse, beginning the eighteenth century as the very definition of the effeminized aristocratic amateur, and the nineteenth as the bogey image of middle-class professionalism. Like a radical noble in 1790s France, the virtuoso shed its aristocratic skin to ensure relevance in the new age.

Virtuosophobia, as an integral element of Romanticism, thus belongs to the general challenge to aristocratic cultural leadership in the eighteenth century. The attack on virtuosity was essentially an attack on style – a bravura mode of music, language, or display – but also on style itself as a description of the performative and ephemeral in art. A central characteristic of what we now describe as high Romantic literary culture lay in its mission to naturalize language in such a way that "style" itself could be said to disappear. Burney and Austen, for example, both looked to Johnson and the middlebrow periodical prose of the eighteenth century as the model for a new form of "standard" English that would transcend class and region. Likewise Wordsworth's linguistic localism was in fact the construction of an alternative standard English, a new literary anti-style the heralded "commonness" of which was both a class and regional description *and* a universalizing prescription: it was a language that all English writers *should* practice in place of the virtuosic "inane phraseology" of the recent past. In short, both Burney's and Austen's prose and Wordsworth's poetry attempted to place literary language outside the space of performance and beyond the reach of fashion, with both of which music culture was intrinsically identified.

In sum: the interdisciplinary purpose of this book is to compose a historical narrative of Romantic literary culture in Britain, and revisions of some of its dominant figures, through the lens of the contemporary music culture those writers inhabited – by which, in some instances, they were wholly absorbed. Anna Seward, for example, was a devoted Handelian, and as passionate a consumer and patron of music as producer of poetry. Likewise Frances Burney lived the first thirty years of her life at the heart of opera culture in London, as a daughter of Britain's leading music historian and opinion-maker. Her first "literary" tasks involved the copying out of her father's music criticism for the press. Wordsworth, meanwhile, from his days at Cambridge, harbored a student's love for the Italian language and the poetry of Pietro Metastasio, both synonymous with the opera house. At the other end of the Napoleonic period, Leigh Hunt's passion for Mozart's operas was integral to the political program of the *Examiner*, while Austen was a lifelong participant in a provincial music culture at precisely the time when the piano revolutionized amateur music-making and came to symbolize female bourgeois domesticity itself. Finally, Byron looms as the arch-virtuoso of British Romanticism. An accidental aristocrat commodified as a scandalous curiosity, Byron (and Byronism) bear the marks of cultural "lateness," in the sense of a novelty grafted upon cultural memory. Just as the Byronist Franz Liszt's pianistic style and repertoire were deeply influenced by the Italian opera, rich in *cantabile* melodic lines, so Byron's notoriety traced its rhetorical origins to the opera stars of the eighteenth century – Thomas Moore once called him a castrato.[31] The Byronic persona accordingly revived a species of old-order aristocratic "uselessness," a virtuoso exhibit brought to commercial realization in the modern space of celebrity colonized by the book trade. My reading of Byron here thus challenges the more conventional opposition between Byronic irony and Wordsworthian sincerity. Indeed, Hazlitt's influential trope of Byronic insincerity, I will argue, shows how the logic of virtuosophobia has been submerged into the very definition of "two-generation" Romanticism as a literary-historical phenomenon, and requires excavation.

III

The continental stereotype of Britain as the "land without music" originated in twentieth-century Germany, and it is the Austro-German dominance of the European art music canon and modern musicology that has, until very recently, maintained that false perception.[32] *Romanticism and Music Culture* joins a tide of recent scholarship in British cultural history that paints a very different picture: of Britain as, arguably, "the most musical country in Europe in the second half of the eighteenth century."[33] Unlike music in Vienna and Paris, both highly regulated by the court, British music culture in the Georgian period was a commercial affair, a free market that attracted the best singers, composers, and instrumentalists of Europe, from Handel and Farinelli to J. C. Bach and J. B. Cramer. For most of the century public music culture among the social elite was dominated by the Italian opera and, later, the Handel oratorio series. In the 1770s and 1780s various concert series emerged to produce a veritable "rage for music" in the capital – documented in Frances Burney's diaries – which was crowned by the tours of Haydn in the early 1790s. In Victoria's first year on the throne a prominent London music journal reflected on "the prodigious impulse given to music towards the close of last century, and which has not yet ceased to operate."[34] Given that London was the first modern music market, and the largest and most diverse in Europe, this study begins with a question. What was the impact of a booming commercial music culture on the development of what we call literary Romanticism? What did Georgian "melomania" mean for Romantic literature?[35]

This book is thus part recovery project, part revisionary history. In addition to a full range of archival sources and current literary scholarship, I have drawn on prominent examples of the so-called "new musicology," which, in Jim Samson's words, "builds the instrument and the performer – the act of performance – centrally into the historical study of a repertory."[36] The politics of music consumption is also central to the new musicological approach. I follow David Gramit's prescription that "meaning" in music history "is constituted not only by the encounter of the cultivated, critical listener with the work, but also by the entire network of relations that bring the privileged moment of critical listening into existence and ensure its privileged status."[37] Accordingly, each of my chapters first establishes a material connection between literary and music culture in the Romantic period, before undertaking a formal literary analysis with that connection in view. The crossing in critical register within each chapter between historicism and poetics is fundamental to the methodological character of the book, which is to approach interdisciplinary aesthetics as a history of style rather than ideas, of rhetoric rather than concepts. *Romanticism and Music Culture* thus reads against the grain of Romanticism itself, which sought to sink performance, and virtuosity especially, in favor of interiority and a sacralization of the "work" as text.[38] In keeping with the new musicology, this book mostly emphasizes cultural analysis of musical practices and reception rather than works; it examines music culture – performers, events, and patrons – more than formal aspects of the current classical repertory. For example, I represent baroque music in Britain through reception of the epochal Handel Commemoration of 1784, and measure the influence of the canonical Viennese figures Beethoven and Mozart as avant-garde stylists enlisted by the middle-class revolution of taste in post-Napoleonic Britain. My readings of Hunt and Austen likewise include references to composers and styles – specifically Italian *opere serie* and obscure 1790s' Viennese composers – that have no place in the current repertoire, but are essential to our understanding of that revolution.

Wordsworth and Shelley routinely invoked a Pythagorean metaphysics of music: "Ocean is a mighty harmonist/thy pinions, universal Air/Ever waving to and fro,/Are delegates of harmony" ("On the Power of Sound").[39] Coleridge in turn echoed Rousseau and the new German idealist writing on music when he proclaimed his frustration with "words [that] halt over & over again," and wished instead for "the Language of Music/the power of infinitely varying the expression, & individualizing it even as it is."[40] Such idealization of musical art and experience is central to European Romanticism, but Romantic ideology nevertheless contained a wholesale rejection of music *culture*, and it is that rejection that, two centuries later, continues to inhibit our interdisciplinary understanding of music and literature in British Romanticism. To help address this interdiscplinary lacuna, I have engaged with the work of prominent new musicologists to whom I hope this book will serve as an introduction for literary historians. They include William Weber and Simon McVeigh on concert life in Georgian London, Ruth Smith on the cultural politics of Handel's oratorios, Carl Dahlhaus and Scott Burnham on the ideology of Beethoven, Leslie Ritchie on women and music culture, and Dana Gooley on the celebrity Liszt. Many of the musicologists important to this book trace their intellectual lineage, to a greater or lesser degree, to the work of Theodor Adorno. Adorno, alone among mid-twentieth-century musicologists, saw that the project of de-romanticizing European (specifically Austro-German) music history after fascism must involve not only a reinvigorated formalism but a critique of musical Romanticism itself, its deconstruction as a sociological field in which innovations in musical form both captured and enabled the emergence of modern bourgeois subjectivity. "Adorno was concerned," writes Tia DeNora, "with how music's *formal properties* evinced modes of praxis that in turn were related to, and could inculcate modes of, consciousness."[41] DeNora's work, like that of Kramer, Gramit, and Michael Steinberg, to name only a representative few, presumes Adorno's belief in "music's power to shape individuality."[42] In this book an argument for the relation of music to subjectivity, and from there to its historical role in shaping Romantic-era social institutions and ideas, informs every chapter. For Seward, Handel's oratorios offered a consensus model of national culture, while for Hunt the operas of Mozart inspired ambitions of middle-class entitlement and reform. In my final two chapters I pay particular attention to the formal properties of both literary and musical works as innovative models of consciousness, linking the famed interiority of Viennese sonata form to Austen's experiments in free indirect discourse, and Byronic irony to Liszt's proto-modernist piano works of the late 1830s.

A principal reward of reviewing canonical Romantic texts through the prism of the sociable, fashion-driven art of music is to expose the politics of style in the production of that canon. To offer one notorious example: Keats's publication of "4000 lines of one bare circumstance," with its bravura disproportion of poetic material and performance, brought the full fury of anti-virtuosic ideology upon *Endymion* in 1817–18.[43] John Wilson Croker intuited the essentially musical corruptions of Keats's method: "He wanders from one subject to another, from the association not of ideas but of sounds . . ."[44] Reconstructing this episode in its music-historical context, the attacks on Keats's style in the Tory periodicals read like any number of eighteenth-century attacks on the Italian opera. Both the verbal glee of *Endymion* and the melismatic vocal techniques of the Italian castrati on display at the King's Theatre folded a vacuous language – "unmeaning absurdity" – into a suspect sexuality – "gross voluptuousness" – and (pseudo-)aristocratic degeneracy – "artifices of vicious refinement."[45] That is, both Keats and the Italian opera presented a regressive image of culture, a brand of extravagant technical display obnoxious enough in aristocratic taste, but wholly insupportable in a barely middle-class wannabe poet in 1817. Conventional Keats criticism has endorsed the terms, if not the tone, of that Tory critique by marginalizing the "virtuosic" *Endymion* as immature and unnaturally beholden to Hunt, while elevating the more stylistically restrained odes and *Hyperion* poems as examples of supreme Romantic virtue. In short, the Tory reviewers' assault on Keats, and the history of Keats criticism, cannot be fully understood outside the rhetorical frame of Georgian virtuosophobia. In this vein, each of my chapters will address a specific politics of Romantic writing and reception – from the problem of Seward's and Burney's "decline" in style and reputation, to Wordsworth's feminine speakers in *Lyrical Ballads*, to Austen's free indirect style in *Emma*, to Byron's "insincerity" – within a historicized account of virtuosity and its phobic expressions in Georgian culture and discourse.

A study of broad historical scope necessarily imposes limits of comprehensiveness. My readings extend neither to popular song and the balladic revival associated with Romantic bardic nationalism, nor the English opera, which incorporated balladic song forms.[46] Romantic balladry was a conspicuously literary enterprise from the beginning, as evidenced by the antiquarian volumes of Thomas Percy (1765), Joseph Ritson (1783), James Johnson (1787–1803), and Walter Scott (1802–3). In today's thriving scholarship, the "scandal of the ballad," in Susan Stewart's terms, is precisely its invention as a literary genre: the Romantic-era ballad industry packaged an oral tradition within enormous best-selling volumes whose very existence embodied the deracinating social forces that doomed their subject.[47]

Little scandal has been attached, however, to the highly contingent relations between lyrics and music of the Romantic ballad. For Johnson's *Scots Musical Museum*, Robert Burns wrote new lyrics for old tunes, while the tunes themselves entered the polite repertoire. From there, "classical" adaptation of the Scottish air, in particular, became a pan-European phenomenon. Such musical genealogies, from the first, show the modern, commercial, and cosmopolitan character of the ballad revival, an economy it shared with music culture at large. In light of this, the declinist narrative that accompanies the standard account of balladry – in which metropolitan polite society placed the dead hand of print literature upon the living song of the streets and countryside – is difficult to sustain.

The busy, porous borders between popular song and polite music culture meant that successful broadside ballads – an ephemeral, single-sheet woodcut print jobs for sale on the streets – were routinely adapted and engraved for purchase by genteel female amateurs. As Kirsteen McCue remarks, the "newly published and polished versions of 'traditional' or 'popular' songs allowed the middle classes to role-play their way into a romanticized peasant culture."⁴⁸ In *Emma*, for example, Frank Churchill's gift to Jane Fairfax places the cosmopolitan J. B. Cramer's sophisticated studies alongside a volume of "Irish melodies." Nor was it simply a matter of bourgeois commodification of folk cultures. Cross-class fertilization tended in both directions. As teachers, performers, and arrangers, Italian musicians based in Edinburgh influenced Scottish popular song from the mid-eighteenth century, while collections of Scottish airs routinely featured the name of the castrato Ferdinando Tenducci – darling of the King's Theatre aristocrats – who was their most celebrated interpreter across a range of venues.⁴⁹ Londoner Leigh Hunt, in turn, recalled how the "delightful airs" of the Italian opera "wandered into the streets out of the English operas that borrowed them, and became confounded with English property."⁵⁰

Hogarth's 1741 print, *The Enraged Musician*, depicts an urban scene in which a destitute ballad singer, accompanied by her wailing infant and a ragged street orchestra, drowns out a well-dressed foreign violinist at rehearsal in his drawing-room. The image vividly opposes a rude, authentic native song tradition to an expensive metropolitan service economy dominated by effete continental musicians. Literary scholarship of the last two centuries has observed the spirit of *The Enraged Musician* in its scrupulous separation of Romantic balladry from a history of cosmopolitan music culture in Britain. As David Simpson has argued, however, binary distinctions between Romantic nationalism and cosmopolitanism themselves can obscure the fact of "the internally diversified nation-state."⁵¹ Handel – a German-born composer trained in Italy, then posthumously nationalized by British audiences – embodies the difficulty of distinguishing musical nationalism in the Romantic period from the "xenophilia" of a deeply cosmopolitan urban scene.⁵² So too does the ballad, in its shape-shifting circuit from oral culture into (and out of) print, crossing between province and metropolis and markets beyond. In short, with all the attention given to balladry as an insurgent nationalist genre within the federated Georgian regime of polite letters, the rivalrous sibling history of music and literature in its larger transnational contexts has remained unwritten: the foreign virtuoso has been left to stew in Hogarth's contempt. It is the purpose of this book to write the history both of his success and of his demonization.

Georgian music culture produced pluralized strains of the British nation and the "other" that lay beyond it (and within). The provincial musical communities of Anna Seward and Jane Austen, for example, depended upon the metropolis, but also enjoyed considerable autonomy from it.⁵³ So too did their fashionable repertoire – a mix of Italian airs, "Celtic" songs, and German sonatas – contain both patriotic and cosmopolitan elements, and offer negotiable distinctions between popular and polite subcultures. My book's title hence makes much of its implied distinction between the problematic category of "British" music and music culture "in Britain," historically the most cosmopolitan and diverse in Europe. To offer a fuller account of music's "prodigious impulse" in the Romantic period, I am thus concerned with the impacts of music culture on literary production observable beyond the well-documented forms of balladic nationalism and the easy donning of a bardic persona. Indeed, the familiar ensemble of Romantic melopoetic tropes – the bard, the balladeer, Pythagorean lyres, and Rousseau's anthropology of melody – is precisely what I wish to bypass here in favor of a more material, transnational study of literary-musical crossings in the late Georgian age.

The dates circumscribing this study are grounded in material developments in British music culture as well as in roughly consensual periodizations of the Romantic movement broadly conceived. The 1770s witnessed the introduction of the modern piano, a boom in music publishing and instruction, and the much-trumpeted "rage for music" in opera and public concerts as well as the domestic sphere. The 1770s also saw the first breach in what Weber calls "the contemporaneity of musical taste" in the eighteenth century.⁵⁴ In addition to antiquarian interest in balladry, the grand scholarly volumes published by Burney and Hawkins in that decade and the new institutional formations around "ancient music" historicized music for the first time, which thus took its place in the broader Romantic turn to history. The canonization of Handel and, later, the introduction of Mozart and Beethoven as representatives of a new "serious" German repertoire also belong to the romanticization of music in the late Georgian period, a project carried out, as I shall argue, according to established literary canons of taste. This included the familiar Romantic strains of idealism and the sublime, attached particularly to Handel and Beethoven, but also its playful, performative counter-current. Hunt, for example, like Seward before him, embraced music as integral to the literary values of what Jeffrey Robinson has called the "counter-poetics" of Romantic sociability, a whole alternative tradition of Regency literary culture that has only recently come into critical view.⁵⁵

Music is the art form historically adapted to group entertainment and the imperatives of sociability. The musical trajectory of my six chapters – from eighteenth-century oratorio and Italian opera to nineteenth-century bourgeois pianism – accordingly traces the "prodigious" expansion of the polite musical marketplace in Britain, and its interpenetration with Romantic literary culture, with an emphasis on its performative, sociable settings. My choice to focus on the opera house and parlor piano is not accidental, but determined rather by the socio-commercial logic of late Georgian music culture, in which a successful song ran the gamut of public and private venues. Beginning on the stage of the Italian (or English) opera houses, and performed by a well-known singer, a favorite air would subsequently be revived at the London pleasure gardens and in genteel concert settings. Its destiny then lay in the music-room of the young female amateur, where it battled the same tides of fashion to which it owed its own existence for a permanent place in her pianistic repertoire.

The dictates of female accomplishment in the Romantic era, built around the explosion in readily available piano literature, have long been an object of ridicule and even disgust, but the dominance of women as both consumers and performers in the booming music industry signifies the piano's centrality to the larger feminization of culture in the nineteenth century. The piano's Romantic-era history is thus the focus of my final two chapters. Beethoven and Liszt literally destroyed the parlor instruments of Austen's youth, helping to stimulate the union of pianism and industrial technology, but for Elizabeth Bennet, as for Liszt, a form of Romantic resistance was necessary to the commodification of the piano as "mechanical muse," and to the commercial standardization of pianistic technique and instruction at the expense of "natural" self-expression.[56] Austen's poetics of sincerity and natural ability in the novel place Elizabeth's unstudied musical gentility in opposition to the Bingley sisters' fashion-driven and exclusive notions of virtuosic accomplishment and class status. The charismatic sensibility Elizabeth transmits from the piano in *Pride and Prejudice* is thus negatively proportional to her modest capabilities on the instrument. To this extent *Pride and Prejudice* tells a classic virtuosophobic tale. That said, by the novel's end the virtuous Elizabeth and the virtuosa-in-training Georgiana Darcy have crossed their respective class bridges to meet on the leveling ground of musicianship, a progressive union of the kind promoted by Romantic reformers of music culture after Beethoven, who came to recognize the necessity of superlative technique for the proper interpretation of the new German repertoire. From this moment the discursive pungency of the opposition between virtue and virtuosity began to recede. Through the 1830s, as I shall describe in my final chapter, the celebrity pianist Liszt aggressively marketed a strategic union of musical virtuosity and literary seriousness unthinkable in the eighteenth century. With Liszt's career, therefore, certain historical limits of the literary critique of virtuosity come into view.

My broad goal in *Romanticism and Music Culture* has been to engage the most current musicological scholarship of the Georgian period – with its particular emphasis on subjectivity, gender, and the cultural marketplace – in dialogue with literary Romanticism, and from there to construct original, revisionary arguments about Romantic-period writers and literary culture more generally. In addition to radically expanding our understanding of Romantic anti-theatricality, the book embraces a wide range of themes dominant in eighteenth-century, nineteenth-century, and Romantic literary studies of the last two decades, including cosmopolitanism and transnationalism; masculinity and the feminization of culture; the rise of the periodicals; nationalism and the politics of spectacle; Byronism and Romantic self-fashioning; the rhetorics of sociability and literary performance; women writers and the professionalization of literature; the aesthetic modeling of liberal subjectivity; and the *embourgeoisement* of British culture.

In addition to constructing intersecting histories of literary and music culture in the period 1770–1840, each chapter will consider how Romantic virtuosophobia has been perpetuated in current criticism in the form of misreadings and omissions. Despite general recognition of Charles Burney's importance to his daughter's career, for example, no serious interdisciplinary study of the Burney family's professional lives – musical and literary – has yet been undertaken. Likewise, the dispute between Seward and Cowper over Handel has never been examined, nor have Wordsworth's translations of operatic arias, nor Hunt's Mozart campaign in the *Examiner*, despite the current renewal of interest in Hunt and the politics of the "Cockney" circle. Austen's critique of female musical accomplishment, to the extent that it has excited interest at all, has been (mis)read at face value, while Liszt's 1840 tour of Britain, with its echoes of Byron's disgrace, has been a source of embarrassment to music historians and is entirely unknown to literary history. Interdisciplinarity, in short – as far as current literary studies in the eighteenth century and Romanticism are concerned – has not extended to music, a situation all the more insupportable given that "it is largely because of its interdisciplinary qualities that music in nineteenth-century Britain has become such a prominent part of the modern musicological landscape."[57] Reasons for this persistent interdisciplinary blindness – on the part of literary historians – lie outside the issue of scholarly competence in literature and music, and beyond the dramatic decline of "classical music" as a commodity of present-day bourgeois taste and education. The scholarly estrangement of music and literature is grounded, rather, in the Romantic-era formation of the disciplines, to the critical history of which this book is designed to contribute. *Romanticism and Music Culture* uncovers the ideological origins of our disciplinary separation of literature and music in a signature Georgian trope – the fear of the virtuoso – and, in historicizing that ideology, seeks to help break its siren spell.

CHAPTER I

Seward's Handelomania

I

In June 1784 the largest musical event in recorded European history up to that time was staged in Handel's honor in Westminster Abbey, with King George III among the four thousand in attendance (Figure 1). No fewer than 525 singers and instrumentalists participated in performances of *Messiah* and other sacred and ceremonial works by Handel. These were not court musicians, but Handel enthusiasts drawn from all parts of the kingdom. Charles Burney, who attended with Joshua Reynolds and James Boswell, recalled that "the effects indeed, upon many were such as modern times have never before experienced. The Choral power of harmonical combinations affected some to tears, and fainting; while others were melting and enrapt, by the exquisite sweetness of single sounds."[1] Some, such as the Whig poet Anna Seward, conceived "Handelomania" as a healer of faction and image of national unity, while others saw the event as a partisan rally for the new cult of monarchy, a congregation of "Rory Tories."[2] To William Cowper's mind the country had gone "Commemoration-mad." Five years before the Revolution in France, the 1784 Handel Commemoration was already a counter-revolutionary assembly, a monarchist choral rejoinder to Burke's "horrid yells and shrilling screams" of the sansculottes, a transcendent order of the mob.[3]

The 1784 Commemoration was the high note of Handel's nationalization, a process that had begun with the Lenten festivals of the 1760s. The popularity of his oratorios, first produced in London (excepting *Messiah*) between 1732 and 1753, spread through these festivals from the capital deep into provincial British music culture. Where history painting and the epic poem had failed, Handelian oratorio, the Commemoration seemed conclusively to say, had succeeded as a genuine national art form. "Is it not, therefore, a subject of national triumph," proclaimed one newspaper, "that, on so worthy an occasion as the memory of Handel . . . we have

Figure 1. Edward Francesco Burney, *The Handel Commemoration, 1784*. View of the orchestra. Westminster Abbey. Frances Burney's artist brother recorded the images for which their father provided the text, another example of the Burneys combining forces to maximize their collective visibility in the public eye.

fixed the greatest achievement of the art in Britain?"[4] The *European Magazine* agreed that the event marked "an aera in the music of Britain," and had effectively canonized Handel as "the muse of the English character. He writes to the masculine genius of a free people."[5] This language of tribute borrows from the memory of the Glorious Revolution – its guarantee of rights and freedoms – and a century of wars during which English freedom was upheld by English arms, by a collective "masculine genius." In 1784 Handel thus claimed (posthumously) a share of cultural-nationalist associations long monopolized by Shakespeare and Milton.

While the 1784 Handel Commemoration was unarguably the most important musical event in Britain in the late eighteenth century, no equivalent claim could be made for the most popular new poem of that year, Seward's epistolary novel in verse, *Louisa*. Literary history, as we know it, skips 1784 entirely, its eyes fixed on the publication the following year of Cowper's *The Task*, the most influential poem of the following fifteen years in Britain. Wordsworth, Coleridge, and Austen all absorbed Cowper's radically ruminative autobiographical text, and his plain, conversational idiom. *Louisa* was no less experimental a poem than *The Task*, at least in its form. Keen to appropriate a share in the popular market for sentimental epistolary fiction, Seward composed an eighty-five-page "poetical novel" divided into four epistles. An entirely original literary genre, it was never to be repeated. Its sentimental evocations of scenic retreat, thwarted passion, the lurid downfall of an heiress, a misbegotten child, and the ultimate triumph of love rehearsed exactly those humid excesses that Wordsworth, in his 1802 Preface to *Lyrical Ballads*, so powerfully traduced. Four lines of the heroine's opening apostrophe to her rural seat will serve for example of how, for Wordsworth, a "gaudiness and inane phraseology" had infected modern verse:[6]

> O ye known objects!—how ye strike my heart!
> And vain regrets, with keener force, impart!
> Slow, thro' the faded Grove, past Pleasures glide,
> Or sadly linger by the fountain's side.   (3)

In her preface Seward concedes, perhaps disingenuously, that "this Poem has little chance to be popular." This she attributes to *Louisa*'s lack of narrative organization, to its being "a description rather of passions than of incidents."[7] Certainly, the integration of the lyric and dramatic do not succeed in *Louisa* according to the example of Seward's idol, Milton. But whatever her apprehensions, *Louisa* was a commercial success: it went through five editions in Britain, was published in America, and consolidated her place as probably the best-known female poet in Britain. Joanna Baillie later remembered the 1780s as a time when "Mr. [William] Hayley and Miss Seward, and a few other cultivated poetical writers, were the poets spoken of in literary circles."[8]

Cowper and Seward, as well as meeting divergent fates in literary history, likewise found themselves in 1784 with conflicting views on Handel. Seward's letters, published by Walter Scott in six volumes in 1811, display already outdated literary enthusiasms, but are indispensable documents for understanding mainstream musical taste in the late eighteenth century.[9] Handel is the presiding genius of Seward's musical life; indeed she has been described as the most "ardent and sentimental" of eighteenth-century Handelians.[10] At the Bishop's Palace in Lichfield, she surrounded herself equally with literati and musicians, and reserved her evenings for the music of Handel. Her intimate friend, John Saville, a well-known tenor, participated in the 1784 Commemoration. Together they attended local concerts dominated by Handel, as well as the larger provincial Handel festivals which originated in cities such as Manchester, Birmingham, and Sheffield in the 1760s, and provided the template for the 1784 Westminster Abbey event (as well as many of the musicians for it). To Seward's circle Handel's oratorios stood for national music, and for the ecstatic possibilities of the religious sublime – as well as its opposite, lyric sensuality.

Cowper, by contrast, deplored the 1784 Commemoration, and devoted some two dozen lines in the sixth book of *The Task* to stating his case against the emerging national cult of Handel. His arguments are not against the music itself, but against the use of Westminster Abbey as a venue for mass tribute to a mere mortal:

> Man praises man. Desert in arts or arms
> Wins public honor; and ten thousand sit
> Patiently present at a sacred song,
> Commemoration-mad; content to hear
> (Oh wonderful effect of music's pow'r!)
> Messiah's eulogy, for Handel's sake.[11]

While Handel himself embodies "a talent so divine," his use of scripture as the libretto for the *Messiah* is a form of "sacrilege." In a letter to the evangelical preacher John Newton on the same subject, Cowper "suppose[d] that in the next year's Almanac we shall find the name of Handel among the red-letter'd worthies, for it would surely puzzle the Pope himself to add any thing to his Canonization."[12] Despite the success of

The Task Cowper's opinions on Handel found little audience. By 1784 the *Messiah* (1742), to which two full days of the Commemoration were devoted, had secured the iconic cultural position it enjoys today, and Cowper's was a marginal voice in opposition. The poet himself appears to recognize this, and concludes his discourse on the Commemoration with a disclaimer:

> But hush!—the muse perhaps is too severe,
> And with a gravity beyond the size
> And measure of th'offence, rebukes a deed
> Less impious than absurd, and owing more
> To want of judgment than to wrong design.   (VI: 653–7)

What Cowper finds "absurd" is not the performance of Handel's music in the Abbey as such, but its spectacular form and the presence of so massive an audience. Cowper's lyric identity in *The Task* depends upon accumulated marks of resistance to such spectacles, characteristic of the "jarring world" of the metropolis:

> 'Tis pleasant through the loop-holes of retreat
> To peep at such a world. To see the stir
> Of the great Babel and not feel the crowd.
> To hear the roar she sends through all her gates
> At a safe distance, where the dying sound
> Falls a soft murmur on th'uninjured ear.   (IV: 88–93)

Something in the idea of musical spectacle itself, of the sociable rituals of public music culture made awesomely manifest at the Handel Commemoration, offended Cowper as an image of the "great Babel" of London from which he sought poetic sanctuary.

Cowper's conciliating conclusion to the passage on the Handel Commemoration was not sufficient to protect him from Seward's wrath. The outraged Handelian composed a poem of "Remonstrance" on what she called "the sarcasms levelled at national gratitude" in *The Task*.[13] The terms of Seward's attack are more political than musical, and more social than religious. She accuses Cowper of a "spleenful heart" (6) educated by "the dark anathemas of Calvin's school" (7). Cowper's objection to the "nation's praise" (8) of Handel is, she says, "fanatic and illiberal" (56). In a footnote added to her collected *Poetical Works*, Seward offers sympathy for Cowper's unhappy life and some praise for his talents, only then to reiterate, in no less energetic language, the indignation she has only just expressed in the poem: Cowper's "illiberal censures" of Handel, she writes, disgrace the interesting and beautiful pages of the Task, [and] teach us, more than ever, to deplore the dire Calvinistic principles, which ruined his peace, and which could so freeze and narrow a heart, which nature had made warm and expansive. They taught him to anathematize for departed genius . . .[14]

Seward's fury at Cowper continues through her letters of 1785–6: "Fanatics have almost always cold hearts," she complains to a sympathetic Anglican clergyman. On the strength of his criticizing the Handel Commemoration in a brief passage of *The Task*, Cowper takes permanent shape in Seward's mind as a "cold-hearted devotionist . . . whose religion is composed of selfishness and terror."[15]

Seward did not publish her "Remonstrance" until after Cowper's death out of respect (she said) for his fragile mental health, and the dispute itself has never earned the attention of literary historians. But what can be made of Seward's rage? Why, on reading Cowper's mild objection to the 1784 Handel Commemoration – one that advanced no new arguments, and to which even Cowper himself appeared only haltingly committed – did Seward feel moved to an *ad hominem* attack on Cowper's religion and personality? What appears to be an argument about religion and religious music, I wish to argue, between Seward the establishment Anglican and Cowper the "methodistical" low churchman, is in fact a political argument over factionalism, and the competing claims of amateur sociability and the new metropolitan professionalism for the future of British literary culture.

My interest here – in linking Seward, Cowper, and Handel – is thus not in the aesthetic relations between poetry and music as such, which Romanticism everywhere presumes, but in the relations between a specific music culture in late Georgian Britain, dominated by Handel, and the production of poetry in that period: the codes, lyric registers, and sense of audience that music culture shared with sentimental and early Romantic poetry. In some respects, this characterization of the dispute between Seward and Cowper over Handel consolidates commonplace literary-historical oppositions between the sociable and the Romantic in the late eighteenth century, and the gendered inflections of those terms. But while the importance of sociability in Georgian political philosophy has been exhaustively commented upon, the practice of sentiment and sympathy at the quotidian, social level remains an elusive phenomenon. Provincial literary culture, whose rituals were so closely associated with the sociable conventions of music, offers a unique venue for its reconstruction. In this chapter I describe the specific politics of sociability in Seward's artistic life, both poetic and musical, as a strategic repudiation of the corrosive spirit of factionalism that, for her, Cowper's *Task* embodied. In this sense, the conflict here is not between Sewardian sentimentality and Cowperian Romanticism at all. For Seward, what is odious in Cowper is not his poetic innovations on the pastoral trope of "retreat," but an all-too-familiar urban-political pose: his satire and "misanthropy" are the calling cards of faction, choice modes of the late eighteenth-century metropolitan literary culture she loathed. For Seward, the anti-metropolitan posture of *The Task* thus masks its essential congeniality to London literary modes and tastes. For her own countervailing task as a provincial, amateur poet, Seward looked to Handel as her cultural model. His oratorios represented a sociable art form with the power, second only to Milton, to renew poetry, drown out the dissonant voices of faction, and constitute a unified national culture.

II

Seward's career, with its busy traffic across the female-dominated spheres of provincial literary-musical salons and public concert-going, is ripe for what Clara Tuite and Gillian Russell have proposed as "a larger investigation of gender and Romantic-period sociability."[16] Women vastly outnumbered men at the 1784 Handel Commemoration. Though Seward was not at that event (she disliked London), she once breakfasted with the conductor and attended countless musical occasions of the type, of a similarly gendered flavor. At home in Lichfield, music was fully integrated in daily life. She described herself to a friend as "living in the almost daily habit of hearing vocal music, in those perfectly fine tones, and with that elegance, pathos, energy, and varied powers, which marries it to poetry."[17] Her letters combine opinions on music and literature with equal facility, and record innumerable domestic entertainments where poetry recitations combined with "music's thrilling pow'r" to animate the social occasion, with herself or another hostess presiding.[18] During the Christmas season of 1786, she recounts a typical visit with a neighboring family:

> A regular morning concert, during two hours, between the three brothers, all musical, and performing on different instruments; with their friend, Mr. Williams, the clergyman of the village, who plays a fine bass-viol; reading aloud from the poetic stores the remainder of the mornings . . .[19]

Seward's Lichfield salon exemplifies a late eighteenth-century domestic literary culture that incorporated music-making with literary performance as "a sociable rather than a solitary experience . . . especially manifested in the regular habit of reading aloud."[20] Her "regular morning concert" embodied sociable principles in its very structure. Before the rise of the new symphonic ethos in the early nineteenth century, the musical offerings at a Georgian concert – whether private, public, or any shade in between – adhered to what William Weber has described as a "principle of miscellany, [which] dictated that members of the musical community had to accommodate one another's tastes and social etiquette. All who entered a concert knew that they were expected to defer to the wishes of others to some extent."[21]

One product of the sociable, melopoetic ethos of Seward's circle was the union of a lyric vocabulary of sentimental expression with a venerating taste for Handel. A revolution in English musical aesthetics coincides with Handel's career in the oratorio. Before 1750 the musical treatises that existed presumed that music, like painting, belonged to the Aristotelean imitative arts. Rousseau then recast music as the speech of the heart, a primal trace of language's originary power, now lost: "It appears that whereas speech is the art of communicating ideas, melody is the art of communicating feelings."[22] In the same decade in Britain Charles Avison's *Essay on Musical Expression* (1752) likewise celebrated music's affective power, as a realm of sensation and unbidden emotional response. Avison's musical vocabulary is not technical or musicological, but rather reads like a synthesis of prevailing aesthetic theories of the sublime, sympathy, and moral sentiments:

[Musical sounds] assume the power of exciting all the most agreeable passions of the soul. The force of sound in alarming the passions is prodigious. Thus, the noise of thunder, the shouts of war, the uproar of an enraged ocean, strike us with terror; so again, there are certain sounds natural to joy, others to grief and despondency, others to tenderness and love; and by hearing these, we naturally sympathize with those who either enjoy or suffer. (3)

Avison's examples – thunder, war, and "enraged ocean" – allude to standard imagery of the oratorio libretti, and the language of "force" and "prodigious" sound is distinctly Handelian. Like Burney's description of the audience's response at the 1784 Commemoration – "tears, and fainting . . . melting and enrapt" – Avison emphasizes the somatic and emotional impact of music, from "joy" to "grief and despondency" to "tenderness and love." Handelian oratorio is thus synonymous, historically speaking, with the romanticization of music as a natural language of the inner life first articulated in the mid-eighteenth century. But unlike its later, individualist expression in Beethoven (see chapter 5), musical sentiment is here inseparable from "sympath[y]" and thus its social function. Music, says Avison, excites "the Sociable and happy passions," a commonplace neoclassical analogy between musical and social harmony expressed across dozens of late eighteenth-century treatises on music.[23]

A 1777 poem from Lady Anna Miller's Batheaston salon, which Seward would soon join, entitled "Ancient and Modern Music Compared, and Their Respective Effects," described the experience of listening to Handel according to Avison's fashionable terms of expression, rapture, and sociability. The Batheaston poet, Sir John More, calls on the composer to

> Again speak sweetly to the feeling heart,
> By nature only, and his genius taught,
> Give the full scope to each impassion'd thought,
> Feel his own strains, and teaching us to feel,
> While o'er our souls the pow'rful raptures steal;
> In pleasing chains our ravish'd fancy bind
> And reign unrivalled o'er the willing mind.[24]   (6–12)

Typical of what I am calling sociable poetry is More's resistance to retreat or exclusivity. His is a Handelian idiom, collective and inclusive, a language of "we," "us," and "our." It is a commonplace of Georgian theory of the sentiments that political faction corrupted the "feeling heart," and endangered the social virtues of friendship and benevolence. More's sentimental language of Handelian tribute is almost identical to that which Seward uses in her preface to *Louisa*, where she describes her ideal reader: "A feeling heart, and a fondness for Verse must *unite* to render it interesting." Both More's poem and Seward's *Louisa* view the arts, poetic *and* musical, as vehicles of sentiment and sympathy and thus, by extension, as instruments of social cohesion.

But how did a German immigrant writing Italian opera for the fashionable aristocrats of London's West End come to embody an ideal of British unity? How did Handel emerge as the St. George chosen to slay the baneful spirit of faction?

Even while still an opera composer catering to an aristocratic elite at London's King's Theatre in the reigns of George I and II, Handel was perceived among the London commentariat as an artist uniquely capable of putting music to work in the cause of ameliorating factional strife. Barely a decade after Handel's arrival in England, a royal chaplain described his performance at the organ as a "Circle of Sacred Sound" with the power to render "Discord of her Rage disarm'd" and "Ev'n restless noisy Faction charm'd."[25] Ten years later, Aaron Hill, that tireless promoter of civic Christian culture in Britain, called upon Handel to abandon Italian opera and

> Teach us . . . to compose
> Our inbred Storms, and 'scape impending Woes:
> Lull our wanton Hearts to ease,
> Teach Happiness to please;
> And, since thy Notes, can ne'er in vain implore!
> Bid 'em becalm unresting Faction o'er:
> Inspire Content, and Peace, in each proud Breast,
> Bid th'unwilling Land be blest.[26]

As Ruth Smith's comprehensive study of the politics of the oratorio libretti has shown, Handel's dozen Old Testament oratorios, from *Esther* (1732) to *Solomon* (1748), succeeded beyond Hill's dreams as powerful rallying points for Protestant national identification.[27] Most importantly, they revived the century-old popular association between Britain and the biblical Israelite nation. As Rev. Thomas Morell, the librettist of *Judas Maccabaeus* (1746) and three other Handel oratorios, observed in sermons during the Spanish War of 1739–40, "our present condition so nearly resembles the ancient State of Israel, that I doubt not but while I was reading the foregoing passages from the History of the Nation, your minds were fixed at home."[28] The anxiety over faction and accompanying calls for national unity only became more intense as Britain entered a period of almost perpetual warfare. Much of the success of the oratorios must be owed to Handel's timely reconsecration of Britain's link to the biblical nation's holy struggle and survival.[29] All the more ironic, then, that Handel's English oratorios, beginning with their first wave of European popularity in the 1770s, would form the basis of an international "classical" repertoire.

The oratorios as a social phenomenon, though full of politics themselves (*Judas Maccabaeus*, for example, was written as a paean to the Duke of Cumberland after his defeat of the Jacobite rebels), thus stood for the neutralization of political division. Samuel Richardson embodied in Sir Charles Grandison the contiguity of musical and social harmony, expressed through a love of Handel that he shares with Harriet. In her 1749 *Epistle for Ladies*, Eliza Haywood likewise recognized the oratorios' power both to create religious consensus and promote sociable behavior. After attending a performance of *Joshua* (1747), her correspondent offers the following advice to her bishop:

I cannot help thinking, but that entertainments of this nature, frequently exhibited, would have an effect over the most obdurate minds, and go a great way in reforming an age which seems degenerating equally into an irreverence for the Deity, and a brutality of behaviour to each other.³⁰

She suggests that oratorios be performed for free throughout the kingdom and to people of all classes.

By the 1784 Commemoration, Hill's call to Handel to "becalm unresting Faction" had, by some measures, been answered. The directors of the Academy of Ancient Music, which produced the Commemoration, were not Hanoverian propagandists but came from all sides of politics (one key figure, Sir William Watkins Wynne, was a well-known Jacobite), as did the subscribers to its annual Handel-dominated concert programs. Listening to Handel, with hundreds of other enraptured spectators, one could forget that one was a Whig aristocrat and one's neighbor a Jacobite, Tory, or Methodist. Indeed, one was obliged to forget it. Seward, a confirmed Whig, sat down with the "Rory Tories," while the Duchess of Devonshire, a central figure in Whig social circles, reckoned the playing of the Coronation Anthem at the 1784 Commemoration "would make me cry my eyes out."³¹ Handel spoke to no one party or sect: he knew no faction. As sublime instantiation of the natural link between God, king, and the people, the new Handelian model of national culture, manifest in the Commemoration, repudiated faction in favor of public and congregational ritual. The full-scale prodution of a Handel oratorio created what no Act of Parliament or royal proclamation could: an environment of affirmation, of consensus-building sociability through the spectacular production of an irresistible aesthetic.³²

III

The Handelian Seward was a sociable poet from the start. She made her public debut as a poet in 1780 at the famous Batheaston salon, presided over by Lady Miller, that produced More's poetic tribute to Handel. For seven seasons the Batheaston villa was the setting for a convivial fortnightly competition in poetry among the fashionable set. Though Lady Miller was herself barely of the upper gentry, and no Lady Montagu in her literary or conversational talents, Batheaston quickly boasted a celebrity cattle call: Frances Burney, Hester Thrale, David Garrick, and the Duchess of Devonshire all made the pilgrimage. Richard Graves, author of *The Spiritual Quixote* (1773), "counted one morning above fifty carriages drawn up in a line from Batheaston . . . with four duchesses."³³ The Parnassian *coup de grâce* of Batheaston, as described by the Bath guidebook writer Philip Thicknesse, was Lady Miller's installation of a Tuscan vase as totem and vessel of the proceedings:

> In one of the rooms of this villa, stands an antique vase, into which the ladies and gentlemen put copies of verses, written on certain given subjects, which being drawn out, and read by one of the company, the majority of them determine which piece has the most merit, and then the author is called upon to avow it; this being done, the lady of the villa present the author with a wreath of myrtle.[34]

The subjects were mock-serious and, in the first years of Lady Miller's "Vase," much energy was devoted to the parlor game of *bouts-rimés*. By the time Anna Seward participated in 1780, however, the "Vase" had begun to attract poets of greater ambition and, beginning in 1776, Lady Miller published annual volumes of the proceedings. In addition, some Batheaston poems found republication in the London periodicals and the anthologies of minor poets. According to Walter Scott, the poems for which Seward first won national attention – her elegies for Captain Cook (1780) and Major André (1781) – found their first audience at the "Vase."[35]

The poetic culture of Batheaston emphasized sociability above originality and community over critique. As Lady Miller stated in her preface to her second volume of "Vase" poetry, "the subjects given out were calculated to preclude all discussion of Party and Opinion – all tendency to Personality – and to discourage every violation of the sanctities of Society."[36] This is not an apolitical manifesto but a critique of factional politics. Lady Miller's sociable ethos adheres to an eighteenth-century tradition – to which Handel's music conspicuously belonged – of the arts as an antidote to partisan spite. As Hill wrote in 1735, "Faction, and the Turbulence of Party Division, can have no Enemy more powerful than Pleasure, and a Disposition to Amusements of Fancy, or Genius."[37] In a similar vein, Lady Miller's language points to her vision of the Batheaston "Vase" as something more than frivolous amusement, though it was certainly that also. Batheaston, in which the "sanctities" of society were preserved above all, served for its constituents as the micro-ideal of a political culture that transcended faction.

In her letters Seward regularly deplored "the arrogance and ignorance of the public critics . . . their strange influence upon the public opinions."[38] Her introduction to this anti-metropolitan ethos was at Lady Miller's villa. The importance of avoiding the jealousy and character assassination endemic to London periodical culture is a signature of the Batheaston volumes. "No partiality to subjects or persons," writes Miller, has directed our choice in the present selection: Such preference would have been as inconsistent with that degree of cordiality and good-will to each other, originating from the like liberal pursuits and intercourse among its members.[39]

Her emphasis on cordiality and "liberal pursuits" implicitly contrasts her amateur literary milieu with the cronyism and ill-will of the London critics whom Seward would later abominate as "hireling authors, whose own works have not merit, or celebrity enough to afford them a maintenance."[40] Sociability, in Miller's political sense, is likewise evident in the great number of tribute poems in her Batheaston publications and in the corresponding absence of satire, the favorite idiom of the periodicals. The exterior of the fabled vase even bore a famous admonition from Pope: "Cursed be the verse, how well soe'er it flow,/That tends to make one worthy man my foe."[41] Even style, if necessary, should be sacrificed to sociability. In her elegy to Lady Miller, published on her sudden death in 1782, Seward articulated their shared ethos regarding provincial amateur literary culture. Leaders of that domain, such as themselves, looked with "calm disdain" upon "Pride's cold frown, and Fashion's pointed leer/On Envy's serpent lie," that is, on the anti-social vices of the metropolitan periodicals. In the poem Seward expressed the hope, vain as it turned out, that Batheaston, where no "noisy strife/Dark spleen or haggard Jealousy were found," might provide her a kind of armature – "Clad in the fine asbestos light attire" – with which to endure "the public fire" of the London reviews.[42]

Inevitably, Lady Miller's salon attracted the mockery of the urban literary press.[43] Frances Burney was lionized at the "Vase," but on her return home wrote her sister that "Bath Easton is much laughed at in London."[44] When Boswell mentioned that an acquaintance had been published in *Poetical Amusements*, Johnson replied, "He was a blockhead for his pains."[45] A satire in the *Gentleman's Magazine* in January 1781 contains a sally typical of the periodicals' amusement at Lady Miller's expense – "You must famish and fume to hear ricketty verses,/And their dull authors bray'em, which exceedingly worse is" – while the *Annual Register* for 1777 ridiculed Lady Miller's "fluttering, noisy crew" for amusing themselves with "mangled poetry and murder'd sense." But that Batheaston should have excited such fascinated scorn from the London periodicals only throws into bolder relief its attempt to stand as an alternative cultural venue for poetry: a poetry defined by public performance and consumption not private reading, and governed by a poetics of tribute, gratitude, humor and entertainment, rather than the socially poisonous "sarcasms" of satire or critique. When a newcomer to

Batheaston once attempted to lampoon one of the company, "the female regent interposed her authority, and restored a little tranquillity, by pronouncing a temporary banishment on the monster, whose satire had thus wantonly o'erturned the harmony of the day."[46] The conventions of literary editing were likewise disregarded. Lady Miller attempted to deflect the scorn of the periodicals by emphasizing that her Batheaston poems "originated amidst the hurry of plays, balls, public breakfasts, and concerts, and all the dissipations of a full Bath Season" and were printed unrevised.[47] Proceeds of sales went to charity, thus relieving the poetical contributors of any taint of professionalism. In Miller's *Poetical Amusements* we find a culture of poetry contiguous with and modeled upon the pleasures of amateur music-making, the concert stage, and the "liberal pursuits" of the Georgian provincial gentry.

Seward fashioned her own poetic career, and her Lichfield circle, after her experiences at Batheaston. She held a lifelong distaste for satire, and was as famous among her set as a dramatic reciter of others' poetry as she was a writer of her own. Scott, after seeing her perform at Lichfield, likened her to Sarah Siddons, and a Romney portrait of her was mistaken for Siddons for almost a century.[48] What Judith Pascoe has described as a style of "Romantic theatricality" characteristic of many women poets of the period applies, comprehensively, to Anna Seward.[49] Seward's circle embodied the music theorist Anselm Bayly's fashionable notion that "there is in no arts a stricter alliance or more intimate correspondence than between those of musick, poetry and oratory."[50] A well-known singing teacher, Bayly mandated that his students learn to recite their texts before singing them.[51] Conversely, Handel's first biographer, John Mainwaring, claimed that Longinus' description of the effects upon an audience of the orator Demosthenes was "so perfectly applicable to Handel, that one would almost be persuaded it was intended for him."[52] The close relation between oratory, poetry recitation, and singing in eighteenth-century aesthetics clarifies Handel's appeal for Seward, who insisted upon the performative, sociable context of her art. In a barely veiled admonition in a letter to Boswell, she "decried the frothy spleen descending so continually upon ingenious composition from the pen of anonymous criticism."[53] The new market-driven periodical journalism – conceived in private, published anonymously, and read with mortification or envy – encouraged "spleen" and promoted faction, while an amateur literary culture modeled on the convivial rituals of music and the stage had the potential to produce precisely the opposite social effects. Seward and Cowper's dispute over Handel thus becomes an argument over the meaning of culture itself: whether poetry's role in the public sphere should adhere to the musical model of sociable art, or to the competitive isolation and Romantic celebrityhood spawned by the new metropolitan world of professional letters, a literary culture Hazlitt would later liken to "a gay coquette . . . followed by a train of flatterers . . . impatient for applause." As Teresa Barnard's recent analysis of Seward's original letters shows, our sense of her antipathy to the London literary scene would be even more vivid were it not for Scott's defensive editorial meddling in the 1811 edition.[54]

Johnson chose a pugilistic metaphor to describe the professional literary culture spawned by the first serious review periodicals, the *Monthly Review* (1749) and the *Critical Review* (1756): "he that writes may be considered as a kind of general challenger, whom everyone has a right to attack."[55] This Corinthian image of public sphere debate soon became tarnished, as must any "naively progressive literary history of eighteenth-century England" that romanticizes the periodicals.[56] Johnson himself acknowledged that "envy and competition have divided the republic of letters into factions."[57] For Blake a half-century later London was not a noble "field of battle" for polemicists, but "a City of Assassinations."[58] Coleridge blamed periodicals for their appeal to the worst of human nature: "as long as there are readers to be delighted with calumny, there will be found reviewers to calumniate."[59] Far from enabling the formation of a rational, democratic public sphere, as Habermas argued, Romantic-era periodicals were perceived by many liberal writers to have become increasingly inseparable from their political affiliation, especially to government. The result was the criminalization of authorship by a "literary police" – in Hazlitt's words – that served as "the engine of party-spirit and faction." The attack on Keats based on his friendship with Leigh Hunt was a conspicuous example, in the post-Napoleonic period, of "that base system of mean and malignant defamation, by which our periodical press has recently been polluted and disgraced."[60] Satire and slander had become a normative rhetorical mode for the periodicals, so much so that William Blackwood set aside a specific fund for combating libel suits, calculating that their expense would be more than offset by the profitable sales of attack journalism.

In the same 1823 essay, Hazlitt describes the venerable *Gentleman's Magazine*, Seward's principal periodical venue, as a bastion of "polite" letters, "the last lingering remains of a former age . . . [a] happy mixture of indolence and study." Seward's attachment to the *Gentleman's Magazine* during her heyday of the 1780s was grounded in its sociable ethos, whereby its readers were also its welcomed amateur contributors in verse, letters, anecdotes, and miscellaneous news of the day: "an alligator stuffed, a mermaid, an Egyptian mummy . . ."[61] From its inception in 1731 the *Gentleman's Magazine* had encouraged the contributions of women in particular. Between 1738 and 1745 Johnson himself served as editor, enhancing its reputation as an intellectual forum appealing to both middle-class and elite markets. But in 1793–4, Seward experienced at first hand the changing character of the *Gentleman's Magazine*, and her own vulnerability to the emerging "rhetoric of professionalism" in periodical discourse, with its pronounced hostility to both women and literary amateurism.[62]

As John Brewer has argued, Seward's critical writings sought to promote and protect "a broadly based critical heritage in which poetry was a sign of higher sensibility and not a professional property."[63] Seward's confrontation with James Boswell over Johnson's reputation in the pages of the *Gentleman's Magazine* serves as a meta-critical lens through which to view the clash between Seward's sociable model of literary culture and the growing professional industry based in London. Seward's relationship with Boswell began around the time of *Louisa*'s publication in 1784, with his attempt to seduce her on a visit to Lichfield. His subsequent love letters, still unpublished, were carefully deflected, and though she spurned his advances, he renewed them at later meetings at Lichfield and in London.[64] The impact of this personal history on their subsequent public quarrel is difficult to judge, but the palpable seeds of the dispute lay in a conversation during Boswell's visit to Lichfield in early 1785, scouring for Johnsonian material. In a letter she subsequently wrote to the poet William Hayley, Seward described how she accused Johnson of "literary jealousy," to which Boswell, unsurprisingly, exhibited symptoms of embarrassment. Seward went on to characterize Johnson's "malevolent" style as a "leveling system of criticism 'which lifts the mean, and lays the mighty low.'"[65] Seward's cultural politics come into clear focus here. Periodical criticism was a "leveling" force, emanating from the metropolis, against which provincial ideals of an elite, leisured, amateur literati must be defended. Clearly unsatisfied by Boswell's response, Seward repeated her claims in the *Gentleman's Magazine* the following year.[66] Writing under the choice name of "Benvolio," Seward defends sociability on difficult terms, that is, as part of an attack on Johnson's indiscriminate "malignance," on the posthumous veneration of a man "who delighted to destroy the self-esteem of almost all who approached him by the wounding force of witty and bitter sarcasm." Predictably, Seward herself was accused, in the following issue, of the same "malevolence" she charged to Johnson, to which she made the following artful reply: "The judge who condemns a criminal upon the clearest proof of his guilt, may with equal truth be called a murderer, as those can be deemed malevolent, who, in the cause of the injured, pronounce Dr. Johnson to have been malignant."

But Seward had less success when she renewed her case against Johnson in 1793 after the publication of Boswell's biography. In his two published replies to Seward, Boswell shifts from defense of Johnson's personality to an attack based on gender. He questions the legitimacy of Seward's very participation in public literary debate: "this kind of conflict is not what I wish to have with ladies." He patronizes her as "my fair antagonist," and apologizes for quoting Latin, knowledge of which her "gentle" education denied her. He concludes by marking a clear line between professional men of letters, such as himself and Johnson, and Seward's "cabal of minor poets and poetesses, who are sadly mortified that Dr. Johnson, by his powerful sentence, assigned their proper station to writers of this description." As recently as 1789–91, the *Gentleman's Magazine* had played host to a long-running dispute over the relative merits of Dryden and Pope in which Seward played a central role, awarded column after column of periodical space to expound her theories of poetry and defend her tastes.[67] Never again would she enjoy such preference. While Seward only ever wrote one paid review, and that at the behest of a friend, the *Edinburgh Review* in 1802 became the first to standardize payments for its contributors, a foundational moment in the professionalization of English journalism after which the London periodicals continued increasingly to enforce Boswell's distinction between the urban professional and provincial "lady" amateur.

Seward's initial literary success in the early 1780s had been built on two patriotic elegies, meditations on the "Nation's woe" at the deaths of Captain Cook and Major André. As befit a Whig, she blamed "haughty Britain" for the war with the American colonies to the extent, she confessed, that she "rever'd her foes."[68] The pre-revolutionary decade being what it was, however, she was able, in the same breath, to uphold André as "a Martyr in the Cause of his King and Country."[69] Seward thus achieved her first celebrity as a national poet, "Britain's muse."[70] Both elegies married a masculine mode of heroic tribute with domestic scenes of female grief and abandonment, a sentimental accounting of the home-front costs of British imperialism, borne disproportionately by women. In *Louisa*, too, Seward crossed between sentimental romance and "imperial georgic."[71] In the rural bower to which the heroine retreats after her betrayal by her lover, she is able to reflect on the baneful effects of economic expansion on the English social fabric: "those gay commercial visions, false and vain" (39). Her "voluptuous" rival, Emira, whom Eugenio marries on account of the failures of his father in global trade, is a gaudy figure for the corruptions of metropolis and empire: "The fair Calypso of a sensual age" (34). Seward's letters and published criticism from the 1780s also contain a nationalist agenda. They focus almost obsessively on the purity of a national style and lineage in poetry, on asserting the claims of "modern" and contemporary poets (Gray, Collins, Hayley, etc.) to the British canon. After 1789, however, Seward's carefully developed public role – as a Whig patriot and guardian of the national taste in poetry – became impossible to maintain. The hostess of a provincial literary salon could no longer command the attention of a metropolitan literary culture fraught with political realignments and their scribbling partisans. The 1790s witnessed a rapid expansion in the number, publication, and readership of periodicals, as Wordsworth famously deplored in his Preface to *Lyrical Ballads*. This metastasizing, highly politicized print culture demanded a very different woman writer, one such as Mary Robinson – a poet, novelist, critic, editor, and celebrator of the metropolis who offered a "resolutely urban, democratic, and cosmopolitan" image both of the new literary journalism of the 1790s and of her professionalized self.[72] In the Jacobin Mary Robinson, Seward's fears of the "leveling" tendencies of metropolitan print culture, and her own irrelevance to it, were spectacularly realized.

In their dispute over Johnson, Seward allowed Boswell the last word. In her conceding the field, we deduce her judgment that the new age of periodical journalism depended upon a "malignant" form of "paper-war" to which personal invective and political partisanship were endemic and she ultimately unsuited. Even the *Gentleman's Magazine*, which had for half a century symbolized the "alliance between the gentry and the *haute bourgeoisie*" in the polite world of letters, could no longer serve as a venue for the policing of sociability.[73] Seward put on a "doublet and hose" for her performance of literary authority – the sociable Benvolio – only to be unmasked by Boswell as a female pretender, a "fair lady" of "uneasy bosom."[74] In the context of her declining presence in the periodicals during the 1790s, and the parallel decline of her literary reputation, it is possible to conceive how the provincial Handelian festivals and her private concerts offered Seward an experience of female-friendly sociability in art, and self-affirmation as a leader of the provincial Whig cultural elite that was no longer available to her in the "leveling," increasingly professionalized literary world of London.

IV

The unique possibilities of the Handel oratorio as a quasi-religious affirmation of social consensus were not immediately obvious. Handel's interest in the genre was a combination of accident and necessity: by the late 1730s, his thirty-year dominance of Italian opera in London had come to an end after a rancorous split with his aristocratic patrons, and he sought a new dramatic musical form that would be commercially viable. It was in this purely practical spirit that Handel's librettist, Charles Jennens, called his *Messiah* an "entertainment," a description that quickly became an embarrassment to its champions, who were called upon to answer charges of blasphemy.[75] The substance of that answer – that Handel's music possesses a "sublimity" that transcends its worldly theatrical representation – came to define the Handelian legacy for the subsequent two centuries. Seward's description of an oratorio performance during the Lenten season in London in 1786 is typical of dozens of Handelian tributes, in prose and verse, recorded across the eighteenth century:

> the sublimity of the harmonies, so full and complete in all those *great* effects which Handel's matchless genius conceived . . . all these admirables produced one grand result, that completely satisfied my imagination.[76]

The musical sublime in Handel should not be confused with Wordsworth's. It was communal not personal, social not spiritual – an aesthetic mandate for British legitimacy, power, and favor in the eyes of God. In Seward's words, Handel's oratorios "exist for the honour of England."[77] By endowing his oratorios with the aesthetic powers of the sublime, Handelian commentators licensed the composer with the power to transcend worldliness of all kinds, including political division.

The sublime – that vaguest of eighteenth-century clichés – was especially flexible in its application to music. In Longinus' brief comment on the sublime in music, the Greek text ambiguously employs a word meaning both polyphony and embellishments – translated by William Smith as "divisions" – designating both the choral "church" style and the decorative ornaments of the virtuoso, both the sacred choruses of *Messiah* and the sensual delights of a Farinelli cadenza.[78] Oratorio itself, built on the interplay of chorus and solo voice, exploited this doubleness, enjoying the best of both worlds, virtue and virtuosity. That said, the sublime owed as much to Handel as Handel did to it: "it became most unusual for ideas about [the sublime] to be expressed *without* reference to choruses by, or in the manner of, Handel."[79] For some, it was all too much. Charles Burney, official historian of the 1784 Commemoration, chafed at what had become the official Handelian liturgy: "one key of Panegyric is all they want," he complained, "fine!—very fine!—charming! Exquisite! Grand! Sublime!!!"[80] Through his association with the sublime, Handel, the highest of high baroque composers, was also the first "Romantic" composer, not in terms of style but of his cultural status. He was the first composer awarded the rank of genius, the first to be grouped with Shakespeare and Milton, the first to be paid homage in Westminster Abbey. In short, Handel himself had to be sanctified before his music could be allowed the power to sanctify, and the relentless employment of the sublime as a *de facto* heroic epithet to the oratorios served that purpose.

Handel did not aestheticize the bible in his oratorios: the aesthetic terms of his musical treatment had already been set by an established discourse of the sublime in biblical commentary. Eighteenth-century critics took for granted that the power of the Old Testament lay as much in its language as its doctrine. Certain passages, such as "Fiat Lux!" from Genesis and the Song of Moses in Deuteronomy, were considered synonymous with sublime power. Handel's music, in setting Old Testament texts, translated this power from the pulpit to the stage, making use in particular of the heartstopping volume of large choruses. The swelling, reverberating effect in an enclosed space, in the presence of royalty and hundreds of one's fellow citizens, could be emotionally overwhelming. "What a glorious spectacle!" reported a correspondent to *The Daily Post* in 1739 after a production of *Israel in Egypt* (1738) attended by the Prince of Wales:

> To see a crowded audience of the first quality of a nation, headed by the Heir Apparent of their Sovereign's crown and virtues . . . sitting enchanted . . . at sounds that at the same time express'd in so sublime a manner the Praises of the Deity itself . . . Did such a taste prevail universally in a People, that People might expect on a like Occasion, if such Occasion should ever happen to them, the same Deliverance as those Praises celebrate; and Protestant, free, virtuous, united, Christian England, need little fear, at any time hereafter, the whole force of slavish, bigoted, united, unchristian Popery, risen up against her, should such a Conjuncture ever hereafter happen.[81]

The oratorio libretti are not concerned with the afterlife and spiritual redemption – that is, *metaphysical* sublimity – but sublimity as material, specifically political power embodied in Old Testament subjects. The relationship between Handel's music and libretti is thus complementary: the libretto laid out the historical antecedents for British exceptionalism as a "Protestant, free, virtuous, united, Christian" nation, while the music granted these material claims the necessary emotional depth through a new choral language of transport and awe.

In essence the eighteenth-century theory of the sublime in music was a theory of meaning: an attempt to accord music a referential power, to secure it from pure sensuality and the degradation of unmeaning, which had been the substance of the English critique of music since Jeremy Collier.[82] By mid-century, the fashionable rhetoric of sublimity had become indelibly associated with certain signature Handelian musical effects: abrupt modulations, dynamic variation, and the monumental harmonic texture of the oratorio choruses. The unadorned style of the oratorios' staging also helped facilitate the Handelian appropriation of the popular discourse of sublimity. Without sets or manifest dramatic action – all the apparatus of spectacle – the oratorios functioned as a kind of "mental opera" (to adapt Byron's description of his plays intended for private consumption). A long essay published on the 1763 oratorio season described oratorio as "a Poem, accompanied with music, where, unincumbered [sic] with the absurdity of a dramatic exhibition, they jointly affect the mind, by a representation of some great and interesting subject, impressed with all the force of their combined powers."[83] The Handelians' answer to the Puritan critique of public performance (revived by Cowper in *The Task*) was to insist on the ability of the oratorio to transcend its theatrical setting and enter the imaginations of its audience as a moral idea.

Enfolding Handel in the aura of the sublime was crucial for another reason. Only the language of sublimity carried the cultural weight required to erase from popular memory Handel's long career with the Italian opera, and its negative associations with aristocratic decadence, foreign influence, and shallow virtuosic splendor. In a letter to Helen Maria Williams recounting her attendance at the Manchester oratorio festival of 1785, Seward is careful to specify her friend John Saville's "unerring power, the energy and pathos of his expression" as exemplifying a proper Handelian style free of virtuosic self-indulgence: "he never aims to dazzle or astonish his audience." She contrasts Saville's performance with the soprano Gertrud Mara, hired from the King's Theatre opera house in London, whose "gay ornaments" marred the Handelian solemnity of the occasion by appealing only to "the false taste of the multitude."[84] Seward and Cowper thus meet in their contempt for London's opera culture. In *Louisa* the hero is cuckolded by an aristocratic opera maven – a "haughty Lord, licentious, false, and vain" – who is himself in thrall to a "swarthy Opera Dancer" (76). The ritual scapegoating of the decadent, elitist, and secular Italian opera was necessary for the production of Handelian oratorio as its opposite: a musical idiom that stood for a virtuous, inclusive, Christian nation state.

v

For Seward the most convenient means of elevating Handel to the ranks of the English sublime was to link his name with Milton's. The eighteenth-century poetical consensus that surrounded Milton – both Seward and Cowper, for example, considered themselves his natural inheritors – provided the model for a similar consensus in music culture built around Handel. To discover in oneself "impulses congenial to those with which Milton wrote and Handel composed" thus represented for Seward the synaesthetic ideal of art. "To produce the united effects resulting from the combination of perfect poetry with perfect music," she wrote in 1788, "it was necessary that Milton's strains should be set by Handel."[85] This, of course, was not simply an ideal. Seward in fact had a specific work in mind: Handel's oratorical setting of Milton's pastoral poems "L'Allegro" and "Il Penseroso," entitled *L'Allegro, il Penseroso ed il Moderato* (1740).

Milton's "Il Penseroso," in its popular Handelian setting, served as the compass point of Seward's taste and her poetic career. Miltonic pastorale was Seward's chief idiom, quite literally from the cradle. She was a literary prodigy, and could recite passages from *Paradise Lost* before the age of three.[86] Then at Batheaston, where literary imitation and parody were stock in trade, "L'Allegro" and "Il Penseroso" were by far the most popular models. Seward's first poem for the "Vase," an "Invocation to the Comic Muse," recalled "L'Allegro," and more than a dozen others of the published poems speak directly to Miltonic pastorale. Little surprise then that at the opening of her most ambitious poetic creation, *Louisa*, Seward explicitly invokes the "matchless strains" of a famous aria from Handel's setting of Milton's "Il Penseroso" as the register of her heroine's own voice:

> Presaging notes my lips unconscious try,
> And murmur—"Hide me from Day's garish eye!"
> Ah! Blest, had Death a shade eternal thrown,
> And hid me from the woes I since have known!
> Beneath my trembling fingers lightly rung
> The Lute's sweet chords, responsive while I sung.   (5)

The union of music, poetry, and oratory described by Anselm Bayly here forms the model for the lyric voice of *Louisa*, who is figured specifically as a Handelian singer. It underscores the complex imbrication of poetry and music in Georgian culture that Handel, in setting "Il Penseroso," did not borrow from Milton's fame so much as create it. As Joseph Warton averred in 1756, "by a strange fatality 'L'Allegro' and 'Il Penseroso' lay in a sort of obscurity, the private enjoyment of a few curious readers, till they were set to admirable music by Mr. Handel."[87] Music, in cultural-historical terms, was the lyric progenitor of Milton's verse. For Seward, the connection between Milton and Handel was not a fanciful analogy but a material, synaesthetic bond.

The union of music and poetry is a key theme of both Milton poems, and "L'Allegro" articulates the fantasy of aesthetic synthesis Seward stages in *Louisa*:

> Lap me in soft Lydian Aires,
> Married to immortal verse
> Such as the meeting soul may pierce . . .
> The melting voice through mazes running;
> Untwisting all the chains that ty
> The hidden soul of harmony.   (136–8, 142–4)

"Il Penseroso," meanwhile, uncannily anticipates Handel himself, or at least the following century's worth of Handelian tribute writing. At the end of the poem, the Melancholic crosses back into the social frame at the hearing of "sweet music." Although he commits himself to "Cloysters pale," his most passionate wish is for something like the Handel Commemoration:

> There let the pealing Organ blow,
> To the full voic'd Quire below,
> In Service high, and Anthems cleer,
> As may with sweetnes, through mine ear,
> Dissolve me into extasies,
> And bring all Heav'n before mine eyes . . .   (161–6)

Here Milton, fittingly enough, produces the template for the Romantic-era reception of Handel. "Il Penseroso," a signature poem of Sewardian sociability, comes with musical accompaniment from its origin, and Seward composes the Miltonic pastorale of *Louisa* with Handel's music, and the poem's reflections on the musical sublime, explicitly in mind.

That said, there is little sublimity in *Louisa*, in the true Handelian sense. The poem's rich sensuality suggests rather a revisionary reading of Handel's career, a return of the operatic repressed. In a letter from 1764 Seward records a lively debate over Handel in the drawing-room at

Lichfield.[88] An unnamed "connoisseur" had argued that for all Handel's superiority in "spirited and sublime composition," he was deficient in "delicacy and tenderness" and unable to rouse "amorous sentiments." For this opinion the guest was roundly abused by both Seward and Saville. Seward concluded the argument with her tale of a squinty, "ill-formed" governess who, on a visit to Lichfield, had moved the young poet to tears with her performance of a song from Handel's *Athaliah* (1733). On concluding her performance, the governess was advised to employ the song as a "weapon of attack" on any future object of her desire. The governess took the cue and, within "a few weeks," had succeeded in marrying her new employer. The erotic power of music to "melt . . . and enrapt" – musical performance as a scene of seduction – is likewise the implicit literary contract between poet and reader in *Louisa*. Taking the model of her own affective response to Handel – "tears of delight streamed down my cheeks" – and in choosing to quote an aria from a non-sacred work, *Il Penseroso,* Seward subtly shifts the stylistic emphasis of *Louisa* from the sublime to "those honied and ever-soothing notes" and "amorous sentiments" of Handel's "pathetic" songs and, by implication, toward his origins in the secular Italian opera.

The operatic style of *Louisa* provoked censure characteristic of antioperatic discourse for almost a century past. *The European Magazine*, heretofore a Seward supporter, featured a lengthy indictment, by turns indignant and sarcastic, directed at the poem's moral and stylistic "obscenity." *Louisa* offered only a "fairy-land of wild, erroneous sensibility, sentiment, and affection," the product of a "sentimentally wild and absurd genius." The reviewer deplored the corrupting effect of "rapturous lines" in which "there is so much billing and cooing . . . so much keen longing, such melting raptures, extacies, and transports, etc., etc." For all its misogynist bias, the *European Magazine* review nevertheless correctly identifies the appeal of the poem in Seward's eroticization of narrative deferral and delay. It is the reader's pleasure, complains the critic, "to *sweetly* pre-suppose that Louisa is yet to be a mother by Eugenio," a literary effect the poet achieves by decelerating the plot through the "excursive Fancy" of lyric effusion while keeping the plot's erotic "*consummation* forever in view."[89] That is, the retarding of the plot shifts the reader's attention to Seward's lyric voice, to a sentimental diction and style pregnant with the narrative consummations the poem withholds.

As Leslie Ritchie has documented, pastoral songs were a fixture of late eighteenth-century polite musical repertoire. The latest compositions of rural melancholy performed at the theaters and pleasure gardens of

London were rapidly disseminated to the drawing-rooms of women amateurs across the kingdom. The songs then found their audience in a multitude of private and semi-private concert settings. Musical accomplishment as a commodity of leisure – the preserve of women of the gentry – harmonized perfectly with the semiotics of pastoral, in which the landscape is inhabited by leisured, not laboring individuals. The "silent Dell" to which the heroine retreats in *Louisa* thus represents a "*locus amoenus* where literary and musical pastoral traditions intersect."[90] Seward's introduction of Louisa as a singer of pastoral in a rural setting is a sentimental overdetermination that both sets the high virtuosic register of the poem and projects beyond the solitary reader-recipient of the "epistle" in the narrative to an imagined concert audience. *Contra* John Sitter's influential study of mid-century poetics, the writers and readers of Seward's circle were not "solitary."[91] For all the atmospherics of loneliness, the domestic concert stage remains the absent-present of *Louisa*: as the scene not of visual dramatic action, but of poetic performance and an essential sociability. Seward is attempting to colonize, through verse, the affective realm of music charted by Avison, specifically its unique power to produce sensual "rapture." To realize the same Handelian affects, however, Seward must employ devices congenial to her own medium. In the first of the poem's "epistles," Louisa's luxurious opening invocation of Handel – "on my lip the ling'ring Cadence play'd" – serves as an elaborate tease to her female correspondent in the East Indies:

> Cease, vain Regrets, excursive Fancy cease!
> Ye only wound afresh my bleeding peace,
> And keep from gentle Emma's anxious ear
> Th'event she longs, yet kindly dreads, to hear . . .   (7)

This state of readerly arousal, stimulated by delay, is transferable across the literary economy of *Louisa*, from Emma's "anxious ear" to the lover Eugenio's "musing, ardent gaze" and "frequent, smother'd sigh," (8) to Emira's "restless blushes, [and] voluptuous sigh," (33) to the heroine's own difficulty in telling her story:

> Thou see'st, my Emma, with what fond delay
> Th'unwilling Spirit loiters on her way . . .
> To stop the sad narration . . .   (11)

Seward's own "fond delay" as author of *Louisa* consists of a gestural, self-conscious poetic performance that resists narrative development, and delights in the teasing powers of sentimental exclamation.[92] Narrative, for Seward, is inimical to passions and their virtuosic lyric expression. Louisa and her lover never meet in the course of the story, and in fact never address each other even in their letters. What appeared to reviewers an absurdity of the plot was a lyric necessity. The heroine's lover must be absent and virtuous, but also simulate betrayal in order to produce the maximum "passion" in the heroine. The reviewer for the *European Magazine* saw in these poetic tactics a kind of "disgustful" soft porn, but *Louisa*'s popularity suggests many readers were less fastidious, and set themselves to enjoy a poem absorbed by the virtuosic demonstration of its own lyric powers, the engine of which is a withheld erotic "consummation":

> All Nature smiles! Nor e'en the jocund Day,
> When festal roses strew the bridal way,
> Darts thro' the Virgin breast such keen delight,
> As when soft Fears with gay Belief unite;
> As Hope, sweet, warm, seducing Hope inspires,
> Which somewhat questions, what it most desires;
> Reads latent meaning in a Lover's eye,
> Thrills at his glance, and trembles at his sigh . . . (9)

The description of Louisa's feelings here articulates the reader's toward the text. The poem's audience – figured as a still unravished bride – "reads latent meaning" everywhere in *Louisa*, which, for more than eighty-five pages, "questions, what it most desires." The poem's state of Keatsian suspension (the terms of the critic's "disgust" anticipate the response to *Endymion* two decades later) is engineered by Seward's own virtuosic technique, a voluptuous excursiveness of language that both models and inspires her reader's ever-intensifying wish for the lovers' union. The result is a lyric style that best satisfies where it is most teasing. For example, Seward's epithets for the virgin's "Hope" – "sweet, warm, seducing" – have the realization of her nuptial longings most decidedly in view.

This passage certainly inflamed James Boswell, who declared himself "warmly delighted" with the poem – words underlined – and set about seducing the author by way of printed encomium.[93] In his effusive review of *Louisa*, he selected the "description of the Delight of Hope," cited above, to exemplify Seward's engaging blend of "delightful Feelings" with "violent Passions."[94] "To those *who know what Love is*," Boswell writes with suggestive emphasis, "[it] will be enchanting." True enjoyment of *Louisa* is not for the sexually uninitiated. Boswell employed the same word to describe his private audience with the author at Lichfield – an eroticized scene of reading/recitation we find in a letter to William

Temple: "Her eyes are exquisite, her *embonpoint* delightful, her sensibility melting. Think of your friend (you know him well) reclined upon a sofa with her while she read to him some of the finest passages of her *Louisa*. How enchanting!"[95] In the context of this letter, and the unpublished love notes to Seward, we are able to comprehend the otherwise obtuse conclusion to Boswell's review of *Louisa*: "I close my remarks upon it, being afraid that I can claim for them but one Half of what Louisa allows to her Lover." If the flattering review constitutes a form of verbal praise of Seward, the other, unspecified "half" allowed to a full-fledged lover would be carnal adoration, which Boswell, taking the role of Eugenio, codedly offers to Seward/Louisa. Whatever one's opinion of Boswell's behavior toward Seward, his unbuttoned reading of *Louisa* is faithful to the text and the basis, I suggest, of the poem's great popularity.

Allied to its eroticized strategies of deferral, *Louisa* also deploys the pastoral device of visual abstraction to shift the reader's focus from lyric content to vocalic medium. In his review, Boswell places *Louisa's* opening Handelian passage alongside the "Delight of Hope" – recalling once again, in coded form, Seward's reading to him while they reclined together on the sofa at Lichfield: "Beneath my trembling Fingers lightly rung/The Lute's sweet Chords responsive while I sung." In the melopoetic "Description of Noon" that follows, which Boswell calls "equal to anything I have read in any language," Seward's word-painting is not intended to produce literal picturesque effects. It invites not the reader's visualization of the scene described but the opposite – an abstraction *from* the visual:

> 'Twas Noon, and ripen'd Summer's fervid ray
> From cloudless Ether shed oppressive day . . .
> My voice, that floated on the waving wind,
> Taught the soft echoes of the neighb'ring plains
> Milton's sweet lay, in Handel's matchless strains.   (5)

Instead of visible fruit, Seward offers "ripen'd Summer"; instead of blue sky, a "cloudless Ether." Likewise, the voice that floats on the wind cannot be seen and the "neighb'ring plains" are empty, no more than a verbal signpost. In keeping with the poetic tradition of retirement, from Milton to Thomson and Gray, the lines train our focus on the formal beauties of the lyric voice rather than the actual landscape. Seward's pastoral language – abstract, redundant, extravagant – is certainly a failure when viewed through a Wordsworthian lens, but can also be read as a performative tactic asserting the privilege of lyric over the demands of visual, action-driven narrative.

Pastoral as a visual poetics of description must therefore be distinguished from its use in *Louisa* as a theatrical mode of gesture and performance. As both sign and supplement of its performative origins, Seward's diction is necessarily over the top, self-conscious, "virtuosic." From the Salisbury home of another prominent Whig Handelian, James Harris, author of a well-known treatise on music, comes an account of a dinner party in 1775 that witnessed a literal enactment of the theatricality inherent in Seward's poetics of retirement. The performer, in a superb coincidence, was Louisa Harris, his musical daughter. On repairing down to the river bank for coffee, the party guests "were supriz'd with a most harmonious invisible sound. The conversation imediately [sic] stopped, and at length we discover'd Louisa had conceal'd herself among the trees and was singing to her harp."[96] For Louisa Harris musical performance offered a modish opportunity for fanciful self-display. Female avatars of late eighteenth-century retirement, such as she and Seward, claimed through poetry and music an interior, pastoral landscape for themselves. By so doing, they were also "creating a new way to be social beings."[97] Beyond the 1780s, however, the stylistic demands of this theatrical, sentimental mode of art and being appeared increasingly alien to a generation of readers raised on such publications as *The Task* and *Lyrical Ballads*, as it did to a growing class of music lovers for whom the pseudo-rural play spaces of the Georgian estates and pleasure gardens, and their musical-pastoral repertoire, were rapidly receding in importance. Thus, in literary-historical terms, Seward's *Louisa* fell between two stools. Her "poetical novel's" ecstatic strains performed a baroque disconnection from the work of narrative and characterization demanded by the actual fiction market she sought to colonize, while the poem's self-conscious virtuosity separated it from the nascent literary virtues enshrined by Cowper and Wordsworth, from "truth" and sincerity as they would come to be understood in Romantic poetics.

VI

With these direct textual and rhetorical links between Handel, Milton, and Seward's *Louisa*, I return to the initial questions I posed concerning Seward and Cowper. Why the divergent fates of their two major poems, *Louisa* and *The Task*, in literary history? And why Seward's apparently disproportionate indignation at Cowper's critique of the 1784 Handel Commemoration? To these questions one more may now be added. Cowper, at least as much as Seward, modeled his poetic style on Milton:

he adopted Miltonic blank verse for *The Task*, and fashioned a persona of moody detachment strongly reminiscent of "Il Penseroso." As poetic tributes to Milton and celebrators of melancholic seclusion, Seward's *Louisa* and Cowper's *The Task* would appear to have very much in common. Why is it that they clearly *don't*?

Differences between *Louisa* and *The Task* are easily identifiable at the stylistic level of the poems themselves, in diction, tropes, and the relative "gaudiness" of phraseology. But I am more concerned here with the ideological and cultural reasons behind those differences. For those, we must return to Seward's letters and her ongoing, one-way dialogue with Cowper's poetics. She was, it must be said, a poor reader of Cowper. Beyond cursory compliments to its "beauties," Seward pays little attention to the poetry of *The Task* itself, and appears to have had no real understanding of its radical innovations. Rather, as we have seen, her critical judgments are overwhelmed by angry reflections on the personality and religion of its author. In a letter from 1800 she bitterly attributes the popularity of *The Task* to the fact it "gratifies the two most general and nurtured feelings of the human mind; its enthusiasm concerning the Deity, and its malice to its fellow creatures."[98] The "malice" of Cowper's satire, more than its pastoral reflections, becomes the brush with which Seward tars the entire poem. On occasion she extends sympathy to Cowper, as "the victim of religious despondency," but mostly she blames his own "depraved and selfish" nature, calling him a "sarcastic misanthropist" and "vapourish egotist."[99]

It is difficult to understand what Seward means by the depravity of *The Task* unless we place her critique in the context of her Handelian ethos of sociability. Seward views the "fanatic and illiberal" tone of the anti-Handelian passage of book VI not as an aberration, but as the spirit of the poem as a whole. Seward's rage toward Cowper smells of literary jealousy, but it originates in deep cultural loyalties and in a specific politics: "Fanatics have almost always cold hearts," she wrote of him, a chill Seward thought characteristic of the "levelling system" of metropolitan literary culture in general, which had produced "the fastidious *coldness* of modern criticism" favored by the London periodicals.[100] Cowper, the periodicals, and their fanatical, leveling, low-church dogma thus combined in Seward's imagination to portend a wintry future for Britain, as harbingers even of jacobinical "terror." For Seward, Cowper and the new class of professional writers to which he belonged had arrogantly excluded themselves from the Handelian model of culture, that is, from the broad Anglican communion, from liberal Whig nationalism, and from the sociable contract that music culture shared with the old order of amateur polite letters. The attack on *Louisa* in The *European Magazine* did not go unanswered. But Seward's defenders characteristically chose verse as their weapon, with poor results. Thomas Whalley in the *Morning Chronicle* and an anonymous odester in the *Gentleman's Magazine* in turn became the object of mockery in subsequent issues of the *European Magazine*. The amateur poets of Seward's circle found themselves increasingly ill equipped to win such literary battles against professional prose-writers, especially on the enemy turf of the periodicals themselves.

Both highly popular poets of the 1780s, Seward and Cowper appropriated the poetry and persona of Milton's "Il Penseroso" to entirely different ends. In *Louisa* the heroine is a pre-Romantic, pastoral figure of melancholy, whose self-conscious identification with Handel's "delicate and pathetic" strains renders her agreeable, indeed attractive, to the norms of sociable art.[101] A melancholy sentiment beautifully expressed is not the same as melancholy as such: in fact, it is nearly opposite in its signification. "Retired Leasure," in Milton as in *Louisa*, is the lyric enactment of a gorgeous departure, an entirely theatrical mode of self-seclusion ("Il Penseroso," 49). A retreat from society to the accompaniment of a Handel air cannot escape its own beauty. As Milton's Penseroso admits, "These pleasures Melancholy give" (175). Seward never loses sight of the figurative essence of pastoral solitude, as a vehicle of virtuoso lyric performance.

Cowper, by contrast, as the self-proclaimed "self-sequestered man" of *The Task*, literalizes the pastoral trope of retreat; he attempts to create a self out of the fantasy of rural solitude. Accordingly for Seward, Cowper's retirement is not a beautiful trope but only the precondition of his satire and the jarring poetic strains of faction. The two registers of *The Task* which critics have often called distinct, even incompatible – the Augustan moral satire and the proto-Wordsworthian exercising of the "philosophic mind" – are, to Seward, entirely of a piece.[102] Cowper's moody recluse is a genuine misanthrope, a modern, fanatical incarnation of Il Penseroso. His solitude produces not pleasure but "egotism," and egotism's consequence is an anti-social sense of superiority, an annoying inclination to mock and preach. "Shield me," Seward protests, "from saints who look upon the world as a den of fools and knaves."[103] The motives for Seward's dark view of Cowper now become clearer. It is not simply a difference in musical taste that is at issue. To Seward, Cowper has repudiated her Miltonic definition of literary performance modeled on music culture, where even the secluded heroine plays and sings to an imagined audience, in favor of "vapourish egot[ism]," the domain of the solitary, sarcastic male writer.

In her "Remonstrance," Seward thus addresses Cowper as a poet who stands outside of the Georgian culture of sociability, one who expressly rejects the Handelian model of congregational faith and nation in favor of an emergent Romantic model: the dissenting, individualized, spiritualized, anti-social voice of *The Task*. In her metaphoric connection between Cowper's frozen heart and the "fastidious coldness of modern criticism" – which she identified principally with the "malevolent" example set by Johnson – Seward in fact prophesied the wholesale politicization of periodical discourse over the following decades, its "sub-division into petty gangs and factions," as Peacock described it in 1818.[104] The disagreement between the two poets over Handel likewise marks the suffocatingly close relation between poetic taste and sectarian and political allegiance in the reign of George III. For Seward, Cowper's attack on the Handel Commemoration is a product of the same anti-national, "meth-odistical" excess as *The Task* in general, and makes visible a connection between Cowper's anti-social poetics and a radical party ideology. While Seward's love of Handel marks her as a Whig monarchist, patriot poet, and champion of the sociable arts, Cowper's rejection of the 1784 Commemoration smacks of Jacobinism *avant la lettre*.

If the rituals of Handelian consensus in Britain endure long into the nineteenth century, amateur virtuosity in poetry does not. The celebrities of Batheaston were quickly forgotten and Anna Seward, in her time one of the best-known poets in England, followed Lady Miller into oblivion (if one does not count the latter's revival as the sapphic Mrs. Leo Hunter in Dickens's *Pickwick Papers*). "Who reads them now?" wondered Hazlitt in 1818, looking back a generation to the vanished fame of Seward and Hayley.[105] With a slew of critical articles in the past decade, and two new biographies, Seward's significance as an influential taste-maker and literary lion of the 1780s is now being revived. Less so her actual poetry. But while there is little prospect of reclaiming *Louisa* for literary anthologies and the undergraduate classroom, it is nevertheless a hugely informative poem from a literary-historical point of view. For the influential promoters of "ancient music" in Britain, Handel's oratorios replaced the decadent Italian *opere serie* with a form of sacred, mental opera, an original English art form to which Seward devoted much time and many superlatives, and identified as the standard of sublimity and sentiment for her own art. For two centuries literary history has adopted a metropolitan disdain for the provincial, amateur literary culture in which Seward thrived and for its Handelian values. Through a musico-cultural reading of *Louisa*, however, we are able to recover at least an outline of the provincial scene of literary sociability that made the poem's sentimental effusions so popular and Seward a celebrated poet of the 1780s. To do more than that, however, is difficult. We must not only enter into the aesthetic protocols of a different *episteme* – the age of the virtuoso literary amateur – but create a reader who is not ourselves: one who recognizes the lyric register of a text modeled on the performative media of music and the domestic stage, and who is capable of reproducing its melancholy pleasures in the act of private reading.

In the new cultural order of the 1790s, the image of the genteel Louisa singing Handel's "Il Penseroso" in the woods soon becomes an embarrassment, recognizable only in the terms Cowper provided in *The Task*, as one of those

> . . . self-deluded nymphs and swains
> Who dream they have a taste for fields and groves . . .
> And crowd the roads, impatient for the town!   (III: 316–17, 319)

By century's end, Cowper's implicit distinction between fake sentimentality (feminine or effeminized) and Romantic sincerity (masculine) was on its way to becoming fully established, to the point where it was almost impossible for anyone after 1800 to "hear" Seward's poetry as her first audiences and readers heard it. In 1783 James Boswell found himself "enchanted" and aroused by Seward's reading of *Louisa*, passages of which he considered "equal to anything . . . in any language," while Walter Scott, preparing a three-volume edition of Seward's poetry for publication in 1810, described it to Joanna Baillie as "absolutely execrable."[106] Around the same time Robert Southey, on a visit to Lichfield, listened to his hostess perform one of the rituals of lyric sociability – a verse tribute to his arrival – and found it deeply ridiculous:

> I took my seat, and, by favour of a blessed table, placed my elbow so that I could hide my face by leaning it upon my hand, and have the help of that hand to keep down the risible muscles, while I listened to my own praise and glory set forth, in sonorous rhymes, and declared by one who read them with theatrical effect . . . The temptation to laugh at a time when you ought not is a terrible one.[107]

Southey chokes back his laughter for the sake of politeness, but his need to do so shows his discomfort with the "theatrical," virtuoso idiom of verse that at one time so affected Boswell. Amateur sociability, and the entire

Sewardian culture of poetry, had become permanently quaint and "risible" barely a quarter century since the heyday of Batheaston and Seward's national fame. Her cherished idea that poetry, like a Handel oratorio, might help the nation at large to transcend faction and the strife of personality, and so preserve "the sanctities of society," would soon become incomprehensible, a nonsense provocation, the very opposite of the mission of modern poetry, of Byronism and its *poètes maudits*.

CHAPTER 2

The Burney baroque

I

Frances Burney idealized her father and music in the same ecstatic language. In her journal of 1773 she describes herself as forever "delighted at the Goodness, the merit, & the sweetness of that best of men." Only pages later, on hearing the castrato Millico perform at the King's Theatre opera house, she has "no Words to express the delight which his singing gave me ... for his Voice is so sweet ... a sweetness that enchanted me."[1] The language is identical in *Evelina* (1778), in which the heroine describes the opera as "of all entertainments, the sweetest and most delightful" (38). To his novelist daughter, Charles Burney *was* music, specifically, the "sweet" *galant* music of the Italian opera he championed in his career and literary productions. For his sake – and the music's – Frances Burney felt compelled to purify them both of the more material odors of music *culture*: its spirit-crushing toadyism, frivolousness, and association with luxury and fashionable *galanterie*.

James Cox, whose exhibition of musical automata the heroine visits in *Evelina* (see the introduction), was a watchmaker by trade, and delegated the musical inventions to his mercurial Belgian partner John Joseph Merlin, "chief mechanician" and manager of the exhibit. Merlin was best known in 1770s London as a piano-maker for the prominent London-based German composers, who included J. C. Bach, Carl Friedrich Abel, and Johann Christian Fischer (Figure 2). He was thus also a natural friend and colleague of Charles Burney. Burney bought at least two of his pianos on which his virtuoso daughter Esther (Hetty) played to audiences (and Frances, occasionally, to herself), while Merlin himself was a regular guest in the Burney parlor. Burney and Merlin traversed the full gamut of Georgian virtuosity, from luxury exhibit to musical performance. Both were collaborators in the up-market business of "polite" music and promoters, for commercial gain, of the virtuoso *galant* style. Merlin provided

53

Figure 2. Thomas Gainsborough, *Johann Christian Fischer* (*c.* 1780). The Royal Collection © HM Queen Elizabeth II. The literary elevation of music is evident in this 1780s' image, where musical instruments serve as luxury props to the cerebral work of musical creation. Friend of Charles Burney, Fischer's expensive, even glamorous persona is artfully balanced between leisure and industry, gentility and genius.

the instruments, while Burney furnished repertoire and instruction to generations of young ladies of fashion.

Georgian London's music industry was unique among the European capitals in its capacity to support a virtuoso community: "only a large market could provide sufficient employment for a specialist; only highly skilled specialists could perform the increasingly difficult music placed before them."[2] Virtuosity was, in this sense, a new and unique aspect of late Georgian life. "My eldest daughter was a better player at 7 years old than I was at 17," Charles Burney admitted to a friend, "but early players were then a Phenomena."[3] In short Frances Burney was born into a family embedded in Georgian virtuoso culture. Her sister Esther was considered one of the best young pianists in London. She married another virtuoso, her cousin Charles, who made a meager living as a pit musician and with whom she performed celebrated duets. Her father exhibited Esther on the family's arrival from King's Lynn in 1768, and it was as her teacher and impresario that Charles Burney first attracted the attention of the fashionable houses, who called on him to instruct their daughters. Her performance of "the difficult lessons of Scarlatti" earned the admiration of the Duke of York.[4] As Burney's fame grew, he was granted the power of musical-cultural imprimatur himself. Everyone, it seemed – from the eager parents of would-be prodigies to established stars of the Italian opera – passed through the Burney parlor on St. Martin's Street hoping for his unofficial preferment. Young Frances, a famous dullard in the nursery, was to be a late-blooming talent in a family of prodigies.

Music abounds in Burney's novels but there is no culture of listening (that would wait for the nineteenth-century bourgeoisie). People of fashion talk over the music they patronize. In *Cecilia* (1782), Mrs. Harrel's "love of the Opera was merely a love of company, fashion and shew," and Mr. Meadows, who sets the fashionable tone at the King's Theatre opera house, declares himself "sick to death of music" (131, 266). In this context the rapturous response of Evelina, Cecilia, and Burney herself to the fashionable music of the opera is not in itself fashionable. Only these reformed, bourgeois heroines are capable listeners: "[Millico] said to my Father, that his *Figliuole* ha[ve] *musical souls.*"[5] A profound element of Frances Burney's lifelong writerly rage for her father was that the fashionable world, of which music was both ritual and emblem, should have degraded them both. Her idealization of her father, her critique of fashionable society, and her various defensive strategies toward music culture – the subjects of this chapter – thus belong to the same impulse.

The reality of life as a service provider in the luxury economy of Georgian music, a fate Charles Burney worked so hard to overcome, could be bleak. Most musicians lived in the city, close to their places of work in the theaters and cathedrals. Their incomes placed them above the laboring class, but not higher than "the most successful of the highly skilled artisans in luxury trades, such as musical instrument makers, jewellers, watchmakers, and fashionable hairdressers."[6] Music was neither professionalized like the law nor offered the earning potential of medical practice. As the composer and organist Samuel Wesley lamented, "I have every day more and more cause to curse the day that ever my poor good father suffered musick to be my profession ... the whole is a degrading business to any man of spirit or any abilities."[7] Frances Burney endorses this conclusion in *The Wanderer* (1814), in which the heroine is an accomplished harpist and pianist who turns to teaching and from there, unwillingly, to the concert stage. For her humiliating experiences in those roles Burney drew upon deep first-hand knowledge of Georgian music culture, and specifically her day-to-day observation of her father's career as a musical professional. While Charles Burney was credited with the rare success of having transcended the artisanal origins of his trade – of elevating himself to the ranks of the literary and social elite – that ascent was never complete in the mind of his daughter, whose attitude to music in her writing became increasingly defensive through her career.

In *The Wanderer*, Miss Arbe, a mediocre amateur musician, manages the fashionable musical circle at Brightelmstone through a shameless exaggeration of her own talents and taste:

She concluded that of all the arts she was completely mistress. This persuasion made her come forward, in the circles to which she belonged, with a courage that she deemed to be the just attribute of superiour merit; and her family and friends, not less complaisant, and rarely less superficial, in their judgments than herself, sanctioned her claims by their applause; and spread their opinions around, till, hearing them reverberated, they believed them to be fame. (225)

As self-appointed impresario, Miss Arbe's dealings with professional musicians themselves are no less fraudulent: "her zeal in return for their gratuitous service had no limit – except what might be attached to their purse" (227). Through the hire of instruments and salubrious rooms, Miss Arbe sinks Ellis in debt, enforcing her consent to become, like Charles Burney, a music teacher to young ladies of fashion, to endure "the minute, mechanical, and ear-wearing toil, of giving lessons to the unapt, the stupid, the idle, and the wilful" (275). Her worst student is Miss Brinville, who languishes in a "darkness of all musical apprehension ... so impenetrable, that not a ray of instruction could make way through it" (236). Despite this, Miss Brinville and her mother are insulted at the suggestion that she not continue her lessons. Ellis's only talented student, Miss Sycamore, is equally trying. She is "presumptuous, conceited, and gaily unfeeling," and holds her teacher and the business of lessons in contempt: "If Ellis pressed her to more attention, she hummed an air, without looking at her; if she remonstrated against her neglect, she suddenly stared at her, though without speaking" (237). For the young women of the *ton*, a music teacher, though necessary, lay beyond the pale of common politeness.

Charles Burney, at the height of the London season, had as many as fifty-five such students, a "business" he carried on for half a century in "the ardour of his desire to obtain self-dependence," as Frances later put it.[8] "Such a hurried, shattered, wornout posthorse as I am at present crawls not on the Earth," Burney wrote to his friend Samuel Crisp in 1775.[9] Even with such labor, and such success, he earned only what would now be considered a modest middle-class wage.[10] Even at the height of his celebrity, he recognized himself as no more than "a drudge amid the smiles of Wealth & Power."[11] When finally, at the age of seventy-eight, he discontinued teaching, he was forced to "relinquish his carriage" and subsisted on a meager pension at Chelsea College.[12]

The business of music, as described in *The Wanderer* and by Charles Burney's career, retained strong elements of patronal culture. Musicians and music teachers were dependent on fashion and the caprices of its aristocratic managers, rather than free agents in a fully commercialized market. When Ellis's respectability is called into question, the fashionable madams drop her instantly, and do not even pay her. Ellis is left, like Mrs. Hill in *Cecilia*, to wait at the doors of her patrons hoping for payment. One tells her to wait until the end of the year like all the other tradesmen. Ellis's dream of "self-dependence" through music is shattered and descends into nightmare when, after failed ventures in a series of other professions, she is reduced to the status of lady's companion, a "toad-eater," the final resort for penniless, genteel young women in distress (275, 520). The emotional abuse she suffers at the hands of her employer Mrs. Ireton – "so humiliating, nay degrading" – is still shocking to read, and argument in itself for a wider readership for *The Wanderer* (527). The fact that the heroine's treatment at the hands of Mrs. Ireton is on a continuum with her experiences as a music teacher suggests how deeply sensitive Burney was to the dependent, "toad-eating" status of her father in the fashionable world, and how eager to allegorize through fiction, and the fictionalization of her father's life, their joint escape from that humiliation.

In her introduction to the seminal 1991 special issue of *Eighteenth-Century Fiction* on *Evelina*, Julia Epstein challenged a new generation of Burney scholars with a critical biographical question: "Did [Burney] succumb to patriarchal constraints and write what she thought her father would approve, or did she deploy a subversive strategy of indirection? How ambitious was she, and how rebellious?"[13] This chapter offers answers to these questions through examination of vital material that has never been brought to the table. As Epstein suggests, the late twentieth-century revival in Burney criticism, with Margaret Anne Doody in the vanguard, has placed her relationship with her father at the heart of her career.[14] Those readings in the Burney family romance have not, however, been extended to a material, genuinely interdisciplinary understanding of Frances Burney's relationship to the music culture in which she was raised and, from there, to a consideration of how her deep ambivalence toward professional musical life – as luxury, as dependency, as virtuosic style – might illuminate a key baffling problem in her *literary* reception, namely, the scandal of her stylistic "decline."[15]

In Virginia Woolf's pointed understatement: "Fanny's attitude to language was altogether a little abnormal."[16] Her nineteenth-century critics were more severe. Macaulay called the contrast between the brilliant metropolitan farrago of *Evelina* and the "broken Johnsonese" of her much-derided late works "a change … unexampled in literary history."[17] This opinion has not gone unchallenged by the current generation of Burney critics who are naturally skeptical of Macaulay and invested in an expanded Burney canon. "Reversing the notion of deterioration posited by early male reviewers," writes Lorna Clark, "feminist critics present Burney's work as a progression of increased radicalisation of ideas."[18] Irrespective of Burney's ideas, however, their simple substitution here for style unwittingly recalls patriarchal logic, whereby "style" is coded feminine and frivolous and therefore beneath consideration, while "ideas" are the preserve of rational, educated men. In this sense, the current defense of the later works uncritically rehearses Burney's own strategic program of masculinization, in which she adopted Samuel Johnson as surrogate father and model for respectable, "serious" prose. In short, the problem of style in Burney is too complex and vital to be dismissed as a misogynist calumny invented by her early Victorian critics. Terry Castle's observation that "it is difficult to connect the end of Burney's fiction with its beginning" identifies the still essential paradox of Burney's career and reputation, and is my principal subject in this chapter.[19] The problem of her prose style and its "gradual and pernicious change" begins, I will argue, with music culture and her famous father, whose career was a quintessentially modern ascent, a triumph of style *as* substance.

Doody has called Charles Burney the "secret addressee" of all his daughter's novels.[20] He finds his way directly into Burney's fiction once, as Dr. Marchmont in *Camilla*, the urbane "man of learning who could deign to please and seem pleased where books were not the subject of discourse," but who is in fact the secret impediment to the lovers' requital, the source of all "conflicts, doubts, suspences, and sufferings" in the novel.[21] The figure of the father, for Frances Burney, was both "sweetness" and "suffering." Michelle Levy has recently offered a mostly benign and progressive account of familial authorship in the Romantic era, in which domestic kindred groups such as the Edgeworths, Shelleys, and Lambs worked collaboratively, inhabiting a subversive relation to the models of authorial genius and literary property encouraged by the booming print marketplace and since reified by literary-critical tradition.[22] To this thesis the Burney family stands as both example and counter-example. As Hester Thrale wrote of the Burney children, "their Esteem & fondness for the Dr seems to inspire them all with a Desire not to disgrace him; and so every individual of it must write and read & be literary."[23] The voluminous exchange of "journal-letters" between Frances and her beloved sister Susan, texts which then circulated broadly among family and friends, is striking evidence of sociable, women-centered manuscript practices and networks enduring into the era of modern mass-print culture. But Frances's writerly relation to her author-father was never collaborative or sociable. It was instead beset by a repetitive drama of agonized obligation, interference, prohibition, secrecy, and sequestration – characterized on the one hand by florid tributes and the overweening "desire not to disgrace him" observed by Hester Thrale and, on the other, by the clandestine composition and violent destruction of manuscripts.

On her fifteenth birthday Frances burned all her writings in a ceremonial backyard pyre. In old age she did the same to the bulk of her dead father's manuscripts. Her famous dedication of the secretly published *Evelina* to her father as "author of my being" thus represents the carefully scrubbed public face of a far more complex familial relation, expressed through embattled modes of authorship and the fate of real texts. The source of Burney's contribution to this oedipal struggle lies, I suggest, in an increasingly defensive repudiation of her father's *galant* style – the modish aestheticization of elegance that governed his music, pedagogy, and prose – and of the dependent mode of social being she observed him perform in his professional capacity as a "drudge amid the smiles of Wealth and Power." As his self-described "ever-favoured daughter," Frances Burney idealized her father, but as a writer she employed every possible weapon – from a satirical critique of fashionable discourse, to a prose style of impossible rectitude, to outright editorial suppression – to erase the *galant* ideal, and music culture itself, from the public memory of her father's career and her own.[24]

II

A central year of the Charles Burney biography is 1776 when, as a newly minted man of letters, he was admitted to Hester Thrale's salon at Streatham, which included his idol Samuel Johnson. What a reader will not learn from Frances Burney's *Memoirs* of her father, or from the censored manuscripts of her own published journals, is that Charles Burney was originally employed at Streatham as a music teacher and only later accepted into the drawing-room as a social companion. For this more genteel employment he was paid £100 a year, approximately three times the dues for a season's instruction at the piano. The two volumes of continental musical *Tours* (1771, 1773) and massive first volume of a *General History of Music* (1776) he produced to earn that promotion established musicology in the competitive world of Georgian letters, and himself in the elite literary circles of London.[25] Charles Burney's removal from the music-room to the parlor was unprecedented for a humble music teacher but, in an important sense, he consummated rather than transcended the demands of his profession. As the nineteenth century progressed musicians were increasingly able to communicate directly with the public through newspapers and to build their careers through an independent machinery of publicity. In the Georgian age, however, "social savoir-faire – the ability to conduct oneself with propriety in aristocratic circles – was every bit as important as technical proficiency or musicianship in building a career."[26] Burney's winning personal style, combined with the cultural capital represented by his scholarship, elevated him beyond his profession to the same celebrity status later enjoyed by his daughter. As Samuel Crisp marveled in 1781: "He is now at the Top of the *Ton*. He is continually invited to all the great Tables, and parties, to meet the Wits and Grandees, without the least reference to Music."[27] In his own drawing-room in St. Martin's Street, Burney's Sunday music parties became legend. English lords, foreign ambassadors, and the London literati applied for admission to these concert evenings, for the opportunity to mix with the cream of imported musical talent of the season, and to preview its operatic delights (Figure 3).

Figure 3. Charles Loraine Smith, *A Sunday Concert* (1782). National Portrait Gallery. Smith's gently satirical print re-creates Burney's cosmopolitan musical circle at St. Martin's Place. Pictured are the castrato Pacchierotti, composer Bertoni, violinist Cervetto, oboist Fischer, and Burney himself at the harpsichord. Lady Mary Duncan was once compelled to burn all copies of a salacious pamphlet linking her name with Pacchierotti's, but is here seated with attentive dignity at the heart of the group of professional players.

Complementing his role as musical patron and impresario, Burney's choice of literary genres likewise furthered his purpose of transcending the abject status of working musician. Unlike his daughter, who adopted the popular, professional idioms of the novel and theater script, Charles Burney represented himself as an amateur man of letters, a kind of gentleman virtuoso whose *Tours* and scholarly *History* both implied leisure time he did not actually possess. As Mary Astell defined the virtuoso a century earlier, "He Trafficks to all places, and has his Correspondents in every part of the World."[28] Burney's scholarly method was virtuosic in this sense – traveling, gathering, corresponding – but was designed to serve the modern urban luxury economy rather than an aristocratic ideal of retirement and leisure: "it is not my Intention to keep in useless obscurity any of the Musical Curiosities I have collected in my Journey."[29]

Burney's prose style likewise embodied the "fusion of courtesy and scholarship" essential to the original amateur model of the virtuoso.[30]

Declaring that he would rather be found trivial than tiresome, he spiced up his lengthy account of music in the ancient world in his *General History of Music* with anecdotes from mythology. A passage concerning the origins of the flute, for example, in a chapter appealingly set "during the Residence of Pagan Divinities," invokes not the archaeological record but Minerva:

She is said by Hyginus to have found herself laughed at by her mother and sister, Juno and Venus, whenever she played the flute in their presence: this suggested to her the thought of examining herself in a fountain, which serving as a mirror, convinced her that she had been justly derided for the distortion of her countenance, occasioned by swelling her cheeks in the act of blowing the flute. This is one reason given for her throwing aside that instrument, and adopting the lyre.[31]

Burney called it "my playful & folatre way of expressing myself," and the ease of his promotion from the back entrance to front parlor at Streatham was facilitated by this absolute continuity between his professional musical wares and personal prose style, be it in conversation or on the page.[32]

This *galant* ideal, conceived as "an inventively varied interplay of contrasting ideas," applied equally to music, prose, and manners.[33] Queeney Thrale's music book exemplifies Burney's agenda in *A General History of Music*, divided neatly between the *galant* composer par excellence, J. C. Bach, whose piano music "resemble[d] bravura songs," and transcriptions of operatic overtures and arias (II: 866).[34] The *galant* repertoire he introduced to Queeney Thrale in the music-room – with its light and unencumbered melodies, quick modulations, and a hint of chromaticism – joined seamlessly with the elegant and varied conversation with which he afterwards entertained her parents. Hester Thrale valued the "Suavity of [Burney's] Manners," remarking to her diary that "few people possess such Talents for general Conversation, and fewer still for select Society."[35] Charles Burney's brother-in-law, the agriculturalist Arthur Young, could not recall "any person who had more decided talents for conversation, eminently seasoned with wit and humour ... His society was greatly sought after by all classes, from the first nobility to the mere *homme de lettres*."[36] The *galant* idiom of Italian *opera seria*, which Burney defines in his *History* as "refinement, delicacy, and invention," (I: 18) thus converged, rhetorically, with the discourse of elegance that governed fashionable manners in the late eighteenth century, at least as an ideal.

The *galant* began, as the word suggests, as a French idiom of manners, a chivalric revival. "He is so French in his manners," a Burney admirer once remarked to his daughter.[37] Only around 1750 did the term come to be applied to a musical style, opposed to the *gebunden* (strict) style of the high baroque.[38] Burney himself draws on the verbal, sociable origins of the *galant* in his *History* when he describes how, in the early part of the century, Handel's operas "became the musical language of the nation, and in a manner proverbial, like the *bon mots* of a man of wit in society" (II: 722). Conversely, "trite and frivolous melodies," by too frequent use, languished like overfamiliar witticisms, "as common and insipid as the flat and stale jokes of Swift's *Polite Conversation*" (II: 720). Since "every age has it's [sic] Phraseology," in music as in conversation, it was the business of the opera house composer to bring with him each season "the new and fashionable musical phrases from Italy" (II: 874).[39]

Something tautologous haunts the *galant* style as a historical phenomenon. What is fashionable is *galant*, and the *galant*, though its precise definition is still debated, "never means anything less than elegant, new, and fashionable."[40] David Sheldon has traced the origins of "galant society" to the francophiles of early eighteenth-century Germany, who placed great stress on literary repositories of conversational wit, namely light verse and letters.[41] Burney's correspondence with Hester Thrale exemplifies the requisite educated, Italianate levity of tone:

Ah, my dear Madam! It is lucky for you that I am not an idle man, for you wd then be *so* pestered with Letters in order to provoke you to quick & ample returns as wd make you rue the Day you ever learned to write or read. As it is, my *Cacoethes scribendi* is kept in pretty good bounds; for perpetually jumbled from pillar to post, by certain, as well as accidental *Diavolini degl'impedimenti*, I am not likely to overwhelm my Friends with Letters; however I may wish to be always scribbling to certain People.

The *galant* energies of his correspondence sometimes verged on raciness, arguably at the expense of good taste. Only months after her husband's death, Burney writes to Hester on the subject of his salary:

And so what a power of business you have contrived to do on this blessed Day!— I need not ax vaat is all dat Schtof?—'tis very ostensible—here's stuff for the Mouth, & Stuff for the Pocket—special *hard wear*—safer & more likely to mend, than mar, my Garments, like your nectareous fruit.[42]

The widow thought it delightful: "how skilful, how elegant is that dear Creature's Pen! But his Mind is so elegant, everything that comes from it, partakes of the Flavour." More than mere "style," the *galant*, in its successful incarnation, was an integrated mode of being designed to please. To his satisfied patron, Burney's poetry reflected the elegance of his mind: his "manners are as sweet as his music."[43]

Likewise as a scholar, Burney used his *General History of Music* not only to showcase the fashionable Italian opera, but to introduce the logic of fashion by which it was governed as a legitimate methodological principle. "The most striking feature" of late eighteenth-century music, Simon McVeigh has written, was "the constant expectation of novelty and thus new repertoire."[44] Burney's *General History* integrated this law of novelty and consumption into a history of aesthetics and taste. Music should be considered an "innocent luxury" and "tranquil pleasure" whose history was one of changing tastes, relative to each era, with a general Enlightenment tendency toward ever-greater refinement (I: 21, II: 7). Burney employed the word "fashion" ubiquitously in his long chapter on Italian opera to describe the ever-shifting vocabulary of musical taste. On several occasions, he literalizes the analogy: "every excellence in Music when it has been pursued to excess, is thrown aside to lie fallow till forgotten; and after a series of years, like a fashion in apparel, it is started again, as a new invention" (II: 814). Burney's chosen case study for musical fashion was not the motivic or harmonic example, drawn from the score of a concerto or symphony, but the virtuosic improvisations of singers in famous performances at the opera house. Burney's text – virtuosic in both taste and character – thus tells a history of performances rather than works. Significant pages of the long chapter on Italian opera are taken up with transcriptions of the vocal improvisations of the most celebrated castrati of each generation, from Farinelli in the 1730s to Pacchierotti in the 1780s: "The divisions and embellishments, which, when a song is new, are its most striking and refined parts, soonest lose their favour and fashion" (II: 683). In short, music *was* fashion, and the essence of fashion was virtuosity.[45] Virtuosic singing was the vocal aestheticization of fashionable discourse, and the aural equivalent of fashionable dress: "the fashionable trimmings of an air ... the furbelows, flounces and vocal fopperies of the time" (II: 725). Changing taste in music in fact represented the machinery of fashion in its most accelerated, breathless form: "a treatise on good taste in dress, during the reign of Queen Elizabeth, would now be as useful to a tailor or milliner, as the rules of taste in Music, forty years ago, to a modern musician" (II: 992).

This glamorizing of musical virtuosity, and the infiltration of English music culture by the international style of the opera house, was not congenial to all. Critics of the *galant* style, who would ultimately include Burney's novelist daughter, considered it a musical reflection of the luxury culture that sponsored it, and thus fully exposed to the disposable logic of fashion:

Novelty and custom, two overbearing tyrants, have given a Sanction to degenerate Harmony, wildness of Air, effeminacy, tautology and affected difficulties, inconsistent with the powers and beauties of Expression. The Luxury of the times, which has produced so many innovations, has diffused itself into our Music.[46]

Music, complained Hannah More, had become "the idol which fashion has set up," and virtuosity, as a pedagogical ideal, a poison to young women's musical education.[47] A virtuosophobic screed published in Bath the same year as *Evelina* noted "the increasing passion for this Art" in society, but lamented the influence of its fashionable "masters" (such as Charles Burney) by whom young women were

fired with emulation on their respective instruments, [and] have extended the powers of execution to such astonishing a degree, as to win the applause of the unthinking part of mankind, and impose mechanical rapidity, and the wonders of difficulty, as the perfection of Genius, and the only triumphs of Music.[48]

Young *virtuose*, such as Esther Burney, were become automata of music, relying on "mechanical rapidity" and "wonder" for their appeal, much like the exhibits at Cox's Museum in *Evelina*. Music as a vehicle of expression and sensibility had been sacrificed to the idol of virtuosic accomplishment (see also chapter 5).

The newfound dominance of the virtuoso *galant* style was likewise anathema to musical antiquarians committed to the establishment of a baroque canon equivalent to the literary triumvirate of Shakespeare, Spenser, and Milton. As the piano prodigy and Oxford don, William Crotch, later recorded: "At this time the musical world of connoisseurs were divided into two opponent parties, the admirers of the ancient and modern styles; the one despising the trifling melodies of the opera, and the other the barbarous and mechanical structure of the fugue."[49] Burney's powers of pleasing were legendary, but it was only with the greatest exertion of self-control that he was able to present a smiling face to the supporters of "ancient music" who, with the intemperate Handelian King George at their head, represented a powerful minority constituency in late eighteenth-century London. Their annual concert series, begun the year Burney published the first volume of his *General History*, featured the concerti of Handel, Geminiani, and Corelli, and no music less than twenty years old. The cause of ancient music was borne, in scholarly form, by Burney's great rival Sir John Hawkins, a friend and biographer of Handel who, in his own magisterial *General History of the Science and Practice of Music* (1776), insisted on music's foundation "in general and invariable laws," that is, outside the regime of fashion.[50]

In his seminal book, *The Rise of Musical Classics in Eighteenth-Century England* (1992), William Weber makes an argument for the political dimensions of the ancient–modern quarrel, with the ancient music movement driven by a resurgent Tory elite, and finding its ultimate expression in the 1784 Handel Commemoration at Westminster Abbey. At the same time, however, the ancient–modern divide was more cultural than strictly party political. Burney, for example, was both a modern and a Tory. The partisans of ancient music represented the conservative principles of continuity and order central to the project of canon formation, but the moderns were not simply their progressive opposite. Their patronage of Italian opera was as much an embrace of a cosmopolitan, aristocratic ideal as it was of modernity, just as the Romantic nationalism of the ancients, while conservative, directly anticipated the European cultural-political order of the nineteenth century.[51]

As a young man, Burney had "worship[ped]" the ancients, but was converted to opera "by keeping company with travelled & heterodox gentleman, who were partial to the Music of more modern composers whom they had heard in Italy."[52] In his *General History* Burney called on the factions of ancients and moderns to leave aside their mutual prejudices – "A chorus of Handel and a graceful opera song should not preclude each other" – but in his private papers he gave vent to his contempt for the ancients' "bigotry for Handel," their unaccountable passion for "the absurdity of Fugue, Canon, & other Gothic Contrivances, in rendering the words of vocal music unintelligible" (II: 8).[53] Burney's major source for his theory of the *galant* was Rousseau's *Lettre sur la musique française* (1753) which championed "unity of melody" against the "confusion and noise" of the baroque contrapuntal style. The battle between the ancients and moderns in London closely rehearses the so-called *Querelle des buffons* conducted between Rameau and Rousseau in the early 1750s, of which Rousseau's *Lettre* was the instigator. Where Rameau championed the supremacy of harmony in French music, Rousseau perceived in the imported Italian opera a reawakened power of melody and return to music's true nature.

Burney sincerely admired aspects of Handel and some instrumental works of Corelli and Purcell but, following Rousseau, he held to an uncompromising belief that the solo voice should be "the first object of attention in a theatre ... never suffocate[d] by the learned jargon of a multiplicity of instruments and subjects."[54] The last significant writings Burney published were a series of musical definitions for Abraham Rees's *Cyclopaedia* (1819). One of his longest entries is under *chiarezza* (clarity), which he nominates among the "essential requisites" of music. The nemesis of melodic *chiarezza*, embodied in Italian opera and its virtuoso singers, was harmonic "confusion," which sacrificed melodic clarity and beauty to the "science" of ensemble instrumentation:

> We speak here of simple melody. But if harmony is added to it, each part increases complication, obscures the principal idea, and it is then that clearness is wanted. Each phrase in music should have a character, and this character arises from the melody. If the accompaniment to this melody forms another melody of a different character ... there will then be a confusion.[55]

The fashionable world chose Burney's book over Hawkins's, unsurprisingly since that world was its essential content. Many of the opera productions Burney memorialized lay within living memory, signifying that his interest lay less in academic scholarship than in "journalistic taste-making rooted in public musical life."[56] Hawkins, by contrast, had not been to the opera in twenty years, considering it "the mere offspring of luxury."[57] More importantly, while Hawkins wrote in a heavy, scholarly prose, Burney, as we have seen, consciously adopted a more accessible, popular idiom: "I could wish to have my Book so divested of Pedantry & Jargon that every Miss, who plays *o' top o' the Spinet* should make it her manual."[58] Burney, for whom "the true characteristic of dramatic Music is clearness," applied the same governing principle of *chiarezza* to his writing (II: 917). The critic for *The Monthly Review*, in pointing to "a certain *amenity*" in Burney's prose as "the diametrical opposite to everything that we call *dull* and *dry*," was making an implicit and by this time standard comparison between Burney and Hawkins, to Burney's advantage.[59]

The importance of the Church as the source of salaried careers for musicians faded markedly through the eighteenth century.[60] As patronage of music was taken up by the fashionable metropolitan class, the material reality of the Church's decline in turn promoted the desire for a new musical aesthetic and a proportionally vigorous repudiation of the *stile antico*: "Church music, by the gay and fastidious frequenters of the opera ... is pronounced to be old-fashioned" (II: 983). Burney likened the instrumental music of Corelli and Handel, with its contrapuntal restatements of brief ideas, to delivering sermons, to "preaching upon or rather, a perpetual repetition of the original text."[61] His rejection of the gothic, fugal style, in both music and literary prose, thus belongs to the wider ideological basis of his class position, exemplified by Shaftesbury's rejection of the Church as the arbiter of public morals in favor of a modern regime of polite manners governed by a cultural elite. Burney's "chief contribution," Weber writes, "was in helping to build a secular and cosmopolitan repertory largely independent of the primarily British school of cathedral music."[62] Burney's *galant* style – a European *lingua franca* of "graceful and airy melody" that stood opposed to "ancient" Church music – embodied the modern secularist outlook and presumed, for the newly ascendant social category of "men of taste," a Shaftesburian entitlement to cultural leadership.

The *galant* continuity of music, manners, and prose style found its ideal embodiment, for Burney, in the figure of the Italian librettist Pietro Metastasio, whose letters he translated, with an accompanying worshipful biography, in 1796. Burney's friend Giuseppe Baretti, a teacher and translator whose place of favor he had supplanted in the Thrale drawing room, nominated *chiarezza* the distinguishing feature of Metastasio's poetry, the signature *galant* endorsement.[63] In parlor games with Mrs. Thrale, Burney, who must rank among the most prolific unpublished poets of the eighteenth century, admitted he would wish to be Metastasio above any other man, perhaps with a view to earning the compliment that he already was. Certainly, Metastasio's extraordinary fusion of literary, musical, and social talents mark him as an embodiment of the *galant* ideal. In his biography, Burney records that in Naples, the birthplace of the *galant* style in opera, Metastasio became

the general and favourite subject of literary academies and assemblies of good taste and polite conversation; where nothing was repeated but the favourite verses which he had sung extempore, and which were remembered by those who had heard them from his own mouth: on these occasions, the order, clearness, and learning, with which he treated the subjects, as well as the beauty of his verses, the sweetness of his voice, the grace of his action, his modest deportment, and the expression of his countenance, were universally extolled.[64]

Verses, voice, action, deportment, and countenance. The Metastasio legend offered an integrated model of personal, professional, and aesthetic style that Burney sought to bring to the fashionable salons of London in the 1770s and 1780s. By the time of its publication in 1796, however, his *Memoirs of Metastasio* upheld the *galant* style no longer as a defense of prevailing fashions but as a mode of nostalgic reaction. The luxury *galant* culture, of which Burney was both conspicuous beneficiary and ornament, had met with the most devastating possible critique, a bloody social revolution in France. Equally devastating, at least within the Burney family itself, was Frances Burney's quiet revolt against the *galant* regime of manners her father so successfully served.

III

In her journal from 1773 Frances records a visit to St. Martin's Street by the *galant* opera composer Sacchini and the castrato Millico (featured in *Evelina*), who were amazed to be greeted by Esther Burney's playing the overture from *El Cid*, Sacchini's latest opera, the score of which had not yet been published: "she had been to 3 Rehearsals, & has gotten almost half the Opera by Ear. Sacchini almost started – he looked at first in the utmost perplexity, as if doubting his own Ears." It was the business of the Burney daughters to amaze the public with what Frances called their "facility," be it for remembering music or "recording," as she did in her journals, the precise details of lengthy conversations.[65] The exercise of this virtuosic facility was modeled by their father, whose *Tours* and *General History* exhibit an extraordinary memory for literally hundreds of performances witnessed over decades. Frances served as her father's amanuensis during his great burst of literary production in the 1770s. She spent countless hours of her youth copying out her father's manuscripts for the printers: "*our* History now requires its secretary & I am almost certain it will not be possible to separate them til the Work is finished." Her first labor as a writer was thus as a virtuoso automaton engaged in machine-like reproduction, something akin to her friend Joseph Merlin's device for musical notation. Her career as a virtuoso copyist subsequently shifted from the reproduction of written manuscripts to verbal conversations. An example of Frances's inherited talent for mental dictation can be found in her journal of 1774 in which she records, as direct speech, a description of a bullfight given by the travel writer Richard Twiss that accords almost word for word with his later published account.[66] The skills she developed in her journals and letters link directly to the idiomatic accuracy and richness of *Evelina*, which is the bravura public exhibition of Burney's particular talent. She was a "girl," wrote Hester Thrale, "of prodigious parts," a prodigy of language, in fact.[67] Like Esther, her performance was virtuosic, and her material the *galant*, what she called in *Cecilia* "the insignificant click-clack of modish conversation" (27).

But Frances Burney's behavior at Streatham, on her elevation there as a celebrated novelist, was the frank opposite of her father's "obsequiousness," which for Hester Thrale had been an eminently forgivable fault: "[By] turning Quality dangler, he lost that Independent Spirit & lofty manner without which no man can please *me* – but in Burney I pardon the want on't." What Thrale could less easily pardon was the daughter's manifest resistance to her dependent status, which violated the *galant* social contract: "She makes me miserable too in many Respects – so restlessly & apparently anxious lest I should give myself Airs of Patronage, or load her with shackles of Dependance." The daughter's attempt to resume the "lofty manner" of independence cheerfully resigned by her father was apparently unsuccessful: it "embarrasses her Talk, & clouds her Mind with scruples about Elegancies which either come uncalled for or will not come at all."[68] It is no coincidence that the ill-fated play Burney wrote while under Thrale's roof, *The Witlings*, concludes with a speech describing "Self-dependance" as "the first of Earthly Blessings."[69] As a family, the Burneys occupied a tenuous position between the professional classes and the fashionable "world." Both father and daughter crossed back and forth, and the anxiety of that crossing became the signature of Frances Burney's authorial personality. Betty Rizzo has noted "the social suspension of her heroines ... who are, like Burney, uncomfortably poised in a world that can sense their fineness but cannot identify their entitlement to it."[70] In *Evelina*, for example, the heroine's greatest fear is neither seduction nor disinheritance as such, but the disgrace of misrecognition, a class fear that, scene after agonizing scene, is granted powers of paralysis. The same apprehension is evident in Burney's dealings with Hester Thrale.

Once famous, Burney attempted to give her desire for independence the more acceptable face of feminine reticence, but with mixed success. Much of her journal from 1778, subsequent to the publication of *Evelina*, is devoted to desperate concern over her anonymity, what she calls her "poor woe begone secret."[71] Even as the truth of her authorship spread, and full public exposure became inevitable, Burney performed for her correspondents a repetitive anguish of denial and, in public, a show of acutely painful modesty. According to the "proper lady" thesis of Georgian women writers, such were the necessary rituals of female virtue with regard to the sexually suspect business of authorship. This reading of Burney, popular in the 1980s, has since come under revision. "The sheer bulk of writing uncovered by feminist scholarship," Terry Lovell has argued, "provides confirmation that emergent bourgeois society must have contained spaces from which women were not only permitted, but actually encouraged and enjoined to write."[72] The late eighteenth century, in particular, "offered unprecedented opportunities for female authorship."[73] Betty Schellenberg places particular emphasis on Burney in her argument against the "separate spheres" analysis of eighteenth-century literary culture and its "binary of oppressor and victim." After making less money than she ought to have from *Evelina* and *Cecilia*, Burney assumed full contractual control over the sale of her subsequent books, conducting herself, as Schellenberg describes her predecessor Frances Brooke, as "a competent literary professional."[74] That said, Burney's relationship to literary professionalism was complex. Her decision to publish her third novel, *Camilla*, by old-fashioned subscription suggests a desire to separate herself from the open literary marketplace, to recover a public space for her fiction in which the gentility of her readers, and her own, would be guaranteed.

Charles Burney was never an enemy to his daughter's authorship, only he understood her "success" in patronal rather than professional terms. When, as her journal records, Frances tremblingly revealed the secret of her novel to her father, he wasted no time on fears for his daughter's virtue. Instead, he was delighted to discover that his second daughter, even to the extent of outdoing the brilliant Hetty, had found her place within the modern economy of talent in which the Burney family lived and thrived, and which was necessary for attaching themselves to "Wealth and Power."[75] Her second "Daddy," Samuel Crisp, likewise thought her reluctance to acknowledge *Evelina* "overstrain'd modesty," while Hester Thrale found it irritating:

If I find you are in *earnest* in desiring concealment, I shall quite scold you!—for if such a desire does not proceed from *Affectation,*—'tis from something *Worse* ... Why an over-delicacy that may make you unhappy all your Life!

For the professional writers in the Streatham circle, Burney's "over-delicacy" regarding authorship had its source not in female virtue but in virtuosity, in her concern to maintain her professional practice as a social satirist. To Samuel Johnson she was a "spy." He called her shyness "slyness" – "[your] pretending to know nothing never took *me* in, whatever you may do with others" – while the playwright Arthur Murphy called her "Miss Slyboots." [76] For Johnson and Murphy, Burney's desire for anonymity represented not the modesty of a conduct-book virgin but a writer's instinct for self-preservation. At the Streatham salon, Burney's was a professional literary ego in formation and still unknown to itself. Romanticism would later elevate writerly solitude from professional necessity to spiritual need but, as a dependent young woman in the 1780s, this ideology was not yet available to her.

Burney's "modesty," in this sense, was a claim for a new, vaguely grasped professional status. In a moving and quietly defiant letter she wrote to her father in 1800, she staked "an hereditary claim" to authorship.[77] But she refused to mystify the literary economy as her father did, where the genteel availability of his books defined the genteel availability of his being. As Catherine Gallagher has remarked, "the father and daughter seem to have had almost opposite orientations toward the literary marketplace." The two generations of Burney writers captured a complex transitional moment in the status of professional letters, "a moment whose mixed messages of authorship pitted patronage against self-determination" in the marketplace.[78] In her desperate, sincere desire for anonymity, Frances Burney separated herself from her books, recognizing them, though not in so many words, as commodities of independence.[79] Hester Thrale remarked on the division in her diary. Burney's novels succeeded in "the truest representation of the very commonest Life: while the Author's Conversation & Behaviour is *all* unnatural, *all* stilted, *all* Affectation."[80] Some part of this much-derided "modesty" – Thackeray called her "that indomitable virgin" – was not her failure to resist conduct-book gender prescriptions, but her repudiation of Augustan forms of patronage in favor of a modern, proto-professional identity.[81]

Burney often expressed "a horrour of a life of attendance and dependence," and almost all her heroines, like she herself, are called "toadeaters."[82] Dependence, far more than reverses in love, marks the nadir of their heroic careers. Burney achieved some financial independence with the success of *Camilla*, but the first spectacular breach of writerly anonymity on publication of *Evelina* had permanent effects on her prose style. First, the *ton* appropriated her satire of fashion as fashionable in itself – one "was reckoned quite unfashionable for not having read it" – and adopted her language into the very discourse she had chosen as her object:

Mrs. Cholmondeley hunted me quite round the Card Table, from Chair to Chair; repeating various speeches of Madame Duval; & when, at last, I got behind a sofa, out of reach, she called out aloud "Polly!—Lord Polly! Only think! Miss has danced with a Lord!"[83]

Evelina entered the fashion economy as a language and a set of modish allusions: "some quotation from it was apropos to whatever was said or done."[84]

Second, Burney herself likewise became "prodigiously *in Fashion*," a "public Character" who was ogled without mercy by the *ton*, as if "they expected to read in my Face all the characters in my Book." The fashionable world demanded her constant attendance, as it had done her father – "Miss Burney is the Heroine now" – and celebrity encroached on the time necessary to her craft: "my opportunities for writing grow less & less."[85] Most fatally, fame introduced a form of self-consciousness that was ruinous to her virtuosic literary method. She could no longer play "Q in the corner," memorizing the conversations around her for future satirical use.[86] Her natural response to being raised from the anonymity of a music teacher's daughter to a literary lion of the Thrale–Johnson circle was to absorb the verbal idioms of that group and reproduce them as satire, which she did in her play *The Witlings*. "Study is a most fatiguing thing!" cries Lady Smatter who, as head of a would-be literary circle, is always misquoting the classics to little purpose: "O how little does the World suspect, when we are figuring in all the brilliancy of Conversation, the private hardships, and secret labours of a Belle Esprit!"[87] When Charles Burney suppressed the play for fear of offending the bluestockings to whom they both now owed debts of patronage (as he saw it), the last of his daughter's writerly resources was taken away. She internalized the prohibition laid on her play with rapidly rising feelings of disgust toward the text and the fashionable discourse it memorialized: "I shall wipe it all from my memory, & endeavour never to recollect that I ever writ it."[88] No longer able to operate as the virtuoso satirist of fashionable discourse, Burney would abandon the idiomatically rich, episodic, dialogue-driven theater of *Evelina* for a literary model she knew would meet with paternal sanction, namely Johnsonian moral discourse. "In an evil hour," Macaulay reflected, "the Author of Evelina took the Rambler for her model."[89] The rhetoric of virtue, specifically a Shaftesburian ideal of "politeness" that Burney had used as a comic foil in *Evelina* and as a defensive ruse for herself upon her elevation to society, would become increasingly reified as style itself, as her own "proper" voice.

IV

Evelina is a kind of virtuoso cabinet of urban wonders, and reflects the generational divide between Charles and Frances Burney's careers.[90] The plot is structured around patronage (or its lack), but the action is generated according to the logic of fashion and the new urban entertainment economy. The novel offers nothing less than, in Deidre Lynch's words, "a Romantic theor[y] of the public."[91] The agents of virtue, Villars, Lord Orville, and Evelina, are shown to be unsuccessful in resisting the desires of Lady Howard, Madame Duval, Sir Clement, and the Branghtons to take the heroine "out" in London, but it is the theatricalizing narrative that actually compels them: "resistance was vain," as Evelina says (286). Virtue is a permeable screen in the novel, an adjunct to virtuosity and the fashionable public sphere against which it protests resistance.

The great novelty of *Evelina* was not its marriage plot, or its conduct-book heroine, but Burney's orchestration of various London dialects in a wild and compelling polyphony. The "polite" discourse of Evelina, Lord Orville, and Mr. Villars functions as a linguistic norm besieged by fantastic speech idioms from all classes of society, from the predatory gallantries of Sir Clement Willoughby to the unstopped naval vulgarity of Captain Mirvan. The hero, Lord Orville, has been imported from "another age" to embody the Shaftesburian secularization of morality into manners, where social values are not issued by royal or priestly edict, but formulated through the rational concourse of enfranchised gentlemen.[92] He is, as Mrs. Selwyn says, "really polite," not simply faking it according to the fashion (283). Lord Orville's polite talk, which on first hearing paralyzes the heroine with its powers of condescension, is guaranteed by the gentility of his birth, and is the novel's only bulwark against the dysfunctional social effects of vulgar and licentious speech.

One of the keynotes of the heroine's virtue is her rejection of the *galant* language of the *ton*, to which her responses range from laughing incomprehension (to Mr. Lovel) to chaste indignation (to Sir Clement): "I must insist upon your leaving me; you are quite a stranger to me, and I am both unused, and averse to your language and your manners" (43). Burney creates a signature comic effect in *Evelina* by the setting of a normative polite language, usually curt, against the prolix and hyperbolic idiom of fashionable gallantry:

"Oh, Miss Anville, did you know what I have endured, the sleepless, restless state of suspence I have been tortured with, you could not, all cruel as you are, you could not have received me with such frigid indifference!"

"*Received* you, Sir!"

"Why, is not my visit to *you*? Do you think I should have made this journey, but for the happiness of again seeing you?"

"Indeed it is possible I might—since so many others do."

"Cruel, cruel girl! You *know* that I adore you!—you *know* that you are the mistress of my soul, and arbitress of my fate!" (329)

Sir Clement is a pure product of the fashionable world: virtuosity as bogeyman. He cuts the verbal figure of libertinism, the rhetorical enemy of virtue. James Fordyce, in a conduct book published the year before *Evelina*, warned young men against the "empty prattle" of *galant* discourse, while his elder brother, Professor of Moral Philosophy at Aberdeen, had earlier composed a moral dialogue on the dangers to young women of the "Arts of Gallantry" and their "Flowers of Speech." A perversion of Shaftesburian politeness, the foppish libertine deployed sociable conversation as "a Conveyance of Lies, and Circulation of Fraud" designed to entrap women.[93] Lord Merton, another callow young man of the *ton* in *Evelina*, captures the latent sexual aggression of *galant* speech in addressing his fiancée: "'You have been, as you always are,'" said he, twisting his whip with his fingers, 'all sweetness'" (280). Such ways of speaking are "strange" and offensive to the linguistically innocent Evelina, as baffling to her as the Italian singers to the Branghtons at the King's Theatre. During the farcical episode where Madame Duval is kidnapped and brutalized by Captain Mirvan, leaving Evelina once again alone with Sir Clement in a carriage, she locates his violation of propriety in his "freedom of speaking": "you must change your style, or I will not hear you ... I beg you not to talk to me so – so strangely" (148). That said, polite speech is equally absurd to the gallants. Sir Clement thinks Lord Orville "cold, inanimate, phlegmatic," and he is not directly contradicted (358). Surrounded in the dark alley at Marybone gardens by a mocking posse of young men, Evelina seeks to negotiate her release in polite terms, only to find that "every other word I spoke produced a loud laugh!" (234). The fashionable language Evelina rejects "with real disgust," the narrator nevertheless offers with manifest pleasure and at great length (43). Even Evelina herself admits that "in large companies, and general conversation, [Sir Clement] is extremely entertaining and agreeable" (159).

In *Evelina* elegant rectitude of language is the comic foil to verbal excess. Politeness thus often recedes into indirect speech, the better to bring the idioms by which it is beset into bolder relief, as in this exchange with her Branghton cousins about Vauxhall:

"For my part," said Miss Branghton, "I like it because it is not vulgar."
"This must have been a fine treat for you, Miss," said Mr. Branghton; "why, I suppose you was never so happy in all your life before?"
I endeavoured to express my satisfaction with some pleasure, yet I believe they were much amazed at my coldness.
"Miss ought to stay in town till the last night," said young Branghton, "and then, it's my belief, she'd say something to it!" (196)

Evelina's "pleasure," to the Branghtons, signifies coldness, just as polite "satisfaction," the opposite of vulgar enthusiasm, expresses not "something" but nothing at all. Polite discourse is a linguistic evacuation of purpose – speech reduced to a genteel pose. The indirectness of Evelina's sentiments is a textual allegory of the unbridgeable social divide the novel polices between the precariously maintained gentility of the heroine and her godawful city cousins. In this, *Evelina* demonstrates a fascination for fashion complicated by a nostalgia for the aristocratic economy of birth.

Johnson's favorite character in *Evelina*, Mr. Smith, exemplified the dangers of leveling, of the *galant* style as a crudely acquired commodity: "I always study what the ladies like – that's my first thought" (188). His speech, a vulgarity that advertises its own "studied" pretension to elegance, was the most contemptible of all, worse than the aggressive insinuations of Sir Clement or the pure verbal rage of Captain Mirvan. As the heroine says, she "should prefer the company of *dullness* itself" (180). There was nothing to stop a talented Mr. Smith from rising in the world, just as there was nothing to stop the talented Burneys who were, after all, in the private opinion of their principal patron, "a very low Race of Mortals."[94] Characteristic of middle-class aspiration in the late eighteenth century is Evelina's contempt (and Burney's) for those who would share her ambitions but neglect to disguise them.

In other words *Evelina* exposes fashion as a threat to class distinction – the substitution of an economy of birth by an economy of status determined by style. The guide at Cox's Museum designates the cultural arbiters of "utility" only as "men of taste," a dangerously diffuse category. *Evelina* is, in this sense, a document of class panic, of fascinated resistance through satire to the lure and mounting power of urban *galant* society. That said, neither Evelina nor Lord Orville questions the necessity of belonging to that elite. The later Burney novels, by contrast, *do* challenge the formation of a social elite regulated by fashion, where admission to the elusive *ton*, as we are told in *Camilla*, "is as attainable without birth as without understanding." It is a new, chaotic social order where members of the fashionable class depend for their popularity and power on the lucky fact that

> some whim has happily called forth imitators; that some phrase has been adopted; that something odd in dress has become popular; that some beauty, or some deformity, no matter which, has found annotators ... But to whichever of these accidents their early fame may be attributed, its establishment and its glory is built upon vanity that knows no deficiency, or insolence that knows no blush. (463–4)

The *galant* style, for Burney, only appeared to be elitist and exclusive. Through her novels, she sought to expose it as a dangerously *inclusive* social regime built on social performances that any budding virtuoso of manners might master. They are cautionary tales describing fashion's threat to succeed birth (or its middle-class mystification, "natural gentility") as the new organizing principle of "the world." The Harrels of *Cecilia* symbolize the dangerous overlap of fashionability and social

The Burney baroque 77

leveling: "no formality was assumed, and no solemnity was affected: everyone was without restraint, even rank obtained but little distinction; ease was the general plan, and entertainment the general pursuit" (22). Here the *ton* mimics radicalism as a promoter of social mobility, with the elusive category of "fashion" as a commodifiable cross-over phenomenon between aristocratic culture and the new mixed urban elite.

Like other purveyors of anti-fashion discourse in the eighteenth century, beginning with Addison, Burney recognized style not as trivial but rather as a new "hegemonic mode of governance" through which "power embeds itself in those apparently non-political and nonideological arenas of everyday life that it represents as unexceptional."[95] Fashion was not the mere play of appearances. It was not *merely* anything, but rather the most formidable antagonist Burney's heroines face. Fashion, which in *Camilla* is likened to a "contagion," is Burney's villain, just as it was the unofficial hero of her father's history of eighteenth-century opera. Frances Burney understood that fashion was invincible to a degree: its logical consummation lay in a fully ironized social being, inscrutable and indifferent to everything, including its own powers. The most fashionable character in *Cecilia*, Mr. Meadows, affects complete indifference to the opera, as to everything else: "There is no making pleasure out of anything. We go the same dull round for ever; nothing new, no variety! All the same thing over again!" (275). And yet his influence on the *ton* is all powerful. As an arbiter of taste and value who wanly disclaims his authority, the irresistible Meadows speaks Truth-to-Fashion and embodies its exhausting, elusive logic. As his brother galant in *Camilla*, Sir Sedley Clarendel, declares, "I begin to tire of *ennui*" (465). In the polite speech of the heroine of *Evelina*, we find the origins of Burney's defensive response to fashionable language and the dangerous, indiscriminate social forces it put in play. After *Evelina*, the polite speech reserved exclusively for that novel's heroes becomes the increasingly dominant idiom of her own narrative prose. Again, we should not read this tactic as a retreat into feminine modesty, but rather Burney's opposing herself, through an increasingly "ancient" literary style, to the cultural empire of the "modern" embodied by her father.

v

After 1780, with the genres of satire and drama effectively disallowed by her father, Burney turned to more subtle, rhetorical forms of opposition to the *galant* style. The first sign of change lies in Burney's increasing reliance on polite speech as the exclusive dialogic mode, rather than as a foil to the excesses of vulgar and *galant* speech. If the juxtaposition of polite speech and fashionable discourse in *Evelina* produced much of its comedy, the reduction of diverse verbal idioms to a uniform polite language in the later novels produces a phenomenon of Romanticism: a gothic obscurity in language, a stalemate of meaning. When two polite characters speak to each other, as in page after page of *Camilla*, they communicate little beyond their own politeness. The following is a typical exchange between the heroine and "the impenetrable Mandelbert":

"You did not, I hope, at least," he cried, "when you had entered it, deem me too rigid, too austere, that I thought the species, both of company and entertainment, ill calculated for a young lady?"

"Rigid! Austere!" repeated she; "I never thought you either! Never—and if once again—" she stopt; embarrassed, ashamed.

"If once again what?" cried he in a tremulous voice; "what would Miss Camilla say?—would she again—Is there yet—What would Miss Camilla say?—"

Camilla felt confounded, both with ideas of what he meant to allude to, and what construction he had put on her half-finished sentence. Impatient, however, to clear that, "If once more," she cried, "you could prevail with yourself—now and then—from time to time—to give me an hint, an idea—of what you think right—I will promise, if not a constant observance, at least a never-failing sense of your kindness."

The revulsion in the heart, in the whole frame of Edgar, was almost too powerful for restraint ... But before he could make any answer, a sudden and violent shower broke up the conference ... (434–5)

Polite speech is almost fully ironized in *Camilla*. Actual signification disappears in a vapor of rectitude and is repeatedly "concluded" only by the happenstance of interruption.[96] Edgar is forever "involved in expressions he knew not how to clear or to finish," leaving the heroine to beg not for love but for clear speech, that he "be more explicit" (298). Terry Castle has called this morbid rhetorical compulsion Burney's "masochistic recoil" against the freedoms of her early style.[97] As Joanne Cutting-Gray observes, in adopting a "style built on Latinate nominalizations," Burney's novels, beginning with *Cecilia*, are "filled with characters who are arrested, stilled in their acts by her own prose style, a style borrowed from the 'Censors' and 'Magistrates' of writing," namely Johnson and his enforcers, Charles Burney and "Daddy" Crisp.[98] In *Evelina* the rhetoric of virtue balanced the novel's virtuosic idioms, in which Burney invested her principal writerly energies. The heroine too embodied virtue in familiar and purely functional terms. But the later novels are increasingly driven by a "wistful, persistent fantasy of flawless virtue," almost a metaphysics of modesty.[99] The representation of virtue then becomes the word-matter of the novel itself – an impacted gothic idiom of ambiguity, protraction, deferral, and delay that is perpetually prey to misprision. Plot and style converge in a common cause, namely "confusion." This is the Burney baroque, a literary anti-style we now begin to recognize as a symbolic repudiation of her father's *galant* mode.

In her late, baroque style, Burney often forgoes reporting speech at all, allowing the forms of polite address she repeatedly rehearses to recede into indirect forms, which themselves assume a kind of bulky opacity. The prototype of politeness in *Evelina*, Lord Orville, was already abstracted from speech. We are told that his "conversation ... is really delightful," but are given no real examples (74). Subsequently through her novelistic career, Burney increasingly flattened out distinctions between the diction of narration and direct speech such that quotation marks ceased to signify any disruption to the rhythmic and remorseless unfolding of polite, anti-*galant* discourse. Even at a moment of high emotion in *The Wanderer*, for example, Ellis speaks with Johnsonian balance, organized by semi-colons: "'I blush to have incurred such a reprimand; but I hope to convince you, by the exertions which I shall not a moment delay making, how little it is my intention to practise any such injustice; and how wide it would be from my approbation" (281). Burney was a virtuoso mimic, but her late style exchanges the imitation of idiomatic speech for the imitation of literary language. *The Wanderer* is written in a strange hybrid borrowing of gothic hyperbole and Johnsonian gravity, for the latter of which almost any passage from the *Rambler* might be selected as a model.[100]

Where *Evelina* was audacious in its virtuosic transcription of recognizable speech idioms, Burney's baroque style increasingly absorbs all idiomatic expression into a ceremonial language that, beyond any specific content, represents the unimpeachable gentility and "literary" pedigree of its author. Burney's "musical" method in *Evelina* – her virtuosic, transcriptive style – has been abandoned. It is no accident, then, that the music concert scene in her last novel breaks down into hysteria and chaos, with the aphasic collapse of the pianist heroine and the attempted suicide of her rival Elinor, all without a note being played: "her voice refused to obey her; her eyes became dim ... her complexion wore the pallid hue of death, and she sunk motionless to the floor" (358–9). The musical *galant* has completed its trajectory in Frances Burney's literary career, from the "delight" and "sweetness" of the opera house she recorded in her early journals and novels, to a ghoulish Saint Vitus' Dance of denial and self-laceration in *The Wanderer*: "The blood gushed out in torrents, while, with a smile of triumph, and eyes of idolizing love, she dropt into his arms" (359). Elinor duly recovers a few pages later, but the *galant* is dead.

VI

In the late 1810s, after the relative failure of *The Wanderer*, Frances Burney turned to the literary task entrusted to her by her dead father – the production of his memoirs. In his long life, a half-century of it spent in the first line of London's social and intellectual circles, Charles Burney had never thrown out a letter or invitation. His study was filled with miscellaneous papers in addition to the twelve bound notebook volumes of handwritten recollections he intended as the substance of his autobiography. For his sixty-year-old daughter it was the overwhelming material remainder of his fashionable life, a deeply oppressive "cloud of words."[101] Her attitude to this long life lived in fashionable music circles shows in how she proceeded with her commission. Charles Burney's "ever-favoured daughter" burned the majority of his loose papers. She then took his notebooks, ripped off the spines, cut up the pages with scissors and committed most of them to the flames as well.[102] The pages she preserved she scored heavily in pen, obliterating hundreds of lines, occasionally filling in the margins with her own editorial revisions of her father's prose, even at times attempting to forge his hand. She had intended to publish three volumes of letters written to her father in his heyday from literary luminaries such as Johnson and Burke, but was thwarted by a change in the copyright laws. What she finally published in 1832 as *The Memoirs of Doctor Burney* consisted of almost none of her father's original writing. Instead, Frances filled three volumes with an idealized, heavily censored account of her father's life organized around sketch biographies of his friends, and often supplemented by long excerpts from her own letters and journals from decades before. The lamentable effect of suppressing, expurgating, and revising her father's own prose, according to his biographer Roger Lonsdale, was "to destroy the true nature of Burney's personality."[103]

Burney wrote her father's *Memoirs* on the supposition that "Literature and its pursuits," were "without rival in his estimation."[104] Accordingly, she almost completely erased the music culture by which her father's life was mostly consumed. Dozens of pages are devoted to his acquaintance with Dr. Johnson, but not a mention is made of his time in Handel's orchestra or his youth playing in the bands at Vauxhall Gardens. His lifetime of teaching music is passed over, as are his compositions. On his removing to London from King's Lynn, we are told he "sent for what, after his lovely wife, he most valued, his books," without any reference to the keyboard that was his livelihood. His first position in London, as music master at a boarding school in Bloomsbury, is quietly omitted. Even the records from the heyday of his fame – such as his close involvement with Haydn during his triumphant London tours – were destroyed, earning Frances the eternal enmity of music historians. The brief chapter she headlines "Concerts," which must stand for the many dozens of famous musical evenings in the house at St. Martin's Street, mentions not a single performer or piece, but rather emphasizes the strictly amateur nature of the events, to remove any odor of professionalism, of music as luxury *trade*. She even disavows her own title for the chapter:

> To style them, however, concerts, may be conferring on them a dignity to which they had not any pretension. There was no bill of fare: there were no engaged subalterns, either to double, or aid, or contrast, with the principals. The performances were promiscuous; and simply such as suited the varying humours and desires of the company; a part of which were always assistants as well as auditors.

Of the dozens of Italian operas her father attended every season, and whose scores he studied in exacting detail, she mentions none by name, and makes reference to her father at the King's Theatre only for the opportunity to invoke the name of the Prince of Wales, "who frequently deigned to call upon Dr. Burney for his opinion upon subjects of harmony."[105]

Burney treated the editing of her own letters and journals upon the same principles as her father's *Memoirs*. The original manuscript of her journal of 1775, for example, a time when she was simply the second daughter of a fashionable music teacher, contains numerous descriptions of musical events and her father's central role as promoter and opinion-maker in the industry:

> Signor Celestini has had a Benefit at Carli[s]le House—to which we all went. The affair concerning him & Madame Giordani has been *Compromized*. He gave a good Concert, but had little Company. He begged my Father to use his Interest for him, which he did, & I believe got off some Tickets for him.[106]

This reference to her father's "interest" – his implied power within the machinery of promotion, and involvement in musical-cultural intrigue – is scored through with the same fierce, obliterating hand she applied to his papers.[107] Charles Burney's business relations with the Thrales and the ingenious instrument-maker Merlin are likewise censored, just as she excises in part or full literally dozens of accounts of her attendance at operas and concerts including, to take but a single example, a 1772 benefit for the fashionable *galant* composer J. C. Fischer: "every great Performer in England, almost, was there—Abel—Fischer—Duport—Ponta—Wendling—Linley—& two sweet singers, Savoi I Grassi."[108] The vast majority of her extraordinarily detailed knowledge of high Georgian music culture – its repertoire, performers, and politics – thus remains irrecoverable, though some equivalent is preserved in her sister Susan's unpublished diaries.[109]

Frances defended her editorial work in the *Memoirs* to her sister Esther, calling their father's recollections "trivial to poverty, and dull to sleepiness." In the *Memoirs* themselves she adverted to her father's "nerveless laxity of expression [and] monotonous prolixity of detail," a criticism that readers of his *Tours* and *General History of Music*, let alone his cracking letters, have found impossible to credit.[110] Contemporary critics of the *Memoirs*, however, focussed their principal wrath on Frances's own prose. Her inveterate enemy, John Wilson Croker of the *Quarterly Review*, wondered whether "what she has suppressed could have been more feeble, anile, incoherent . . . than that which she has substituted for it." Macaulay called it "the worst style that has ever been known among men," capable only of producing "mirth, shame, and loathing" in her once-admiring readers.[111]

In the *Memoirs of Doctor Burney*, his daughter refers to herself, ubiquitously, in an elevated and remote third person. The text, taken whole, represents the apotheosis of polite speech in Burney, the summit of her baroque late style. The *Memoirs* offer almost no direct speech whatever, allowing her prose to recede to the point of absolute rectitude. As Doody has observed, "awkwardness of style" in the *Memoirs* increases whenever the narrative treats matters internal to the Burney family, suggesting repression in the classic Freudian sense.[112] She records the fact of the fashionable wit with which her father was surrounded, and to which he was a celebrated contributor, but not its actual language. Though in possession of numerous examples among her father's papers, and no doubt many more in her own recollection, her tribute to Hester Thrale as "a star of the first magnitude in the constellation of female wits" likewise contains not a single example, but only the suffocating assurance that she was capable of "sallies of wit and gaiety, and the happiest spontaneous epigrams."[113]

Prose style itself is the protagonist hero of Frances Burney's "last novel."[114] This romance of writing finds an allegory in the fantasy memory she records of the dying Johnson's tender preference for her company. The satisfaction is all her own, though she grants it to her proud father: "Dr. Burney was daily more enchanted at the kindness with

which his daughter was honoured by Dr. Johnson." Enchantment here doubles as emasculation and oedipal revenge. Johnson displaces Charles Burney in the *Memoirs* as its heroic figure just as Johnson assumed a kind of internalized paternal authority over his daughter's prose. The enfeeblement of Johnson is thus both the matter and the medium of Burney's farewell romance:

He then suddenly and expressively looked at her, abruptly grasped her hand, and, with an air of affection, though in a low husky voice, murmured rather than said: "Good morning, dear lady!" but turned his head quickly away, to avoid any species of answer.

  She was deeply touched by so gentle an acquiescence in her declining the confidential discourse which he had indubitably meant to open, relative to this mysterious alienation. But she had the comfort to be satisfied, that he saw and believed in her sincere participation in his feelings; while he allowed for the grateful attachment that bound her to a friend so loved; who, to her at least, still manifested a fervour of regard that resisted all change; alike from this new partiality, and from the undisguised, and even strenuous opposition of the Memorialist to its indulgence.[115]

The second paragraph reads as an impenetrable fusion of abstractions and subordinate clauses. The long sentence is divided by three semi-colons, each more grammatically tenuous than the last. The meaning of the whole is self-repudiating: Burney's resistance to his "partiality" is directly contradicted by the paragraph itself in its massive Johnsonian bulk. Such prose is Burney's final symbolic rejection of her father's aesthetic, of the modern *galant* style and its vaunted clarity. What Macaulay called her "broken Johnsonese" would better be understood in socio-political terms as middle-class Tory – as a fugal, gothic, "ancient" style opposed to modern metropolitan elegance – for it is in the original musical-cultural context of the *galant* that Burney first formed her opposition to the culture that had made and, in her eyes, degraded her father, before the salvation of letters. Thus, her erasure of music culture from her father's biography was effected not only by outright censorship, but through the high Church baroque idiom with which she replaced her father's modern, secular voice. Here she describes her father's return from his continental tour in 1772:

With all the soaring feelings of the first sun-beams of hope that irradiate from a bright, though distant glimpse of renown; untamed by difficulties, superior to fatigue, and springing over the hydra-headed monsters of impediment that every where jutted forth their thwarting obstacles to his enterprise, Dr. Burney came back to his country, his friends, his business, and his pursuits, with the vigour of the first youth in spirits, expectations, and activity.[116]

Burney's idealizing diction – here taken to a dizzying heroic extreme – is in fact an act of rhetorical violence, only pretending to purify. Her lifelong critique of her father's career is submerged beneath its hyperbolic, unendurable opposite, the hagiographic apology. In the *Memoirs*, Frances the amanuensis revenged herself on her father, dictating what he would say, publishing her words under his name. She finally committed the crime for which she had always felt guilty since publishing *Evelina*. She usurped the place of the "author of my being," and struck his *galant* presence from the cultural record.

VII

In 1785, after thirty-three years under her father's roof, Frances Burney's life became a sequence of enforced removals and seclusions – first at court, followed by marriage in a rural "hermitage," then exile in Paris. That is, her life became increasingly romantic at the same time as her literary productions became less popular. After *Cecilia*, Burney shifts in our imagination from a writer to a quasi-novelistic character, Madame D'Arblay, whose destiny, by an uncanny set of happenstances, was to be a close witness to world-historical events: the madness of King George, Napoleonic Paris, the battle of Waterloo. Even her son became a kind of tragic Wertherian figure. Embedded in that world-historical sequence we call "Romantic," Madame D'Arblay came to assume a proportional contempt for her father's outmoded *galant* simplicity, as well as her own early virtuosic style.

The new virtuoso of the late eighteenth century embodied, in extreme form, the demands of the new professionalism, defined as the disciplining of raw human capabilities into marketable skill. The word "virtuoso" itself – which described Frances Burney's father, sister, cousin and, I suggest, her own early writerly practice – tracked a critical social shift from belletristic, connoisseur culture to professional specialization and technical proficiency characteristic of the emerging bourgeois regime. In *Evelina* the virtuoso is a hidden figure of self-conscious authorial practice – the professional who both performs and is absolutely conscious and critical of the mechanical demands of that performance. The castrato Pacchierotti, a real-world image of virtuoso professionalism, was the Burneys' favorite singer and a family intimate. He makes an appearance in *Cecilia*:

> She found herself by nothing so deeply impressed, as by the plaintive and beautiful simplicity with which Pacchierotti uttered the affecting repetition of *sono innocente*! His voice, always either sweet or impassioned, delivered those

words in a tone of softness, pathos, and sensibility, that struck her with a sensation not more new than delightful. (65)[117]

Pacchierotti's "innocence" is both a joke – he produces a coded sexual awakening in the heroine – and a poignant biographical irony. From the evidence of Susan Burney's diaries, the singer cherished a frustrated passion for Frances Burney herself. Nor is his voice "innocent," as such, but rather the purest possible vehicle for innocence, aesthetically realized. The most celebrated male soprano of 1780s London combines virtuosity, sensibility, and professionalism in an artistic ideal that is the model of Burney's own early style.

Burney's own virtuosic practice was worked into *Evelina* itself as the heroine's paralyzing self-consciousness. Later, with her professional anonymity breached, and removed from the musico-cultural surroundings of her youth, Burney's virtuosic self-consciousness receded, to be replaced by the defensive necessity of "modesty" – by a desire to consolidate her family's precarious respectability upon the palpable foundation of an elevated prose style that opposed itself to the leveling social aesthetic of the *galant*. Burney accordingly substituted the transcriptive, inclusive, virtuosic methodology of *Evelina* with a literary method that was deeply exclusive, that denied all possibility of linguistic and class division. This literary turn to Johnson was artistically disastrous because, as Macaulay perceived, "It was not ... by reading that her intellect was formed," but rather, as I have argued, by music and sociable music culture.[118] Her late style thus came to embody the moral, specifically "literary" virtues once mistaken for her personality. The strategic "shyness" documented in her early journals eventually dissolved, leaving only virtue's empty shell – derivative, defensive, ideological writing. Viewed through the prism of music culture and her father's career, however, we are able to understand Burney's late style not merely in the terms handed down to us by Croker and Macaulay, but as her final statement in a lifelong melopoetic struggle with her father and the *galant* culture he represented. To his modern *chiarezza* she opposed her own increasingly fugal and impenetrable solemnity, a kind of Romantic seriousness whose utility might always be opposed to mere popularity or critical acclaim, and which could never be mistaken for fashionable writing.

Frances Burney began her writing career as her father's dutiful amanuensis, and ended it the most tyrannical of his editors. So identifiable was her youthful hand to London publishers that she felt obliged to write in a disguised script when preparing to submit *Evelina*. After that novel's success, Charles timed his own subsequent literary productions with hers. He bullied her into completing *Cecilia* so that it might pave the way for the second volume of his *General History of Music,* and *Camilla* subsequently came out the same year as his *Memoirs of Metastasio*.[119] Unfortunately, Charles Burney viewed his daughter's writing only as symbolic capital, not actual revenue. Her financial independence was simply not important, or even conceived of: the goal, for the Burneys' beloved *paterfamilias,* was to attract whatever epithets of status he could through his children, be it virtuoso pianist, fashionable novelist, or queen's companion. The theme of patronal dependency in Frances Burney's novels and journals is central to our understanding her persistent critique of fashionable society and *galant* music culture. But the deeper truth of her resistance, and its most powerful expression, lies in the writing itself, which could never literally acknowledge or thematize its own rebellious motives. That is, the precise objects of Burney's critique of fashion are obscured within a critique of style, beginning with the satire on fashionable language in *Evelina,* continuing with the adoption of a baroque, anti-*galant* politeness in her fictional prose, and concluding with the systematic editorial suppression of music culture in *The Memoirs of Doctor Burney.*

"Nothing can be more general than the reciprocal Follies of Parents & Children," wrote Samuel Crisp to Frances Burney, after he and Charles Burney had combined to suppress *The Witlings.* He was describing the plot, but Frances the writer saw only the criminal folly of her two "Daddies." Her description of their "Hissing, groaning, catcalling Epistle" is found in the bitterest letter of the many hundreds she wrote.[120] Henceforward, the Burneys, father and daughter, had a destructive impact on the other's career and legacy. He inflicted the pathologies of patronage on her, she the pathologies of middle-class gentility on him. Frances's career as a playwright was snuffed out, and her novel writing either postponed or placed on crippling deadlines at her father's behest. A prototype of the modern literary professional, Burney was nevertheless haunted by the elusive prestige of leisured gentility. Her prose style became a baroque monument to the independence and respectability Charles Burney would or could not guarantee her. She, in turn, drastically diminished his place in English cultural history with the destruction of his papers and, through the devastated *Memoirs,* introduced the still-persistent image of him as a social climber whose principal object was literary recognition. To see these writerly antagonisms simply as symptomatic of deeper "real" conflicts of gender and generation is to join the ranks of those who have reduced Burney all along, from her deserved status as a ground-breaking professional novelist "of prodigious parts" to Thackeray's "indomitable virgin." Frances Burney idolized her father in their family life and in her journals, but their deeper, unspoken relationship played itself out as a melodrama of writing: a bloody family romance of coercion and rebellion, writing and destroying texts, born in music and conducted through the pen.

CHAPTER 3

Wordsworth castrato

I

In a group portrait of opera superstars from the mid-eighteenth century, the incomparable castrato, Farinelli, sits center stage with the soprano Castellini at his right hand (Figure 4). The artist, Jacopo Amigoni, places himself in the most intimate relation to Farinelli – leaning over him, hand on his right shoulder – but in actuality it is the figure furthest away, to the rear on the left margin of the painting, who could lay greatest claim to Farinelli's confidence and to an almost equal share of his fame. The librettist Pietro Metastasio (see chapter 2), Farinelli's correspondent and collaborator for over thirty years, holds a quill, as if he has just finished transcribing the score that Farinelli has in his hand. That score, of which a fragment is just visible, shows Farinelli's own setting of Metastasio's famous *La Partenza* (1749) – "Ecco quel fiero istante" – a signature piece of the great male soprano, a text repeatedly set over the next fifty years by the most prominent composers in Europe including Haydn, Mozart, and Beethoven.[1]

If Metastasio's *La Partenza* looms large in European music history, however, its place in British *literary* history has been forgotten. Wordsworth translated this very portion of the poem, with four other Metastasian texts, for the *Morning Post* in 1803. That the tantalizing journey of Metastasio's *La Partenza* from Farinelli's hand to Wordsworth's has never been traced is typical of the embarrassed silence that historically surrounds the intersection of opera and literature. The disregard is mutual. Metastasio's marginal relation to Farinelli in the Amigoni portrait reflects the subservient relation of text to performance in opera culture, while the near-illegibility of the text Farinelli holds in his hand mirrors Metastasio's invisibility in Wordsworth criticism. My purpose in this chapter is to break the silence between baroque opera and British Romanticism by setting what are arguably Wordsworth's most obscure

Figure 4. Jacopo Amigoni (1682–1752), *The Singer Farinelli and Friends* (*c.* 1750–2). Oil on canvas. National Gallery of Victoria, Melbourne, Australia. Felton Bequest. While in England in the 1730s, Amigoni attached himself to musical patrons, earning commissions from the Duke of Chandos, Covent Garden, and the King's Theatre. He accordingly attracted virtuosophobic attention from the press: in 1743, the *Weekly Register* attacked his florid, continental style, contrasting it to the moral realism of neglected native artists.

verses – his translation of Metastasian arias for the *Morning Post* – alongside the *über*-canonical *Lyrical Ballads*. Italian opera was and is the most stylized art form in mainstream Western culture, a bastion of style in a long age of realism that Wordsworth himself presides over as a kind of fathering vapor. Reading Wordsworth through Metastasio thus presents the scandalous suggestion of operatic registers in *Lyrical Ballads*, a text historically characterized by decidedly anti-operatic notions of realism, restraint, and moral seriousness. A juxtaposition of opera and Romantic poetry, set at the conclusion of the "century of the castrato," has the potential likewise to shake our assumptions regarding Wordsworthian masculinity, to address what Adela Pinch has called the perennial difficulty in "assign[ing] a fundamental place to questions of gender and sexuality" in *Lyrical Ballads*.[2]

In "The Brothers," a long dramatic poem first published in the 1800 *Lyrical Ballads*, Wordsworth makes strategic use of a masculinist language familiar to his wartime readers. The "Priest of Ennerdale" mistakes Leonard, a returned sailor, for an effeminate Lakes tourist, a "moping son of Idleness." His "tears," "fancies," and "solitary smiles" represent to the Priest a masculine deficiency, a neglect of industry and martial vigor. This (mistaken) description of Leonard is also strikingly evocative of Wordsworth's own balladeer, and by extension the poet himself:

> 'Tis one of those who needs must leave the path
> Of the world's business, to go wild alone:
> His arms have a perpetual holiday,
> The happy man will creep about the fields
> Following his fancies by the hour, to bring
> Tears down his cheek, or solitary smiles
> Into his face, until the setting sun
> Write Fool upon his forehead.   (103–10)

Through the Priest, Wordsworth articulates with surprising relish the masculinist critique of the Romantic man of feeling. He is not a hero of solitude, but the inverse: an effeminate idler, a deserter of "the world's business," a "Fool." The pun on "arms" points to a more specific charge: the poet-figure is on "perpetual holiday" from his principal masculine responsibility, namely defense of the nation. The irony of the Priest's misrecognition – the reader knows that Leonard has in fact spent his life at sea furthering the empire's business of war and trade – compromises the force of his masculine indictment, but incidental details of the narrative conversely suggest its truth: Leonard, for example, frequently bursts into tears. The association between tears and femininity, and hence unmanliness, is commonplace across centuries of English literature – consider Macduff's fighting back tears in *Macbeth*: "O, I could play the woman with mine eyes/And braggart with my tongue. But, gentle heavens,/Cut short all intermission" to which Malcolm approvingly replies, "This tune goes manly" (IV.iii.230–2, 235). Adam Smith applied the same standard to himself as a member of the theater audience:

when we attend . . . a tragedy, we struggle against that sympathetic sorrow the entertainment inspires . . . If we shed any tears, we carefully conceal them, and are afraid, lest the spectators, not entering into this excessive tenderness, should regard it as effeminacy and weakness.[3]

Theatricality pervades the eighteenth-century discourse of effeminacy, in which tears figure both feminine weakness and a critical self-consciousness, the dangers of publicizing the self as "show." Leonard's double identity – as both manly hero and tearful poet-surrogate – embodies a pervasive anxiety over public effeminacy in *Lyrical Ballads*, and over Wordsworth's own relation, as poet and man of feeling, to the performative codes of Georgian masculinity.

In his Preface to *Lyrical Ballads*, Wordsworth's principal defense against imputations of effeminacy lies in his famous self-advertisement as "a man speaking to men."[4] He aggressively champions a "plainer and more emphatic language" (*P* 1800: 70), belonging implicitly to men, against "the gaudiness and inane phraseology of many modern writers" (*P* 1802: 55), its (ef)feminized opposite. As critics have pointed out, Wordsworth launched his career in a poetry marketplace increasingly populated by women, as both writers and readers.[5] The Preface thus presents his *Lyrical Ballads* as an antidote to poetic fashion, to those poets, female or feminized, who "have indulge[d] in arbitrary and capricious habits of expression in order to furnish food for fickle tastes and fickle appetites of their own creation" (*P* 1800: 88–9). Gaudiness, inanity, caprice – Wordsworth's argument against the fashionable poetry of sensibility borrows directly from the language of misogyny. By means of this veiled attack on women poets, and his own contrasting "manly" style (*P* 1800: 493), Wordsworth employs the Preface to protect himself "from the most dishonorable accusation which can be brought against an Author, namely that of an indolence which prevents him from endeavouring to ascertain what is his duty" (*P* 1800: 59–63). For duty as an author, read *duty as a man*. In late 1792 Wordsworth was obliged, for financial and political reasons, to return to England, leaving Annette Vallon and their small child in France. In book x of the *Prelude* he recalls the suicidal thoughts and dire feelings of emasculation to which he fell prey on his return: "A Poet only to myself, to Men/Useless" (234–5). As we shall see, indolence and uselessness belong to an eighteenth-century discursive history linking effeminacy, virtuosity, and artistic labor. The strained defense against indolence in the Preface to *Lyrical Ballads* marks the fine line between masculinism and masculine self-loathing in Wordsworth. In his Preface, the poet assumes the role of the newly returned Leonard in "The Brothers," whose conspicuous attention to "honor" and "duty" automatically repudiates charges of effeminate "indolence," whatever appearances to the contrary.

If Wordsworth's intention in his Preface was to reassure readers of his masculine credentials, he succeeded with William Hazlitt. In two closely related essays – "On Effeminacy of Character" (1822) and "Mr. Wordsworth" (1825) – Hazlitt implicitly accepts Wordsworth's argument that literary masculinity should be determined by style not subject matter. For Hazlitt, Wordsworth's revolutionary "plainer" language in *Lyrical Ballads* stands for "the manhood of poetry," a heroic foil to the "tinsel pageantry" of the "effeminate style." Hazlitt contrasts the poetry of sensibility, with its "cumbrous ornaments of style and turgid commonplaces," to the "simplicity of truth and nature" of *Lyrical Ballads*.[6] The word "ornament" – a commonplace in music discourse to describe a singer's virtuosic embellishments of the melody in the *da capo* section of an aria – is a rhetorical yoke linking a century-old virtuoso-phobic discourse in England and the revolution in poetic diction conventionally located at that century's end. In the mid-eighteenth century Hume had identified the slippery slope by which the "ornamental" speech recommended by modern politeness might descend into effeminate "affectation and foppery," while both Eliza Haywood and Mary Wollstonecraft used the same word to impugn the manliness of the Army officer corps and Edmund Burke, respectively.[7] By dint of his *un*ornamented, manly style, Wordsworth has compensated for the sentimental concerns of his poetry and insulated himself, in Hazlitt's eyes at least, against the "dishonorable" association of effeminacy.[8]

Despite the masculinist rhetoric of Wordsworth's Preface, and its reiteration by Hazlitt, not all contemporary critics were convinced of the poetic manhood of *Lyrical Ballads*. One of the volume's first reviewers, Charles Burney, called *Lyrical Ballads* a "*poesie larmoiante*, more plaintive than Gray himself," a stinging pre-emptive dismissal of the Preface, where Gray serves as Wordsworth's prime example of what Hazlitt termed "effeminate style."[9] In 1807 the journal *Le Beau Monde* upped the rhetorical volume, labeling *Lyrical Ballads* the work of "an historical [sic] schoolgirl." These hostile, gendered readings were echoed by Francis Jeffrey in his better-known attack in the *Edinburgh Review* in the same year, where he charged Wordsworth with "extravagances" and "unbridled indulgence," also Georgian code-words for effeminacy.[10] The uncertain status of masculinity in "The Brothers" thus also constitutes an original fault-line of critical opinion on *Lyrical Ballads*, where Wordsworth is figured as both traitor and champion of manliness.

The question naturally arises: who is more right, Hazlitt or Burney? Is the Wordsworth of *Lyrical Ballads* "a man speaking to men," or a crying schoolgirl? The question is the more pressing given that the canonical aura of Hazlitt's reading, and the invisibility of Burney's, has mostly survived the recent feminist turn in Romantic studies, in which Wordsworth has assumed a multitude of pejorative masculinist identities, as, in one critic's summation, "a rapist, a conqueror, a cannibal, or a capitalist."[11] Marlon Ross places Wordsworth's image of the poet as "Hannibal among the Alps" (from his 1815 "Supplementary Essay") at the center of British Romanticism and its "world of aggressive desire and conquest." No poet before Wordsworth, Ross argues, "associates the achievement of poetic identity so closely with the passage to masculine maturity."[12] Alan Richardson has identified an even "more insidious" form of male poetic imperialism in Wordsworth's appropriation of the feminine language of feeling, an act which aggressively "colonize[s] the conventionally feminine domain of sensibility," exposing at once his fear of the rising popularity of women poets, the poverty of his masculine resources, and himself as a grand emotional plagiarist.[13]

A strong feminist counter-charge to these late 1980s masculinist readings of Wordsworth has come from Susan Wolfson, who identifies gender ventriloquism in *Lyrical Ballads* not with a "colonization" of female sensibility but with an anxiety over masculinity, in her words, with "a male subjectivity being eroded of its manliness."[14] In a similar vein Judith Page has argued that to employ Wordsworthian masculinism as a wholesale "interpretive grid" fails to account for how the poet, so often in his early poetry, "stages a drama in which the feminine continuously transforms masculine experiences."[15] Adela Pinch, at the outset of the current gender debate, formulated the central, still-pertinent question regarding gender ventriloquism in *Lyrical Ballads*, namely "why a [male] poet would find letting feminine suffering inhabit and speak through him to be a source of poetic pleasure and power?"[16]

At the most literal level, masculinist readings of Wordsworth depend upon the dismissal of his chorus of female speakers and tearful, ineffectual males from *Lyrical Ballads*, whose mere presence would seem to contradict them. A significant portion of Wordsworth's "manly" language in the ballads is actually spoken by women – such as the Female Vagrant, the Mad Mother, and the Forsaken Indian Woman – or by grieving, hapless men such as the shepherd in "The Last of the Flock." But the deeper drama overlooked by a masculinist reading of Wordsworth is the battle over masculinity that Wordsworth waged with himself. As Tim Fulford has written, Wordsworth's female voices "are new to poetry and more piercing than most invented at the time by women writers." In this chapter I follow Fulford's revisionist suggestion that masculinity, for Wordsworth as for other Romantic writers, was an "elusive and questionable" trope of power.[17] At the same time, I do not restrict myself, as Fulford does, to the "masculine" metaphorics of the sublime in Wordsworth and the poet's explicit reflections on Burke, Milton, and power. These are the last places we can fruitfully investigate Wordsworthian sexuality because they are programmatic and, therefore, "public." Wordsworth internalized the complex forms of the eighteenth-century debate over masculinity in which the Man of Feeling claimed the right to weep but met with a fierce backlash in publishing them, as Burke discovered with his tears for Marie Antoinette and Coleridge for his on behalf of the Revolution, for which he was accused of "shrinking softness."[18] My argument here is that the ambiguous critique of effeminacy we find in "The Brothers," where masculinist language is undone by irony, and masculinity's image by tears, exemplifies a Wordsworthian compromise on masculinity, a symbolic model for the mutual constraints operating between (so-called) manliness and effeminacy in *Lyrical Ballads* as a whole.

In his discussion of meter in the 1800 Preface, Wordsworth theorizes an economy of form and content in gendered terms.[19] The importance of poetic meter, he argues, lies in its "restraining" effect on "excitement [that] may be carried beyond its proper bounds" (*P* 1800: 505, 502). Meter as pleasure principle, in which the machinery of form acts as a restraint on the improper excitations of sentimental content, rehearses the gender distinctions of Wordsworth's earlier polemic on poetic diction: just as his "plainer" language will rescue English diction from "the gaudiness and inane phraseology" of the sensibility poets, so meter performs a disciplinary, masculinizing role on improper subjects, specifically, on Wordsworth's female and effeminate voices. Note too that Wordsworth's theory of meter is essentially performative. The "restraining" effect of meter cannot be understood outside the sensual workings of poetry as an oral medium: as words uttered, tones heard, pulses felt. This performative power Wordsworth grants to meter suggests a specific historical context for *Lyrical Ballads* – a context that links Wordsworth's early career, his critic Burney, and the Georgian debate over masculinity – namely, the Italian opera.

As Herbert Lindenberger has observed, post-Enlightenment critical orthodoxy places opera and literature squarely at odds. The opera, as an "*extravagant, gestural, ceremonial,* and *performative*" art form, privileges sentimental effect over "literary" concerns for verbal restraint, mimetic truth, and psychological depth.[20] Lindenberger's binary categories naturally extend to gender, to a historically traceable opposition between operatic effeminacy and literary manliness. The association of music and effeminacy dates at least to the Elizabethans, and the writings of the puritans Phillip Stubbes and William Prynne.[21] The Italian opera's spectacle of luxury, transvestism, and the male soprano crystallized the equation in the Georgian mind. From its arrival in England in the first decade of the eighteenth century, Italian opera endured a harassing buzz of associations with effeminacy and English cultural decline. Charles Burney, biographer of Metastasio, was its first reputable historian (see chapter 2). The fact that Burney was also the first to detect the effeminate strains of *Lyrical Ballads*, and that Wordsworth himself shared Burney's susceptibility to Italian opera in the texts of Metastasio, represents a natural starting point for a reconsideration of Burney's heterodox description of *Lyrical Ballads* as *poesie larmoiante* – "crying" poetry – and its implications for our understanding of gender and masculinity in Wordsworth.

My first duty will be to return the librettist Metastasio to the English literary-cultural orbit to which he belongs, a place he would have occupied in Wordsworth's mind as he translated five of his lyrics for the *Morning Post* in the winter of 1802–3. To then compare Wordsworth's "literary" answer to the problem of operatic extravagance with that of the period's most prominent English Metastasian, John Hoole, is to undertake an object lesson in the distinction between the so-called manly and effeminate styles, a distinction everywhere implied but only poorly exemplified in the Preface itself. Lastly, as an extreme example of manly style adapted to effeminate content, Wordsworth's Metastasian translations will provide a novel, "operatic" context for my readings of select poems of *Lyrical Ballads*, in particular their complex proprieties of female voices and manly tears.

II

Hazlitt defined effeminacy of character as "a prevalence of sensibility over the will." The classical figure of the *effeminatus* returns in the shape of the Regency avatars of sensibility, who "lie on beds of roses, and spread their gauze wings to the sun and summer gale."[22] For Hazlitt, the modern *effeminatus* is vain – "completely wrapped up in [himself]" – but his symbolic function is principally negative: he represents ineffectuality and inaction, a dangerous "deficiency in masculine energy." Effeminacy, in its Regency sense, should thus not be confused with femininity or homosexuality.[23] While consistent with effeminacy, these are not the principal object of its critique, which is to uphold what Hazlitt describes as the energetic and "hardy spirit" of masculinity against its modern nemeses: fashion, self-love, and indolence, all historically associated with music culture.

Linda Dowling has formulated effeminacy in its broad Georgian sense as a "civic incapacity, the dissolution of social categories which occurs when community itself has begun to dissolve into an aimless and self-regarding egoism." In the context of demoralizing reverses in the decades-long struggle with France, it was a moral commonplace, exemplified by words delivered from a Newcastle pulpit in 1759, to contrast men "who choose Dangers in defence of Their Country" with those who abjure the responsibilities of manhood for "the unmanly pleasures of a useless and effeminate life." For the clergyman John Brown, in his best-selling mid-century diatribe, effeminacy and its companion vices, "luxury," "vanity," and "novelty," stood as master-tropes of national degeneration: "the Character of the Manners of our Times . . . appears to be that of a *vain, luxurious*, and *selfish* EFFEMINACY."[24] The metonymic proximity of luxury here points to effeminacy as a corrupting symptom of commercialization, thus subsuming it within the dominant Georgian trope of the nation and its perceived changing character. "A history of luxury and attitudes to luxury," Paul Langford has written, "would come very close to being a history of the eighteenth century."[25] That this connection between the scandal of effeminacy and luxury consumerism mostly disappeared by the mid-nineteenth century suggests that the Victorians enjoyed "a much easier relationship between normative masculinity and the values of commercial society."[26] Throughout the Georgian period, however, the critique of effeminacy was a ubiquitous subject of pamphlets and treatises, and belonged to a pervasive, sometimes hysterical indictment of the debilitating effects of the new commodity-rich metropolitan lifestyle on the fighting readiness of British men.

The introduction of Italian opera in the first decade of the eighteenth century became synonymous with England's cultural decline into effeminacy. Michèle Cohen, an influential historian of British masculinity, has defined the scandal of effeminacy almost exclusively as a reaction against the threat of French manners, but early eighteenth-century sources often identify the decline of manliness more closely with Italian culture, the importation of opera in particular.[27] "Curse on this damn'd *Italian* Pathic Mode" – wrote Henry Carey in his "Satyr on the Luxury and Effeminacy of the Age" (1729) – "To Sodom and to Hell the ready Road."[28] The first Italian singers had barely reached English shores before the critic John Dennis perceived English manhood "dissolv'd in the Wantonness of effeminate airs." The resultant sympathetic chorus was long and loud: in the 1720s Jonathan Swift singled out the opera for his complaint that "we are over-run with *Italian Effeminacy*"; Aaron Hill decried "our emasculating present Taste, of the Italian luxury and Wantonness of Musick"; while the anonymous author of a 1749 pamphlet declared that "since the Introduction of Italian Operas here, our Men are grown insensibly more and more *Effeminate*." The opera-going dandies of London recalled the decadent youths of Rome, who had "lost their Spirit of Manhood, and with it their Empire," who had exchanged "their Liberty to preserve their *Effeminacy*."[29] The equation of manliness and liberty – and its antithesis, effeminacy and tyranny – was automatic to the Georgian mind. The "effeminate" Italian opera, for Hill, in particular its male sopranos, represented a clear and present danger to heterosexual norms, warlike vigor, and by extension to British liberty: "the Martial spirit of our Nation is effeminated, and gradually relax'd, by the Influence of this softening Syren." How did this "Influence" operate? The castrato's voice was not a model of effeminate weakness to be imitated. The threat lay, rather, in the dynamic, eroticized relation between singer and audience. The castrato's penetrative power – relocated from missing organ to melismatic voice – opened his auditors, male and female, to the pleasure-horizon of submission. In Roland Barthes's words, "The voice is a diffusion, an insinuation, it passes over the entire surface of the body, the skin . . . it possesses a special hallucinatory power."[30] A vocal style of "effeminate trills" and cadenzas seemed to glory in music's independence from text and consumable meaning, advertising itself as pure luxury, outside any economy of need or use. Music, lamented John Brown, "now concerns not the Expression . . . but the Tricks of the Performer . . . when he runs the compass of the Throat."[31] Hill cites a warning from Cicero's *De legibus*, in which musical taste represents an essential index of civic strength, or its lack. In early Georgian texts such as Hill's, we find anti-Italian virtuosophobia, suffused with sexual panic, to be a central theme of neoclassical republican discourse.

The effeminate taint of opera communicated itself to Italian poetry. In the 1750s a group of Italian literati led by Giuseppe Baretti, a member of the Johnson and Burney circles, sought to establish a canon of Italian literature among the growing constituency of English connoisseurs and grand tourists. Baretti's first duty as he saw it was to rehabilitate the Italian epic tradition – Dante, Ariosto, Tasso – from the charges of effeminacy brought against it by Voltaire. Dante's verses "are so little effeminate," protested Baretti, "that every one who hears them read . . . will be convinced by the Sound, that they are as strong and sonorous as those in any other language."[32] In the more difficult case of Metastasio, whose name was synonymous with the King's Theatre opera house, Baretti argued that if any effeminate association existed the fault lay with the house composers, who "either slacken when his poetry requires to be expressed with forcible notes or sink into effeminacy when it demands but softness." Baretti's efforts notwithstanding, the effeminate associations of Italian poetry in general, and Metastasio in particular, endured well into the nineteenth century. As the *Quarterly Review* reflected in 1820, the rise of Metastasio in the eighteenth century "rapidly confirm[ed] the prejudice, that effeminacy was the distinguishing character of Italian literature."[33]

Given the Hazlittian consensus endorsed by the first generation of feminist Romantic criticism, which defines Wordsworth as the manliest of poets, it is surprising to find him absorbed in the sexually tainted literature of opera libretti the very year he first published his definition of English poetry as "a man speaking to men." Late in life, Wordsworth recalled how in his first year at Cambridge he

got into rather an idle way; reading nothing but Classic authors according to my fancy, and Italian poetry. My Italian master was named [Augustine] Isola . . . As I took to these studies with much interest, he was proud of the progress I made.[34]

The critique of effeminacy informs Wordsworth's retrospection: he makes an intuitive connection between "idleness" and Italian poetry. Wordsworth returned in the winter of 1802 to his old college textbook of Italian verse, bypassing Petrarch and Tasso for the most effeminate of them all, Metastasio. The five Metastasian poems Wordsworth published in the *Morning Post* in October and November 1803 have been so little regarded by Wordsworth scholars that they were not republished until 1947 (in an appendix to the Selincourt edition), and Wordsworth's translation from *La Partenza* ("Laura, farewell my Laura!"), the text featured in the Amigoni portrait, was not identified until 1962, an event in the English literary canon that passed entirely unnoticed.[35]

Though obscure now to all but opera buffs and Italian specialists, Metastasio was not so to Wordsworth, or to any educated Georgian. In fact, he was one of the most famous men in eighteenth-century Europe. "Everything of epochal importance to the history of music . . . around the middle of the eighteenth century," Daniel Heartz has written, "happened first in Italian opera. It could not have happened without Metastasio, whose incomparably mellifluous poetry and universal appeal so often provided the necessary scaffolding."[36] Handel was the first to set a Metastasian libretto for a King's Theatre production: *Siroe, Re di Persia* in 1728. For the rest of the century Metastasian texts dominated the King's

Theatre stage as they did the opera houses of Europe at large, where his twenty-seven libretti received some 850 different musical settings by the principal opera composers of the age, including Vinci, Scarlatti, Gluck, and Cimarosa. Largely because of his fame at the King's Theatre, Metastasio was the most translated and arguably most read Italian poet in England in the second half of the eighteenth century, exceeding even Dante and Petrarch. At least sixteen volumes of translations of his libretti were published, and individual Metastasian lyrics (including *La Partenza*) continued to appear in both Italian and English translation in literary periodicals and the publications of minor poets into the first decades of the nineteenth century. Already by 1759 Oliver Goldsmith could call Metastasio "well known in England, and ... universally admired."[37] In the ensuing half century Metastasio's prominence only increased, culminating in Charles Burney's *Life and Writings of Metastasio* (1796) and John Hoole's expanded three-volume edition of his dramatic works, *Dramas and Other Poems of Pietro Metastasio* (1800). Given this wide influence, Wordsworth's translation of a selection of Metastasian lyrics for the *Morning Post* in 1802–3 did not demonstrate arcane scholarship or an unusual taste, but rather belonged to the mainstream of minor literary production in the late Georgian period.[38]

When sitting down to his Italian texts in late 1802, Wordsworth could not have known that Metastasio's reputation had peaked. A. W. Schlegel was a chief engineer of its decline. In his 1808 lectures in Vienna, the scene of Metastasio's glory only a generation before, Schlegel condemned the librettist's lyrics for their "total absence of the romantic spirit," calling them "a brilliant surface without depth," and tainted by "an indescribable something, which seems to show that they were designed for the flexible throat of a [male] soprano singer."[39] For the Romantic reformers of the early nineteenth century, the opera house – synonymous with castrati, ephemerality, and the ruination of poetic texts – was inimical to the new poetics of interiority and the imperatives of middle-class literary canon formation. Schlegel's contempt, and the modern literary-critical categories he helped establish, consequently effected the almost total erasure of the baroque Metastasio from European Romanticism, and with it the embarrassing image of Wordsworth in his Grasmere study poring over eighteenth-century opera libretti. The operatic Wordsworth is well worth reviving, however, as a counter-image to the Romantic, masculinist Wordsworth we have inherited from Hazlitt, with its potentially misleading emphasis on an interiorized literary self purified of performance and theatricality: "His poetry is not external, but internal."[40]

Wordsworth's translations of Metastasio – "poetry designed for the flexible throat of a soprano" – belong to operas in which, according to the conventions of Italian *opera seria*, cross-gender casting was routine and the popularity of castrato singers in heroic roles meant that the portrayal of masculinity, and male heterosexual desire, was consistent with a high vocal register. A distinctly "operatic" confusion of speakers thus prevails in the lyrics both in terms of theatricalized sexual identity and the direction of romantic desires. The poem Wordsworth translates as "To the grove, the meadow, the well" ("Alla selva, al prato, alla fonte"), taken from the opera *Il Re Pastore* (1751), is an aria sung by a woman character to a shepherd traditionally performed by a woman *en travesti*. In a similar vein, his selection from the well-known *Ezio* (1728), "Oh! bless'd all bliss above" ("Quanto mai felici siete"), translates an aria in which a woman pines for a hero played by a castrato. Another, "The Swallow, that hath lost/His Mate and lover" ("Rondinella, a cui rapita"), from *Semiramide Riconosciutta* (1729), is a lament sung by a castrato character, Mirteo, for *his* lover. In addition to "Laura, farewell my Laura" ("Ecco quel fiero istante," 1749), Wordsworth translated another of Metastasio's incidental lyric songs, entitled "Gentle Zephyr" ("Placido zeffiretto"), a text which showed no greater promise than the arias for a hetero-normative consummation of desire, it being excerpted from a cantata entitled "Amor Timido." Four of the five Wordsworth translations thus belonged in their musical origins to the soprano voice, be it male or female, and the other to a timid, effeminized male speaker.[41]

On one level, Wordsworth compensated for the femininity (and effeminacy) of his speakers, their "soprano" register, through the act of translation into English itself. In 1835 Thomas Moore recorded a discussion with the elderly poet on the subject of Italian and English as "poetical languages" and, indirectly, their respective gender associations. Wordsworth argued that although English was "unmanageable," costing the poet immense labor to mine its sonorities, it was more conducive to "thought" than the "music" of endlessly harmonizing Italian vowels:

[he] repeated a stanza of Tasso to show how naturally the words fell into music of themselves.—it was one where the double rhymes "ella "nella" "quella" occurred, which he compared to the meagre & harsh English words "she" "that" "this" &c. Thought, however, that on the whole there were advantages in having a rugged language to deal with, as by struggling with words one was led to give birth and dwell upon thoughts, while, on the contrary an easy & mellifluous language was apt to tempt by its facility into negligence, and to lead the poet to substitute music for thought.[42]

For Wordsworth, English is "rugged" and concentrates the manly mind, while Italian is "easy and mellifluous" as a siren song. This formulation suggests that Wordsworth considered his translating Metastasio a form of masculinizing transformation whereby he would subject the insinuating feminine rhymes of the romance language to the "rugged," "meagre," and "harsh" constraints of Anglo-Saxon demonstratives: "that, this &c." That the manliness of the English tongue compared favorably with the "musical" facility of Italian was a Georgian commonplace. Addison – in an essay included in the handsome eight-volume edition of the *Spectator* published in 1799 – found in Saxon monosyllables "the genius and natural temper of the English, which is modest, thoughtful, sincere." The genius of the Italians, by contrast, "which is so much addicted to music and ceremony, has moulded all their words and phrases to these particular uses."[43] An English contemporary of Wordsworth took similar satisfaction in his native tongue as unmusical and unvirtuosic, the very opposite of Italian. English required no "facility, through the mouth" to speak it, and was "neither made for music, nor for those flowery and sonorous beauties which, in some other languages, charm and run away with us by the ear."[44] This gendered coding of English and Italian is historically relative, however. It is contradicted by Dryden, for instance, who reversed the equation in the preface to his own English opera *Albion and Albanius* (1685), calling the pronunciation of Italian "manly and sonorous," and English, with its tricky, sibilant consonants, "effeminate."[45] To a Georgian or Victorian, such an assertion would have seemed perverse. That Dryden could make it without qualm just prior to the introduction of Italian opera in England suggests that *opera itself* came to define the Italian language as "effeminate" to English ears after 1700. Wordsworth and his poetry existed in a culture of specific and transient linguistic associations. Italian was "musical" and "effeminate," which is to say, quite literally, that it was operatic.

Wordsworth's masculinist notion of translation accords with the stated agenda of the contemporary English Metastasians – principally Burney and Hoole – who opposed literary translation of Metastasio's poetry to the eviscerated form of his libretti. According to William Popple of *The Prompter*, the "unnatural tones" of a "mutilated" opera singer (i.e. a castrato) could never convincingly express human emotion because "'tis impossible to suppose he can feel them within himself . . . to *move* one must feel."[46] Strategically borrowing from this anti-operatic discourse, Hoole drew an implicit analogy between Metastasian texts transformed into libretti and the castrati singers who performed them: "not only the dialogue is *mutilated*, but the action is precipitated, the catastrophe *unnaturally* brought on, and the whole rendered *cold and unaffecting.*"[47] The language of "mutilation" is ubiquitous in Georgian anti-operatic discourse, and readily transferred from the scandal of castration to the hostile relation between text and performance, literature and opera:

> those [texts] of the elegant Metastasio have been mutilated and massacred, according to the caprice of the composer; and how barbarously they have been sacrificed to the conveniency of his *adagio* or *allegro*. But the truth is, that the musicians of Italy care little about the poetry they set.[48]

The 1800 King's Theatre production of Metastasio's *Zenobia* serves as a pertinent example of textual "mutilation" as its published libretto may be placed side by side with Hoole's translation of the same year. The title page of the King's Theatre libretto represents it as "Poetry altered from Metastasio," which understates the extent to which almost every scene of Metastasio's text, as it appears in his published works and in Hoole's labored but faithful translation, has been abridged, rewritten, or cut altogether. In the final scene, barely a line of Metastasio's original text remains.[49] For Hoole, and the circle of Italian literature scholars and connoisseurs to which he belonged, Italian opera represented the emasculation of Italian literature. It was the task of literary scholarship, and translation in particular, to restore the "mutilated" Metastasian text.[50] Hoole's masculinist claims notwithstanding, his translations, when compared to those of Wordsworth in the *Morning Post* just three years later, will provide a compelling example of the conceptual instability surrounding the so-called effeminate style of poetry: if Hoole's goal was to masculinize Metastasio, then Wordsworth effectively masculinizes Hoole.

III

John Hoole cut a figure on the Georgian literary scene as a translator of the Italian poets.[51] At Cambridge, Wordsworth read his translation of Tasso, *Jerusalem Delivered* (1764), alongside the Italian edition of his tutor, Augustine Isola.[52] He was intimate with Johnson and friends with Burney, Reynolds, and Glover; but the writers of the succeeding generation, Wordsworth's peers, were not charitable to his posthumous reputation. Walter Scott called his translation of Tasso a "flat medium," and mocked his prolific output: "he did exactly so many couplets day by day, neither more or less; and habit made it light to him, however heavy it might seem to the reader." Macaulay shared Scott's contempt, placing

Hoole's versifying style in a context by which we can usefully compare him to Wordsworth:

> coming after Pope, [he] had learned how to manufacture decasyllabic verses; and poured them forth by thousands and tens of thousands, all as well turned, as smooth, and as like each other as the blocks which have passed through Mr. Brunell's mill, in the dockyard at Portsmouth.[53]

In short, Hoole, a third-rate follower of Pope, made a middling career of precisely that brand of versified "Rope-dancing" that Wordsworth famously abominated in his Preface (*P* 1802: 340).

Hoole's translation of "Quanto mai felici siete" will serve as an example of his effeminate style, synonymous here with *bad* style. The aria is taken from Metastasio's *Ezio* (anglicized as *Aetius* in Hoole's translation), one of Metastasio's "most popular librettos."[54] Honoria, the emperor's sister, is secretly in love with his bitter rival; at the end of the first act she laments her predicament. First, the Italian:

> Quanto mai felici siete,
> Innocenti pastorelle,
> Che in amor non conoscete
> Altra legge, che l'amor.
> Ancor io sarei felice
> Se potessi all'idol mio
> Palesar come a voi lice,
> Il desio di questo cor.

In his translation, Hoole does not indulge the personifications Wordsworth singled out for criticism in his Preface (published that same year), but his choices in rhyme and meter produce ugly Latinisms as well as examples of that "arbitrary" and "capricious" diction that Wordsworth condemned in favor of his own manly style:

> Harmless nymphs on rural plains,
> Happy is the lot you prove,
> Whom in love no law restrains,
> Save the gentle laws of love.
> How blest! Could I my suffering tell
> To him whose virtues cause my smart,
> And unconstrain'd, like you, reveal
> The flame that preys upon my heart.[55]

The pitfalls of elevated diction are all too apparent here. In the first stanza, Hoole's nymphs "prove" their "lot" – an idiomatic wrong note – in order to produce a rhyme for "love." Likewise, in the second quatrain,

Honoria's secret torment must be reduced to a mere "smart" in order to agree with "heart." Hoole also shows a poetaster's tin ear for metaphor. The "flame" of love is clumsily put with the hounds, to "prey" upon the heart, where in Metastasio's lyric there is no metaphor at all, only the simple "Il desio di questo cor." Hoole's concern to retain Metastasio's four-beat lines and a comparable rhyme scheme likewise exposes what Wordsworth later called the "unmanageability" of the English language in comparison to the "easy and mellifluous" Italian. Metastasio's tripping "innocenti pastorelle" becomes the leg-locked (and topographically inept) "Happy nymphs in rural plains," while "idol mio" is transformed into the pig-latin monstrosity, "To him whose virtues cause my smart."

By contrast, Wordsworth's solution to the problem of English Latinate wordiness is to contract Metastasio's line to three beats throughout, thus imposing a fundamental metrical restraint. The effects of this contraction on Wordsworth's diction are necessarily dramatic. Five of the nine lines consist solely of monosyllables:

> Oh! bless'd all bliss above,
> Innocent shepherdesses,
> Whom in love no law distresses,
> Who have no law but love.
> Could I, as ye may do,
> Who, conceal'd, adore him,
> Tell what love I have for him;
> Bless'd were I too
> All bliss above.

"Bless'd all bliss above" is Wordsworth's creative and highly musical measure of exactly how happy ("Quanto . . . felici") his shepherdesses are. "Bless'd," contracted into a single syllable, almost collapses into "bliss" on first hearing, then immediately does in a tantalizing pseudo-repetition. In one sense Wordsworth contradicts his poetics of plain language by displacing the prepositional "above" to the end of the phrase. But the momentum, indeed the joy of the line depends entirely on the repetition of the phoneme "bl" on its first two beats. The doctrinally sound alternative, "Bless'd above all bliss," would seriously weaken the interior of the line as it waited for the strong beat of the noun. Wordsworth's is a musical choice, governed by the non-semantic imperatives of sound and rhythm. The musicality of the phrase, however, does not approximate Metastasio's "easy and mellifluous" Italian; we hear instead the percussive "roughness" and fizz of Anglo-Saxon roots and their unique economy, what Addison called "that *hissing* sound in our language, which is taken so much notice of by foreigners."⁵⁶ Wordsworth's translation thus defends English poetic diction on two fronts: against the "foreign splendour" of ornaments and inversions Hoole tunelessly indulges, and against *foreignness* itself, in this case the effeminate musicality of the Italian language (*P* 1802: 277).

That said, Wordsworth's very success in translating Metastasio raises questions for readers of *Lyrical Ballads* and its famous prefatorial advertisement of "a man speaking to men." In publishing an aria from one of Metastasio's most popular operas, Wordsworth exposes himself to the effeminate contamination of that provenance. Moreover, the dramatic context of the scene demands further concessions to a virtuosic effeminacy: the male poet must ventriloquize a heroine expressing love for a male soprano. A more "mutilated" text, in terms of masculine poetic norms, is hard to conceive. Why would the Wordsworth of 1802, the "manly" poet of the ballads, take such care translating a pastoral trifle of love and bliss, distress and shepherdesses, a lyric best known to English audiences in its operatic form as a controversial spectacle of cross-gender confusion and desire? The same question, and with it the specter of effeminacy, arises with the poem Wordsworth published four weeks earlier in the *Morning Post*, on November 15. "Placido zeffiretto," a nine-line lyric that concludes "Amor Timido," repeats the in-love-in-vain motif of "Quanto mai felice":

> Placido zeffiretto,
> Se trovi il caro oggetto,
> Digli che sei sospiro,
> Ma non gli dir di chi.
> Limpido ruscelletto,
> Se mai t'incontri in lei,
> Dille che pianto sei
> Ma non le dir qual ciglio
> Crescer ti fè così.

Wordsworth's translation takes pains to preserve (or restore) the manly dignity of the speaker. As if to compensate for the personifications that open each of the stanzas, Wordsworth restricts himself to the blandest of verbal palettes thereafter. There are no exclamations (Hoole's translation is dotted with them), and the entire poem is more a whisper than a declamation:

> Gentle Zephyr,
> If you pass her by,
> Tell her you're a sigh;
> But tell her not from whom.

> Limpid Streamlet,
> If you meet her ever,
> Say, with your best endeavour,
> That swoln with tears you come;
> But tell her not of whom.

Wordsworth maintains an austere discipline through the first stanza, both in diction and grammar. Lines two through four perfectly represent the principle put down in the Preface that there is "no essential difference between the language of prose and metrical composition" (*P* 1800: 249–50). In the second stanza, however, the diction begins to swell as if in sympathy with the timid lover's tears. In line six, "ever" is displaced to the end of the line, and two lines later Wordsworth inverts the verb and adverbial phrase: "That swoln with tears you come." The translation as a whole suggests an unstable compromise formation or, in rhetorical terms, an economy of license and restraint. The emotion swells up and Wordsworth's "prosaic" discipline stretches accordingly.

In sum: Hoole's translation of "Quanto mai" shows the dangers of allowing dramatic content to dictate too literally, too naively, to form. The operatic intensity of the heroine's yearning, which Hoole seeks to match through some commensurate register of English diction, produces only "gaudiness and inane phraseology." Hoole's approach recalls the discredited virtuoso poet of the Preface, who merely "describes and imitates passions" and is thus "altogether slavish and mechanical." The same robotic condition afflicts Wordsworth's "translator," who "substitutes excellences of another kind for those which are unattainable by him; and endeavours occasionally to surpass his original, in order to make some amends for the general inferiority to which he feels that he must submit." To admit this inferiority as a necessary relation not only between a translation and its original, but between poetry and experience itself is, for Wordsworth, to "encourage idleness and unmanly despair" in poets (*P* 1802: 315, 333–7).

In contrast to Hoole's "unmanly" poeticisms, the austerity of Wordsworth's translation from "Amor Timido" artfully restrains the operatic gesture at the heart of the lyric, the emotional extravagance of the lovesick speaker and his tearful, effeminate "timidity." As Wordsworth observes in the Preface, the regulatory effect of meter combined with unelevated or "plainer" diction has the power to produce an effect of passion greater than its parts, and far greater than those "transitory and accidental ornaments" conventionally employed to communicate high feeling (*P* 1802: 416). Still, the evident strain between speaker and diction in "Bless'd all bliss above" and "Gentle Zephyr" embodies both the terms *and* problems of Wordsworth's argument for the reformation of English poetry. The gendered economy of license and restraint in his Metastasian translations mirrors the rhetorical instability between his masculinist Preface to *Lyrical Ballads* and the sentimental poems it so ambiguously defends (*P* 1800: 521). More particular to my purposes here, the two Metastasio translations likewise betray Wordsworth's general fascination, observable in *Lyrical Ballads*, with what might be called "effeminate effects" in the lyric crossings of gender and voice, specifically female ventriloquism and the confessions of the tearful male.

IV

The Preface's famous formula for the psychological conditions of poetic creation – "emotion recollected in tranquillity" (*P* 1800: 538) – syntactically and conceptually places memory at the heart of Wordsworthian poetics. "Tranquillity," however – shorthand for the restraining exercise of poetic technique on "emotion" – is no less integral to Wordsworth's lyric practice. Issues of technique in the Preface suffer because of their association with artifice. The actual labor of the poet is hidden behind a rhetoric of natural feeling and "real language" (*P* 1800: 3–4). But in a reference to meter in the same paragraph, Wordsworth presents his verse as a product of aesthetic principles and craft, not the unfathered vapor of imagination:

Now if Nature be thus cautious in preserving in a state of enjoyment a being thus employed, the Poet ought to profit by the lesson thus held forth to him, and ought especially to take care, that whatever passions he communicates to his Reader, those passions, if his Reader's mind be sound and vigorous, should always be accompanied with an overbalance of pleasure . . . [in] the music of harmonious metrical language. (*P* 1800: 546–51)

Poetry consists of lessons learned in the careful art of "communication" and should aspire, in its metrical shape, to the "balance" of music. Technique, not time, mellows the raw emotion into art. I have called this theory of form in Wordsworth "performative" because of the analogy it suggests with the vocal arts. As his Metastasian translations suggest, Wordsworth was interested in the forbidden crossing between opera and literature, specifically in the peculiar challenge of the aria as a lyric genre.

In eighteenth-century Italian *opera seria*, the aria disrupted the natural temporality of the drama, stopping the action so that a hero or heroine might give voice to the specific strong feelings produced by the preceding scene. Arias were performed in the liminal space of the *proscenio* between stage and audience and were accompanied, gesturally, by stylized poses. The aria's design was to "transcend the banalities of plot and action" and invite the audience into "the formally closed, suprarational realm of song."[57] As such, the aria form offered Wordsworth a model for the lyric stylization of feeling. Like the Romantic lyric poem, it served as a vehicle of intense, momentary emotion, but this compressed content imposed both dramatic and technical demands. Because a singer, to be appreciated, cannot both cry and sing at once – both truly feel and make art at the same time – the performance of the aria depended on a set of highly formalized protocols that adapted the physiological demands of vocal production to the dramatic representation of feeling. Without this accommodation, the vocal-emotional outpouring would appear, in Wordsworth's terms, "pathetic beyond the bounds of pleasure" (*P* 1800: 509–10).

Between the formal demands placed on a lyric singer and those Wordsworth submits himself to as a lyric poet are differences of degree rather than kind. True virtuosity in poetry, as in opera, requires restraint, the artful "tempering" of "excitement." The poet of *Lyrical Ballads* understood as well as any vocal artist this difference between real speech and art-speech, between language and song. Wordsworth's theory of a "plainer" poetic language in the Preface should thus be understood, rhetorically, as a catachresis whereby he re-tropes matters of technique and formal choice as a mimetic necessity, as the record of romantically "vivid sensation" (*P* 1800: 4). The examples of Wordsworth's formal restraint I will now consider in specific poems of *Lyrical Ballads* are those he employs to regulate the "operatic" speakers we have already met in his translations from Metastasio, namely the lamenting women and tearful, effeminate men who are most in danger of carrying "excitement . . . beyond its proper bounds." As we shall see, Wordsworth's *poesie larmoiante* in *Lyrical Ballads* allows for no schoolgirl hysteria, but has strict rules governing its performance.

Wordsworth's figure of masculine failure, his poet *larmoiant*, arrives early on the scene in *Lyrical Ballads*. A tearful wandering youth alone in a pastoral setting, reminiscent of Metastasio's timid lover, features in Wordsworth's first contribution to the 1798 volume, "Lines left upon a Seat in a Yew-Tree." Burney jokingly called the poem "a seat for Jean-Jacques" – Wordsworth's youth displays a Rousseauean capacity to produce dynamic exhilaration from the still contemplation of scenes of nature:

>   He would gaze till it became
>   Far lovelier, and his heart could not sustain
>   The beauty still more beauteous.   (32–40)

This is Wordsworth's poet of the Preface: "a man . . . possessed of more than usual organic sensibility" (*P* 1800: 105). But something is amiss. The tearful youth is more a Narcissus figure than a true visionary. Gazing across the lake, he discovers not in nature but himself "the beauty still more beauteous." The man of feeling is a "lost man" who never graduates from precocious talent, "by genius nurs'd," to the office of poet. The youth's visions produce tears rather than poems:

>   On visionary views would fancy feed,
>   Till his eye streamed with tears. In this deep vale
>   He died, this seat his only monument.   (41–3)

In *Lyrical Ballads* tears must cease for poetic utterance to begin. The youth's feelings never discover the creative constraints of lyric speech and so pass beyond the bounds of pleasure into improper excitement: "his heart could not sustain/The beauty" (33–4). The youth knows rapture but not "the silent hour of inward thought," emotion but not tranquility. His tears, therefore, are less an expression of emotion than a symptom of speech unheard and unwritten, a visionary blockage that ultimately kills him. Wordsworth then concludes the poem with an image of himself as the alternative youthful visionary who has properly matured, who has chosen to have his visions constrained by the "monumental" labor of writing poetry:

>   True dignity abides with him alone
>   Who, in the silent hour of inward thought,
>   Can still suspect, and still revere himself,
>   In lowliness of heart.   (57–60)

"Dignity" and "lowliness" mark the character of him who, like Wordsworth, has resigned the "useless and effeminate life" of a visionary to become a professional poet. They likewise invoke Wordsworthian style, as code-words for the "manly" and "plain" in poetic language.

Both "The Brothers" and "The Childless Father" also conform to this operatic logic of *Lyrical Ballads*, whereby the capacity for speech depends on the drying up of tears, on "tranquillity" or "restraint." At the conclusion of "The Brothers," Leonard cannot even thank the Priest on account of the "Tears rushing in." They part "in silence" with Leonard's own tale still untold. Leonard later sends a letter of explanation, the language of which captures his ambiguous relation to the Priest's masculinist attitudes. It is not the *strength* of overpowering feelings on learning of his brother's death that struck him dumb, he says, but "the weakness of his heart." The affective meaning is the same but not its gender significance. Our last image of Leonard echoes our first, that is, of a weak, effeminate man, a "moping son of Idleness." Likewise Timothy, the father who six months ago lost his last child, is another man whose high emotion, represented by tears, renders him silent. The balladeer, in tranquil mood himself, must ventriloquize his thoughts:

> Perhaps to himself at that moment he said,
> "The key I must take for my Ellen is dead"
> But of this in my ears not a word did he speak,
> And he went to the chase with a tear on his cheek.   (17–20)

The balladeer's ability to project the unspoken feelings of the tearful male suggests an almost suffocatingly close identification with him, a kind of voyeuristic sympathy or sentimental spying.

The balladeer describes a more open encounter with a crying man in "The Last of the Flock." He begins by emphasizing the scandal of manly tears. Public tears in "A healthy man, a man full grown" signal an embarrassing breach of masculinity's social codes:

> In distant countries I have been,
> And yet I have not often seen
> A healthy man, a man full grown
> Weep in the public roads alone.   (1–4)

As if he expects his reader to still doubt the possibility of such a thing, the balladeer insists that "such a one, on English ground,/and in the broad high-way, I met" (6), and repeats the extraordinary fact that, for all his manly sturdiness, "His cheeks with tears were wet" (8). The stranger, a shepherd and father of ten carrying his last lamb to market, feels the shame as acutely as the masculinist code upheld by the balladeer would dictate: "He saw me, and he turned aside,/As if he wished himself to hide" (11–12). But the balladeer – whether from a sympathetic or disciplinary motive – pursues and confronts him. The shepherd, unlike Timothy and Leonard, is then granted a voice with which to tell his pathetic tale, but not before he has dried his tears and acknowledged his lapse into a shameful effeminacy:

> Then with his coat he made essay
> To wipe those briny tears away.

> I follow'd him, and said, "My friend
> What ails you? Wherefore weep you so?"
> —"Shame on me, Sir! This lusty lamb,
> He makes my tears to flow.   (13–18)

The story that follows, of starving children and a diminishing flock, is told in the simple ten-line balladic stanzas that Wordsworth preferred for his most plaintive tales, including "The Mad Mother" and "The Complaint of the Forsaken Indian Woman." Unlike the balladeer-narrator, Wordsworth's direct surrogate, who often enjoys the relative freedom of blank verse and the educated language of philosophical reflection (see "Tintern Abbey"), the feminine and effeminized voices of *Lyrical Ballads* speak its plainest idiom. The sing-song meter, simple rhyme scheme, and plain, mostly monosyllabic diction in "The Last of the Flock" restrain the shepherd's deeply sentimental "woes," an effect I have described as performative or operatic, and which Wordsworth insists upon in the Preface as necessary for the maximum emotional impact on the reader. A truly lamenting shepherd, a threnodic shepherd, would carry emotion "beyond the bounds of [aesthetic] pleasure," that is, beyond poetry itself.

Wordsworth offers a narrative allegory of his principle of formal restraint at two separate moments in "The Last of the Flock." As we have seen, the balladeer begins by rehearsing the assumptions of English masculine reserve, which the shepherd himself answers by an expression of shame and wiping away his tears. Later, the shepherd provides the psychological grounds for his current relative composure. As his flock has dwindled, so has his capacity for love and feeling:

> Alas! It was an evil time;
> God cursed me in my sore distress,
> I prayed, yet every day I thought
> I loved my children less;
> And every week, and every day,
> My flock, it seemed to melt away.   (85–90)

Formal restraint in *Lyrical Ballads* is thus not artificially imposed, or a mere effect. Wordsworth provides a psychologically credible rationale for why his characters speak in the simple balladic forms they do. We meet the shepherd not at the summit of his despair, but at a moment of relative "tranquil" reflection: he stands at a solemn, almost dazed traumatic distance from truly woeful feeling.

"The Female Vagrant" performs a similar correlation between psychological and rhetorical restraints. After losing her husband and all her children "in one remorseless year," the vagrant woman tells the balladeer that her "every tear/Dried up" (133–4). She resumes crying only when finished telling him her tale:

> She ceased, and weeping turned away,
> As if because her tale was at an end
> She wept;— because she had no more to say
> Of that perpetual weight which on her spirit lay.   (267–70)

As in the examples of Leonard, Timothy, the shepherd, and the youth of "Lines left upon a Seat in a Yew-Tree," speaking and crying do not mix in *Lyrical Ballads*. In each case, an aesthetic necessity for the poet is troped as a physical impossibility for his characters. For the vagrant woman, furthermore, speech takes on the therapeutic power of a talking cure. She weeps not because the pain of her memories has returned, but because she has temporarily ceased to relate them and thus lost the palliative power of speech. The regulatory power of language keeps emotion within proper, operable "bounds," an effect which, for Wordsworth, is intensified by a metrical, unornamented, "manly" poetic idiom, as signified by the Vagrant Woman's "*artless* story" (2). Just as the youth's tears in "Lines left upon a Seat" did not express feeling but blocked it, the vagrant woman's tears are illegible, anti-poetic. Only when her tears are "dried up" does she tell her tale. When that storytelling ends the tears and high emotion rush back, canceling speech, and the poem stops. The woman's narrative thus adheres to the protocol of "emotion recollected in tranquillity." The woman's tale is a formal double, or allegory, of the ballad by which it is framed.

"The Complaint of the Forsaken Indian Woman" presents another dry-eyed, tragic speaker. Abandoned on the forest track, she tells her absent child "do not weep and grieve for me" (43). The austere form of her speech implicitly carries with it the same injunction. Instead of exclamations and other extravagant lyric indices of weeping, the Indian woman's "complaint" consists of sing-song lines, balladic stanzas, and the barest monosyllabic diction:

> My fire is dead: it knew no pain;
> Yet is it dead, and I remain.
> All stiff with ice the ashes lie;
> And they are dead, and I will die.   (11–14)

The poet's "plainer" language here borders on pidgin. Wordsworth has taken his exotic subject seriously in accepting the dual obligations of female ventriloquism and "translation" from the Indian woman's native tongue. In fact, her idiom, both plain *and* exotic, represents an ideal Wordsworthian vehicle. More convincingly than an English speaker, male or female, the Indian woman's otherness automatically legitimates an "experimental" cross-gender register of manly feeling/feminine restraint that elsewhere in *Lyrical Ballads* must necessarily attract suspicions of effeminacy, that is, an undue identification with female experience and the "feminine" language of feeling.

In poems such as "The Female Vagrant" and "The Complaint of the Forsaken Indian Woman," Wordsworth demonstrates an interest in cross-gender voices that he never admits to, in fact stridently denies, in his Preface. In "The Pet Lamb," however, a poem near the end of the second volume of the 1800 *Lyrical Ballads,* Wordsworth retrospectively acknowledges his interest in female ventriloquism and its "operatic" registers. The relation between a male poet and his female speaker becomes a poetical question in itself, one that Wordsworth clearly could not address in the prose medium of the Preface with its binding disclosures, but was able to commit to within the more secure frame of an enigmatic, fairytale-like episode between a little girl and her pet lamb.

In "The Pet Lamb," as in so many poems from *Lyrical Ballads,* the balladeer assumes the role of lyric opportunist, recording chance encounters on the public way. From his "shady place" where he is "unobserved" (17–18), the sentimental spy finds himself fascinated by the scene of pained departure between little "Barbara Lewthwaite" and her pet lamb. He studies the "workings" of regret in the girl's face, which in turn fire the machinery of sympathetic identification and his ventriloquizing powers. The next ten stanzas are not reported speech, but the voice of the balladeer explicitly adopting the sentimental tones of the "little Maid":

> If Nature to her tongue could measur'd numbers bring
> Thus, thought I, to her Lamb that little Maid might sing   (19–20)

The vocal transposition is marked immediately by a sequence of intense questions. Barbara's first "line" itself contains three, the second no more than a truncated, one-word exclamation: "What ails thee, Young One? What? Why pull so at thy cord?" (21). The compression of syntax, and the rising interrogatory inflections are formal indices of female ventriloquism, of the girl's higher emotional register.

An operatic climax occurs at the beginning of stanza thirteen when Barbara interrupts her plaintive second-person address to the lamb to utter a self-conscious, dramatic aside: "It will not – will not rest!" (49). This desperate exclamation, in stark contrast to her reassuring speech to the lamb, transforms the balladeer's secret witness of the scene, and ours with him, into full-blown theatrical spectatorship. Again, its truncated, reiterative form – "It will not – will not rest!" – signals a dangerous crossing toward improper "excitement" and the silence beyond. But the poet pulls back from the brink. Barbara's high pitch of (ventriloquized) feeling produces instead a climactic realization of the lamb's sentimental predicament. He is one of the *Lyrical Ballads*' many dejected orphans: "poor Creature can it be/That 'tis thy Mother's heart which is working so in thee?"

The balladeer having reverted to his own voice, "The Pet Lamb" concludes with a reflection on the poetic labor of the *Ballads* themselves:

> As homeward through the lane I went with lazy feet,
> This song to myself did I oftentimes repeat,
> And it seem'd as I retrac'd the ballad line by line
> That but half of it was hers, and one half of it was mine.   (61–4)

Introduced by the pun on "lazy feet," the wandering balladeer dissolves into an image of the poet himself working over his texts "line by line," unsure even as he revises them which belong to him and which to the girl whose voice he has assumed. The confusion is deepened for the reader at line 60 by the absence of closing quotes separating Barbara's imagined voice and the speaker's own. It is a lexical slip perfectly consistent with the poet's own stated confusion:

> Again, and once again did I repeat the song,
> "Nay" said I, "more than half to the Damsel must belong,
> For she look'd with such a look, and she spake with such a tone,
> That I almost receiv'd her heart into my own.   (65–8)

Here in "The Pet Lamb," we are a long way from poetry defined as "a man speaking to men" – much closer, in fact, to a "poetry designed for the flexible throat of a soprano," as Schlegel described Metastasio. As such, the balladeer's moment of vocal misrecognition – is it my voice or Barbara's? – represents Wordsworth's female ventriloquism not as an "insidious . . . colonization" of female language, but rather as an operatic porousness of gender and voice, as the virtuosic workings of a "flexible throat" that belie the masculinist poses of Wordsworth's Preface and much of the criticism it has inspired.

v

The gendered poetic objectives of Wordsworth's Preface to *Lyrical Ballads* – to introduce a new "manly" voice to English verse through the use of "plainer and more emphatic language" – have a revealing parallel in the history of Italian opera in England. In the very year of the Preface's first publication, the century-long occupation of the King's Theatre stage in London by Italian castrato singers came to an abrupt end. Opera patron and composer Richard Mount-Edgcumbe records in his memoirs how during rehearsals for his setting of Metastasio's *Zenobia* in the 1800 season, the resident castrato and *primo uomo* of the King's Theatre, named Roselli, was found inadequate to the part.[58] The role of Tiridates was subsequently transposed and given to the tenor Viganoni. It was an event little remarked on at the time, but the dismissal of Roselli marked an epochal shift in the staging of Italian opera in England. After 1800 castrato roles were given to female sopranos and contraltos or transposed for tenors who, by 1830, had become the standard heroic male voice of the new Romantic opera.[59]

In 1800, then, both the King's Theatre opera house and Wordsworth's Preface to *Lyrical Ballads* proposed reformation of vocal register as the answer to the problem of public (and published) effeminacy. The operatic male soprano was a travesty, William Popple had argued, because he could not *feel* the emotions he expressed. In that sense the castrato was a monstrous theatrical personification of what imperiled English poetry for Wordsworth in the work of Gray and the Della Cruscans, namely the divorce of style and feeling. Just as the castrato substituted virtuosic vocal display for genuine expression, so the poets of sensibility relied on "a motley masquerade of tricks, quaintnesses, hieroglyphics, and enigmas" ("Appendix," 62–3) in place of language "really used by men" (*P* 1802: 64–5). Wordsworth's Romantic theory of poetic virtue thus shares its opposition of "ornament" and "feeling" with Georgian anti-virtuosic discourse. The bone of contention for both was effeminacy, specifically as expressed by verbal/oral extravagance. In short, the worlds of poetry and opera, historically at odds in British culture, synchronized precisely at the beginning of the nineteenth century, when both elevated poetic diction and its operatic equivalent, the male soprano voice, were summarily banished from the scene. But the analogical relation between Wordsworth's poetry and Italian opera is also a mirror image, doubled and reversed: what appears to be a problem of masculinity at the opera is at root a problem of realism (the castrato's "unnatural" voice), while what appears to be a problem of realism addressed in *Lyrical Ballads* is at root a problem of masculinity.

Translating the poetry of Metastasio in late 1802, Wordsworth submitted the effeminate music of the Italian language to the "rough . . .

thought" of English: an act of sexual-linguistic domination. These excursions into the effeminate, aristocratic world of the opera, seemingly inimical to his promotion of a new "manly," rural poetics in the Preface, in fact recall the structural anxieties of *Lyrical Ballads* precisely, where Wordsworth must translate the feminine-identified language of feeling into a masculine register. In both cases Wordsworth is tainted by the act itself, by the attraction the translation acknowledges. Reading Wordsworth through Metastasio, we are better able to trace the powerful tension between sentiment and style in the poems of *Lyrical Ballads* according to an economy of gender license and restraint. The Preface's advertisement of masculine diction confesses, in that very act, that masculinity is at issue, under threat.

Wordsworth's translations of Metastasio serve as both act and metaphor for a new understanding of *Lyrical Ballads* because their crossing between the operatic and literary, or from effeminacy to the "manly style," is never clean or complete. That is, Wordsworth's participation in the rescue of a "literary" Metastasio from opera culture and its effeminacies is as ambiguously successful as his attempt to rescue English poetry from a similar fate. As Charles Burney uncannily foresaw, the Preface attacks most vehemently those poets of sensibility whom Wordsworth, as a poet *larmoiant*, most resembles. For Wordsworth, manliness and effeminacy thus represented no more than a useful, though ultimately illusory binary. There was no choice to be made between them, only the opportunity to act out the rescuing of one from the other. Wordsworth seized this opportunity in his Preface not because "the real language of men" reflected the masculinist content of his poems, but because it did not (*P* 1800: 3–4). The Preface focusses on issues of style rather than subject because it is there that Wordsworth can magnify a rhetorical distinction between *Lyrical Ballads* and the poetry of sensibility even while their emotional content bears such striking similarities. As Burney observed, Wordsworth sounds "more plaintive than Gray himself." In short, the Preface to *Lyrical Ballads* stages a performance of masculine authority but does not enforce it in the ballads themselves.

To his future in-laws the unemployed and little-known poet Wordsworth was little better than a "Vagabond."[60] Placed in the context of the Georgian critique of effeminacy, manly style in *Lyrical Ballads* should not be thought of as truly manly, or its sentimental content as truly effeminate, except in the strategic, rhetorical sense in which Wordsworth employs these terms to "defend" himself and his poems from masculinist critique in a time of war, a time when he himself, like

Leonard in "The Brothers," was at risk of being called an effeminate do-nothing, a "moping son of Idleness." That said, the merely strategic, gender-political interpretation of Wordsworth's "manly" style risks paying too little credit to the poet. Although masculine anxiety surely played its role in producing Wordsworth's plain diction in *Lyrical Ballads*, it is also comprehensible as the product of a lucid and disinterested aesthetic choice. Drawing on his own theory of meter as a model, we see that Wordsworth employs plain language not pathologically, as a means of repressing sentimental affect, but as an aesthetic vehicle for maximizing that affect. Tears, shed by women and men alike, flow as plentifully in *Lyrical Ballads* as in any Italian opera, and according to similarly strict expressive rules. Just as the sympathetic stream bears Metastasio's timid lover's tears to his beloved, but "tells . . . not," so, in *Lyrical Ballads*, Wordsworth's characters cannot cry and speak (or "sing") at once. It is a narrative allegory of the conditions the poet has set himself for lyric composition, as "emotion recollected in tranquillity." For both Wordsworth and his many surrogate speakers, the subsiding of tears into tranquility, the restraint of "excitement" within "proper bounds," is the condition for telling one's tale of woe. That the Preface represents that melopoetic principle in masculinist terms – as a manly restraint on the excesses of feminine sensibility – had less impact on the extraordinary gender experimentation of *Lyrical Ballads* than on masculinist misreadings of Wordsworth in the two centuries since.

CHAPTER 4

Cockney Mozart

I

The week that Mozart's *Don Giovanni* made its famous, and famously belated, debut on the London stage, Leigh Hunt, editor and opera critic of the *Examiner*, found himself marooned in Buckinghamshire. From there he sent a letter to his friend Vincent Novello, the composer and music publisher, who had tickets to the opening night. We "envy you the power of seeing *Don Giovanni*," he wrote wistfully.[1] Hunt had good reason to be jealous. The April 1817 premiere of *Don Giovanni* at the King's Theatre in the Haymarket marked "a red letter in the operatic annals" of England, a production that permanently changed the nature of opera and opera-going in London.[2] The triumph of the 1817 *Don Giovanni*, and Hunt's excitement, nevertheless prompt a question. Why was Mozart's most celebrated opera, which premiered in Vienna and Prague in 1787, not produced in London for a full thirty years? The generation delay in the debut of *Don Giovanni*, at the most prestigious Italian opera house in Europe after La Scala, opens up the political history of Mozart reception in England I wish to pursue here, specifically the struggle between the Mozartians of the Hunt circle and the aristocratic, anti-Mozart "cabal" at the King's Theatre.

In a series of opera reviews he contributed to the *Examiner* in 1813, Thomas Barnes, Hunt's old schoolfellow and long-time editor of *The Times*, made a strident case for middle-class control of opera repertory at the King's Theatre based on the argument that superiority of rank in Regency society stood in inverse relation to taste and education:

The King's Theatre is almost exclusively visited by the highest rank and fashion of the nation, and yet these superb aristocrats are delighted with a style of performance which would disgust the lower orders. What is the reason of this? It is simply, that the highest orders of society, with very few exceptions, are worse educated than the inferior ranks of the middle portion of the community: that with respect to intellect and mental cultivation and everything but manners, they are semi-barbarians, the consequence of which is the utter absence of that best characteristic of a gentleman, a well-instructed taste. (May 9)

It is a measure of the confidence of the new radical bourgeois press, and the *Examiner's* undaunted class rage during Hunt's imprisonment, that an aristocrat might be described in its pages as a "semi-barbarian," or worse, as failing to meet the requisites of a gentleman. To make taste rather than rank the standard for gentlemanliness was as potentially revolutionary a proposition as universal enfranchisement. My argument in what follows is that the Hunt circle's sense of mission as taste-makers in English music culture took shape in the 1810s with their campaign for professional productions of Mozart's operas at the King's Theatre. The opera house's resistance to Mozart came to represent the stifling hegemony of aristocratic taste, inspiring a Cockney sense of injustice as keenly felt as any betrayal by the Prince Regent, bad review from the Tory press, or parliamentary waffling on reform.

The audience for the 1817 *Don Giovanni* extended far beyond the aristocratic habitués of the King's Theatre in the West End. The press recorded unprecedented crowds at the April 12 premiere:

Long before the commencement of the Overture the Pit was literally crammed, and hundreds who subsequently arrived were obliged to return disappointed, or ascend the gallery, which also was completely filled. Belles and beaux were seen indiscriminately huddled together at the sides of the Pit, endeavouring to catch a glimpse of what was passing on the Stage; and it was remarked as a somewhat rare occurrence, that not a single box in the house remained unoccupied.[3]

The box subscribers soon chose to scorn Mozart, but for a few opera-crazed months in the spring of 1817, the King's Theatre presented a spectacle of class chaos and intermingling reminiscent of Burney's *Evelina*, but increasingly rare in the Regency period. Audience demand for Mozart was so great that democratic reform was literally forced (however temporarily) upon the proprietors of the King's Theatre: "So great, indeed, has been the overflow from the Pit, that it has been found necessary to throw open such of the Upper Boxes as remain unlet, in order to accommodate in some degree those who are unable to obtain seats below."[4] In an age when operas rarely played more than a few nights in a season, *Don Giovanni* ran a record twenty-three times to "overflowing houses," and would have played more often had not the aristocratic subscribers insisted on a conventional baroque *opera seria*, Paer's *Agnese*, to break the Mozartian monopoly. "There never was exhibited to the musical world a more consummate feast," concluded *The Times*, "than *Don Giovanni*" (January 12, 1818).

For two of the *literary* figures of the Hunt circle, the 1817 *Don Giovanni* was a conversion experience. "I am in your debt for a very delightful evening," wrote Charles Lamb to the King's Theatre manager, his friend William Ayrton, "and I am almost inclined to allow Music to be one of the Liberal Arts: which before I doubted."[5] Lamb requested three more gallery tickets for the next week's performances. Meanwhile, Thomas Love Peacock persuaded Percy Shelley to accompany him to see *Don Giovanni* that same season:

> Before it commenced he asked me if the opera was comic or tragic. I said it was composite, more comedy than tragedy. After the killing of the Commendatore, he said, "Do you call this comedy?" By degrees he became absorbed in the music and action ... From this time till he finally left England he was an assiduous frequenter of the Italian Opera. He delighted in the music of Mozart.[6]

Given that Lamb was, on his own admission, unmusical – "I have no ear" – and Shelley so often an unhappy theater-goer, their absorption in Mozart's *Don Giovanni* speaks volumes for the broad, literary nature of the opera's appeal.[7] For Lamb, Mozart's opera represented music's claim to admission among the liberal arts, and the long-suffering Mozartians of the London press worked hard to produce a critical vocabulary commensurate with that new status. *Don Giovanni* "is a perfect whole," wrote the *British Stage and Literary Cabinet*, "the master-piece of the master of his art, the presiding genius of harmony, the Shakespeare of composers" (May 1817). The reviewer at the *Theatrical Inquisitor* extended the pantheon still further: "It is one of the most stupendous works of human genius, and fitted to rank with the Iliad of Homer, the Eneid of Virgil, or the Macbeth of Shakspeare" (April 1817). "Such music," wrote Richard Mackenzie Bacon, "is surely the highest intellectual enjoyment within the reach of mortals: we bowed in silent admiration before the divine genius of the German Bard!"[8] Most importantly for these critics, Mozart opera did not depend on spectacle and virtuosic singing. It did not merely "astonish" the ears and eyes of the audience, but offered a psychological truth of character through music that required from the audience an intellectual commitment more often associated with reading the great poets. Comparisons to Shakespeare and Homer aside, the more pertinent literary analogy to Mozartian opera was the emerging bourgeois novel, in which character, the dramatic ensemble, and the formally integrated work were pre-eminent. "The production of Mozart's *Don Giovanni* in 1817," Rachel Cowgill has written, "marked a decisive swing toward work-oriented values at the King's Theatre."[9] *Don Giovanni* was the first

Mozart production in London in which no arias from other operas were inserted or its text rearranged. Ayrton, the director, took charge of the publication of the opera's libretto and composed a worshipful preface according to standard literary practice. After a century of ephemeral, virtuosic *opere serie* at the King's Theatre, Mozart's operas opened a new and permanent vista of musical possibility because their genius lay not in the performance but in the score, a musical text that was reproducible on stage, at the drawing-room piano, and in the imagination.[10] For the London critics, writing mostly for Whig and radical publications, Regency music culture was to be reformed according to literary canons of taste. There was now nothing to choose between Shakespeare and Mozart. Both were "intellectual" in the broadest, transdisciplinary sense; both were "Bards."

Mozart, no less than the Elizabethan poets, served as a principal muse of the Hunt circle and as one of its liberal causes. As Hunt wrote in his April 1817 letter to Novello, "I would have Mozart as common in good libraries as Shakespeare and Spenser, and prints from Raphael." In 1820 Hunt proposed to Novello that they collaborate on a book consisting of Mozart songs and airs, with commentary provided by Hunt. Hunt opens "Musical Evenings" by imaginatively recalling the scene of many impromptu musical affairs he and Novello enjoyed with their circle at Hampstead and Oxford Road.[11] He sets out a sequence of songs and readings for his ideal musical evening with the Cockney favorite Spenser featuring prominently alongside excerpts from *Le Nozze di Figaro*, *Don Giovanni*, and *Così fan tutte*.[12] Music and poetry are once more placed conspicuously on the same footing:

In this country of books, and piano-fortes, and poets, and firesides, and fair faces . . . how many soft or manly voices are reading a favourite poet to hushing rooms:—how many fair hands are going over keys or strings, culling sweet sounds as they would flowers:—how many fathers, husbands, brothers, and lovers, are standing beside them, with flute or violin, falling in, as the song requires, with their bending and smiling accompaniments.[13]

Poetry and music serve here as the enabling language of highly formalized erotic play, but also of a radical, progressive social formation. The melopoetic evening functions as a meeting ground for the sexes in which the strict regulation of gender roles produces a general harmony. Both "soft" and "manly" voices may read poetry, but "fair hands" play the piano and harp. Hunt's 1832 poem "The Lover of Music to the Pianoforte" eroticized the piano as the instrumental locus for domestic "bliss": "No fairy casket, full of bliss/Outvalues thee:/Love only, waken'd with a kiss,/More sweet may be."[14] The early nineteenth century saw the rise in popularity of keyboard sonatas with only nominal violin accompaniment, a reversal of the situation a century earlier when the amateur male violinist dominated the domestic scene. "The establishment of a different kind of relation in the music," Stanley Sadie has argued, "may well be seen as linked with, or symbolic of, changing attitudes toward the role of women."[15] Here, the women of the Hunt circle are the designated masters of the domestic music sphere while the men of the party accompany them, a subordinate role they submit to "bending and smiling."[16]

As "Musical Evenings" attests, Mozart's operas had been a staple of Hunt circle life for a decade before the 1817 *Don Giovanni*. A Hunt poem first published in the *Examiner* in 1816, dedicated to Hazlitt, described the melopoetic atmosphere at Hampstead:

> Then take down an author, whom one of us mentions,
> And doat, for a while, on his jokes or inventions;
> Then have Mozart touch'd, on our bottle's completion.[17]   (41–3)

The letters and memoirs of the group are likewise full of vivid exchanges and reminiscences. In an 1814 letter from Surrey County Gaol to Mozart neophyte Charles Cowden Clarke, Hunt recommends a list of arias, promises to consult with friends to extend the list, and offers detailed advice on procuring scores. He also encloses two songs from *La Clemenza di Tito* with the letter.[18] Novello's daughter Mary, who married Cowden Clarke, possessed a lock of Mozart's hair, and remembered *entire days* singing his operas around the piano at Oxford Street: "Mornings and afternoons witnessed numerous 'goings through' of Mozart's *Così fan tutte, Don Giovanni, Nozze di Figaro*."[19] Since the advent of Italian opera in London, music publishers had been quick to establish a direct route from the stage of the King's Theatre to the homes of the musically literate. From there, the music of hit operas such as *Don Giovanni*, through the repetition of favorite airs in band concerts, music halls, and café and street performances, eventually percolated through every layer of society.[20] Indeed, as Thomas Christensen has argued, the prolific repackaging of opera scores for the domestic market shaped musical literacy and ideology in powerful ways, and ultimately undermined aristocratic control of polite music culture. The vast reach of piano-vocal scores throughout the kingdom brought Italian opera from its elite audience into the public sphere and, as we shall see in this chapter, "made possible the reconfiguration of opera as an object of public criticism."[21]

The Cockney Mozartians gathered around Hunt's piano read like a who's who of early nineteenth-century music culture in Britain: Thomas Alsager, opera critic for *The Times* and founder of the Beethoven Quartet

Society; Keats's Enfield classmate Edward Holmes, who was to be music critic for the *Atlas* and the author of the first serious Mozart biography; Cowden Clarke, future editor of *Musical World*; Thomas Attwood, a composer and student of Mozart; Henry Robertson, an "agreeable bass singer" and treasurer at the Covent Garden theater who became the *Examiner*'s first opera critic; and Novello himself, composer, publisher, and impresario.[22] Lamb, Shelley, and Hazlitt numbered among the audience for these casual concerts, and Mary Cowden Clarke remembers John Keats leaning against the organ, "one foot raised on his other knee" – a semi-supine position that evokes her last sight of the fatally ill poet "half-reclining on some chairs" at Hunt's house on the eve of his sailing for Italy.[23] In a letter to the Novellos, Hunt describes another tragic Italian refugee of his circle, Mary Shelley; the widow was as "quiet as a mouse" and an avid listener "ready to drink in as much Mozart and Paeisiello as you choose to afford her."[24]

For the Hunt circle communal worship of Mozart functioned as a form of group consolation, a binding, constitutive pleasure. They elevated listening to Mozart to a poetics, a shorthand for the Cockney sublime. A poem from *Foliage* (1818), which Hunt directs as "written to be set to music by Vincent Novello," describes the unique power of music to both speak to the "individual spirit" and enliven group feelings, to at once transmit the inner life and function as an essentially sociable art form:

> When lovely sounds about my ears
> Like winds in Eden's tree-tops rise,
> And make me, though my spirit hears,
> For very luxury close my eyes,
> Let none but friends be round about
> Who love the soothing joy like me,
> That so the charm be felt throughout,
> And all be harmony.[25]   (1–8)

Jeffrey Robinson has identified the sing-song tetrameter as a prosodic signature of the Cockney poets, long disdained by the anthologizers of literary history. Here the light, disarming couplets challenge the reader to shake off her melancholy and embrace the seriousness of pleasure, a "luxury" of the senses – in music and poetry – that produces neither excess nor degradation but "harmony," personal and social.[26] In short, the Cockney love of Mozart represents rich historical evidence for what is now recognized – following Robinson, Cox, and a growing body of revisionist criticism – as the Regency counter-tradition of "Romantic sociability." The Cockney Mozartians offer a link between the Waterloo generation and anterior modes of melopoetic communality, such as Anna Seward's

Lichfield circle (see chapter 1), that conventional literary history has submerged beneath the high Romantic canon. The common thread linking Lichfield in the 1780s and Hampstead in the 1810s is the integral role of music to the literary community, as a model of the sociable production and consumption of art, but also of a new politics. For both Seward and Hunt, their ideological differences notwithstanding, "sociability was a first step in healing the fissures of the commonwealth," and music the unifying, sociable art to which literary production should aspire.[27]

In his 1815 poem "A Thought on Music," Hunt describes the act of listening to music in almost religious terms:

> To sit with downward listening, and crossed knee,
> Half conscious, half unconscious, of the throng
> Of fellow ears, and hear the well-met skill
> Of fine musicians—the glib ivory
> Twinkling with numerous prevalence,—the snatch
> Of brief and birdy flute, that leaps apart—

Hunt mixes impressionism and word play ("birdy flute") with philosophy. He hails the restorative power of music to make

> … the sickliest thought, that keeps its home
> In a sad heart, give gentle way for once,
> And quitting its pain-anchored hold, put forth
> On that sweet sea of many-billowed sound.[28]

What Robinson calls Hunt's "counter-poetics of the Fancy" are here on dazzling display.[29] The Cockney style is, above all, a poetics of variety, of mixed tones and mercurial tenors. The simplicity of "sad heart" and "gentle way" gives way to the solemn and wholly poetic surprise of "pain-anchored hold." All simplicity and solemnity are then instantly forgotten in the fanciful invocation of the "sweet sea" and its "many-billowed sound."

In keeping with the *politics* of Cockney Fancy, Hunt's evocation of the listening act and its powers speaks to a specific historical moment. The "downward listening" of the opening line suggests both a concentrated, head-bent pose and the mental act of concentration itself: the "Half conscious, half unconscious" state produces for the listener in a Hampstead drawing-room a pastoral vision of himself "floating and floating in a dreamy lapse,/Like a half-sleeper in a summer boat." This is not the dreamy suburban escapism vilified by the Tory critics. Hunt's "sad heart" is consoled neither by fantasy nor the merely sensuous experience of the music – by "the notes alone, or new-found air,/Or structure of elaborate harmonies" – but by its sublimity: the power of music to produce "Out of the very vagueness of the joy/A shaping and a sense of things beyond us,/Great things and voices great." The "great things and voices great" are not specified, but they are not merely musical. At the opening of Hunt's 1815 masque, *The Descent of Liberty*, Liberty's divine medium is a sound of "strange delightfulness, and something/Of a new freshness in the air about us," a new music that "bode[s] good" to the suburban shepherds (1. 76–8).[30] Music for Hunt, like the poetry he featured in his radical journal, cast shadows of futurity on the political present, impressing the "sad heart" of post-war disillusion with an image of "great things" to come, "a shaping and a sense" of change, an operatic allegory of Reform.

What most infuriated the Tory reviewers about the Hampstead writers was that they represented "Reform" not simply as a political goal but as a lifestyle. For the Cockneys, the liberal "love of sociality" might be lived before it was ever legislated.[31] Choosing to sing Mozart all day with friends, like composing sonnets for each other, was a political form of leisure, an act of class self-identification. Mary Shelley, writing to Hunt, fantasized a kind of renovated Hampstead at Susa. She imagined the drowned Percy again with them, and Mozart as their natural accompaniment: "we will do all our work keeping time to Hunt's symphonies ... and when we are tired we will lie on our turf sofas, while all our voices shall join in chorus in *Notte e giorno faticar*."[32] Mary Shelley's "turf sofa" is a quintessentially Cockney image of suburban recreation, a witty conjugation of pastoral indolence and bourgeois luxury with erotic overtones. The image belongs both to the internal vocabulary of the Hunt circle – a shared set of memories and inside jokes – and to its public voice: the published verse that *Blackwood's* described as "easy, courtly, and Italian" at its best and, at its worst, as a lexicon of "glittering and rancid obscenities." The vision of Hunt and his friends lying exhausted together on the grass singing Mozart is both operatic and orgiastic, the kind of joking, loosely sexualized Cockney self-image that Lockhart meanly interpreted as "the extreme moral depravity of the Cockney School."[33]

The Cockneys' "depravity" was synonymous with their love for Italy, and Mozart's operas perfectly represented that love.[34] Composed in Italian by an Austrian, the operas stood not for Italy itself but the outsider's perfected desire for Italy, his longed-for "Italianization." In Hunt's King's Theatre reviews for the *Examiner* (1817–21), Mozart represents the ideal modern synthesis of the Italian and German musical traditions, with the Italian in the ascendant: he is "German by nation, and Italian by nature" (March 22, 1818). His fanciful biographical explanation for this unique synthesis – "Mozart was in Italy while a boy, and at that early period perhaps caught the fine spark from the southern sunshine" – described exactly what Hunt wished for himself, and so reached deep into the Cockney psyche (March 23, 1817). After seeing *Don Giovanni*, Hunt elides the northern origins of Mozart entirely, calling him "the genial intellect of the South," as if, with that extraordinary proof of southern sensibility, Mozart's Italian metamorphosis were complete (July 27, 1817).

In 1823, while Hunt himself was living in Italy, his friends, including Mary Shelley and Jane Williams, Holmes, Clarke, and Robertson, gathered at the Novellos' to celebrate his birthday *in absentia*. In a letter Mary Novello wrote with guests still lingering at the door, she flatters Hunt with her account of how his name "ran through the room like a charm," and the effervescent Cockney style of "badinage, raillery, and compliments . . . broke loose." But "above all," she records, "music was triumphant," with Mozart motets and arias creating an "atmosphere of pleasure." From London then, in the damp of October, Mary Novello describes a self-consciously *Italian* scene of sentimental tribute and pleasure-driven commingling, with Mozart as presiding genius: "Your health was drunk *con amore* . . . and particularly during the singing of *Ah, Perdona*, many tears were shed by friendly eyes."[35] Mozart's achievement in opera for the Hunt circle was not merely to create a rich fund of domestic entertainment, but to have performed an exemplary cross-over from northern reaction to the liberal south. The struggle to stage Mozart's operas at the King's Theatre thus belongs to what Marilyn Butler has described as the larger "battle in defence of the classical and Mediterranean South stoutly fought for a decade from 1812 by a generation of liberal English writers who believed they were fighting for their political principles."[36] Frustrated by their cultural marginality in England and energized by Italian yearnings, the cosmopolitan souls of the Hunt circle found an ideal image of themselves in Mozart, the bourgeois striver from Salzburg who transcended class and national origins to become Italian through his art.

II

Mozart's Italian librettist, Lorenzo Da Ponte, came to London in 1791 only to discover that there was little appetite at the King's Theatre for Mozart. In his memoirs Da Ponte bitterly recalled the short shrift he received:

> it was more than three months before I saw Taylor [the manager] or he me. That was at the performance of Gazzaniga's *Don Giovanni*, an opera suggested by Federici and given to the public on his advice, in bestial preference to the *Don Giovanni* of Mozart, brought to London and proposed by me.[37]

William Taylor, like a succession of King's Theatre managers after him, followed the *galant* tastes of their imported house composers (Vincenzo Federici, in this case) and, more crucially, their Italian star singers, who rejected Mozart's music and united with their aristocratic patrons against him to form what came to be known in English operatic history as "the Italian cabal."[38]

Novello raised the subject of the Italian cabal with Mozart's widow and son on his "Mozart pilgrimage" through Europe. Vienna in 1829, he learned, was no different from London before 1817: "while the Italian singers are there, there is no chance of hearing Mozart's operas, when they leave they are performed." Constanze Mozart blamed the Italian prejudice against Mozart squarely on the singers' poor musicianship. Most Italian singers could not read music, she told the Novellos, and the intricacies of a Mozart score, with its difficult ensemble sections in particular, were beyond what "their indolence and ignorance can manage." Mozart's son singled out the incompetence of the famous soprano Angelica Catalani, expressing "contempt" for her career built on the learning of "a few songs by memory."[39] The Mozarts' mention of Catalani would have resonated strongly with the Novellos. Sheridan's hiring of Catalani at Covent Garden at an exorbitant rate had helped trigger the Old Price riots of 1809. The *Examiner* vigorously supported the protestors, and its sustained editorial campaign against Catalani began with the "OP" affair. The soprano's excesses, both musical and financial, during her tenure as *prima donna assoluta* at the King's Theatre in the 1810s provided a lightning rod for Henry Robertson's attacks on the aristocratic management of the opera house. With Catalani's controversial London career, we find the simmering conflict over control of the Italian opera in London, and the frustration of the Mozartians, brought to a head.

"Harry, my friend, who full of tasteful glee,/Have music all about you, heart and lips." The intimate apostrophe that begins Hunt's 1818 sonnet to his trio of fellow Cockney Mozartians – Henry Robertson, John Gattie, and Vincent Novello – announces it as a Hampstead coterie poem, while "tasteful glee" and "music all about you, heart and lips" offers a rhetorical-erotic exuberance characteristic of sociable Cockney verse. Robertson was an indispensable member of the Hunt and Novello circles, valued for "his tenor, his joke, and his breathing nod of acquiescence."[40] The Cowden Clarkes remembered him as the essence of Cockney musico-sociability, as "one of the very best amateur singers conceivable . . . always in tune, invariably in good temper."[41] As opera critic at the *Examiner*, Robertson took up his pen at the height of Catalani's fame, and in some forty reviews in the seasons of 1808–13 produced a damning critique of virtuoso diva culture and its abuses at the King's Theatre. Robertson's opera reviews were faithful to the character of the *Examiner* in general: skeptical, sarcastic, and set in opposition to an established, conservative order patronized by the social elite. Before the *Examiner*, opera reviewing amounted to little more than puffs in the dailies and lists of the fashionable in attendance. None of the serious political periodicals paid any attention to opera whatever. As Hunt attested in his preface to the 1808 *Examiner*, Robertson's King's Theatre reviews thus constituted "the first criticism of the kind worthy the attention of sound readers." Moreover, Robertson's reviews stand as the first serious criticism of Italian opera made in operatic terms, that is, a form of critique that did not seek simply to abolish opera altogether, as eighteenth-century critics from Dennis onward had done, but to reform its culture from within according to an alternative, literary, Mozartian set of operatic standards.

The core of diva culture at the King's Theatre lay in the traditions of eighteenth-century operatic form. The baroque *pasticcio*, which accounted for the overwhelming majority of productions, was essentially a star vehicle for virtuoso singing in which the drama, and even the orchestra, played a distinctly subordinate role. As George Hogarth remembered, Catalani "appeared chiefly in operas composed expressly for her, in which the part for the *prima donna* was carefully adapted to the display of her various powers … [that] enabled her to exhibit all the wonders of her voice and execution."[42] Few of the operas performed at the King's Theatre before 1817 exist in original score, and of the 250 opera productions at the King's Theatre between 1760 and 1800, only some forty were new works by the house composer.[43] The concept of an operatic repertoire itself had not yet been established, nor had the Romantic notion of an integrated and inviolable artistic "work."[44] As the Italian *galant* style stipulated, melodies and their orchestral accompaniments were spare and simple, affording maximum opportunity for the singer's improvised embellishments and bravura variations. A new production was most often stitched together by the house composer from various, often dramatically incongruous sources, then discarded or altered beyond recognition for its next performance. Favorite arias from the *prima donna*'s repertoire (called *arie di baule*, or "suitcase" arias) were interwoven with hastily sketched recitative and the occasional aria for subordinate singers. Two acts of an opera might be switched at the diva's whim, or the action halted for the inclusion of the latest popular air.

For an Italian *prima donna* such as Catalani, Mozart's music threatened to subordinate the freedom of the singer guaranteed by the *galant* pastiche tradition to a Germanic orchestral regime and the strict prescription of the musical text: "Mozart, in his scores, frequently treats his singers as instruments, as if they formed part of the orchestra; hence they have often to contend either against passages and intervals of great difficulty, or against the overpowering effect of the wind instruments."[45] The vocal line was *primus inter pares*, but the singer could not simply overwhelm the orchestra, especially when singing in ensemble, nor alter the tempo to allow for improvised cadenzas. Catalani accordingly "detested Mozart's music ... which keeps the singer too much under the control of the orchestra, and too strictly confined to time, which she is apt to violate."[46]

Robertson's criticism of Catalani centered on her virtuosic technique: "Madame Catalani becomes more and more a singer of mere trick," he wrote in the *Examiner* in 1808, in what was probably the first published criticism of the untouchable diva: "There is nothing pleasing in the retention of a note till she is as breathless as the exhausted receiver of an air pump, nor in the chromatic runs which are introduced on every occasion of joy or sorrow" (May 1). Robertson acknowledged Catalani's "fascinating talents," but insisted on a distinction between opera as an exhibition of machine-like vocal ability – "air pump" – and its larger dramatic and musical possibilities as an art form. The "[b]ravura-style of singing" is of an "inferior class," he argued, because it depends on relentless self-display. Virtuosity, unlike Romantic notions of character, cannot exist in the hidden form of credit, but must be lavishly spent. The diva is obliged to produce all her "tricks" at every opportunity regardless of the dictates of character or dramatic mood. A breathtaking chromatic run by Catalani does not "mean" joy or sorrow, it means only Catalani: "The Mischief of exuberant ornament is, that it levels all music to one character, and produces a fatiguing monotony ... it is to exhibit the whole extent of their talent on every occasion, without accommodating their style to the nature of the composition" (June 5, 1814). Catalani's sacrifice of dramatic truth to technical display meant that Robertson routinely complained of her indifferent acting, in particular her tendency "even in the most critical situations, to preserve a countenance of philosophical serenity or grinning mirth" (May 13, 1810).

Ornament was more than mischievous in the singing of Mozart: it amounted to artistic sacrilege. When Catalani chose to insert an aria from *Die Zauberflöte* into a production of Fioravanti's *Giocondina* in the 1808 season, Robertson put aside his usual contempt for the conventions of the pastiche form to praise the diva for her "taste," but criticized her for indulging in her usual bravura improvisations on the theme: "the variations were in themselves unpleasing and injudiciously introduced. The air is beautiful for its simplicity, and as indifferently adapted to flourishes as the hundredth Psalm" (June 12). By her relentless indulgence in ornament, Catalani was, according to Robertson, guilty not merely of lapses of taste in her own solos and failing to properly represent her character, but of structurally undermining the entire production through the relentless demands of vocal pre-eminence. In one of his first reviews, he complained that Catalani

was resolved to prevent the other performers from being heard, and exerted her Stentorian voice with all the force of which it is capable. This is unmerciful: it is like a strong man shewing his power by knocking his friends down. The principal art in singing in parts is the accommodation of the strong voices to the weak that the whole may be heard distinctly. (March 6, 1808)

Robertson here casts his musical criticism in political terms, as an abuse of power. The spectacular presence of the diva was maintained only through a kind of theatrical tyranny, by the suppression and belittlement of other performers.

Catalani's reign at the King's Theatre set an unsurpassed standard for diva excess. When the King's Theatre manager objected that her salary demands would leave no funds for him to pay the rest of the company, Catalani's husband reportedly replied, "You want an opera? My wife and four or five puppets – that will do." Within a few years, the singer's salary had leaped to £17,000, which did not include the money she earned from giving private concerts for her aristocratic patrons.[47] In Regency diva culture, the languages of profit-taking and virtuoso music-making overlapped. Robertson deplored the various conspiracies worked up by Catalani and the manager to designate frequent "benefit nights" for the diva, for no purpose but to fill the house and coffers: "No one appears to understand the art of money getting better than Madame Catalani, whose invention is continually on the rack for some expedient to increase her already exorbitant profits" (July 3, 1808). Catalani's avarice is as "exorbitant" as her singing, and as dependent upon "invention." Robertson makes the metaphorical connection himself when he describes her virtuosic style as requiring "many notes but very little specie" (February 18, 1810). Catalani's voice represents a kind of speculative currency of music; it sounds like money. The mob at Covent Garden in 1809, at the outset of the extraordinary two-month struggle over ticket prices, intuited the intrinsic connection between Catalani and currency, specifically their own: "'Off! Off! Old prices!' were the cries;/'No Catalani' and 'No rise!'"[48] The diva's virtuosity took on the character of her salary: an endless, extravagant production of notes. She transcended the musical score according to the same principle she exceeded all rational monetary value, that is, as a "star" who paradoxically never turned a profit for her employers. We saw in chapter 3 the synonymity of virtuosity and luxury in eighteenth-century moral discourse – how the Italian vocal style stood for the corrupting influence of wealth and conspicuous consumption. Catalani is the last imported Italian star to the London stage to embody that precise conjunction so offensively. The profusion of ornament and virtuosic embellishment in a Catalani performance, her "fantastical excess," was a kind of runaway expense account of art: "Her powers are nearly confined to a wonderful voice and rapid execution which, unrestrained by musical knowledge, have run wild and indulged in every extravagance that false taste could adapt" (May 19, 1811).[49]

Three years into Robertson's tenure at the *Examiner*, the first cracks in the diva-driven operatic establishment began to appear. Both *Così fan Tutte* and *Die Zauberflöte* (produced in Italian as *Il Flauto Magico*) premiered on the King's Theatre stage in 1811. Robertson deplored the dramatic "absurdity" of *The Magic Flute* that marred its "wonderful music," but with *Così fan Tutte* he could express unfettered joy over the apparent defeat of the "Italian cabal" at the hands of the Mozartians:

The lovers of good music have at last been relieved from the dull repetition of the productions of Pucitta, Trento, Guglielmi, and others, who have so long strove, with too much success, to suppress those operas of sterling merit, which would have exposed the poverty of their invention, and consigned them to merited oblivion. (June 16)

It is tantalizing to imagine Robertson and his fellow Cockney Mozartians at a full-fledged production of an opera they had so often rehearsed together at the piano in their homes. Robertson's euphoria at *Così fan Tutte* is obvious, and he seizes on this rare opportunity to expand on the sublimities of Mozart:

To convey by words an idea of the electrical effect this music produces is impracticable, and to recommend any particular compositions to those unacquainted with the opera would be useless, where the whole is one collected mass of excellence. It is only by hearing such music that an adequate conception can be formed of the exquisite beauty and variety of the airs, the uncommon richness of the harmony, or the genius displayed in the accompaniments, which sport through all the mazes of science; at one time flowing with a calm solemnity, and at another bursting forth in modulation as unexpected as inspiring. (May 19)

Robertson lists the Mozartian virtues: melodic originality, richness of orchestral accompaniment, consistency of musical standard, and emotional depth and variety. Mozart commands a broad vocabulary of feeling through music, from "calm solemnity," to the "bursting forth" of inspiration. Thomas Alsager later wrote in reference to *Don Giovanni* that Mozart's genius was to have created through opera a new dramatic language of feeling, "a more perfect eloquence, a medium for sentiment, and passion of the most exalted kind: he seems always to take the tone suited to the occasion, and to transfer the emotion to the mind of the hearer."[50] It is this Romantic aspect of Mozart's music that Mary Shelley later evoked in *The Last Man* (1826) for a scene of erotic tension between Perdita and Raymond:

> Among the other transcendent attributes of Mozart's music, it possesses more than any other that of appearing to come from the heart; you enter into the passions expressed by him, and are transported with grief, joy, anger, or confusion, as he, our soul's master, chooses to inspire.[51]

Mozart speaks to Perdita, and to the Cockney sensibility more broadly, like a great poet. He inhabits that exclusive realm where aesthetic language dissolves into contradiction: he is both "transcendent" and master of the "passions," an artist of the intellect and heart, sublime and sensual. That said, the 1811 season proved to be a false dawn for the Cockney Mozartians. *Così fan Tutte* was repeated only twice that season and did not reappear at the King's Theatre for a full five years. The resistance of the Italian singers and their aristocratic patrons to the production of Mozart was not yet broken.

Objective judgment of the "Catalani seasons" at the King's Theatre is difficult because her supporters, by virtue of their class, were little inclined to the writing of memoirs, let alone periodical criticism. It is important, therefore, not to overstate the influence of the *Examiner*'s criticism of the King's Theatre, at least in the immediate term. Catalani's extraordinary success is the best evidence we have that Robertson's views were not mainstream in these years but, like the *Examiner* in general, oppositional. A letter published in the *Examiner*, seemingly written by a member of the "Italian cabal," mocks Robertson for the "refined taste" that moves him to "vent his spleen" and "censure indiscriminately" everything he sees at the King's Theatre. The writer assures the editor Hunt

> that the whole town is not of his opinion ... for the Opera still continues to be frequented – the King's Theatre still boasts a fashionable and crowded audience ... and the Catalani, who gives voice to the music your writer is pleased to reprobate, still receives the applauses of the cognoscenti of the day.

He suggests class resentment as the reason for Robertson's attacks: they "must either be the effect of ignorance, of envy, or of prejudice" (July 1, 1810).

The opera subscriber Allatson Burgh went beyond the mere suggestion of class conflict at the opera. He called "barbarous and unfashionable" those amateurs who dared to criticize Catalani for her alterations to Mozart's music.[52] Such strong language suggests that Robertson did represent an irritating constituency of reformist opinion among opera-goers, and that the ongoing controversy in which he and the *Examiner* played a leading role was divided along class lines: on one side the traditional "fashionable" audience, made up principally of seasonal residents from the aristocratic West End for whom the opera house had been a premier forum for social mingling and display for a century past, and on the other a growing audience of "barbarous and unfashionable" city professionals with a more or less serious interest in the musical and dramatic content of opera. These two groups even divided the schedule between them: Saturday night was dominated by the *bon ton* in their boxes, while on Tuesday the amateurs appeared in force in the pit and gallery. Robertson's reviews represent a first public bid for power by these musical *arrivistes*, the rising professional middle class of London whose tastes were as neglected at the King's Theatre as their political aspirations were in Parliament and at court.

Opera performances at the King's Theatre before the advent of Mozart should properly be considered an extension of Georgian court culture. The theater itself was by far the largest in London with a capacity of over three thousand. The auditorium, lavishly rebuilt after a fire in 1792, was dominated on its second and third tiers by a catacomb of luxury boxes divided into three sections – the Prince's Side, the King's Side, and the Crown Gallery – that mirrored the triangulated political divisions of Regency England with its divided court and unstable ministry (Figure 5). The theater likewise maintained the visible character of St. James's Palace or Carlton House. Patrons were required to wear court dress: knee breeches and *chapeaux bras* for the men, full evening dress for the ladies. In the pit sat a mix of "amateurs" and "professors," but its most important constituency remained standing in the aisles – so-called Fop's Alley – from where, like courtiers, young men of fashion could offer ocular tribute to the female quality in the boxes above them.

Angelica Catalani served as a kind of vice-regent to this *ersatz* court, and the impression of her vocal power and authority was articulated in

Figure 5. Biagio Rebecca, *The Opera House: The Auditorium* (c. 1792). The Royal Collection © HM Queen Elizabeth II.

monarchical terms. She was an "arbitrary empress," an "image of resistless power," who "reign[ed] triumphant" from her King's Theatre "throne."⁵³ When Hogarth described Catalani "in the meridian of her course, and the full effulgence of her splendour," he employed a cosmic hyperbole historically reserved for feudal kings.⁵⁴ At a time of great liberal agitation, the Regency nobility patronized the Italian opera to participate in a group reaffirmation of the rituals of servile wonder on which their own power rested, with themselves in the role of subject courtiers paying homage to their "empress."⁵⁵ Catalani returned the compliment. Her 1826 contract with the King's Theatre was designed to secure her total authority and insulate her from any conceivable challenge to it: "Madame Catalani shall choose and direct the operas in which she is to sing; she shall likewise have the choice of performers in them; she will have no orders to receive from anyone . . ."⁵⁶

But like British royalty in the Regency period, Catalani had her liberal detractors. "Like the Athenian demagogue," proclaimed the Whiggish *Theatrical Inquisitor*, Catalani "must corrupt wherever she is caressed" (August 1817). Robertson and other critics of the opera house saw its diva, and the aristocratic management that "caressed" her, as part of the greater social and political corruption affecting the country. "The English . . . pay singers like princes," Ayrton later wrote, "while they are content to let their labouring classes subsist upon charity."⁵⁷ Catalani's "royal" status at the King's Theatre was thus more than simply metaphoric. There was a direct, visible link between her and the larger social injustices produced by the aristocratic order that sustained her. The first English critic of Italian opera had made the same liberal judgment a century earlier. "Wherever operas have been a constant Entertainment," wrote John Dennis in 1706, "they have been attended with Slavery."⁵⁸

In other words, Catalani's status as *prima donna assoluta* functioned quite literally. Her "absolute" power expressed itself in her dominance over the management of the theatre, while her rights to those powers were ritualized on the stage itself, where her bravura performance symbolized a kind of Napoleonic self-crowning. The critic John Sterland remembered Catalani's virtuosity as a kind of "spell" cast upon her audience:

Hours after hearing her—in the calmness of the closet—you might tremblingly question the purity of her taste, or even the correctness of her intonation; but while present to your eye and ear, she carried you by storm, even against your better judgment.

The psychological effect of Catalani's vocal exhibition is violent, almost a rape of reason. The listener is "enchained" by sound, "carried . . . by storm." Later, "in the calmness of the closet," the diva's merits and faults assume proportional shape, but in the moment of performance itself Catalani's "energy" disables the workings of critique. It is the operatic enactment of feudal majesty, whose legitimacy resides not in reason and principle but in the awe-inspiring exhibition of power itself.

No accident then that in her debut performance, as the heroine of Portogallo's *Semiramide*, Catalani chose the moment when Semiramis declares "I am a queen," to first reveal the full extent of her vocal prowess and thus establish, both symbolically and substantially, her dominion over the London opera-going public: "She dropped at once the double octave ... and finally astonished all ears, by running, for the first time within the memory of opera-going man, the chromatic scale up and down."[59] Catalani's virtuosic announcement, "I am a queen," was no ordinary speech act: its truth was not conferred by some pre-existing claim or endowment, but by the brilliancy of the utterance itself. In diva culture superfluity is substance, a paradox through which we observe the afterlife of feudal sensibility in the modern culture of spectacle and its cult of "talent." The diva's power resides not in birthright but the intangible form of virtuosity, a commodity whose value can only be recognized in moments of "fantastical excess."

Tyrannical arrogance of power; resistance to reform; dizzying spectacle; nepotism and greed; excess, waste, bad taste, and luxuriance. Such is the language of the *Examiner's* campaign against Angelica Catalani and the Italian opera house. But it might just as easily describe the *Examiner's* contemporaneous attack on the Prince Regent for his betrayal of the Whigs and the cause of liberal reform. Hunt's bitter satire on the Prince Regent on May 15, 1812, "The Regent's First Levee," describes the court rituals of the Regency as a kind of bad Italian opera. We see the Prince emerge from his boudoir like a diva onto a stage, a dazzling "Brother of the Sun." Robertson's resistance to the charismatic power of Catalani enabled him to expose her "tyranny" of bad taste at the King's Theatre. Similarly, Hunt is impervious to the image of feudal majesty at the levee and turns the spectacle of the Regent's face into a sarcastic advertisement for the necessity for Reform:

> it is easy to conceive the delicious sensations with which he advanced into the levee-room, and how delightful he must have appeared in all other eyes as well as his own. What promise of brilliant days and sunshine must have been in that look! What amends for all our past darkness and deprivations!... The clouds of war and of sorrow roll away from before him; peace and prosperity look forth from his happy face; a prospect, all radiance and renovation, bursts open upon the eyes of the people and turns their despondency into rapture!

Hunt ironically adopts the style of courtly flattery, but it might also be read as the tired hyperbole of a theatrical puff, a form of promotional doublespeak in which a disastrous performance is represented to the public afterwards as a triumph, simply because the interests of management are served in saying so. Robertson had criticized the King's Theatre for just this "impertinent mode of opposing the public opinion" (May 21, 1809).

In "The Regent's First Levee," Hunt figures "Reform" as one of the Prince's "early friends" who now stands unacknowledged in the corner, "in a desperate condition for want of assistance." According to the liberal logic of the *Examiner*, the embattled cause of reform was analogous to that of Mozart, whose music had likewise suffered from the criminal neglect of an all-powerful Regent surrounded by sycophantic courtiers. Like the forgotten figure of "Reform" at the levee, the shadow of Mozart's unheard music at the King's Theatre represents a denial of progressive bourgeois rights and a rallying point for class identification. The *Examiner*'s campaign for reform of the Italian opera house thus harmonized closely with its larger reformist goals. Diva culture at the King's Theatre, and its anti-Mozartian "cabal," stood in symbolic parallel to the reactionary administration of post-war Britain.

Mozart's operas did not merely symbolize change for Hunt and the *Examiner*. Their aesthetic content suggested the longed-for democratic order itself. On the most basic level of plot, both *Don Giovanni* and *Le Nozze di Figaro* delivered a decisive come-uppance to licentious noblemen (Thomas Holcroft's production of the latter Beaumarchais play at Covent Garden, as *The Follies of the Day*, was alluded to at his treason trial in 1794). At a more profound musical level, however, to listen to these operas was to experience transformative human possibility itself, "A shaping and a sense of things beyond us,/Great things and voices great." First, Mozart's scores carried the textual authority of a constitution or bill of rights, never to be altered or amended according to the whim of an individual singer or manager. Second, Mozart's emphasis on "concerted music" shifted the focus from the vocal powers of a tyrannical diva to the broader ensemble, where the "strong" voices might accommodate the "weak." Mozart's operas proved to Alsager that

> the distinctions of *prima donna* and *primo uomo* should absolutely merge in the general excellence of the whole *corps*. With the sublime composer of *Don Giovanni* ... whether we choose to bestow on the orchestra, or the singers, our exclusive attention, we may imbibe a distinct perception of beauty.[60]

This is the Cockney democratic ideal itself, where "distinctions" of rank merge into a "general excellence," and no class of society has a privileged claim on "beauty."

This deep metaphorical connection between Mozart and political reform is not a product of hindsight cleverness, but was explicitly articulated at the time. The aristocratic patrons of the King's Theatre did not welcome the reformation of their opera house, and in 1824 Mount-Edgcumbe lamented the new fashion for Mozart and Rossini – what he called "modern opera" – where "each individual singer has little room for displaying either a fine voice or good singing." From the viewpoint of a newly disenfranchised elite, the new repertoire carried with it a familiar political threat: "In these levelling days, equalization has extended itself to the stage and musical profession; and a kind of mediocrity of talent prevails."[61] Mount-Edgcumbe's opera memoirs went through multiple editions, but the opinions of the old order at the King's Theatre were drowned out by the chorus of liberal music criticism, modeled on the *Examiner*'s progressive agenda, that flourished in the 1820s and saw in the respected amateur composer and connoisseur Mount-Edgcumbe only "one of that class of dilettanti who took near twenty years to consider whether Mozart was worthy of a hearing."[62] The pre-eminent music journal of that decade, *Harmonicon*, marked Catalani's return to the London stage after a decade's absence with reflections on the "great change" in operatic taste, whereby "the public are no longer satisfied with one, or at the most, two good singers … The whole must be nearly equal, and *mourceaux d'ensemble*, well performed, are absolutely essential."[63] In the eyes of the emerging liberal commentariat of Regency London, of which the Hunt circle is a prime exemplar, delays in the production of Mozart had come to resemble delays in social reform itself. Their ultimate triumph in the long-awaited debut of *Don Giovanni* in 1817 – a year in which the clamor for parliamentary reform reached unprecedented heights – produced all the exhilaration and *éclat* of a dynastic overthrow.

III

Much like Henry Robertson, two other members of the Hunt circle central to the 1817 *Don Giovanni* production at the King's Theatre, Thomas Alsager and William Ayrton, have been entirely forgotten by literary historians.[64] Alsager was an intimate member of the group, remembered in Hunt's *Autobiography* as "the kindest of neighbours, a man of business, who contrived to be a scholar and a musician."[65] Ayrton, meanwhile, stands in a more tangential relation to the Hampstead circle, as a member of Hunt's broad, liberal London acquaintance. In an *Examiner* piece written from Italy, Hunt remembered him as an intimate of Charles Lamb at his whist evenings on Russell Street: "the most well-bred of musicians, who hates a paradox like an unresolved discord" (April 4, 1824).[66]

Ayrton was the son of an assistant director of the 1784 Handel Commemoration. His operatic credentials lay with his King's Theatre reviews for the liberal *Morning Chronicle*, in which he struck a common chord with Robertson at the *Examiner* in both his championing of Mozart and his sarcastic treatment of the diva Catalani. In his review of the 1813 premiere of *Le Nozze di Figaro*, Ayrton wrote that Catalani "so amply supplied with embellishments Mozart's music, that it had, at least, the merit of being quite novel to those who are intimately acquainted with his works … let the public be the judge between her skill as a *composer*, and that of Mozart" (March 11). Also in keeping with the reformist rhetoric of the *Examiner*, Ayrton viewed the management of the opera house as an anti-Mozart conspiracy, a tyranny of taste:

Managers and performers now govern the public; they are suffered to control the taste and judgment of every audience, and they will finally destroy both if some powerful hand is not raised to protect them. This protection may be afforded by the press, and we call on our brother journalists to aid in our efforts for this purpose. Our desire is not to injure individuals, but to support the Arts … (26 March)

Simply to describe the Italian opera as an "Art" belonging to "the public" amounted to a declaration of war against the "Italian cabal," and we can only speculate on Ayrton's surprise that history would so soon choose him as the "powerful hand" to be raised against it.

By the end of the 1816 season the financial demands of Catalani and the other *primi donne* and *uomi* had virtually bankrupted the King's Theatre. Despite the price of a box rising almost 100 per cent during the Catalani seasons, from 180 to 300 guineas, no manager had been able to turn a profit. In 1817 the management committee of aristocratic patrons turned in desperation to Ayrton, a man with an impressive record as first manager of the Philharmonic Society concert season begun in 1813 (see chapter 5). Ayrton was a sensible choice in terms of management experience but risky as regards operatic taste, and the noble committee members soon came to repent it. On the news of Ayrton's taking up the management of the King's Theatre in 1817, Hunt, who had now assumed the responsibility for opera reviews at the *Examiner*, welcomed the prospect of "better things from the known taste and talents of the gentleman who is understood to have undertaken the management of the principal departments" (January 19).

Ayrton had his heart set on bringing out *Don Giovanni*. He traveled immediately to Paris in order to recruit Giuseppe Ambrogetti, the most famous "Don Giovanni" in Europe, and a corps of singers of sufficient depth to properly surround him. As the Sheriff's Court later heard, after Ayrton had sued the opera house owner for his expenses, "Every pains were taken by Mr. Ayrton to form a complete *corps dramatique*, in which one particular person should not stand before the rest, but where every part should be equally eminent."[67] In doing so Ayrton struck his first blow against the diva culture of the King's Theatre. "The sovereignty of the *prima donna*," wrote Sterland, "was threatened with annihilation" (246). Predictably enough, murmurings from the "cabal" arose almost immediately. Ayrton insisted on the right to cast the singers himself, so that "many of them were not satisfied." There were also an unprecedented number of "very long" rehearsals. These did not include the many private rehearsals for which Ayrton took it upon himself to visit the houses of the principal female singers, to accompany them through their parts on the pianoforte. Such detailed attention to the preparation of a score and the command of individual parts was unknown and decidedly unwelcome. "Intrigues of every kind were resorted to," Sterland records,

nay, if all that was whispered at the time be true, even representatives of royalty "mingled in the dance," and denounced the theatrical damnation of Don Juan to be as certain as the shower of fire which closes his mimic existence.[68]

The royalty in question could not have been the Whig sympathizer Princess Charlotte, who attended the 27 May performance.[69] Perhaps the Prince Regent himself, that "libertine . . . and despiser of domestic ties," found the prospect of a revenge opera representing the destruction of a high-born philanderer before an audience of enraptured city radicals too much to bear.[70]

Ayrton was close friends with Alsager, a factory owner and trader whose literary posterity rests on his being the owner of the Chapman's Homer that found its way into the eager hands of Keats, and as one of the principal organizers of Hazlitt's lectures at the Surrey Institution in 1818. He was a friend of Wordsworth as well as Hunt, and stayed at Rydal Mount only months after the *Don Giovanni* debut. Alsager's offices stood in Southwark next door to Horsemonger Lane prison, where Hunt enjoyed the hospitality of the Crown from 1813 to 1815. He was a regular visitor to Hunt's "cell" and, on his release, the nervous and sickly prisoner first stopped at Alsager's to accustom himself to the shock of his freedom. To show his gratitude, Hunt sent Alsager a miniature portrait accompanied by a melopoetic sonnet, expressing his appreciation for "the fine pleasure/Of lettered friend, or music's mingling art,/That fetches out in smiles the mutual soul."[71] As in his sonnet to Henry Robertson, Hunt equates literature with music and defines both in sociable terms as a single "mingling art," a cornerstone of Cockney friendship and fellow feeling.

Hunt's description of Alsager as a "man of business" as well as a "scholar and musician" marks him as a quintessential new man of the city. From 1817 he was employed at *The Times* as a reporter on both finance *and* opera. His participation in the world of business and trade went hand in hand with radical bourgeois cultural aspirations, among them the promotion of Mozart.[72] In fact, recent research into the early history of Mozart reception in England has shown that Alsager was a key figure in what was technically the first production of *Don Giovanni* in London, an amateur concert performance in a floor-cloth factory in Whitechapel Road that took place more than ten years before the opera's professional debut at the King's Theatre.[73] Alsager helped copy out the score, and almost certainly arranged the performance space. He was a freeman of the Clothworkers' Company of London, and would have known the owner of the historically notable factory, an otherwise obscure city "amateur" named Thomas Hayward.[74]

An anonymous member of this first *Don Giovanni* cast published his reminiscences of the event in Ayrton's journal *Harmonicon* in 1831. The "Amateur Singer" describes himself as "an ardent, almost idolatrous admirer of Mozart's operas" and recalls the deep "regret" among the amateurs of the city in the first years of the nineteenth century "that Portogallo and Catalani should unite to prevent our enjoying his masterpieces then where they ought to have been heard – in the King's Theatre." His account of the unofficial production of *Don Giovanni* in Whitechapel Road in 1805 (or 1806) reads like a triumphant episode in the history of an underground resistance movement:

with the exception of the *Clemenza di Tito* . . . the first opera of Mozart's ever heard in this country was got up by a party of amateurs, and performed, oratorio fashion, without action, amidst the mingled effluvia of canvas, oil, and turpentine.[75]

A more symbolically resonant debut for Mozart's opera is hard to imagine. The rich odor of the City – the "effluvia" of manufacture and trade – hangs over *Don Giovanni* from the beginning. Mozart's music, like radical politics, Italianate poetry, and the *Examiner*, first takes hold not in the theaters, terraced houses, and pleasure parks of the West End, but in the City, among the "canvas, oil and turpentine" of a Southwark factory.

There is evidence too of Alsager's close collaboration with Ayrton in the 1817 *Don Giovanni* in his role as opera critic for *The Times*. He attended at least one of the many rehearsals, in response to which he sent a letter to Ayrton full of notes and suggestions. However compromising it might appear to journalistic scruples today, the director and the critic felt no qualms in meeting for dinner less than a month before the premiere and then rehearsing the opera together at the piano.[76] Alsager also promoted the performance in *The Times* for weeks leading up to the April 12 opening and concluded their collaboration by declaring "the success of *Don Giovanni* eminent and complete" in his April 14 review.

The Hunt–Alsager–Ayrton connection does not occupy a central place in literary histories of the Hunt circle, just as the 1817 *Examiner* is far better remembered for its role in the promotion of Keats and Shelley than for its Italian opera column. But the triumph of the *Don Giovanni* premiere in April of that year, and the *Examiner* circle's role in bringing that remarkable event about, demonstrates no less powerfully the collaborative networking of a broad "Cockney" intelligentsia in the advancement of progressive, middle-class urban taste in Regency culture, and the integration of music with literature in a general enterprise of cultural reform. This network stretched from suburban Hampstead to the factories of Southwark to the newspapers of Fleet Street, where *The Times* and *Morning Chronicle* joined their radical brother, the *Examiner*, in a City-based, pro-Mozart campaign against the cultural hegemony of the West End nobles.

IV

One problematic aspect of the 1817 premiere of *Don Giovanni* was Hunt's decision to grant the privilege of reviewing the production to Hazlitt, a critic with a questionable ear for music and little appetite for the baroque spectacle of the King's Theatre. Hazlitt described his principled antipathy to the Italian opera most fully in a polemical piece for the *Yellow Dwarf* the following year. His argument is not made on musical grounds but against the spectacular form of the opera *in toto*:

Every object is there collected, and displayed in ostentatious profusion, that can strike the sense or dazzle the imagination; music, dancing, painting, poetry, architecture, the blaze of beauty, "the glass of fashion, the mould of form"; and yet we are not satisfied—because the multitude and variety of objects distracts the attention, and by flattering us with a vein shew of the highest gratification of every faculty and wish, leaves us at last in a state of listlessness, disappointment, and *ennui* . . . It is an illusion and a mockery, where the mind is made "the fool of the senses," and cheated of itself. (May 23, 1818)

Hazlitt's critique of the "vein shew" of visual art is as old as Plato. If Italian opera requires an indulgence in purely sensual pleasures of virtuosic singing or, as Hazlitt memorably puts it, "a species of intellectual prostitution," then the implied contrast is with the virtues of poetry, a textual art that does not rely on "distraction" and "illusion." Hazlitt's language is very close to Addison's, whose dismissal of Italian opera in the *Spectator* – "its only design is to gratify the sense, and keep up an indolent attention in the audience" – established the template for a century's worth of middle-class anti-operatic sentiment.[77] Another early operaphobe, John Dennis, perceived in the new "entertainment" a threat to poetry itself and to the human "spirit" (what Hazlitt called "mind" or "intellect") enlarged by poetry:

Now if we can shew that Poetry augments this Spirit wherever it finds it, and sometimes begets it where it was not before, and that mere Musick, such as is that of our Operas, is so far from begetting this Spirit, where it was not before, or from augmenting it where it meets with it, that it has a natural Tendency to the diminishing it, and destroying it; then I hope it will be readily granted, that since publick Entertainments of mere Musick and Poetry are incompatible, and that we must banish one and retain the other, it will be reasonable to banish the Opera, and not Poetry.[78]

The scene-painters and musicians of the opera must be "banished" from the British realm as from Plato's Republic, if its proper neo-Augustan spirit is to be preserved.

For a revival of *Don Giovanni* in 1828 Hazlitt returned once more to the King's Theatre as opera critic for the *Examiner*. Instead of the performance, he reviewed the audience. We can only speculate as to what specific indignity Hazlitt suffered during the course of the evening, but it translated the next day into a 2,000-word diatribe against "the *figurantes* at the Opera" in which Hazlitt's class sensitivities exhibit themselves red raw:

We import Opera-singers, dancers, kings! Liberal land! That knows its own deficiencies in what is refined and elevated! Happy, that it finds others so ready to oblige it! All they get from us, is hard blows or hard cash: all that we get from them, is politeness and luxury! (May 4)

Hazlitt jostles with the dandies in Fop's Alley, squints upward at the dazzle of the *beau monde* in the boxes, and feels his blood boil. Through his devastating critique of "fashion," which the King's Theatre historically embodied, Hazlitt's night at the opera becomes a hellish vision of class-ridden England at large. Fashion, for Hazlitt, is England's new slavery, a cultural economy powered by the machinery of class distinction and hostility, immured to "human sympathy," where all commodities begin to lose their value for the elite at the very moment they become popular with the general public.

Hazlitt's contempt for the "fashionable," who "are solely occupied in thinking how they themselves look, whether their coat is of the right cut, their cravat properly tied," is in part undoubtedly correct observation, but is also a projection of his own intensely self-conscious class anxiety. When he blames the audience for being distracted from the opera itself by the question of "whether their next neighbour is good enough for them to speak to," Hazlitt reveals himself *as* that neighbor, the visitor to the opera house who just might not belong there. Everywhere you turn, he writes, "you hear an elegant discourse on 'the higher and lower orders.'" The spectacle of class pretension and hostility in the audience out-dazzles the production on stage, and corrupts its pleasures through the all-consuming vanity of "refinement." The consequence is the operatic manifestation of a deep cultural malaise:

In England our object is not the pursuit of pleasure, but to run away from the pleasures of others; and when a taste for the drama or anything else becomes a little common, we grow sulky and insensible by way of being spiritual and refined. We see no other refinement in the case, unless the getting rid of thought and feeling is a proof of refinement; and the *figurantes* at the Opera are an intermediate link, a soft imperceptible gradation, between the grossness of human passion and the absence of all human sympathy.

Jennifer Hall-Witt has shown how the rapid increase in titled ranks in the late eighteenth century transformed the King's Theatre from an elite venue indispensable to the display rituals and deal-making of an intricate patronage system to a more competitive and exclusionary arena in which aristocratic women in particular exerted their powers as social gatekeepers, in order to preserve a core elite network from encroachment by noble *arrivistes*. Thus, even at a time of self-conscious reform among some elements of the aristocracy, the King's Theatre was its weak flank, host to an obnoxious intensity of "status performances" that might be publicly condemned by journalists such as Hazlitt, thereby "reinforc[ing] the sense of a political system in need of reform."[79]

Hazlitt was thus far from alone in his resentments. The middle-class Mozartian revolution at the King's Theatre demanded reforms in audience behavior, specifically the nobility's. For instance, Alsager at *The Times* suggested that the practice of applauding *during* the singing be discontinued because of its distracting effect on the necessary Mozartian absorption:

There is one custom ... we should be very glad to see reformed; we mean that of yielding (in a way very honourable, no doubt, to taste and feeling) to the impulse of admiration excited by a fine passage, and interrupting it by an applause which, however judicious in itself, is perfectly ruinous to the effect (April 16, 1817).

There is evidence also that the new Mozartian constituency of the King's Theatre began attempting to police the time-honored liberty to engage in loud conversation during performances, with a pause only to listen to the diva. The Norwich manufacturer and avid musical amateur William Gardiner recalled how on his visit to the King's Theatre to see *Don Giovanni*, he had found it necessary to tell two members of His Majesty's Cabinet to please shut up:

Lord Castlereagh and Lord Warwick were on the bench just before me, conversing so loudly upon the income-tax, that I said, "Gentlemen, your talking prevents my hearing the music;" which remark seemed to give pleasure to a party on the seat behind me, for I silenced the senators.[80]

In such anecdotes we discover traces in the growth of a distinctly bourgeois public music culture in Britain, which, increasingly through the nineteenth century, demanded an atmosphere of almost religious devotion at the public performance of serious music, what Hunt had called "downward listening ... Half conscious, half unconscious" (see chapter 5).[81] The role of the King's Theatre as an extension of court culture – more a place of "upward talking" as it were – came increasingly under threat from the Mozartian amateurs. Indeed, by mid-century, the nobility had largely deserted the opera house as part of their general retreat from social power and those public venues – the licensed theaters, St. James's Park, etc. – that had been their display spaces.

Perhaps thinking that the *Examiner* was in danger of failing the historical moment, Hunt himself wrote two follow-up reviews of the 1817 *Don Giovanni*. Where Hazlitt seemed to damn the pleasures of Mozart's opera – its "gaiety, tenderness, and sweetness" – by disadvantageous comparison with the literary "grand expression" it mostly lacked, Hunt allows the democratic equivalence of music and literature, and promotes Mozartian pleasure itself as a fanciful form of sublime "transport":

the notes are struck up to love, and gaiety, and coquetry, and all the intensities of pleasure ... When he gets into this vein, he turns criticism into mere admiration and transport. One has nothing to do but to reckon the songs in succession, and panegyrize them as they go by, like a dance of beauties. (August 3)

He then opens a debate over the dramatic propriety of the final scene where Mozart, ill advisedly according to Hunt, "got his statue off the horse" and in doing so "spoiled him." Whereas the scene in the cemetery, when the Commendatore first speaks to Don Giovanni, "present[ed] a combination than which nothing can be more grand or fearful," the finale divested the ghost of his solemn majesty through an overabundance of "motion" and "noise." Hunt's grammatical gyration – "than which nothing can be more grand" – echoes Kant and the rhetorical protocols of the sublime. Though Hunt proceeds to show how the opera's finale fails the Kantian standard, his argument is based on the very presumption disallowed by Hazlitt and Dennis: namely that opera should be capable of sustained "grand expression" and of providing intellectual satisfaction equivalent to those poets Hunt calls "Mozart's brethren."

By contrast with Hazlitt, Hunt's opera criticism in general shows a man bent on enjoying himself.[82] While Hazlitt is not sure what a good radical such as he is *doing* at the opera, Hunt casts himself as a reformer from within. At a production of Paisiello's *La Molinara*, three weeks before the premiere of *Don Giovanni*, Hunt declared himself

heartily glad to see this Theatre fill so well, for we like Italian, and music, and dancing, and beautiful mythologies, and the sight of spectators from various countries amicably mingling together, and are even extrinsic enough to admire the flounces and flowers in the boxes—not to mention a small predilection in favour of the fair wearers. (March 23, 1817)

Hunt allows himself to enjoy the ostentatious self-display of the cosmopolitan upper classes, and embraces "fashion," which Hazlitt abominated, as a natural object of middle-class desire. In the preface to *Foliage*, published the following year, we find Hunt's confident credo of pre-Victorian bourgeois sensibility and desire, in which he claims the right of "cheerful leisure," and prescribes an ethics of "enjoyment," "cheerfulness," and "sociality" as a necessary antidote to the "yellow atmosphere of money-getting" among the rising merchant and professional classes. In this account the language of bourgeois aspiration takes the place of Hazlitt's class rage. Indeed, Hunt credits "the fashionable world" with an ability to "see a great deal farther into these … pleasures," music in particular, and upholds their leisured "refinements" as objects of emulation.[83] Hunt's positive predisposition at the opera house – his "hearty gladness" – forms the basis for his appreciation of Mozart's operas, which constitute the spectacular manifestation, the objective correlative of his own enjoyment:

Mozart's tendency was to feel all that he said, to be conscious of every idea in the shape and touch of a positive pleasure. He is therefore always at his best in direct enjoyment—in love, in pastoral pleasure, in joyous anticipation, in deep and actual delight. This was his faculty, his peculiar self ... (July 27, 1817).

For Hunt, the public act of enjoying Mozart represents an ideal, performative mode of Cockney "social sentiment."[84]

While Hazlitt reads the pleasures of Mozart's operas as necessarily trivial, for Hunt, gaiety and moral seriousness no more contradict each other in Mozart than in radical journalism. In his preface to the 1808 *Examiner*, Hunt had promised stylistic reform as the natural accompaniment to political opposition:

as Theatrical Criticism is the liveliest part of a newspaper, I have endeavoured to correct its usual levity, by treating it philosophically; and as Political Writing is the gravest subject, I have attempted to give it a more general interest by handling it good-humouredly.

Hunt employs the same ironic reversal in his description of the opera house as "a palace of pleasure, even in its tragedy. Bitterness there cannot but speak sweetly."[85] For Hunt there was no choice between seriousness and pleasure, between "frivolity" and "the grave realities of life," between, by extension, the operatic and the political. In a review of *Il Flauto Magico* in 1819, Hunt disavows Hazlitt's "preconceived" equation of pleasure and triviality, arguing that "enjoyment" and "gladness" are the properties of art and genius as much as moral depth:

We are not sure, for our own parts, that we do not admire it more than any of his operas, if we could candidly rid ourselves of a preconceived notion that Mozart's powers were chiefly confined to the gayer part of enjoyment—a misconception to which all men of various genius seem to have been liable, in return for their bestowing gladness.

Hunt here makes his own modest claim to be numbered among the "men of various genius" who have had their style "misconceived."

Hunt's reputation is only now recovering from the charges of dilettantism and frivolousness first leveled at him almost two centuries ago by *Blackwood's* and its Tory cronies. As Nicholas Roe, Jeffrey Cox, and other current Hunt scholars have rightly argued, it will not do simply to reiterate these politically motivated prejudices in our own judgment of Hunt, or to rehearse the high Romantic ideology in Anglo-American academic culture that has historically diminished the Cockney phenomenon. Reading Hunt's opera criticism, we recognize that dilettantism and frivolousness are integral to his "Mozartian" style of opposition. *Don Giovanni* and *Le Nozze di Figaro* both offer critiques of aristocratic power and license, but they are also vehicles of pure aesthetic pleasure and style. In the same way Hunt's 1812 attack on the Prince Regent in the *Examiner* takes the form of a sequence of elaborate farces, highly enjoyable even in their serious legal consequentiality. Consider, for example, the dream sequence in his article "Princely Qualities":

I ran over the history of the last fifty years; and so complete was my abstraction, that I was in a hundred points of time and parts of the kingdom at once; I was at motions in Parliament about money; I was at Brighton, I was at Blackheath, I was at Newmarket, I was at Mrs. R.'s, Mrs. C.'s, and Mrs. F.'s—at my Lady J.s and my Lady H.'s; I was two hours in company with a hatter and three with a tailor; I was surrounded with duns and blue devils; I was at the payment of sundry pensions to noisy, ill-looking fellows, who the moment they got the money clapped their hands upon their mouths; I was keeping it up till four-o'clock in the morning; I sunk under the table and fell asleep, and then I began dreaming … things as incongruous, for instance, as supposing one's self to be a beast and a man at one and the same time, or a jackass and Alfred the Great, or a Prince and a box of peppermint. (March 8)

"Princely Qualities" transcends the formal definition of satire where the frivolous corresponds to and inverts the "grave reality" in a one-to-one system of relation. Hunt's zany narrative instead marks a deconstruction of seriousness itself, a truly radical irreverence, politics *as* style. Lockhart and the other Tory critics sought to deny Hunt and his circle the right to idle poeticizing, unsystematic self-education, and "round table" style opinions – in short, to non-material labor, to frivolousness. If the government was offended by the insolent freedom of Hunt's portrayal of the Regent, it was truly scandalized by his so obviously enjoying it. It was Hunt taking his pleasure where he wished – be it in his journal or at the opera house – that constituted his true threat to the social order, the reason why he, not Hazlitt, ended up in gaol.

To pursue this point: the eagerness of Hunt's Tory critics to brand him a vulgar misfit took the shape it did precisely because Hunt laid claim to aristocratic privilege not in the tangible assets of land, wealth, and rank, but the new cultural consumables of modernity, namely leisure, entertainment, and taste. Hunt's surprising embrace of the aristocratic Italian opera in the pages of the *Examiner* accordingly stands for a strategic politicizing of pleasure. Hazlitt was also attacked by the Tories, but because he took on the more familiar shape of the radical as the angry, disenfrachised outsider, he represented a manageable, symmetrical figure of opposition. Hunt's breathless delight in the opera signals him as a more dangerous agent of middle-class aspiration: a bourgeois *bon vivant* who not only expresses a desire to enjoy the privileges historically reserved for the nobility but pretends *to be enjoying them already*. Mozart and the opera house were integral to the public display of Hunt's "counter-poetics of the Fancy," a politics of taste and leisure that elevated "the supposedly trivial and the immature, the ephemeral and the light, the casual and playful, the scurrilous and immoral, the contradictory."[86] Hence the pleasure Hunt takes in Mozart at the King's Theatre is a form of class defiance at least as powerful as Hazlitt's denunciation of opera culture in the *Examiner* in 1828. By enjoying himself at the King's Theatre, Hunt is fighting for the right to redefine operatic art and for his constituency's access to its pleasures. His Italian opera reviews are thus not extrinsic to the program of the *Examiner* but perfectly congruous, indeed exemplary. The role of reformer and taste-maker at the King's Theatre was one Hunt sought rather than scorned not because Italian opera was ever a serious matter, but precisely because it was a luxury.

Twenty years after the controversial and long-anticipated debut of *Don Giovanni* at the King's Theatre, the class battlelines at the opera house were still apparent, but newly redrawn. Reviewing an 1837 revival of the opera, the Novellos' journal, *Musical World*, remarked on *Don Giovanni's* enduring power to draw

> that large and increasing body of classical amateurs (and which is composed almost exclusively of the middle class in life) to hear such music as *they* prefer. The majority of that immense audience the other evening, to all appearance, came from the East of Pall Mall. (5 May)

In 1813, Hunt's *Examiner* had described the Italian opera house as a public venue "almost exclusively visited by the highest rank and fashion of the nation" (May 9), who still adhered to a *pasticcio* aesthetic of opera and defined the musical experience of the King's Theatre, as Charles Burney had a generation earlier, exclusively by its virtuosic singing. Then came the revolution: drama, character, ensemble singing, fidelity to the score, and orchestral richness of effect. These were the Mozartian values that converged with the cultural ambitions of the professional journalists and music lovers of the greater Cockney circle. Their Mozart campaign against the "Italian cabal" and their aristocratic patrons at the King's Theatre was so successful that, by the late 1820s, "the purity and the integrity of

Mozart's operas in performance were policed by critics and audiences alike."[87] The quarter century since 1813 had marked enormous changes in the English social landscape, nowhere more visible than at the entertainment venues of London's West End. By 1837, the King's Theatre was in the business of addressing the preferences of its "middle-class" patrons, a "large and increasing body." In the year of Victoria's ascent to the throne, what remained of Hunt's music-loving circle could look with satisfaction upon the "immense" city audience for Mozart at the King's Theatre, and see there the operatic shape of Regency reform.

CHAPTER 5

Austen's accomplishment

I

In 1775 – while James Cox exhibited his luxury musical automata at Spring Gardens for the delectation of Burney's Evelina (see the introduction) – a family of Swiss inventors, the Jaquet-Droz, placed two "human" robots on show in Covent Garden. Both were fully realized mannequins with clothes and wigs and a complex mechanism of some four hundred parts accessible through a door in their backs. The first represented a boy in the act of writing at a desk, the other a girl playing the harpsichord. The *Ecrivain*, according to the prospectus, "moistens his pen himself, shakes off the excess, and writes distinctly and correctly everything one cares to dictate to him ... When he has completed one line, he moves on to the next." Meanwhile, his companion, the *Musicienne*,

> performs on her harpsichord, by herself, various pieces of music in two or three parts, with considerable precision ... she glances equally at her hands, at her music, and at her spectators ... her breast alternately swells and falls, in order to show her breathing.[1]

The Jaquet-Droz robots belong to a rich popular history of the automaton in the eighteenth century, a Georgian fad and cultural motif borrowed promiscuously by philosophers and conduct-book writers alike to illustrate everything from the nature of human rationality and free will to the dangers of automatized femininity through improper education.[2]

The year 1775, a banner year for London automata, is better known to literary history as the year of Jane Austen's birth. Austen would later belong to a generation of writers whose accredited achievement lay in their production of original rhetorical techniques, including Austen's free indirect discourse, which glamorized a psychologically layered human subjectivity. If the Jaquet-Droz exhibition suggested a new, possibly toxic proximity between writing and mechanical virtuosity in popular culture, the intensity of the "Romantic" turn in literature around the turn of the nineteenth century bears all the marks of cultural reaction. The Jaquet-Droz robots defined virtuosity in both its historical senses – as a luxury exhibit and a mechanical mode of performance – while capturing also, in their visual equation of writing, music-making, and mechanics, the specter of virtuosity as it would come to haunt Romantic literary culture.

Aspects of both Austen's fiction and the avant-garde orchestral music of London in the new century, centered around Beethoven, can be described as Romantic repudiations of virtuosity and its mechanized image of culture. Austen and Beethoven were both creatures of the 1790s who came to public notice in Britain in the 1810s. Growing up, Austen learned the fashionable Viennese piano music that was the young Beethoven's *lingua franca*. Later, she published *Pride and Prejudice* in the same year, 1813, that the newly formed Philharmonic Society of London premiered Beethoven's Fifth Symphony. In *Emma* (1816) Jane Fairfax receives the gift of a Broadwood piano, clandestinely, from her lover Frank Churchill. The following year, the Broadwood company sent a piano to Vienna as a gift for Beethoven, hoping to garner publicity from association with Europe's most prestigious living composer. They succeeded. Beethoven's Broadwood looms large in nineteenth-century musical mythology as central to his elevation of the piano from the amateur sphere of the parlor to the professional concert-stage. Through its connection to Beethoven and his new pianistic values of expressiveness, the Broadwood piano belongs also to the new musical discourse of the 1810s that contributed, in historically specific ways, to "the modern articulation of subjectivity."[3]

As a ubiquitous article of furniture charged with competing tropes of labor and leisure, privacy and performance, sensibility and seduction, class ambition and personal freedom, the piano offered a mirror to modern bourgeois female aspiration and its attendant anxieties. Austen, for her part, in her creation of the Broadwood-playing Jane Fairfax in *Emma*, participated in the imagined professionalization of female accomplishment in the post-Waterloo period, and integrated music into the larger artistic project of the novel: the narrativization of Emma's "inner life" through free indirect discourse. In short, this chapter casts Austen and Beethoven as fellow technicians of the Romantic-humanist subject. Each developed, in their respective media, the raw materials of modern, bourgeois, "psychological" art. The hidden figure of Beethoven in the text of *Emma*, and the historical convergence of Austen's published novels with Beethoven's introduction to London audiences, presents an opportunity to explore the poetics and politics of lyric interiority that Austen's fiction shares with the Viennese music she knew so intimately, and which Beethoven adapted to his own heroic dimensions.

In generations of novels, commentary, and visual representations across the nineteenth century, the piano hums and vibrates with possibility like nothing else in the bourgeois domestic sphere. The most important disseminating medium for commercial music, the pianoforte fulfilled a range of roles: as an emblem of newly leisured status, a magnet for sociability organized around the performance of fashionable songs, and a lightning rod of subjective desires in which the paradox of bourgeois individualism – both market bound and "free" – was daily played out. From the age of twelve, Jane Austen practiced the piano most mornings and performed for her family in the evenings, until her fatal sickness forced her to discontinue.[4] She was still taking weekly lessons and learning new repertoire at the age of twenty – "I practise everyday as much as I can" – unusual even for accomplished women of her class.[5] Despite the limited income of the Austens after the death of her father, a good-quality piano was hired for her at Southampton and later at Chawton.[6] Printed music could be expensive, so Austen belonged, as did innumerable amateur musicians of her time, to an informal, woman-driven network of music copyists and borrowers. Austen's experience of domestic music culture ran in parallel with the sociable literary culture she enjoyed, in which "the purchasing, lending, and borrowing of books were closely connected with other social networks."[7]

The piano music in Austen's possession at the time of her death, some half of it copied out meticulously in her own hand, amounts to nearly fifteen hundred pages. Music historians charged with cataloguing Austen's collection have remarked on its "sheer scope and variety," which demonstrates "just how rich the public (and private) musical life of Britain must have been."[8] Her repertoire included drawing-room songs, opera transcriptions and dances, but also a strong sampling of 1790s' solo piano music imported from Vienna – Schobert, Pleyel, Hoffmeister, Steibelt – as well as the London "school" of Clementi, J. B. Cramer, and J. C. Bach.[9] Music was the most cosmopolitan of the Georgian arts, as Austen's musical repertoire reflects: "the German sonatas," wrote pianist and teacher Charles Dibdin in 1791, "are now universally a fashion."[10] The collection also suggests that she was a fine amateur pianist. The most difficult of the sonatas in the Chawton books – if they were at Austen's command – would rank her among her own female characters, if not at the near-professional excellence of Jane Fairfax, then certainly higher than Emma Woodhouse. Marianne Dashwood and Anne Elliot perhaps best represent her own standard.

Figure 6. John Smart, *Misses Elizabeth and Harriet Binney* (c. 1806). Victoria and Albert Museum, London. That both Binney sisters are featured suggests this portrait by Smart, an in-demand society miniaturist, was intended as a family keepsake and not for the delectation of a suitor. The curtain has been raised as if to announce a musical concert, but the self-possession of the sitters suggests that we have happened upon the daily domestic ritual of piano practice.

The piano music of the 1790s is not an idle footnote to Austen's world and fiction. The first questions put to Mr. Elton about his bride in *Emma* require him "to tell her Christian name, and say whose music she principally played" (162).[11] Music repertoire functioned as an indispensable shorthand of taste and character; music was, as Leon Plantinga puts it, "woven into the very fabric of social interaction: it was part of the system of signs by which people communicated with each other" (Figure 6).[12] In *Sense and Sensibility* Edward Ferrars speaks of books and music in the same breath, as do Elizabeth and Colonel Fitzwilliam in their conversation at

Rosings Park in *Pride and Prejudice*. Jane Fairfax waxes lyrical about post offices in *Emma*, where she receives secret letters from Frank Churchill but where, as a committed pianist, she would also have collected the latest instalments from an increasing array of music periodicals distributing the most fashionable new music to all corners of Europe and its empires. Recent studies have shown the extraordinary reach of the music revolution in Romantic-era Britain, measured in the sales of sheet music, pedagogical literature, and musical instruments. The music boom was not confined to the social elite. For middle-class women, according to Leslie Ritchie, "music was neither as expensive nor as exclusive as has been thought."[13] Jane Austen's close involvement in the increasingly sophisticated and accessible music industry of her day is expressed in her letters, where she talks about music as much as she does books, and in her voluminous collection of printed music. And yet, for all this, her musical life remains at the margins of Austen biography and academic criticism of her fiction.[14]

One reason for this marginalization is the ambivalent image of music in the novels. Marianne Dashwood's pianism is anti-social, a symptom of her melodramatic self-absorption. Sir Thomas Bertram blames his daughters' dissipation on their education in accomplishments rather than morality. Mary Crawford plays the vixen at the harp, while Elizabeth Bennet's relaxed attitude toward piano practice contrasts appealingly both with Mary's sullen anxiety for "display" and Georgiana's sequestration following the failed elopement with Wickham, for which she punishes herself with scales. Willoughby and Frank Churchill employ their musical talents for mischief-making and seduction while, most insidiously of all, Jane Fairfax's flawless performances at the piano suggest a proportional emptiness of personality, a woman whose identity has been consumed by the imperatives of female accomplishment, of which she is the cold paragon.

Austen's disapproval of musical accomplishment in her fiction appears to contradict her own personal commitment to the piano, but – like her appropriations of Gothic novels, picturesque landscape theory, conduct-book manuals, and so much else – it chimes with a popular discourse of the 1790s, namely, the debate over female education. Jane Fairfax was an object of more than just Emma's anxiety. She embodied a widely published concern about the inflationary effects of female accomplishment on young women's education. Hannah More decried the "frenzy for accomplishments," as did Maria Edgeworth, Erasmus Darwin, Clara Reeve, John Burton, and others. Mary Wollstonecraft expressly opposed female "accomplishments," as vehicles of virtuosic self-display, to the cultivation of intellectual and moral "virtues."[15] In Edgeworth's 1814 novel, *Patronage*, the Miss Falconers employ their musical proficiency with a view only to displaying their own fashionable tastes and placing themselves conspicuously within the view of rich male suitors. In Austen's unfinished *Sanditon*, the Miss Beauforts likewise delight in those "showy acquirements" that More deplored, which were sought after by young women hoping only "to make their fortune by marriage."[16] According to this critique, accomplishment was a relic of court culture, with women defined solely by their power to captivate through exhibition: Miss Beaufort looks for "praise and celebrity from all who walked within the sound of her Instrument" (374). The emerging professional middle-class ethos represented by the 1790 reformists of all ideological stripes demanded, in place of virtuosic identity, a non-performative, inward, rational, essentially literary self. For women, argued Wollstonecraft, "the grand end of their exertions should be to unfold their own faculties and acquire the dignity of conscious virtue."[17] Austen's novels, in their enforcement of anti-virtuosic standards and innovations in psychological depth, stand as exemplary agents of this reformist agenda.

To the limited extent that it has taken up the issue, recent criticism has selectively rehearsed the "full-scale attack on female accomplishments" advanced in the 1790s with which Austen's fiction belatedly seems to concur.[18] That untroubled consensus is typified by Richard Leppert, who places "the domestic production, hence consumption, of music ... among the 'accomplishments' that made females fit for the marriage market and thereafter for reflectors of their husbands' station."[19] For Gary Kelly, "singing and playing music displayed the young woman's body and bearing at social occasions to attract a suitor." Mary Poovey likewise nominates piano-playing as one of the "only thinly disguised opportunities for the display of personal charms," which served as "an acceptable version of men's personal competitiveness."[20] While such language is faithful to the viewpoints of More and Edgeworth, it deflates the controversy into settled fact and is dubious in its sweeping generality. Most of the 1790s' critique of accomplishment focussed on the proper employment of private time. Defenders of accomplishment, such as Catharine Macaulay and Thomas Gisborne, perceived music's utility in "supply[ing] hours of leisure with innocent and amusing occupation."[21] Allatson Burgh, writing in the 1810s, went further, advocating the discipline of musical study as a "means of preventing that vacuity of mind, which is too frequently the parent of libertinism ... an antidote to the poison insidiously administered by innumerable licentious Novels."[22] Likewise collaboration, not competitiveness, might be considered the hallmark of

Georgian women's music culture – as Jane Austen's borrowing of music and encouragement of her piano-playing nieces attest. It is even more certain that private practice, not public performance, formed the greater part of a Georgian woman's musical life. As to the actual *pleasures* of music – which Colonel Brandon experiences during Marianne's performance in *Sense and Sensibility* – or musicianship as an expression of self and its autonomy – as Anne Elliot, who "in music ... had been always used to feel alone in the world" (47) – current literary criticism is resolutely deaf.[23]

Obscured in the critique of accomplishment, past and present, are the dramatic class ramifications of music's wholesale entry into the domestic realm after 1790, to the point where families of the mercantile class and lower might be expected to own a piano: "the Daughters of Mechanics, even in humble stations, would fancy themselves extremely ill-treated, were they debarred the indulgence of a pianoforte."[24] Music catalogues that in the 1760s contained a hundred items by 1790 had thousands, and by 1820 could offer selections from tens of thousands of available musical scores.[25] This explosion in the music industry is a powerful expression of British modernity and its global primacy in the Romantic era: "the main reason for Britain's leadership of the boom in piano manufacture and sheet music publishing was that it was the only country that had the wealth and technological advances to make them possible."[26] With such a vast literature came a new language of repertoire, composers, singers, and music theory – an entire new discursive dimension of middle-class life – that is abundantly documented in Austen's novels. "Musical" Mrs. Weston, with her modest origins, enjoys command of an aesthetic vocabulary denied to women of her class only a generation before. She is thrilled by Jane's Broadwood and grills her about it, "having so much to ask and to say as to tone, touch, and pedal" (197).[27] As early as 1798 Edgeworth declared that female accomplishments "are now so common, that they cannot be considered as the distinguishing characteristics of even a gentlewoman's education."[28] Music was no longer the preserve of the elite, no longer even a safe distinguisher between the gentry and mercantile classes. The middle-class amateur musicians, and the aristocrats they sought to emulate, played the same repertoire of German sonatas, Italian songs, and such "Irish melodies" as Frank Churchill includes in his anonymous gift to Jane Fairfax.

Though favorite tunes and lyrics traversed class lines in promiscuous fashion, the drawing-room music Austen played was distinguishable in its protocols from the popular songs of the music halls and street corner balladry. As an international language representing the emerging aristocratic-bourgeois coalition of Europe, drawing-room songs could be multilingual but were without "all the distinguishing marks of working-class music: no dialects, no vulgarity, no low humour."[29] Austen's own prose followed the same prescription, as a new form of standard "polite" English that made no distinctions between region and class and, in doing so, asserted a middle-class and distinctly female sovereignty over the practice of fiction. The latter-day critique of accomplishment fails both to recognize the convergence of interests in middle-class literature and music of the Regency period and to look forward into the nineteenth century, where the consequences of large-scale bourgeois female pianism, formerly an object of satire, "became more complicated; women's aspirations for genuine education and high culture had to be taken more seriously."[30] More destructively, it perpetuates an interdisciplinary blindness, a partisan literary-cultural representation of the Georgian music culture to which Austen and her fictional heroines belonged, viewed exclusively through the ancient negative paradigm of vanity and visual display, and updated with a veneer of gender politics that diminishes both women and music. The countermanding image to the anti-accomplishment critique – of the empowerment of middle-class women by the technological and commercial advances in music culture – is exemplified by Austen herself: a Georgian woman privately absorbed by the demands of an artistic discipline and whose musical life, like her heroine Anne Elliot's, lay entirely outside the more vulgar demands of accomplishment.[31]

Mary Hunter has shown how piano pedagogy in the early nineteenth century offered "a kind of simulacrum of Romantic subjectivity," while subtly reclaiming the principle of technical excellence from the stigma of virtuosity. Regency piano treatises, by combining technical exercises with musical examples, "separated technique from expression, but then taught expressive gestures as if they comprised a branch of technique."[32] More broadly, piano-playing, and in particular the regimen of practice, positioned British women such as Austen at the vanguard of a new, disciplined approach to time management and mechanical efficiency that was the domestic analogue of their male counterparts' education in the professions. Austen's late novels, as Janet Todd has observed, all "display marriages between professional working men, whose work is central to their characters, and women who are suited through experience and temperament to be their wives and part managers."[33] The corresponding *personal* rewards for successful self-discipline in musical accomplishment were what one critic called, in Beethoven's contemporaneous symphonies, a drama of "psychological development," the privilege of Romantic interiority that is the subject and matter of Austen's novels.[34]

As the foregoing sketch suggests, the argument of this chapter situates the piano, and female pianism, alongside women's writing at the vanguard of what Nancy Armstrong has described as the feminization of nineteenth-century culture. The perception of that feminization was an established trope well before the Victorian age, as the eighteenth-century discourse on effeminacy illustrates.[35] Since the mid-1700s women had enjoyed increasing influence in English music culture across a continuum of private and semi-private settings. With the massive advance of the piano into the domestic sphere at the turn of the new century, where women could act as both patrons and performers, that power enlarged exponentially. Likewise in the public sphere, women's contributions to Romantic-era music culture – as performers, composers, and publishers – "increased dramatically."[36] In short, Austen's pianism, like her fiction, belonged to what More called a "revolution of the manners of the middle class," a revolution strongly influenced by women's increased visibility.[37]

Austen, for all her satire of young "prodigies," takes the disciplines of accomplishment seriously enough to cite Emma's lack of "steadiness" in learning music and drawing as an adumbration of her larger character deficiencies (39). Piano-playing was only partly about women as domestic ornament, as the 1790s' critics themselves recognized. "We condemn only the *abuse* of these accomplishments," stipulated Edgeworth, while More made a clear distinction between the intellectual benefits of musical training and the pitfalls of performance: "the watchful mother must have the talents of her daughter cultivated, not exhibited."[38] The fact that Mrs. Elton claims to be "passionately fond" of music but refuses to play (as does that other recent bride Lady Middleton) is a more telling character indictment than Marianne Dashwood's self-indulgence at the piano or Jane Fairfax's irritating perfection (248). For Austen failure to meet the minimum terms of accomplishment is worse than their abuse. The sterner critics of accomplishment such as More trivialized music, but their stridency only confirms the magnitude of the cultural revolution taking place. With the new movement in serious music in the 1810s, embodied in Beethoven, began the gradual rehabilitation of domestic music-making from the battering it had received at the hands of the education reformers of the 1790s. In Austen's novels the entry of her heroines into the "world" mirrored the admission of young Regency males into the professional ranks. The new Viennese repertoire Austen and her heroines played, and the discourse of self-expression that surrounded it, was likewise a central means by which, as the century of the piano progressed, British women of the middle class participated in the broader professionalization of culture and "could step forth as an object of knowledge."[39]

II

In place of an inner life Jane Fairfax offers only a collection of alienated epithets. She is the "really accomplished young woman" – an ideal Elizabeth Bennet protests never to have met with – whose superior performance at the piano inspires Emma to practice for an hour and a half (a unit of time no serious musician would use to quantify her practice). But she is also a woman of "such coldness and reserve" that Emma, for all her good intentions, cannot properly befriend her. Nor is the reader, on first reading, given much latitude to disagree that "her composure was odious" (148, 236). Virtuosity is pure exteriority, while Austen's novels are grounded in the virtues of interiority. That said, the tension between Jane and Emma is as much founded on their uncanny similarities – same age, same gentility, same accomplishments – as on their differences. As Knightley observes, Emma sees in Jane Fairfax a feminine ideal she herself fails to meet. The two women are different expressions upon the same principle.

In the terms provided by the anti-accomplishment discourse of the 1790s, a direct correlation exists between Jane's virtuosity at the piano and her "unbecoming indifference," her apparent lack of feeling (236). In a fictional dialogue in Edgeworth's *Practical Education* that evokes the Jaquet-Droz *Musicienne*, the author asks a lady of fashion, anxious for the proper education of her daughter,

> would not you ... consent to have your daughter turned into an automaton for eight hours in every day for fifteen years, for the promise of hearing her, at the end of that time, pronounced the first private performer at the most fashionable, and most crowded concert in London?[40]

The lady demurs. Charles Dibdin gives a practical insight into what the acquisition of a serviceably fashionable piano technique for young women involved:

> An eternal repetition of four semiquavers, or three quavers, with the left hand, by way of an accompaniment to an insipid succession of notes with the right—and these modulated into a variety of extraneous keys, so dissonant and irrelative ... make up now the whole of their studies.

Truly "superior" performance at the piano, it was feared, required a too slavish application to digital motor skills, to "a mechanical exertion, tasteless and insipid in its effects."[41] Edgeworth worried about young women becoming "mere machines" through excessive attention to practice, while James Fordyce, who actually defended music education against what he acknowledged as the "prevailing opinion," expressed a consensus concern about the "vast expense of time" by which women "lose the labour of years, that might have been directed with lasting benefits into some other channel."[42] To some, femininity itself appeared to be at stake, in the sense of how women's bodily movements appeared at the piano. "To be graceful," Burke had declared, "it is requisite that there be no appearance of difficulty."[43] If grace inspired admiration, virtuosity threatened the opposite: the empty "wonder" of mechanism, the de-feminization of women, and the cultural obsolescence of beauty itself. In Burney's *Camilla* (1796), the doll-like Indiana Lynmere is, like Edgeworth's fictional pianist, called an "automaton," shorthand both for superficial beauty and a criminal deficiency in self-reflection.[44] In *Emma* the culprit is not vanity but too much practice. The demands of accomplishment have turned Jane Fairfax into a Jaquet-Droz robot: "Oh! The coldness of a Jane Fairfax!" (242). Jane embodies the uneasy slip, the subtle moral deterioration from accomplishment to virtuosity. In her scandalous secret we trace a narrative allegory of the female pianist's always incipient "fall" from sentimental being into automatism.

The relation between time, mechanization, and the larger enterprise of nineteenth-century industrialization is clearly evident in the music culture of the 1810s, and bears upon the anti-virtuosic ideology of *Emma*. Johann Mälzel, inventor and charlatan, patented the metronome the year that *Emma* appeared, and Beethoven was among the first composers to indicate metronome markings in his published music. A more spectacular, though less enduring, musical-industrial development in the mid-1810s was Johann Logier's so-called "chiroplast," an elaborate wood-metal contraption, reminiscent of the stocks, which held the student pianist's hands in proper relation to the keyboard (though it enabled no lateral movement). Amazingly, the invention, which Celia Applegate has called "one of the biggest frauds to sweep across musical Europe" in the nineteenth century, received the endorsement of both Johann Baptist Cramer – the composer mentioned in *Emma* – and his famous teacher, Muzio Clementi.[45] The chiroplast itself could not have made Logier's fortune without his creative extension of a mechanized digital technique to the booming business of teaching piano. According to Logier's "system," the discipline of the chiroplast, supplemented by mass-produced textbooks, would enable music professors to teach whole groups of students at once, playing in unison. The older students could assist the beginners, as in the Lancaster method, and instead of the long-standing practice of informal one-to-one lessons, academies of piano instruction could be established to maximize profits. Michel Foucault has located the emergent ideal of bourgeois discipline, with its emphasis on the mechanization of the body, in the Prussian military culture of the late eighteenth century.[46] Bodily discipline, as a new phenomenon of *domestic* culture, is crudely evident in the Logierian system, which made rapid progress in provincial England and was successfully exported to the continent. By 1816, dozens of Logier academies had been established in towns like the fictional Highbury across England and the empire. If Logier is to be believed, sales of his instruction manuals were in the tens of thousands in Great Britain alone.[47]

In 1817 a backlash formed, led by the professional avatars of serious music at the new Philharmonic Society of London. Their motives were twofold: an aesthetic mistrust of mechanization and its corollary, virtuosity, and a more prosaic concern for their own livelihoods.[48] They worked diligently in the press to expose the expanding Logier industry as "open quackery," as "a false and ridiculous system of Musical Education."[49] In doing so, the Philharmonic Society was acting as a body of self-described "professional men" vested with disciplinary power to define codes of conduct and de-certify imposters.[50] Again, the bogey-image of the automaton was invoked. "Many a parent," warned one professor, "when their little darlings will exhibit … will find that they have got little better than a species of musical automaton, possessed of no more feeling or sensibility than the instrument upon which it performs."[51] The Logier system integrated the machinery of the piano with the performing body, a bold stroke that could not but meet with the full sentimental force of virtuosophobia, since it expressed so literally the underlying logic of that critique. The Philharmonic Society's campaign mostly discredited Logier, who left England for Prussia, where his system received the endorsement of the state and generous funding.

The Logierian system, designed principally for women amateurs, represented a difference in degree, not kind, from the rapidly expanding mainstream of music education in the early nineteenth century. Mary Bennet studies the thoroughbass – it might be Logier's own well-known manual on the subject – and no doubt would have owned one or more of the primers in piano technique that flooded the market after 1800, led by Clementi's best-selling *Introduction to the Art of Playing on the Piano Forte* (1801).[52] Clementi, a celebrated virtuoso who renounced the concert platform in order to build a musical empire embracing all aspects of the industry, from piano manufacture to publishing to pedagogy, was intent upon building a permanently expanding market for music beginning with texts for children.[53] After Clementi, no rising musical pedagogue could be without his own instructional textbook combining theories of fingering, harmony, and the proper practice regimen with practical musical examples.⁵⁴ Austen herself owned his student J. B. Cramer's *Instructions for the Piano Forte* (1813) on which he built his reputation as "one of the first teachers in Europe." His professional prestige was commodified, like a modern celebrity author, into a publishable "how-to" format and sold by the thousands worldwide.⁵⁵

By the 1810s the domestication of virtuosity, as the critics of the 1790s had feared, was complete. With the great proliferation of instruments and performers, and the professionalization of pedagogy, skill levels rose dramatically. The social effects of this are felt at Mrs. John Dashwood's "small musical party" in *Sense and Sensibility*, where "the performers themselves were, as usual, in their own estimation, and that of their immediate friends, the first private performers in England" (218). The competitive tension evoked here concerns the ambiguous place of musical performance and criticism between the domestic sphere of "immediate friends" and the greater public approbation of "England," which the unnamed performers bravely claim. With public concerts in decline during the Napoleonic Wars, genteel music culture continued under the semi-private auspices of society hostesses, where professionals and highly skilled amateurs increasingly crossed paths. Emma's anxiety over Jane Fairfax's "superior playing" belongs to this historical moment of music's incipient professionalization, when amateur musicians of the old order "tended more and more to become listeners."⁵⁶

Reading Jane Fairfax's pianistic accomplishment in this light – where Logier represents only an extreme example of a newly industrialized music culture – her training appears closer to Foucault's description of the modern technologized self than to a Regency governess. The bodily discipline represented by pianistic accomplishment, and its temporally exacting ratio of practice to performance, points to a proto-professional, disciplinary understanding of time, to "the principle of a theoretically ever-growing use of time: exhaustion rather than use; it is a question of extracting, from time, ever more available moments and, from each moment, ever more useful forces."⁵⁷ As a proleptic image of the new female professional, Jane Fairfax is the most modern character in all Austen, until the end when she lapses into a more archaic pose: like that other ill-starred Austen pianist before her, Marianne Dashwood, she wanders the meadows alone and wills herself ill. The consummation of this reverse is achieved in the theatrical disclosure of her secret engagement: her inner life, rather than non-existent, turns out to be the hidden mechanism of the plot itself, with an unwritten richness Emma can only meditate on in wonder. The virtuoso foil of *Emma* turns belated heroine in a tale of virtue besieged.

Only in our second reading of the novel, when we know in advance of Jane's engagement, do we pay attention to signs of her psychological complexity, the most unequivocal of which is a series of musical clues, heretofore unremarked, that contradict her reputation for soulless virtuosity. In their discussion of the recent dinner party at the Coles', Harriet and Emma touch upon the exhibitions of Emma and Jane at the piano. The narrator specifies that they were the only two performers, and Harriet's relation of the event situates the episode firmly within the historical opposition of virtue and virtuosity, here called "taste" and "execution." Says Harriet: "Mr. Cole said how much taste you had; and Mr. Frank Churchill talked a great deal about your taste, and that he valued taste much more than execution" (208). The discursive imperative to place musical virtue and virtuosity in opposition, and to embody them in a "contest" between two representative performers, represents a foundational trope of music mythology and criticism across the centuries, from Apollo and Marsyas to Rubinstein and Horowitz. In Austen's lifetime, the most famous piano "duel" took place between Mozart and Clementi at the palace of Emperor Joseph II in Vienna in 1781, "won," of course, by Mozart, who derided Clementi as "a mere *mechanicus*."[58] Any number of similar examples could be cited, including a German newspaper account of Beethoven in 1791, which elevated his "weight of idea" and "expression" over the "astonishing execution" of his rival Vogler.[59] According to the impromptu court of musical opinion at the Coles' party, an opinion crafted by Frank Churchill, Emma plays Mozart/Beethoven to Jane Fairfax's Clementi/Vogler.[60] In Fordyce's terms, Jane's "execution" is inseparable from "affectation."[61] Emma's lack of technical proficiency at the piano, like Elizabeth's in *Pride and Prejudice*, is actually a virtue, a testimony of taste and time better spent (as Darcy says), while Jane's virtuosity is necessarily at the expense of taste, because in acquiring her pianistic technique she has mechanized herself beyond the reach of natural feeling. Mary Wollstonecraft declared, as an almost theological truism, her preference for "expression to execution," and that "a person must have sense, taste, and sensibility, to render their music interesting. The nimble dance of the fingers may raise wonder, but not delight."[62] The sheer number and formulaic repetitiveness of such comments suggest that the opposition between virtue and virtuosity served less as an actual description of the world than a kind of discursive compulsion, a rhetorical twitch that disfigured aesthetic discourse throughout the eighteenth century and beyond. It was a definitive Georgian formulation beyond Wollstonecraft's, Highbury's, or Austen's powers to resist: Jane's superior pianism is discursively inseparable from a moral deficiency, from her "disgusting ... reserve" (150). Such is the Highbury opinion, at least, but Emma, to her great credit, will not allow it to stand. When Harriet attempts to commend her taste above Jane's execution, Emma replies, "Ah! But Jane Fairfax has them both." The correctness of this judgment is born out by Jane's redemption at the conclusion of the book: she is heartstricken, not heartless. With the help of a musical-historical lens, however, we need not simply take Emma's word but can extrapolate her aesthetic judgment (as she does not) into more generous expectations of Jane Fairfax's character.

At the very middle point of the novel Jane receives the mysterious gift of the Broadwood piano. In the history of the piano industry, Broadwood was the first industrial giant, selling pianos at eight times the volume of the largest Viennese company, "and participating fully in the gradual change that saw the efforts of individual craftsmen replaced by the specialized labor and high production of a factory."[63] In the brief period in which Austen published her novels, the Broadwood company almost doubled in value to about £140,000 and was one of the largest consumers of wood in London. The "large square" piano Frank buys for Jane was the Broadwood staple. While the quality of Viennese pianos was patchy, and individual pianos themselves uneven in tone, Broadwood focussed its design innovations on creating homogeneity and "depth" of tone, and broadening the piano's expressive capability: "what they desired above all was the richest possible aural presence."[64] The symbolic exchange integral to bourgeois commodity value – where a standardized, mass-produced item bears the utopian promise of individual expression – is embodied both in the Broadwood piano and in Beethoven, Broadwood's most famous client. That is, the mythology surrounding the Beethoven Broadwood is inseparable from his supposed artistic "choice" to reject the brilliant *galant* tone of his Viennese Streicher pianos, with their shallow keys designed for virtuosic runs, for the sluggish but more expressive Broadwood. Tia DeNora has argued that Beethoven did not respond to new technology; rather, the new Beethovenian values of depth and expressiveness drove piano engineering toward acceptance of Broadwood as the international standard.[65] In *Emma*, Jane Fairfax's association, through Broadwood, with Beethoven, immediately casts doubt on her role as the heroine's nemesis of accomplishment and as the virtuosic bogey of the text in general. Indeed, Beethoven's Broadwood, on which he redefined technical difficulty as a quality of artistic seriousness, points toward a final supersession of the eighteenth-century opposition of virtue and virtuosity.

Beethoven's Broadwood exemplifies the true modernity of the piano, which traversed national boundaries and colonial spaces alike, speaking a new global language of capital, luxury consumption, and continental bourgeois music literature. But wrong notes abound in the history of Beethoven's Broadwood as in the pianos of Austen's novels. Beethoven increasingly cannot hear his; Marianne Dashwood cannot face hers after her break-up with Willoughby; for Mary Bennet and Georgiana Darcy, pianism mingles with self-loathing; while Jane Fairfax's Broadwood does not speak a common language at all, but carries with it the lovers' secret that is the guilty heart of *Emma*'s plot. The piano, a signature bourgeois commodity promising accessibility, affordability, and self-expression is, in Austen, also a frequent site of frustration, failure, and the illicit emotions deriving from a painful secret or memory. Reminiscent of Beethoven's exported Broadwood, the conspicuous mobility of Austen's pianos – shipped from London to Highbury and Pemberley, from Norland Park "by water" to Devonshire, etc. – signifies the social displacement of characters, the dubious operations of conspicuous consumption, and a class system in flux.

In standard music histories the Broadwood piano is associated with Beethoven's so-called "late style" music – some of the most dense, enigmatic repertoire in the European canon. Almost a century after Austen created Jane Fairfax, E. M. Forster's Lucy Honeychurch, in *A Room with a View* (1908), plays Beethoven's "late style" Opus 111 sonata not as an expression of accomplishment or marriageability, but of the unimpeachable seriousness and potential of her free self: "If Miss Honeychurch ever takes to live as she plays, it will be very exciting – both for us and for her."[66] Beethoven received his Broadwood the year he devoted almost exclusively to the composition of the monumental *Hammerklavier* sonata; the following year he chose it as the vehicle for his Diabelli Variations. The latter exemplifies Beethoven's late style, which abstracted the Viennese tradition of the late eighteenth century into the syntactic units of musical convention, mixing archaic elements with an avant-garde sensibility. The Variations dissect a banal waltz into its minutest elements – entire variations are constructed on a single interval or ornament in the original text – and include allusions to Bach, Cramer, Handel, and Beethoven himself. Like the *Hammerklavier* sonata, they offer an ironic critique of the language of drawing-room music and, by extension, of amateur accomplishment itself. The variations mark a historical rupture between the amateur pianism of the salon and the professional concert repertoire of the future, but in the form of a parodic homage to the pre-Napoleonic era.[67]

Irony, in Austen and late Beethoven, is thus directed toward essentially the same historical object: the parlor-room culture of the 1790s. Just as Beethoven's Diabelli Variations deconstructed the salon music of that decade, Austen's novels revisit the fashionable discourses of her youth: the gothic, the picturesque, anti-Jacobinism, the conduct book, the reform of the aristocracy, the debate on accomplishment, etc.[68] In terms of literary language, Austen likewise manufactures a middle Georgian idiom – her own "late style" – for the purpose of educating the reader in the powerful conventions of the new middle-class politeness, with its subtexts of self-interest, materialism, and ignorance, the implicit suggestion being that we resist our own uncritical incorporation within that discursive regime. The construction of Jane Fairfax's "reserve" in *Emma* as an item of received wisdom is a subtle example of how the conventions of polite talk – in this case anti-virtuosic critique – shape perceptions with such fluid immediacy that only an authorial intervention has the power to expose the "truth."

If middle-period Beethoven – the "heroic" Romantic of the symphonies – is synonymous with a new humanistic discourse of music, his "late style" is the opposite: a highly technical, even abstract revision of the Viennese music of his formative years. Until her Romantic recuperation, Jane Fairfax *is* late style in *Emma*, a disintegrating parlor-room subject who offers, like Beethoven's late "Broadwood" piano music, only the "rigid, inexpressive face of convention:"[69]

The like reserve prevailed on other topics. She and Mr. Frank Churchill had been at Weymouth at the same time. It was known that they were a little acquainted, but not a syllable of real information could Emma procure as to what he truly was. "Was he handsome?"—"She believed he was reckoned a very fine young man." "Was he agreeable?"—"He was generally thought so." "Did he appear a sensible young man; a young man of information?"—"At a watering-place, or in a common London acquaintance, it was difficult to decide on such points . . . " (151)

As "late style" ironizes fashionable music, so Jane embodies forms of politeness disengaged from the social contexts that originally guaranteed their meaning. She is "indiffer[ent] whether she pleased or not," a phantasmic character whose unsociable "reserve" precedes her as a form of negation, an empty subject into which Emma pours her own inchoate and objectless anxieties. Jane's robotic conversation, through its sheer, affectless banality, threatens to expose the rhetoricity of Emma's own talk, the discursive limits of her much-valued "openness." No wonder "Emma could not forgive her."

Jane's Broadwood is accompanied by the music of J. B. Cramer, a musical synonym for Beethoven's historical reconciliation of virtue and virtuosity. Cramer's relationship with the Broadwood company anticipated the terms of modern commercial endorsement. His published scores, along with other composers of the London school such as Clementi and Dussek, "were closely linked with the robust sound and greater resonance of English instruments," and the latter two virtuosi made European tours performing upon and promoting the Broadwood brand.[70] Cramer's name likewise doubles Beethoven's through a series of historical associations.[71] "Glorious John," as he was known to his English admirers, introduced Beethoven's sonatas to the cognoscenti in private settings in London through the 1810s.[72] At Beethoven's death editions of Cramer's famous *84 Études* were found in his library of scores, one of them annotated in detail for the use of Beethoven's nephew Karl.[73] The influence of Cramer's *Études* is audible in several of the Beethoven sonatas.[74] Beethoven, furthermore, who knew Cramer personally, had immense respect for his virtuosity, reportedly preferring his playing to all others.[75] Austen does not give us the title of the Cramer work, but given Jane Fairfax's advanced technique, and their fame, the *84 Études* are the most likely candidate for Frank's gift. That Frank then pretends not to have heard of Cramer is proof that virtuosity, of character as of music, will always deny its own name.

Like Broadwood and Beethoven, Cramer's name points toward a new model of musical seriousness that synthesized musical virtue and virtuosity according to the imperative of bourgeois professionalism, which required both advanced technical specialization and an ethos of subjective expression and individual depth. The either/or rhetoric of the eighteenth-century piano duel, pitting taste against execution, was replaced, in a figure such as Cramer, with a new synthesizing logic. Chopin mandated study of Cramer's *Études* for his students, while Victorian editions of *Grove's Dictionary* commended the *84 Études* for their "balance between artistic and didactic values," as an "intimate combination of significant musical ideas with the most instructive mechanical passages."[76] The specific form of this critical endorsement endured into the twentieth century, where the *Grove* entry on Cramer quotes Robert Schumann calling the *84 etudes* ideal training for "head and hand." Indeed, at its very first appearance in 1809, reviewers remarked on the uniquely satisfying synthesis of the Cramer *Études*: "The *Etudes* are of highly intrinsic value and merit due to their musical inventiveness and taste, *and* by virtue of their formal execution and design – spiritual, intellectual, and mechanical."[77] The conjunctive grammar of these reviews directly addresses the eighteenth-century opposition between virtue and virtuosity with a view to declaring its redundancy in the new age.

Playing Cramer's *Études* on a Broadwood piano, therefore, Jane Fairfax should not be mistaken for a musical automaton. That said, the residents of Highbury, in codifying her by these terms, are not "wrong." Jane, alone among the women of Austen's fiction, faces a life of work rather than marriage. The text limits her vocational prospects to governess, but the subtext expands them in the direction of the modern female professional, of Jane Fairfax as working concert pianist. Austen's novels belong to a period when a third of public piano concerts in London were given by women, at which Cramer "featured prominently amongst the music they performed."[78] Among other things, virtuosophobia expressed anxiety over the professionalization of culture, of which Jane Fairfax is the "odious" female proto-image. Jane as soulless paragon, as working Jaquet-Droz doll, is the abjected other the Romantic heroine Emma creates both to assure herself of her own uniqueness and to certify her leisured status. According to the internal logic of *Emma* – on its *first* reading – one may have the rich inner life of a genteel woman *or* to be merely accomplished. On second reading, these choices for Austen's women appear more as a form of exchange: Jane and Emma are transformed from opposites into *doppelgängers*, a composite figure of the new bourgeois woman of the professional class for whom the promised riches of an autonomous inner life served as reward for her disciplined relation to time and skill acquisition, otherwise called "accomplishment."[79]

III

The hidden figure of Beethoven in *Emma* opens up the musical-cultural revolution of the 1810s that witnessed the introduction of his middle-period music – the nine symphonies and best-known sonatas – as the representative repertoire of an emerging constituency for "serious" new instrumental music in London. The formation of the London Philharmonic Society in 1813 marks a decisive episode in the importation of aristocratic, avant-garde Viennese music – Haydn, Mozart, Beethoven – to serve as the aesthetic imprimatur of music's professionalization, and as the substance of the new broadly middle-class canon.[80] After the "rage for music" of the 1780s, which reached a euphoric high-point in the early 1790s with the tours of Haydn, the number of public concerts in London had declined significantly. The Philharmonic Society addressed itself specifically to this problem in its charter, but its unwritten motives were more important: to offer a bulwark against a perceived decline in serious domestic music (the sonata, for example), and against the mass proliferation of new musical genres, such as the Irish and Scottish melodies Mary Bennet, Caroline Bingley, and Jane Fairfax play, the innumerable sets of variations on popular airs, and programmatic *tours de force* like the ubiquitous "Battle of Prague."[81] The Philharmonic's focus on symphonic music, and initial banning of both vocal and concerto music, was a direct challenge to the virtuosic principle of the miscellany that had governed concert programming for a century past.[82] In institutional terms, the orchestral concert set itself against the King's Theatre opera as the new forum of enlightened and progressive musical taste. The goal of the Society was the reformation of polite culture through the promotion of a body of canonical works whose seriousness resided as much in the aura of the "work" as in the performance (see chapter 4). With the founding of the Philharmonic Society, the prestige of music itself began to usurp the prestige attached to its patrons.[83] The introduction of the new Viennese canon also began what Jim Samson has called the historical "marginalization" of virtuosity, displaced by "a view of the musical work that coalesced historically and analytically around Beethoven's heroic style."[84]

We have already seen with their intervention in the Logier controversy an example of the professional mandate the Philharmonic Society assumed. As "probably the world's oldest concert organization founded and maintained upon professional initiative," the Philharmonic Society's symbolic importance to the bourgeois cultural revolution of nineteenth-century Britain can hardly be overstated.[85] Its desire to separate itself from the forms of eighteenth-century opera culture and its system of aristocratic patronage was reflected in its directors – prominent musical professionals such as Cramer, Clementi, Kalkenbrenner, Viotti, and the critic and manager William Ayrton; in its governance on democratic, professional lines; and in its concert repertoire, which championed the symphony over vocal music and the virtuoso concerto. The symphony, in particular, "in which no individual or section is singled out for very long, was the perfect embodiment of the egalitarian political ideal ... [of] professional autonomy and democratic process."[86] The members of the Society elected their own directors, shared the responsibilities of administration, and took turns leading their concerts: "There shall not be any distinction of rank in the orchestra."[87] This egalitarian flavor extended to women who, soon after the Society's founding, were admitted as "female professors" and later as orchestral players. The old distinction at the opera house between the "professors" and the fashionable audience was superseded at the Philharmonic concerts by a new category, the connoisseur, who crossed traditional class and gender lines: "The audience at the Philharmonic are neither 'the great vulgar nor the small' – they are the cognoscenti."[88] In the eighteenth century, "even the public concert still formed part of patronal culture," but with the introduction of disciplinary reforms characteristic of the new bourgeois regime at large – including the regulation of ticket sales, enforcement of punctual attendance at rehearsal, and mandated silence during the performances – the Philharmonic Society made a decisive break from aristocratic control while continuing to solicit support from valuable titled patrons.[89] The social politics of the Society's formation, whereby a new professional middle-class institution formed an alliance with aristocratic power, thus reads much like Austen's *Pride and Prejudice*, published the same year, which tells the story of mutual concessions between a representative aristocrat and a middle-class heroine, and heralds their sharing of cultural leadership into a revolution-free future.

Silent listening, in particular, was a crucial regulatory item in the new musical regime. It introduced the defining bourgeois ethos of politeness to a music culture hitherto guided by the more sociable, performative audience protocols of the nobility, and was analogous to the regime of silence beginning to be instituted in the public libraries opening all over Britain.[90] Austen herself marks this historical moment in "the sacralization of secular musical life" in Marianne's performance at Barton House, where only Colonel Brandon pays her "the compliment of attention," while everyone else chats away (30).[91] Serious listening, in Brandon's case, is a code for Romantic depth, and for the new standards of middle-class politeness to which the old-style Tory Middletons are oblivious. For the audience at a Philharmonic Society concert, their silence advertised a collective subscription to a new ideal of aestheticized selfhood, insulated by politeness, which served as symbolic compensation for the highly regulated disciplines of their professional lives, in turn embodied in the Society's structure and codes. This exchange may be generalized as a defining aspect of Romantic cultural production. To cite just one example, Andrew Elfenbein locates Byron's marketplace success in his radical subjectivization of style, "whereby the book trade responded to the mass market's anonymity by offering readers a simulacrum of intimacy."[92] Silent listening likewise represents an exemplary exchange of the new bourgeois culture: virtuosic performance, and the accompanying chatter of the audience, were disclaimed in favor of a new social code of restraint that embraced both performer and audience, leavened with the Romantic rewards of the rich inner life produced by absorbed listening. "The goal of the concert," as David Gramit puts it, "was nothing less than to cultivate the audience to the point of full humanity."[93] It is a reward structure analogous to the conclusion of *Emma*, where the consummate new professional man, Knightley, embraces bourgeois domestication in return for the symbolic dowry of an inner life embodied in the heroine.

The Philharmonic Society championed Beethoven's music ahead of all other living composers and took upon itself the heretofore aristocratic responsibility of commissioning works, including the Ninth Symphony. Beethoven, the Society recognized, "freed music from the fetters of fashion," and his borrowed prestige elevated their own status from indentured professionals to connoisseurs and custodians of a new bourgeois avant-garde in music.[94] In the conventional terms of music history, "Beethoven virtually in one fell swoop, claimed for music the strong concept of art ... to stand on a par with literature and the visual arts."[95] In melopoetical terms, Beethoven's appeal was irresistible. Adorno has identified the connection between Beethoven's music and a heroic form of bourgeois interiority in his radical expansion of the possibilities of sonata form, which functioned, he argues, as a musical transcription of this new middle-class social contract. The listener's experience of dramatic subjectivity and "freedom" in development of the melodic subject discovers, in the recapitulation of that subject, its natural destiny within a collective, organic whole.[96] Beethoven's symphonies – the consummation of his middle-period, "heroic" style, and a staple of Philharmonic Society programming in the 1810s – enacted *Bildung*, the "musical analogue of the free individual," a uniquely convincing aestheticization of freedom and subjectivity as they were imagined in the tumultuous European scene around 1800.[97] In sonata form, difference was realized, blissfully elaborated, then assimilated within a larger structure of repetition.

First associated with the Viennese composers of the 1780s, including Mozart and Haydn, sonata form marked the historical moment in European art music where "structure replaced ornamentation as the principal vehicle of expression."[98] For "ornamentation" read "virtuosity." Repudiating the *da capo* structure as a vehicle of virtuosic display, music in sonata form, as modernized by Beethoven, integrated the idea of repetition within a greater theory of organic form. Lawrence Kramer has called the technique "expressive doubling," for instance, in the modified *da capo* structure of the third movement of the Fifth Symphony in which thematic material emphatically presented earlier in the movement by the horns returns in a much softer register, "like a musical image for a haunting memory ... the musical equivalent of the past."[99] The organization of musical materials maps the organization of mental life, in this case, memory. Beethovenian form appeared not to rely on abstract principles – as in the case of an operatic aria or a baroque fugue – and yet was nevertheless comprehensible. As such, it seemed to imply the existence of an engaged, rational listener, and to enact a drama of "psychological development."

Records of impressions of the first performances of Beethoven's symphonic music at the Philharmonic Society are scant. To fully understand the appeal of Beethoven's innovations in sonata form to a self-constituted group of middle-class professional musicians in London in the 1810s, one looks to Germany, where the most advanced school music curriculum in Europe produced a "mature market ... for serious music journalism among professional readers" a full generation before Britain.[100] As Austen sat down to write *Emma*, the young Schopenhauer recognized the power of modern symphonic music to represent for the listener "all the possible events of life and of the world passing by within himself."[101] A few years later, in his lectures on aesthetics, Hegel would define music as uniquely capable among the arts of expressing "the object-free inner life, abstract subjectivity as such."[102] Outside of the academy, in the musical press, Beethoven's reception followed the same terms. As the editor of the *Berliner Allgemeine Musikalische Zeitung*, Adolph Marx, described the effect of the *Eroica* Symphony: "it poeticizes the feeling of a specific moment in [the listener's] existence that he is just now living or has lived."[103] This same sentiment is expressed again and again, with striking uniformity, through a century of Beethoven commentary: "the whole of Beethoven reception can be read as if it were 'one book written by one author,' the prevailing theme of which is the 'human element' in Beethoven's music."[104] The content of Beethoven's music was, in some essential way, the human itself, a musical enactment of *Bildung*, of the subject emerging into self-consciousness. Beethoven's music constructed the listener as an organic, "authentic" subject.

Beethoven's heroic style, in the contemporary language of German idealism, represented cognition without object. The mind encountered itself in the temporal act of making sense of the music, and anticipating the next musical event. In Charles Rosen's words,

> Beethoven was the greatest master of musical time. In no other composer is the relation between intensity and duration so keenly observed ... the power that can be drawn from repetition, the tension that can arise from delay.[105]

A characteristic Viennese technique adapted by Beethoven was to create continuity through the overlapping of musical phrases that act, at their cadential hinge, as both the resolution of the prior idea and the introduction of fresh material: each musical moment thus refers to both to past and future, giving the listener a palpable sense of forward motion. The structure is processual, Hegelian.[106] The focus of post-Kantian German philosophy on themes of change and temporality thus found its musical analogue in Beethoven who made the experience of time – musical events in ebb and flow – the signature of his compositional style.[107] The form of the music did not determine its temporality, but rather seemed to assume the temporal shape of cognition itself, what E. T. A. Hoffmann psychologized as "inexpressible longing."[108] As Hegel described the effect of organic development in sonata form, "the self is in time, and time is the being of the subject himself."[109] What Adorno called "the illusion of pent-up time" in Beethoven – as in the first movement of the *Eroica* Symphony or the Arietta of Op. 111 – granted the listener an experience of possibility and power that functioned, symbolically, as a reward for his submission to the demands of disciplinary, segmented, and ever-diminishing time under the new bourgeois order (119). Beethoven, according to this reading, spoke the language of modern liberalism to its principal beneficiaries, the professional bourgeoisie, as the emergent ruling class of Europe. As an education in middle-class self-awareness, and its heroic destiny, listening to a Beethoven symphony would become as instructive as reading Kant's *Critique of Pure Reason* (1791) or Mill's *On Liberty* (1859).[110]

Or, for that matter, Jane Austen. In the 1790s, when Austen's piano technique and tastes were established, pieces in sonata form "were very popular among the increasing numbers of middle-class amateur musicians in cities like Vienna, Leipzig, Paris and London." By one calculation, some two thousand pieces with at least one movement in sonata form were published in her piano-playing lifetime.[111] Both Austen's "psychological" fiction and Viennese sonata form are thus rooted in the 1790s, when serious interest in sonata form as a critical category emerged.[112] With the appearance of the modern German music periodicals in the early 1800s, and the influential critics Hoffmann and Marx, sonata form, as a language of musical interiority, claimed more general currency. Austen's position as a music consumer in the new cosmopolitan marketplace, which was marked by a new discourse of Romantic interiority surrounding sonata form, mirrors her literary moment where, through innovations in free indirect discourse, she constructed her heroines as organic, interiorized subjects, and made their psychological development the dramatic content of her fiction. "Development," or *Bildung*, is thus the principal structure of both sonata form and modern free indirect discourse as conceived by Austen. The materials of both are dialectical, that is, each is built on the processual interplay of contrasting materials – call them "subjective" and "objective" – that powerfully suggest the organic self-creation of the work rather than its formal construction.

The opening of *Emma*, for example, is remarkable for its introduction of a consciousness in place of plot, and for its radical subjectivization of time. The family governess has married, a reception has taken place at Hartfield and, with her father nodding off to sleep, the heroine is left in the company of her thoughts:

The event had every promise of happiness for her friend. Mr. Weston was a man of unexceptionable character, easy fortune, suitable age and pleasant manners; and there was some satisfaction in considering with what self-denying, generous friendship she had always wished and promoted the match; but it was a black morning's work for her. (4)

Thus the subtle work of free indirect discourse in *Emma* begins, with its occasional marking of mental agency ("considering"), interwoven with unmarked shifts between the stale language of conventional wisdom ("Mr. Weston was a man of unexceptionable character"), Emma's personal rationalizations ("self-denying, generous friendship"), and judgments we must attribute to the diffuse presence of the narrator, such as when Mr. Woodhouse is described on the next page as "a valetudinarian all his life, without activity of mind or body." The effect is not a settled integration of subjective and objective viewpoints, but a constant, sometimes imperceptible dialectic. When the valetudinarian awakes, two paragraphs later, the reader does not stop to consider how long he has napped, or to judge the relation of nearly two pages of Emma's thoughts to the lapse of real time. Time is instead subjectivized, embedded in the created consciousness of the heroine. Austen then grants Emma the quasi-authorial power to ventriloquize her father's thoughts. Free indirect discourse here describes Emma's own representation of her father's mental life to herself:

Matrimony, as the origin of change, was always disagreeable; and he was by no means yet reconciled to his own daughter's marrying, nor could ever speak of her but with compassion, though it had been entirely a match of affection, when he was now obliged to part with Miss Taylor too; and from his habits of gentle selfishness, and of being never able to suppose that other people could feel differently from himself, he was very much disposed to think Miss Taylor had done as sad a thing for herself as for them, and would have been a great deal happier if she had spent all the rest of her life at Hartfield. Emma smiled and chatted as cheerfully as she could, to keep him from such thoughts; but when tea came, it was impossible for him not to say exactly as he had said at dinner, "Poor Miss Taylor!" (5–6)

Emma's smiling and chatting with her father occurs simultaneously with these interior projections of his thoughts. Her untranscribed "chat" serves as a real-time context for the proper narrative business, namely the construction of interiority, the powers of which include imagining the thoughts of others. The authenticity of Emma's inner life depends on free indirect discourse not simply as a repository of thoughts but as a vehicle of temporality, of the subjectivization of time against which real-world events – dozing, waking, chatting – appear as abstract, metronomic points of reference, as part of the realness effect. Like Beethoven's middle-period style, which opened up "a perspective simultaneously subjective and objective" on its musical materials through the temporalization of form, Emma's character is simultaneously narrated and enacted, and the impression of her subjectivity is a function of time."[113]

Much has been made of Austen's skeptical rendering of Emma's inner life. As Marilyn Butler has argued, the novel, on its larger thematic canvas, erodes our trust in imagination, intuition, desire, and many other cherished aspects of Romantic sensibility.[114] But whatever the epistemological skepticism of the novel, its ontological foundation in Emma's inner life, established in the opening pages, is never in doubt. The celebrated realism of Austen's technique, first observed by Walter Scott, lies not in her choice of subject matter, or in her deliberate plainness of diction but, like Beethoven's innovations in sonata form, in her radical temporalization of self through the expanded use of free indirect discourse.[115] The reader experiences the character of Emma not narratively but phenomenally, as a "self in time," a temporal rather than rhetorical effect, which is why Austen is so difficult to catch in the act of greatness. This phenomenon of reading produces a "truth" in Emma that is untouched by any ironic depiction of her fallibility. Austen's skepticism toward the operations of private thought only masks more effectively the extraordinary naturalization of bourgeois subjectivity and psychological development that occurs in the text.[116]

"Development," in fact, is an inadequate description for this technique, just as it is for Beethoven's treatment of sonata form structure. Development implies an original thematic statement that is then elaborated, whereas, for example, the theme of the *Eroica* Symphony's first movement is never given but rather "is entirely absorbed into the process for which it provides the substance."[117] In middle-period Beethoven, thematicism itself is ironized. Analogously, the authorial exposition of the Romantic "subject" at the beginning of *Emma* lasts only four short paragraphs. The narrator points to dangers for Emma that are "unperceived" by her, then abdicates her omniscient authority for good (4). Thereafter, Austen relies on a formal technology of self, a processual language combining subjective and objective viewpoints that situates the "character," Emma, in unfolding time. The realness effect – the overwhelming sense of authentic subjectivity in both Austen and Beethoven – derives from this technique. The new Romantic art-subject of the 1810s – be it "Emma" or the theme of the *Eroica* – is not made to stand out against a background or "form," but is the very texture and material of the medium itself. And the effect, as generations of readers and listeners have attested, is distinctly "natural."[118]

The hidden figure of Beethoven in the text of *Emma* suggests what the work of the novel will be: to show, as sonata form does, the material limits of individual freedom by naturalizing its integration within larger discursive, social structures. The marriage to Knightley is the most obvious such ideological moment, where Emma's correction at his hands shows the necessity for the inner life to be brought under the regulation of the new liberal, professional ethos, "the wedding," as Gary Kelly describes it, "of 'masculine' and 'feminine' aspects of gentry-professional culture in the national interest."[119] Emma's shock realization that "Mr. Knightley must marry no-one but herself" (370), whereby she relabels the unuttered wishes of the Highbury community with the name of her own desire, is equivalent to the moment, in the Beethovenian recapitulation, when "the objectivity of form becomes palpably embodied in the subject."[120]

But this integration of Emma into the social order does not begin with her engagement to Knightley. Austen's free indirect discourse represents a characteristic form of Romantic women's writing in which interiority, as a linguistic realm, is always already permeated with mass-produced, "social" idioms: with gossip, cliché, and conventional wisdom.[121] Casey Finch and Peter Bowen make the same point in starker terms reminiscent of Adorno's reading of middle-period Beethoven: the permeation of private and public discourse in *Emma* is a "violation," a "mechanics of power by which the disciplinary agenda of a community is internalised as the private wishes of the individual."[122] Austen, however, appears to have judged the power relation in opposite terms, as the renovation of a social order and institutions by a bourgeois female subject endowed with Romantic depth and authenticity. From the viewpoint of diction, Austen makes no distinction between interiority and civic discourse: it is a single language of middlebrow Georgian politeness. Subjectivity in Austen should be distinguished from more simple romanticisms of self and selfhood, defined in opposition to the object or social world. The "subjectivity" put into play by free indirect discourse, like Beethovenian sonata form, "resides at the borders of autonomy and integration," where language is not the medium between self and world but its ironic matter, the constituter of terms and limits by which the romanticisms of the text might be enjoyed.[123] The social function of "development" in Austen is to naturalize the individual's relation to social change by internalizing its possibility, as occurring organically from "within." Austen's accomplishment in the history of the novel is that, after her, such moments of imagined autonomy come to define fiction itself, and that personal development was principally the prerogative of women belonging to the emerging professional classes.[124]

Virtuosity is a code-word for triviality, and has been the grounds for neglect of Austen's participation in Regency music culture, a culture apparently so at odds with the literary virtues she was in the process of establishing through her fiction. But Austen's rich musical life, and especially her lifelong absorption of Viennese sonata form, was entirely consistent with, not opposed to, the Romantic project of interiority she advanced in her novels. *Emma* can be understood to dramatize the same social contract as Beethovenian sonata form, both at the structural level of the marriage plot and at the rhetorical level of free indirect discourse, which marries, dialectically, the subjective and objective viewpoints of character and narrator. From her earliest years at the piano, Austen was exposed to the new musical language of sonata form and its social possibilities just as she enacted, in her conscientious, lifelong practice regimen, a ritual of para-professional discipline that was the hallmark of her class and gender, and integral to British middle-class women's apprenticeship as the domestic partners of professional men. These features of Austen's musical life, language, and sensibility appear in her novels in literary translation, as in her creation of Jane Fairfax and her experiments in free indirect discourse. The processual power of free indirect discourse, like that of sonata form, was to represent "the act of animation, of being endowed with soul, over and over." The business of Beethoven's heroic-period music and Austen's fiction – which appeared simultaneously on the British cultural scene – was to "mak[e] the inner life intelligible to itself" through the aesthetic naturalization of a union between self and world.[125]

We would be wrong, therefore, to accept Austen's critique of musical accomplishment in her novels at face value, especially in *Emma*. As a paragon of style living on the margins of polite culture with only her accomplishments to recommend her, Jane Fairfax is the closest figure we have for Austen herself – a proto-professional women living by her talent. Both possess the modern professional's armor, a shell of reserve, an "indifference whether she pleased or not."[126] Charlotte Brontë, adapting Emma's view of Jane Fairfax, complained of a lack of "warmth or enthusiasm" in Austen's prose.[127] But Jane Fairfax's secret is also Austen's. Neither are mere virtuosi, bereft of an inner life. Both possess execution *and* taste. Austen's focus on authenticity and sincerity as moral measures of her characters is a narrative compensation for the performative "insincerity" – call it Romantic irony, or virtuosity – of her own prose. Jane Fairfax, as rehabilitated virtuoso, mirrors Austen's own phantasmic presence in the text as a figure of pure style – the accomplishment ideal – that is both empty and replete. The narrative dictates that Jane Fairfax must be each of these things in turn, but the unique satisfaction of reading Austen's fiction is to experience both at once, to wonder how it is that while so little appears to be said, nothing is left unaccomplished.

In biographical terms Jane Fairfax's predicament doubles Austen's own, as a parlor-room ornament whose choices beyond it lay in marriage, disgrace, as a governess confined to the nursery or, at a now just conceivable future time, as a working professional in the new bourgeois regime. One critic has called female accomplishment a "mytheme" in which "we see the formation of the middle-class feminine subject under consumer capitalism."[128] The accomplished female was a compromise formation of the Georgian age, pointing backward to an idea of woman as courtly exhibit, but also forward to one who advertised herself, through her "disciplined" private life, as a suitable partner for a professional man and, more distantly, as a prototype for the middle-class professional women of the following century. The rewards of that ambiguously realized future depend on one's attitude to such terms as "professionalism," "middle class," and "consumer capitalism." This is not Austen's language, but the trajectory of her heroines into the future – as full-fledged, humanized subjects – is clear. There are no professional women in Austen, but her novels point emphatically to their readiness for professionalization. Who is to say that Jane Fairfax, as the new Mrs. Churchill, did not rediscover her late-style taste? That, sitting at her Broadwood one day, she did not think to take up Beethoven's *Hammerklavier* sonata and drive Frank out of the house, crashing chords and a demented fugue her manifesto of professional independence and best revenge on his outworn parlor-room gallantries?

CHAPTER 6

The Byron of the piano

I

A nineteenth-century celebrity, on whom monographs are still regularly composed, lies in the grass at Newstead Abbey on a hot day in September. He is the talk of London, both for his art and his scandalous personal life, and he is known to be a close friend of the notorious Lady Blessington. He has a talent for dividing opinion and making aristocratic women forget themselves. "Hysteria," as a phenomenon of modern celebrity culture, is said to begin with him. But he is unhappy in England, unappreciated, and looks forward to leaving ...

No, not Byron in 1816. I refer, in fact, to Franz Liszt, who visited Byron's estate in 1840, and whose tour of Britain and Ireland that year was a kind of professionalized Romantic wandering interspersed with concert dates, as if Childe Harold himself had discovered a medium for his ennui at the piano in cascading arpeggios and operatic transcriptions.

Liszt's visit to Britain and Ireland in 1840 (with several months in 1841) is typically remembered only as the historical origin of the melopoetic term "recital" to describe Liszt's solo performances. Otherwise, the British tour has been an embarrassment to the Liszt legend and its keepers. The great biographers, from Lina Ramann to Alan Walker, pass over it in a few breaths, while British music historians make tepid apologies. The Victorian Francis Hueffer acknowledged the "artistic rebuff" the young Liszt had received and even Walker, while quoting at length from the few positive reviews Liszt received in London, admits that his performances there attracted "the worst press notices of his career."[1] David Allsobrook describes an air of "desperation" on the visit, best evidenced by Liszt's decision to sign on to two long provincial tours as part of a company of musicians and comic singers, like any common salaried professional or "saltimbanque," as he himself put it, "in a band of travelling players."[2]

Liszt rarely risked highbrow repertoire on such tours. His fellow musicians were baffled by one performance of a Beethoven violin sonata he accompanied, and he was reduced largely to his standard pop-virtuoso repertoire, which included a transcription of the *William Tell* overture, operatic airs, Hungarian marches, his *Grand galop chromatique* and, if an orchestra were available, Weber's famous *Konzertstück*.[3] He drew the occasional large audience, such as at York, but often played to less than half-empty halls, as at Hull where 160 saw Liszt in a room capable of holding 800. The schedule was exhausting, the receipts "mediocre," and the normally extrovert and publicity-hungry Liszt became strangely withdrawn. He complained in a letter to his lover Marie d'Agoult of his "invincible ennui" while on tour, of an "exterior life" that was "the most monotonous in the world." From Birmingham in November, he communicated a moody disaffection worthy of Childe Harold: "I am totally removed from everything around me. I read, write, and play the piano, rendering to everyone, according to the occasion, indifference for indifference." At the conclusion of this letter, he reminded Marie of her promise to send him his volume of *Childe Harold* and *Don Juan*. By the end of the tour, he barely left his room.[4]

For a man accustomed to being lionized in society on a nightly basis, and chaired through the streets by roaring throngs of German students, the "indifference" of the British public must have been galling.[5] "I am terribly tired of the English public," he wrote in the last days of the tour. His inability to connect with that public appears to have had a poisonous effect on his well-being. An artistic and professional "rebuff" in Britain translated, in his own mind, into a Byronic language of alienation: "I am utterly sad and exhausted ... I feel completely atrophied ... and the future seems to me gloomy and hopeless." As the London press duly noted, the tours were a "failure." The impresario Louis Lavenu had lost a small fortune promoting the most famous musician in Europe to audiences who had never seen him: "to live in a business country without doing business," Liszt observed, "is a terrible thing."[6]

The reviews of Liszt's performances in Britain in 1840 indicate that the tour was by no means an unmitigated critical failure, however. His reception is best described as deeply ambivalent. The two most influential London critics, Henry Chorley at the *Athenaeum* and John Davison of *The Musical World*, took up battle positions from Liszt's first significant concert appearance, with the Philharmonic Society on May 11. The cosmopolitan Chorley exulted in "the bright, eager, elevated poetical genius to be heard in every tone and touch," while Davison, a nationalist and notorious curmudgeon, declared Liszt "a delirious posture-maker" in whose playing he was "unable to detect an atom of genuine feeling."[7] Davison elaborated on his objections in an editorial for *Musical World* a month later in which he labeled Liszt's prodigious "mechanical acquirement" a vice: "the cultivation and encouragement of this kind of semi-miraculous handicraft exerts a most baneful effect ... it enslaves the understanding to the ear – it draws attention from the composer to the player." Davison's symphonic values rehearse the early nineteenth-century Romantic principle of *Werktreue* – and its virtuosophobic premises – in the clearest terms: to the "written creations" of Beethoven and Mozart "belong alone the soul-humanizing capabilities ascribed to music," while "the feeling [Liszt] excites is what we should term animal astonishment."[8] The cultural threat of the 1840 Liszt lay not with his foreignness as much as his being a stateless cosmopolitan in a period of heightened musical nationalism, the subtext of Davison's critique. At his London performances, according to the composer Charles Salaman, Liszt approached his audience "with the gracious condescension of a prince."[9] Liszt's aristocratic demeanor harked back to an obsolete demographic economy outside the terms of the early Victorian nation state, to a pre-revolutionary paradigm of international relations where the ruling classes of Europe identified with each other more than their native peoples. Just as Byron trafficked in the aura of a fading aristocracy, Liszt flaunted himself in the concert rooms of London as the glamorous dauphin of a traveling court, making a fashion of the outmoded.

The disagreement between Chorley and Davison is inherent to the structure of virtuosity itself, borne out time and again in the early nineteenth-century reception of Catalani, Liszt, Paganini, and others. The virtuoso produced a double-sign – sincerity and insincerity, expression and mechanistic emptiness – irresolvable in the minds of the public. As Susan Bernstein has observed, "Liszt's most disturbing trait [was] probably his ability to simulate the genuine with the same ease as he produce[d] the hyperbolically artificial."[10] John Keats understood the chimerical character of virtuosic style. In a letter, he challenged Reynolds to "pick out some lines to Hyperion and put a mark X next to the false beauty proceeding from art, and one 11 to the true voice of feeling ... I cannot make the distinction."[11] A Liszt concert, like Keats's Miltonic exercises in *Hyperion*, was truth and fakery, perilously, at once, which is also to say that it was Byronic. The entry on Byron in the 1834 *Encyclopédie des gens du monde* defined the poet in like mercurial terms: "In Byron, there is no central point ... [but rather] two sides to everything, good and evil, negation and affirmation ... the ridiculous and burlesque side-by-side with the sublime."[12] Byron was the great thematizer of virtuosity as an artistic and social predicament: he called it "truth in masquerade" or "mobility." His celebrated vindication of society hostess Lady Adeline in canto XVI of *Don Juan* is the most convincing defence of virtuosity ever written:

> So well she acted, all and every part
> By turns—with that vivacious versatility,
> Which many people take for want of heart,
> They err—'tis merely what is called mobility,
> A thing of temperament and not of art,
> Though seeming so, from its supposed facility;
> And false—though true, so surely they're sincerest,
> Who are strongly acted on by what is nearest.[13]

Byron is describing himself, as he implicitly confesses in a note. Picked up by Leigh Hunt in his 1828 memoir, Byron's "mobility" – his multi-faced, "merely" technical brilliance – became a keynote of his nineteenth-century reception, whereby "sincerity" was decided upon as the scandalous deficiency of *Don Juan*.[14] Here, Byron collapses the opposition between sincerity and virtuosic "facility" as a form of pre-emptive strike (vain, as it turned out) against his critics.

The Chorley and Davison reviews set the template for Liszt's critical reception while on his national tours in the autumn and winter of 1840–1. Provincial reviewers from Southampton to Leeds hewed to the lines laid out by the London critics and, for all the thousands of words written, did little to advance the argument or clarify Liszt's impact on the British public. More significant than the reviews was the often disappointing size of Liszt's audiences and, more largely, the lack of any lasting cultural influence produced by his presence in England for more than seven months at the very height of his fame.

In this chapter I pinpoint Liszt's self-conscious Byronism as a principal cause of his failure in Britain. To make this argument requires the elucidation of several distinct cultural contexts: first, Liszt's mostly successful struggle to transcend the taint of virtuosity during his early career in Paris in the 1830s; second, the often embattled character of Liszt's Byronism, particularly evident from his Romantic travel-writing in Switzerland and Italy; and third, the corresponding British inhospitability to Byronic self-fashioning in that decade, the result of a broad critique of Byron in the press that borrowed heavily from virtuosophobic prejudices originating in Georgian music culture. In the 1830s, I will argue, Byron was read and condemned as a virtuoso poet – a castrato, as Thomas Moore once playfully described him.¹⁵ I will then put my argument for a Byronic Liszt to work in a reading of *Childe Harold* III to show how wholesale appropriation of the poem by Liszt, both as persona *and* poetics, profoundly affected the development of European modernism in music and how, in turn, a Lisztian reading of *Childe Harold* offers a fresh and historically enriched account of Byron's own literary modernity.

II

English virtuosophobia achieved perhaps its last, fullest flowering during Liszt's tour of 1840. His style, habitually exoticized by his critics as "French" and "Romantic," was said to sacrifice melodic continuity to a variety of virtuoso effects. "There is little melody in a whirlwind," complained the music critic for the *Hull Packet*, for whom Liszt produced "no chord which had struck a responsive tone in human feeling, no passage of delicious and soothing melody, which sank at once into the heart to remain there for ever."¹⁶ So too the *Norfolk Chronicle*, whose critic "listened in vain for one strain of pure and sustained melody."¹⁷ The living example of the Clementi school, J. B. Cramer (another foreigner), was likewise vivid in the mind of the writer for the *Doncaster Gazette*. The integrity of melody (here called "subject") is again the sticking point, with Liszt faring poorly by comparison with the "native" Cramer:

> But we question the merit awarded to the school of music which degenerates into a mere display of mechanical dexterity, or brilliancy of execution. Those who have carefully minded the performance of any really grand subject by Cramer and have paid the same attention to a similar effort on the part of Liszt, must come away convinced that Cramer loses every thought of self as he proceeds evidently absorbed in the desire to accomplish a noble end; but with Liszt, the wish seems to be more for the display of rapidity of invention, than for a rigid adherence to whatever subject he may have before him.¹⁸

With his emphasis on what has been sacrificed, musically speaking, at the altar of self-"display," "dexterity," "execution," and "rapidity of invention," the Doncaster critic is not guilty of provincialism or a specifically English virtuosophobia. He is rehearsing an international anti-virtuosic creed that had been vigorously enforced in the leading French and German music periodicals for more than a decade.¹⁹

The 1830s was the first great decade of public instrumental virtuosity, a phenomenon that has been linked to the rising participation of the middle classes in public concerts and huge growth in the commercialization of piano literature and manufacture.²⁰ By one estimate, over three hundred piano manufacturers were operating in Paris, Liszt's headquarters, by 1830; by 1845, there were 60,000 pianos in a city of fewer than a million people.[21] "It seems incontrovertible," writes Dana Gooley, "that the middle bourgeoisie was the core of [Liszt's] audience."[22] But, or hence, the 1830s and early 1840s was also the period of greatest critical backlash against virtuosity in the elite musical periodicals, which waged "war against the piano music industry."[23] "You can hear it ring in every house, in every company, both day and night," complained Liszt's fellow Parisian and Byronist Heinrich Heine, who blamed the "reigning bourgeoisie" for "the universal rage for thumping the piano." Pianistic virtuosity, for Heine, mirrored the cultural moment in which industrialization and bourgeois philistinism were horribly merged. He deployed, like Maria Edgeworth and so many others before him, the bogey image of the automaton: "the piano has at last killed off all our thoughts and feelings … and marks the victory of the mechanical arts over the spirit. Technical perfection, with the precision of the automaton … is the transformation of Man into a humming instrument."[24] Placing Liszt's early career in the context of the international anti-virtuosic critique of the 1830s, advanced by leading European critics such as Heine, François Fétis, and Robert Schumann, is crucial to understanding Liszt's treatment by his English audiences.[25]

The important point regarding Liszt's reception in Britain in 1840 is not the presence of anti-virtuosic prejudice in the reviews of Davison and others but its degree and timing. Charles Rosen has described Liszt's early works as "vulgar and great," a precise rendering of the historical dialectic of virtuosity, and identical in character to Davison's 1840 review: "Liszt's playing is certainly at the extreme of beauty as his music is the perfection of ugliness."[26] Liszt was acutely aware of this tenacious critique, and had worked single-mindedly throughout the 1830s to distinguish himself from "les virtuosi ordinaires" of Paris by re-creating himself as a utopian artist-philsopher, man of letters, and avant-garde composer.[27] His transcriptions of Beethoven symphonies and performances of his sonatas both exhibited his acceptance of the new symphonic values of musical seriousness, and made an implicit argument for the necessity of technical prowess for full pianistic "interpretation" of such works. "Virtuosity exists," Liszt wrote, "only to permit the artist to reproduce everything that is expressible in art."[28] He likewise mystified his practice regimen, obscuring the demands of digital repetition to construct an ideal of almost priestly preparation for the keyboard: "Technique creates itself from the mind, not from mechanics," was his constant refrain.[29] By redefining virtuosic discipline and performance in cerebral terms as the necessary corollary of authorial genius, Liszt attempted an ambitious reconciliation of what Dahlhaus has called the "twin styles" of nineteenth-century music: between the virtuosic, event-based tradition embodied in Rossini's operas, and the new "literary" or hermeneutic model of the Romantic symphony that challenged the listener "to decipher, in patient exertion, the meaning of what had taken place in the music."[30] In elaborately staged, hieratic performances of Beethoven, virtuosity assumed its place as the indispensable vehicle of genius, and Liszt gained in every way by the association. Reviewing a performance of Beethoven's *Hammerklavier* sonata in 1836, Berlioz described the playing of "the new Liszt" as "elevated throughout to the plane of the composer's thinking."[31] In the context of reviews such as these, the question in mainland Europe appeared to have been settled in Liszt's favor by 1840. The verdict was that he had "transcended" virtuosity.[32] In the words of a Viennese critic on the eve of his British tour, Liszt's "style of playing is not the mere straining for effect, but the expression of his most private being and the feelings that overpower him … it is this that sets him apart as a true artist."[33] After such encomiums as this, to meet with the old, familiar criticisms once more in England, and in a greater volume than he had ever seen in Paris, must have seemed to Liszt a distasteful anachronism, an unwelcome blast from the past. And he was not slow to resent his treatment publicly. He foresaw in the bourgeois machinery of English taste, evidenced by his bad reviews, an emergent "aristocracy of mediocrity" from which his genius, like Byron's before him, was destined to be exiled.[34]

And yet the burden of artistic proof, as Liszt knew well, lay always with the virtuoso. His predicament in 1830s Paris, and again in Britain in 1840, was that his public image as an artist was perpetually at risk of being obscured by his medium of representation, namely the virtuoso performance. Virtuosity dissociated sign and meaning: in the eyes of its critics, it reduced music to display, a melodically rich score to pure sound.[35] Virtuosity was, by definition, insignificant, or deficient in significance. Because of this, the virtuoso Liszt was in continual need, throughout his concertizing career, for some form of thematic supplementation beyond the concert performances themselves to sustain his image as a credible artist and public figure. Recent influential studies have located that supplementation in Liszt's body. For Lawrence Kramer, public fascination centered on the mesmeric contraries of the Lisztian body, erotically labile in its movements and transfigured in its expression. In the emerging bourgeois public sphere of the 1830s and 1840s, Liszt represented "the vexed relationship between virtuosity and visuality," and between virtuosity and sex.³⁶ In the popular culture of mid-century Europe, which Liszt so deeply touched, his anatomization was rendered in a peepshow of constantly circulating fetish objects: the Liszt hair, the Liszt fingers, the Liszt clothes.³⁷

In a recent book that revolutionizes Liszt studies, Dana Gooley has dramatically extended our understanding of virtuosic supplementarity in Liszt by showing his reliance on a variety of extra-musical personae to penetrate public consciousness in the different locales on the virtuoso circuit: "Liszt became one of the most widely admired figures of his time not because his enormous musical talent made such popularity inevitable, but because his audiences made symbolic demands upon him that he was willing and able to fulfill."³⁸ These symbolic roles sometimes contradicted each other and landed Liszt in trouble. In Paris, he was man of letters, a reformist and utopian associated with the political left. In Hungary, by contrast – where, in a notorious episode, he was presented with a saber by representatives of the derelict feudal nobility – he found common cause with the Magyar nationalist movement. Later in Germany, he allied himself with more militant, authoritarian nationalists, infuriating the Parisian press in the process.³⁹ On other occasions, in stark contrast to the symbolic uses of militant nationalism, his success was built on his reputation as a humanitarian, most notably in his 1840 concerts in Vienna for relief of the flood victims in Pest, but also, as Gooley has reconstructed, in Berlin in 1842. The image of Liszt radiant with almost Christlike charity, we find, was essential to German "Lisztomanie." In each case Liszt galvanized public interest in his performances by cultivating a persona – utopian, nationalist, humanitarian – independent of his actual concertizing, but which could be used to help elevate those performances from mere concerts to cultural events in which the audience participated in the affirmation of a collective ideal.⁴⁰ In the studied cultivation of his multiple public images, we find Liszt "solving th[e] problem of bringing the self into the public" at a time when the lived experience of European urban modernity was increasingly that of mixing with strangers. The rapid growth in print and visual media, communications, and ultimately the railway expanded individual consciousness of a transnational public sphere, and of one's own anonymity within it.⁴¹ In his hectic career across the metropoles of nineteenth-century Europe, Liszt offered a model for cosmopolitan identity, while also trafficking in nationalism. The strategic manufacture of "personality" for public consumption is an eighteenth-century phenomenon perfected by Liszt, who saw in Byron an archetype of pan-European celebrity.

Figure 7. Josef Danhauser, *Franz Liszt am Flügel* (1840). Nationalgalerie, Staatliche Museen zu Berlin, Germany/Art Resource, NY. In Danhauser's superb melopoetic confection, the portrait of Byron above Liszt's head completes the trinity of Romantic inspiration with the marble bust of Beethoven. The image celebrates the literary consecration of music, but is also rife with interdisciplinary tension: George Sand, on the leather chair, closes Alexandre Dumas's book for him, suggesting music's transcendence of the word.

Liszt's extra-musical personae – and their problems – are essential to understanding his 1840 tour of Britain. Only months before his arrival, Liszt had been hailed in Pressburg as "the musical Byron." Another German magazine published a poem dedicated to him that began "I hereby christen you Byron, the All-Powerful."[42] Two years later, the Berlin poet and music critic Ludwig Rellstab reported a conversation with Liszt in which the pianist named Byron "both the poet of his choice and the one to whom he has most devoted himself. So far as his intellectual development is concerned, the choice is crucial."[43] When Chorley hailed Liszt, after his Philharmonic debut in May 1840, as the "poet of the pianoforte," there could be little doubt in anyone's mind as to which poet he meant. Indeed, it comes as no surprise to even the most casual student of nineteenth-century cultural history to be presented with the conjunction of Liszt and Byron (Figure 7). Only when we realize that we make the association because Liszt wanted us to, that he set out deliberately to invoke Byron as part of his larger campaign for cultural seriousness in the 1830s, do we see the necessity for re-creating the specific historical texture of the Byronic Liszt in Britain. Liszt's 1840 tour, I wish to argue, marked the uncanny return of Byron to the country he left in controversial circumstances in 1816, the return of a full-blown Byronism with all its cultural baggage to the British public sphere. Reinforcing the deep-set virtuosophobia of critics both in London and in the provincial towns, Liszt's expressly Byronic image in England brought him into dangerous proximity with the scandal of virtuosity itself, and was thus insufficient, indeed counterproductive, as an extra-musical persona with which to attract the interest and goodwill of the British public.

III

In the summer of 1835 Liszt left Paris with his married lover, the Comtesse Marie d'Agoult, for Geneva, and the couple spent much of the next three years on an extended sojourn in Switzerland and Italy. Their itinerary adhered to the now well-established rituals of Romantic tourism, trodden by Goethe, Byron, and Heine before them. By the 1830s any educated traveler's opinions of Lake Geneva, Mont Blanc, the Simplon Pass, and Venice could not but be filtered through dense layers of poetry and travelogue prose, whose set-piece landscape descriptions converted readily into souvenir prints available in shops and on street corners across Europe. In one of his open letters from his travels published in the leading Parisian musical journal, *La Revue et Gazette Musicale*, Liszt gamely attempts to distinguish himself from the tourist herd with their popular guidebooks.[44] With an anxiety more than familiar today, and no less hopeless, he exclaims from Milan,

> Do you think I rush off to see the cathedral, the museum, the library? No, my God, no! Nothing like that, I do not read Valéry's guidebook; I have absolutely no idea how to travel profitably and go about ticking off one's admirations, classically and methodically.[45]

After six weeks in the Alps, the Comtesse d'Agoult, in her memoir of the tour, likewise exhibits sure signs of Romantic fatigue, with its telltale disgust for landscape:

> We have crossed eleven cantons, engraved four mountains, navigated three lakes; and exhausted by this optical debauchery we have arrived at a complete indifference for the "beauties" of nature. I find myself not entirely exempt from a certain irritation for romantics and poets ...[46]

Of all the poets who acted as their virtual guides, Byron was omnipresent. Dozens of implicit or explicit references to Childe Harold in particular mark the couple's various accounts of their tour.[47] This, for example, from one of Liszt's letters to George Sand, also published in the *Revue et Gazette Musicale*:

It behooves an artist more than anyone else to pitch a tent only for an hour and not to build anything like a permanent residence. Isn't he always a stranger among men? Isn't his homeland somewhere else? Whatever he does, wherever he goes, he always feels himself an exile. He feels that he has known a purer sky, a warmer sun, and nobler beings. What then can he do to escape his vague sadness and undefined regrets?[48]

The harboring of "undefined regrets," in particular, was a familiar Byronic signature, adapted from the aura of secrecy and transgression attached to Harold's famous exile:

> And dost thou ask what secret woe
> I bear, corroding joy and youth?
> . . .
> What is that worst? No, do not ask—
> In pity from the search forbear.[49]

Liszt, Sand, and their circle were all products of the Byronic wave in French culture that dated from the Pichot translations of the early 1820s and Alphonse de Lamartine's tribute poem, "Le Dernier Chant du Pèlerinage d'Harold" (1825). Sand herself, like Liszt, was both explicitly indebted to Byron and routinely likened to him.[50] Only weeks after the lovers' hasty, clandestine departure from Paris, Liszt wrote to his mother to send his books, including Byron. The next spring Liszt negotiated with Berlioz to transcribe for piano his own tribute to Byron's alter ego, *Harold en Italie*, a project that occupied Liszt for two years. In 1838 Liszt described himself to his Alpine traveling companion Adolphe Pictet as "in the grip of an unbelievable passion for [Byron]," a fact he reminded him of only months later, where the Byronic passion was characterized as "beautiful and lasting."[51] In Milan, Liszt briefly joined Rossini's circle, and was struck with that composer's choral tribute to his idol, *Il Pianto delle Muse in Morte di Lord Byron* (1825). Then in Venice, he was delighted to find a gondolier who claimed to have met Lord Byron, visited the palazzo where the poet lived with his own mistress, the Contessa Guiccioli, and imagined himself installed there with Marie. Later, he visited the island of San Lazzaro and made himself comfortable in the chair "in which Byron sat during that impetuous, hotly passionate period when he bound himself to the study of Armenian."⁵² In a subsequent letter to the *Revue et Gazette Musicale* from Venice, he "longs for those fine days when *conversazioni* were held at the Benzoni, Albrizzi, and Cicognara residences," all literary salons frequented by Byron, whose names he reels off with the shorthand confidence possible only in a true Byronist.⁵³ Liszt's correspondence, both published and unpublished, as well as his musical output in the 1830s, makes obvious that Byron was indeed "crucial" to his "intellectual development," as Rellstab attested. For Liszt, as for so many European Byronists, a copy of *Childe Harold's Pilgrimage* in one's pocket, and ready quotations on one's lips, was a kind of passport to self-realization literalized in the act of touring.⁵⁴

Byron may have been an inescapable reference point for the self-fashioning Romantic, but Byronism, as a cultural phenomenon, represented an increasing threat to its satisfactions. As Liszt's close friend and collaborator Berlioz put it, mere imitation of Byron could only be "pitiful."⁵⁵ Byron was too popular, too readily quoted in verse and dress to retain the necessary aura of exclusivity. As Gooley has described, Liszt's public concerts, in which his aristocratic patronesses grouped about him in an intimate circle on the stage, were not structured as bourgeois events, but as theaters of aristocratic self-display to which the bourgeoisie were invited.⁵⁶ Byronism, in a similar way, created a cultural sphere easily permeated by the general populace where, as Matthew Arnold observed, class differences might, on the strength of an open-necked shirt and a cultivated look of disdain, be erased.⁵⁷ After a generation of the wildest speculations in Byronic imitation, Byronism's value plummeted, at least in the eyes of the cultural avant-garde. In his 1855 poem, "Stanzas on the Grand Chartreuse," Arnold wondered

> What helps it now that Byron bore
> With haughty scorn which mocked the smart,
> Through Europe to the Aetolian shore
> The pageant of his bleeding heart?   (133–6)

Victorian critics looked back in horror at that social "calamity" whereby "every particular of Lord Byron's history was jealously treasured up, all his personal habits were greedily noted and carried to the profoundest, most foolish, and most disgusting excess of servile imitation."⁵⁸

An incipient disgust toward Byronism is integral to Liszt's own Byronic self-fashioning. In an open letter from Venice addressed to "the German Byron," Heine, Liszt begins with the celebrated opening line of canto IV of *Childe Harold's Pilgrimage* – "I stood in Venice, on the Bridge of Sighs" –

as if there were no other possibility for introducing the subject, then instantly laments, "Ah! My God, yes, just like Byron and like the thousands of imbeciles who came after him, following his footsteps in order to glean some scraps of poetry, which their rough hands immediately transformed into appalling commonplaces."[59] One such "imbecile" soon presented himself at George Sand's villa where Liszt describes the company as beset by "Byronian-styled pilgrims," whose objects were, presumably, Sand and himself as inheritors of the Byronic mystique. A lengthy and rather sadistic anecdote follows in which the Childe Harold wannabe is humiliated and leaves town: "People like him have vanished from Nohant," Liszt wolfishly concludes, "and by now the whole race has apparently been exterminated."[60] Vulgar Byronists threatened misrecognition of the true Byron, or the truth-in-Byron, whose proper name was Franz Liszt. Hence the homicidal tone of Liszt's anecdote, the more so since it comes just before one of the most famous passages in Lisztiana, where he asserts himself as the true Byronic poet of music. Liszt textualizes the piano as a kind of private journal or lyric autobiography:

> My piano is to me what a ship is to the sailor, what a steed is to the Arab, and perhaps more because even now my piano is myself, my speech, and my life. It is the intimate personal depository of everything that stirred wildly in my brain during the most impassioned days of my youth. It was there that all my wishes, all my dreams, all my joys, and all my sorrows lay. Its strings quivered under all my passions, its docile keys obeyed my every whim.[61]

Liszt's readers would have recognized in the images of the sailor and rider an allusion to the opening of canto III of *Childe Harold's Pilgrimage*:

> Once more upon the waters! yet once more!
> And the waves bound beneath me as a steed
> That knows his rider.   (10–12)

Harold's embarkation at sea is Byron's metaphor for his own resumption of his poem, and is the presiding figure for the entire narrator-hero relation. Liszt, perhaps the closest reader of *Childe Harold* in the nineteenth century, borrows it whole. The self-image Liszt manufactured for the *Revue et Gazette Musicale* quite deliberately transcended musical associations into the sphere of Romantic literary idealism. His piano was his "speech" and "life." His model for describing the piano was not Beethoven's or Mozart's feelings for their keyboards, but Byron's relationship to his own "intimate personal depository," *Childe Harold's Pilgrimage*, a work Liszt himself had, via Berlioz, translated into the new Romantic language of the piano. "Hugo called Virgil Homer's 'moon,'" he wrote to Marie some years later: "When I am in the mood to flatter myself, I tell myself that perhaps one day I will be Byron's moon."[62]

It is under the same imperative that Liszt, during his years in Swizterland and Italy, undertook his first serious compositions for the piano, a volume of which he subsequently published under the title of *Impressions et poésies*, then collectively as *Album d'un voyageur* (1839), but which after 1840 began to bear the collective title *Années de pèlerinage*, a further express invocation of Byron's *Childe Harold*. In his foreword to the 1841 edition, Liszt describes the piano suite as "a poetic language able, better than poetry itself perhaps, to express our inner life, and everything that passes beyond the usual bounds." The two-volume structure of the *Années* follows the itinerary of Childe Harold, and Liszt's own in 1835, from Romantic Alpine Switzerland to sensuous Italy. In addition, no fewer than five of the first volume of "Swiss" pieces bear epigraphs from Byron's poem, all from canto III. The best-known piece, "Vallée d'Obermann," has earned an uninterrupted place in the concert piano repertoire since its publication. Its Byronic epigraph is also the longest, the famous stanza ninety-seven where the poet describes his response to a storm over the Rhône:

> Could I embody and unbosom now
> That which is most within me,—could I wreak
> My thoughts upon expression, and thus throw
> Soul, heart, mind, passions, feelings, strong or weak,
> All that I would have sought, and all I seek,
> Bear, know, feel, and yet breathe—into *one* word,
> And that one word were Lightning, I would speak;
> But as it is, I live and die unheard,
> With a most voiceless thought, sheathing it as a sword.

Poetry – the famous Byronic lines attached to the score – here functions as a defense against the threatened unmeaning of virtuosic music, the merely mechanistic production of wonderful sound. Liszt's Byronic allusions are thus not merely fashionable but necessary and strategic, his self-inoculation against virtuosophobia. Stanza ninety-seven is especially pertinent, and ironic, as it defends virtuosity at its point of greatest weakness, namely "expression." Davison, we remember, found not "an atom of genuine feeling" in Liszt's performance at the Philharmonic Society. The risk of virtuosity was that it disclaimed the inner life.[63] Byron's Childe Harold, by contrast, offered pure interiority-without-content, the inner life in its negative, most Romantic form. His appeal lay in his very refusal to perform "feeling." His heroic epithet is "unmoved" (for example, I: 811, II: 282).

Expression, in Byron's poem, is left to the unnamed narrator, while the aura of the hero Childe Harold is built, paradoxically, on expression's absence. For example, the narrator mourns the ravishment of Greece by time and empire in the famous opening to canto II while Harold remains a blank: "Little reck'd he of all that men regret . . . /And left without a sigh the land of war and crimes" (II: 138, 144). The poem was the essence of Romanticism, and was recognized as such by readers like Liszt, because it traded not in specific expression but "expression" in the unwritten abstract, in all its glorious potentiality. The unspeakable was Byron's "poetic capital."[64] What Harold would say, were he moved to, is all the power there is in the poem. That the sentimental and expressive narrator spoke for, but never finally exposed, Harold's inner life created a fascinating "game of candor and obliquity" in verse, a novel literary effect that became the Byronic signature in the poetry of his years of fame, from *The Corsair* to *Manfred*.[65] Harold's "secret" remains undisclosed, as both the narrative engine of his Romantic exile and a tantalizing negative description of his lyric identity: "And he himself as nothing" (IV: 164).

Liszt faced serious difficulties, however, in adapting the mysterious Childe Harold for his virtuosic persona. The affective corollary of Harold's secret is, precisely, his affectlessness. Harold's lure as Romantic icon is the tragic incommensurability of expression and identity in the poem, a "voicelessness" that finds phantasmic embodiment in the hero's faceless torpor, his bare textual presence. The virtuoso, however – feel that Romantic incommensurability as he might – cannot resort to affectlessness on the concert platform; rather, he must ceaselessly *display* himself and his "art."[66] A cavalcade of sounds-as-signs must leave nothing in his technical acquirements to be guessed at, nothing in reserve. He is incapable of representing "voiceless thought," but must be committed to the full expenditure of his technical resources. As Heine observed, there are no unrecognized virtuosi.[67] And because there is no existence for virtuosity outside of performance, the virtuoso's predicament is fatally close to that of the Byronist, who must display his Byronic affiliation at every opportunity – Venice, the Alps, on the boulevards of Paris – or else risk passing unrecognized (which is no fun at all).

Virtuosity, then, as a semiotic double-term – the performance of a sincere feeling that dangerously invoked its opposite – was mirrored in Liszt's relation to Byron, which was both serious *and* mocking, sincere *and* cynical. Liszt idolized Byron but feared the Byronist in himself: that "sterile, absurd, and worthless Byronism" that sometimes afflicted him "when [he was] not in the proper state of mind to make like Childe

Harold."⁶⁸ Virtuosity cast the same strange shadow, both enabling and thwarting the aspirations of "genius." Byronism and virtuosity merged in the figure of Liszt; the poet and pianist were, in the historical encounter I am staging here, the names or definitions of each other. In another published letter from his Italian tour, Liszt recalled a dream in which the image of a stranger, uncannily resembling Childe Harold, appeared to him on a beach. In the dream, he is drawn to "the serious and pensive figure" as if by "magnetic force," and filled with an instant conviction that he must possess or consume this stranger, that "he and I had to merge with and transform each other."⁶⁹ Here Liszt takes on the role of the enraptured spectator to Byronic virtuosity who, like the popular image of the female fan at his own concerts, might just be taken for a hysteric or a fool. As for Marie d'Agoult, she came to regard Byron as her rival, a narcissistic envelope of Liszt's creation she could not penetrate. In a letter to him from 1844, as their relationship was unraveling, she dared to suggest that Byron's day had passed, that Byronism had become "respectable." Liszt's furious response makes no distinction between the injury done to Byron and to himself: "You no longer believe in my words, you no longer want to understand or justify the sad demands of my life ... What can I say to you? Why should I write to you?!"⁷⁰

In sum Liszt's great anxiety, through the 1830s, was for originality and distinction as an artist and, at the same time, to penetrate popular consciousness in a manner that would enable him to transcend the status of a professional virtuoso. Both his medium and one of his most vivid personae, however, adhered to perilous models: first, the itinerant piano entertainer could easily be confused with what Liszt himself called, in his frequent, strategic deployment of self-loathing, a "useless clown"; second, and in analogous fashion, his Byronic persona constantly threatened to collapse into the "imbecility" of Byronism.⁷¹ To defend himself against this always incipient collapse, Liszt adopted a complex rhetorical strategy: namely, mocking degraded versions of himself – the clowning virtuoso, the imbecile tourist – whose fake homage to art would, in the same breath, be contrasted to that authentic commitment, his own, which they so breathtakingly resembled (if only in appearance).⁷² Liszt's difficult task, as a "true" pilgrim of Byron deep in the cultural landscape of *Childe Harold's Pilgrimage*, was to assure himself and his public that his Byronic identity transcended Byronism, and was an authentic reproduction (no mere copy) of the original. Liszt's avant-garde landscape tone-poems, *Années de pèlerinage*, inspired by Byron, were the result, and the Paris critics at last certified his claim to the status of serious artist. In Britain in

1840, however, the *Années* suite was as yet unknown. Moreover, his appropriation of the cultural property called "Byron" proved far less stable at its point of issue than on the continent – its native meanings beyond even Liszt's extraordinary musico-rhetorical powers to control.

IV

We know from a letter written to Marie d'Agoult that Liszt was acquainted with Lady Blessington's *Conversations with Lord Byron* (1832–4), a popular tell-all memoir of her time with Byron in Italy that was published in French that year. Lady Blessington's open intimacy with the Comte d'Orsay was a perennial London scandal. As Liszt described to Marie in a letter on his arrival in May 1840, "Lady Blessington is at loggerheads with Society here, but receives social lions and people of talent … D'Orsay sets the tone with his waistcoats and cravats. Milady's attire and her furnishings are likewise at the forefront of fashion."[73] With their combination of unorthodox domestic arrangements, dandyism, worship of the arts, and a form of celebrity evident in the popular imitation of their "attire" and "furnishings," Lady Blessington and the Comte d'Orsay represented, compositely, a Byronic cultural phenomenon familiar to and embodied in Franz Liszt.

But Liszt was wary at first of invitations to Gore House where the notorious couple presided. Two days after his concert at the Philharmonic Society, Liszt wrote to Marie that "My success here is unparalleled," and that he had therefore "refused to be introduced at Lady Blessington's, having no need of anyone at all."[74] Liszt was apparently unaware of the troubled state of the Philharmonic Society, that it had fallen, as Davison said, "out of fashion with the aristocracy."[75] His brilliant debut there did not, as he thought, settle the question of his celebrity in London. Nor was the Gore House set to be easily denied. Within a week Liszt records that "D'Orsay came to see me and invited me to their house (that's Lady Blessington's). They long to know me. Probably someone had told them that I did not particularly want to visit."[76] Liszt's reluctance to be introduced to Lady Blessington was entirely consistent with his standard publicity strategy, perfected in Paris and other European capitals, whereby he first brought himself before the public in the salons of aristocratic hostesses and only then, with their support, booked venues for the larger, fee-paying public. Lady Blessington was a famous titled lady but a fallen woman: "I have seen no-one from Society," Liszt wrote. The milieu at Gore House contained a smattering of nobility, but was mostly bourgeois-professional and mildly bohemian, the world of "editors and artists."⁷⁷ To court Lady Blessington was to snub the indispensable hostesses of London society at large.

But these hostesses failed him anyway, and Liszt began to feel the chill of possible defeat in London. He was lionized well enough, but bohemian soirées were not paying affairs. Liszt came to London with avaricious intent – "A single idea preoccupies me here, to make money" – and he planned to charge 30 guineas apiece to perform at society salons, as was his custom in Paris.⁷⁸ As William Weber has documented, virtuosi such as Liszt usually "came and went from prestigious households in brisk, business-like fashion, preferring to play their market for as many profitable contacts as possible rather than settle into tight relationships with one or two families."⁷⁹ Liszt's almost exclusive intimacy with Lady Blessington's salon may thus be seen as an enforced departure from his normal practice and a sign of his troubles. The truth must be that Liszt was snubbed by London society.⁸⁰ According to the Victorian pianist and critic Alice Mangold Diehl, who remembered the tour from her childhood spent as a member of one of London's most prominent musical families, a passing moment of "Liszt fever" quickly "died out" at the behest of the "acknowledged authorities."⁸¹ Since the critics were divided, this must have been a more silent, social form of assassination. Perhaps the Victorian hostesses of 1840 were unwilling to risk a repeat of the hysteria shown by their mothers toward Byron a generation earlier, when the poet had cut a swathe through the drawing-rooms and marriages of the *bon ton*.⁸²

At least visiting Gore House (and later, actually residing there) gave Liszt fruitful access to the critic Chorley, whom Lady Blessington's Victorian biographer has described as "very intimately acquainted" with her.⁸³ Chorley himself was something of a dandy in dress, and had published tributes to Lord Byron. Another habitué of the Blessington circle was Edward Trelawney, arguably the original Byronist, a close friend of Byron in his Italian years whom the poet had once called "the personification of my Corsair."⁸⁴ Within two weeks of his arrival, Liszt was dining on an almost daily basis at this Byronic enclave in Kensington. "Lady Blessington's salon," he wrote to Marie, "gave me a lot to think about," including, we can assume, her observation that he resembled Lord Byron and Napoleon.⁸⁵ This was almost a redundancy. Napoleon was "the first of Byron's historical self-projections," and Gaspard de Pons's "Bonaparte et Byron" (1825) one of the foundational texts of French Byronism.⁸⁶ The coincidence is tantalizing. Only days after Lady Blessington's flattering comment, the latter-day Childe Harold signed a lucrative contract for a provincial tour with the impresario Lavenu and embarked on a Napoleonic campaign through provincial Britain.⁸⁷

Liszt's rejection by London society recalls the fate of his hero. George Sand, who had a great distaste for English prudery – what she called "le fluide britannique" – pulled a face when told by Marie d'Agoult of her plans to join Liszt in England, and made an explicit allusion to Byron and his mistress Teresa Guiccioli, as if she and Liszt would certainly share their fate in English social opinion. Biographer Sacheverell Sitwell agrees that Victorian uptightness was the principal reason for Liszt's struggles in English society: "the moral code took such a stern view of the pianist and his irregular union with Madame d'Agoult that his concert tour was a failure." Sure enough, when she did finally arrive, Marie was kept at a distance in Richmond for fear of "embarrassing" Liszt, and the couple were miserable.[88]

If Liszt's "exile" from London had analogies with Byron's disgrace, the Byronic tone of the provincial tour was set early on by a visit to Newstead Abbey, a detour made specifically at the pianist's request. On the eve of his visit, he wrote to Marie that

> my fellow feeling—I would almost say affinity with—Lord Byron remains the same ... he is the sole being to whom I feel intimately drawn. I know not what fantastical, burning desire comes over me sometimes to meet him in a world in which we shall at last be free, powerful, and living a real life.

He identifies, specifically, with Byron's feelings of persecution at the hands of society – an important feature of the French myth of Byron – mixed with a trademark ennui. The letter that follows, describing his experience at Newstead, is no less rhapsodic:

> At Newstead Abbey I lay on the grass in the bright sunshine. Flocks of ravens were cawing above my head, and for a long time I listened to their funereal music. Then I entered the rooms. They showed me the cup which Lord Byron had had made from the skull of a monk, and the grave of his dog. As I left, the moaning of the pine trees awakened the harmonies of my soul, and I sang silently as I meditated aloud. I shall write all that down one day.

Literary ambitions rise in Liszt, first in the Gothic interior of Newstead and then in the grounds, concluding in a Pythagorean invocation of soulful harmonies. He leaves the Abbey, unsurprisingly, with a fever. As we have seen, Liszt's letters to Marie of this period often adopted a Harold-like pose of impenetrable indifference. He refused to describe the landscape he was passing through because "all this nature ... says nothing to me." But Newstead was the glorious exception: "The only place which has made an impression on me is Newstead Abbey – because of the man associated with it." Later in the same letter, he describes a "dire thirst for

Italy," a Byronic code for the *locus amoenus* both of Harold's pilgrimage and Byron's own exile.[89]

Liszt's identifications with Byron were of the body as well as spirit. He quickly developed an admiration for the Byronic fashion statements of the Comte d'Orsay. About the time of his first introduction at Gore House, he directed Marie to send him his "fleece Hungarian frock coat, the Hungarian bedrobe, and that sort-of turkish pantalon in blue, as well as those other morning pants of the same type in white," in addition to some jewelry. "Pacha!" responded Marie – an allusion to the Albanian brigand made famous in *Childe Harold*, and whose dress Liszt seemed to want to imitate – "to hear is to obey!"[90] A wardrobe more at odds with the popular sensibilities of early Victorian England is difficult to imagine. For the winter leg of his provincial tour, Liszt brought a "great Hungarian coat with him, composed of Skins & ornamented with different coloured leather" that, according to his musical colleague on that tour, the singer John Parry, astounded the men of Wales. Later, Liszt astonished Parry himself with his purchase, after consultation with their female companions, of two poplin waistcoats woven with "gold thread."[91] Sitwell, echoing Chorley, blames Liszt's failure in Britain partly on these "affectations of his dress, manner, and deportment."[92] In addition to Byronic outfits, Byron's poetry was much on Liszt's mind during the long months of the provincial tour. He told Marie to buy the new French translation of Byron and put it on her bedside table. From Birmingham in November, he asked her to send him his volumes of *Childe Harold* and *Don Juan*, then reminded her again before the letter was finished. The Byron volumes become a running theme of their correspondence. Everything, even Marie herself, "reminds" Liszt of Lord Byron. In Liverpool, Liszt "sighs" for his Byron, which he does not finally receive until the end of December.[93]

From this fragmentary evidence, taken collectively, we see the outlines of Liszt's British strategy. Arriving in London in 1840, knowing almost no one and little of the language or culture, and after a disappointing reception from society, Liszt found that he had no immediate resources with which to galvanize public interest in his tour. Nationalism, utopianism, a humanitarian or popular cause – Liszt found nothing in his usual inventory to vault his public exposure beyond the narrow realms of the musical press. What followed – Liszt's intimate connection to Byron's memoirist Lady Blessington; his apparent rejection by society for reasons of sexual scandal; his embarking so precipitously on a provincial "pilgrimage"; the idealized account of his visit to Newstead; his constant references to Byron in his letters and in his dress; his reading and writing in the mode of *Childe Harold* – all form the basis for speculation about Liszt's attempt to "do business" in Britain in 1840. In short, for want of any other extra-musical persona with which to impress himself on the English public, Liszt chose Byron. Or, at least, he chose to accentuate his already fastidiously cultivated Byronism as a means of imposing himself on public notice. But in vain. For all the effort and exposure of an eighty-stop campaign across thousands of miles of Britain and Ireland, Liszt remained a mere touring pianist like Döhler, Herz, and Thalberg before him, and was judged by comparison with them, never becoming a trans-musical figure of the greater public imagination.

v

Why did Byronism fail Liszt in Britain? The Byronic legend, in its homeland, was a fallen angel narrative, with the years of fame darkened by digust over the details of Byron's divorce and the disgrace of exile. As Chorley wrote, in his role as literary critic, Byron was "followed out of England by popular opprobrium as an incarnation of evil – an outlaw without the pale of humanity."[94] Even more serious than this notoriety, however, had been the decline in Byron's literary reputation in England since 1824, when his glorious martyrdom in Greece was followed by a sustained period of Byronic revisionism.

Even during Byron's years of fame, Keats and Hunt thought him merely "theatrical." Lockhart, in 1821, had sneered at *Don Juan* as "the only sincere thing you [Byron] have ever written," meaning that the poem was sincere only in its insincerity.[95] Because sincerity was considered a distinctly British virtue – "Spoke with the sincerity of a Briton!" exclaims the heroine in Samuel Foote's play *The Englishman in Paris* (1753) – *in*sincerity belonged to a chain of associations that included foreignness, fashion, effeminacy, a corrupt cosmopolitan aristocracy, and virtuosity.[96] With the Byronic corpse barely cold in its grave, Hazlitt's essay in *The Spirit of the Age* (1825) gave official stamp to the trope of insincerity. Meaning in Byron's poems, Hazlitt argued, was subordinated to rhetoric: "He seldom gets beyond force of style." The comic effects of *Don Juan*, for example, were the product of a style based "in the utter discontinuity of ideas and feelings," which is to say, cynicism. In terms indebted to the century-old critique of virtuosity in music – and strikingly reminiscent of the *Examiner's* recent campaign against the opera diva Catalani (see chapter 4) – Hazlitt describes Byron's relationship to his poetic materials as opportunistic, in which the choice of inferior content only better serves to bring his bravura technique into focus: "he thinks he shows his superiority of execution in this ... It is not the value of the observation itself he is solicitous about; but he wishes to shine by contrast – even nature only serves as a foil to set off his style."[97] Hazlitt's readers would have been more familiar with the term "execution" from the opera columns of the *Examiner* or *Harmonicon* than from the literary periodicals. Hazlitt crosses disciplines to write of Byron in musical, specifically anti-virtuosic terms.

For Carlyle, writing later in the decade, the impact of Hazlitt's critique was far-reaching. Byron's Romantic persona, to which he was in thrall as a young man, had been exposed by *Don Juan* as "theatrical, false, affected." And the cynicism of *Don Juan* had infected his reading of the rest, including *Childe Harold's Pilgrimage*. "All the poems," Carlyle declared in retrospect, "had a certain falsehood, a brawling theatrical insincere character." Byronic revisionism intensified through the 1830s.[98] At the outset of that decade, Macaulay could already mourn "the magical potency which once belonged to the name of Byron," while Edward Bulwer-Lytton wrote in 1833 of "an unjust and indiscriminate spirit of depreciation springing up against that great poet." At Cambridge there was a "revolt against the worship of Byron." A popular book of aphoristic commentary, authored by members of the Cambridge Union, labeled him a "prince of egotists" capable of "fine sounding lines" but little else.[99] In similar terms, John Henry Newman criticized "popular poems" in the Byronic style, which had "mistake[n] mere eloquence for poetry," while the playwright Henry Taylor, in a lengthy indictment from 1834, described Byron's technique as "little more than poetic diction, an arrangement of words implying a sensitive state of mind, and therefore more or less calculated to excite corresponding associations."[100] While readership of Byron remained strong through the 1830s and 1840s, and Byron himself one of the "public gods," the literary elite turned against him. Byronism, Taylor later recalled in his autobiography, had become a "dead body."[101] "The rejection of Byron," as Andrew Elfenbein describes, "became one of the nineteenth century's master narratives, the *Bildungsroman* of the Victorian author."[102] The high water mark for Byronic "insincerity" was reached by Thackeray in 1846, who famously judged that Byron "*never* wrote from his heart. He got up rapture and enthusiasm with an eye to the public."[103]

The terms of Byron revisionism in the 1820s and 1830s are very familiar to any reader of European music criticism in the same period. Hazlitt considered Byron's principal object to be to "display his own power" and "astonish the reader." The language of "display" and "astonishment" is, as we have seen throughout this book, integral to the long-standing critique of virtuosity in Georgian cultural commentary. Hazlitt, and the critics who followed his lead, found that critique pertinent, in fact indispensable, to their reading of Byron. To reduce poetry to "diction," "mere eloquence," and "fine sounding lines," was identical, in aesthetic terms, to the crime of the piano virtuoso, who reduced melody to the "whirlwind" of arpeggiation, music to unmeaning sound. These virtuosi, both poet and pianist, produced a simulacrum of feeling only, "calculated" mechanical effects that did not express the "sensitive state of mind" but merely "corresponded" to it, theatrically. Liszt, recalled an observer of his London recitals, appeared as the sum of his "affectations and eccentricities."[104] The impact on the listener was only an arrested, bastardized feeling of "wonder," a ubiquitous description of Liszt's performances in Britain: "As a pianist ... he is indeed a wonder ... [but] we return from hearing Mr. Liszt with much the same feeling as we should return from seeing an accomplished conjurer or posture-master." Likewise for Hazlitt, "the colouring of Lord Byron's style ... is in itself an object of delight and wonder."[105] Wonder and mere "style" were synonymous with virtuoso performance. Be it in verse or on the concert stage, virtuosity was corrupted by its too-ready absorption into what Taylor called the "intensity of self-love" characteristic of both Byron and Byronism.

Liszt was unaware of the decline in Byron's reputation in England because no equivalent reassessment had occurred on the continent. Byron's skepticism had never found favor with French moralists, who thought him a kind of English Voltaire, an atheist avatar of "l'idée encyclopédique."[106] By virtue of a rush of translations and a famous death, however, Byron's literary influence in France in the 1830s was at its acme just as it was waning across the Channel. For Hugo, Leconte de Lisle, Alfred de Musset, and Flaubert, "Byron" named the melancholy predicament of liberal French sensibility in the 1830s, when a generation of war and revolution had succeeded to the restoration of a discredited monarchical order. Byronic pessimism was a natural affectation and his defiant individualism a kind of politics.[107] There is, of course, no better evidence of the persistence of Byron in Parisian culture than Liszt himself. In continental Europe, England's resistance to Byronism was a kind of scandal. Goethe "castigated the English for judging their great countryman so meanly, and in general having understood him so little."[108] So too Guiseppe Mazzini, the Italian patriot, who remarked at the irony that "the foreigner who lands upon her shores should search in vain ... her national Pantheon, for the Poet beloved and admired by all the nations of Europe."[109] In England in 1840, Franz Liszt found himself that disappointed Byronic pilgrim.

We have seen that the reviews of Liszt's concerts in London are characteristic of a virtuosity that bears within it its own critique. That is, Chorley's impression of truth and "expression" in Liszt's playing sits – necessarily – alongside Davison's critique of the same performance as mere "unsentimental ... display." A broader cultural context for Liszt's unhappy visit to England in 1840 – a context that helps to explain the intensity of criticism Liszt faced – is that the decline of Lord Byron's reputation in Britain in the 1830s was effected in terms identical to the contemporaneous critique of virtuosic pianism. As a touring virtuoso pianist, with a Byronic persona, Liszt stood therefore in double jeopardy. His "failure" in England, by these terms, appears almost inevitable. Where the question of Liszt's "sincerity" as an artist had been largely settled in Paris and Vienna by 1840 – by distinguishing his pronounced literary sensibility at the piano from "les virtuosi ordinaires" – his explicit identification with Byron had precisely the opposite effect in England. Instead of elevating his claims to artistry and social relevance, it sabotaged them by drawing him into association with a Byronic persona and artistic style recently pronounced to be "theatrical, false, affected," that is to say, virtuosic.

In other words, not only did Liszt's Byronism fail to ignite interest in Britain because of the long-standing native ambivalence toward the poet, but his reception became overdetermined by that very poetic association he had encouraged since the mid-1830s. Both poet and pianist were guilty of insincerity, of valuing mere display over genuine feeling. By bringing his Byronic persona with him to England, and moving in Byronic circles, Liszt not only failed to insulate himself against English virtuosophobia but exposed himself to it in the most spectacular way. Long after memory of his actual concerts had receded, he passed into Victorian popular history as an image of virtuosity's corruption, "a thin, gaunt, long-limbed man," whose "aim seemed more to startle and to astound than to charm."[110] The standard eighteenth-century language of virtuosophobia is here applied not to Liszt's playing but to his appearance, to his persona in general. It is an example of how the semiosis of virtuosity can pass from its aesthetic vehicle, be it poetry or music, into a promiscuous and adhesive cultural sign-system designating vulgarity, charlatanism, dehumanization and foreignness – a sort of free-floating, malignant Other. It is also a clue to how the taint of virtuosity could pass so easily between Liszt and Byron, to the point where the pianist's 1840 tour might usefully be read as Byron Redivivus, the uncanny return to Britain of its dead poet-celebrity and his disgraced mode of being.

At a loss after two weeks of tepid reception in London, Liszt threw in his lot with his fellow Byronists at Lady Blessington's little realizing that, once across that threshold, the script for the remaining months of his British tour was as good as written, its terms decided as much by the Byron revisionists Hazlitt and Carlyle as by the music critics Chorley and Davison. Liszt was, like his hero Byron, insincere, a fake – his virtuosity, like Byron's poetic gifts, degraded. For the "acknowledged authorities" of London society, any repeat of the Byron hysteria of 1812–13 was not to be thought of. "Liszt fever," such as it was, promptly "died out" almost before the great virtuoso had played a note. The irony is that Liszt was to some degree an unwitting orchestrator in this – his usually keen instinct for publicity deserted him – and he played his role in the failed Byronic revival of 1840 no more convincingly than at Newstead Abbey where he reclined on the lawn, considered writing poetry, and wished himself anywhere but in England.

VI

So much for culture: but what of form? In 1828, Liszt's friend Berlioz was hailed on the streets of Paris as "the Byron of music," and the overture to his opera *Les Francs-juges* as his "Childe Harold."[111] Liszt transcribed the overture for piano in 1833. Berlioz later literalized the Byronic associations of his music by composing a major orchestral suite, *Harold en Italie* (1834), which Liszt dutifully transcribed while on his own Haroldian pilgrimage through Switzerland and Italy. Then, of course, came Liszt's own Byronic tribute, the *Années de pèlerinage*. But the reception of the overture to *Les Francs-juges* is most crucial: it was called "Byronic" in the absence of any explicit programmatic association with Byron or his poetry. The Byronism of *Les Francs-juges* must thus have been recognizable to its first auditors in the music itself, and be describable in formal or aesthetic terms. In what way did the new French Romantic music of the 1830s, including Liszt's, formally adopt Byron's poetics rather than merely trade in the cultural currency of Byronism as I have discussed thus far?

In 1828 Berlioz had not yet been properly introduced to Beethoven's symphonic music, which would so decidedly influence his *Symphonie fantastique* (1830). His debts in the overture to *Les Francs-juges* belong more to his French classical tuition and French opera. But the work was nevertheless "uncompromisingly modern."[112] It contained a wealth of innovative orchestral effects: vertiginous ascending figures; brief lyric units interrupted or overwhelmed by tremolos and droning bass figures; a disregard for sonata form; and a corresponding emphasis on gestures of orchestration such as repeated arpeggiated flashes in the treble, dark chromatic movement in the bass, and breathless dotted rhythms. Lyricism, like form, was ironized: often, melodic lines sound almost overheard against the orchestral business, like a dramatic citation rather than lyricism proper.

Berlioz's Byron-inspired *Harold en Italie*, written at the height of his fame, was first commissioned by Paganini as a concerto for viola (virtuosi, it seems, were naturally drawn to Byronic subjects). But when he saw the frequent rests given the viola in Berlioz's score, Paganini demurred: "I should be playing all of the time," he said, a statement that may stand as the most succinct possible definition of the virtuoso worldview. The celebrity violinist came to reconsider on hearing the work – he offered to go down on his knees to Berlioz – perhaps because he understood its profound Byronism and thus its more radical modernity.[113] Just as Byron collapses his narrator and hero in *Childe Harold's Pilgrimage*, Berlioz in *Harold en Italie* takes Byronic license in uniting Haroldian scenes with his own experiences of Italy in a loose four-movement collage. The first and longest movement, "Harold aux montagnes," introduces the hero's theme in a series of fragments that reappear irregularly throughout the subsequent movements in company with a haunting pilgrims' march and energetic adaptations of Italian folk songs. The Harold theme is never "developed" in the orthodox, classical sense, and sometimes can barely be heard. Just as Byron's Harold is so difficult to distinguish in his role as phantasmic observer, and is eliminated entirely from the fourth canto, by the fourth movement of *Harold en Italie* the hero's melodic motif is attenuated to the point where it is virtually unrecognizable; it is then abandoned before it is half complete. Harold stands at an enigmatic distance, "unmoved" by the noisy exertions of the brigand's orgy. As in the overture to *Les Francs-juges*, the structural emphasis is not on motivic development but on rhythmic gestures – there is much experimentation with competing pulses set across different parts of the orchestra – and sonic texture: the harp, the basses and the timpani play extraordinarily individuated and complex roles. The most imposing effect, once more, is that of "style" defined as a set of musical gestures and sound effects rather than an unfolding melodic idea or functional harmonic argument within a conventional contrapuntal or sonata form. Individual musical episodes are mostly brought to an abrupt conclusion without formal cadence. For the listener, such orchestral effects were experienced virtuosically, that is, they drew the composer himself into focus as a material music-maker like a Paganini or Liszt.[114] The popularity of Berlioz acquired, accordingly, the character of cultish adulation.

Like Berlioz's Byronic music, Liszt's *Années de pèlerinage* contains a radical critique of classical structures and marks a definitive turn toward a material, performative conception of the piano. The suite is made up of six episodes without thematic continuity. Characteristic of Liszt's transcriptive, citational approach, many of the melodies are borrowed from a compilation of Swiss folk songs.[115] These are modal in character, assisting his departure from diatonic logic. "Vallée D'Obermann," the long piece at the heart of the suite, drifts from E minor to C, then obliquely to E major.[116] As in many of the pieces in the suite, modulation is achieved chromatically or enharmonically rather than through diatonic progression. Key identification is initially obscured by the Chopinesque languor of the opening – a minor seventh chord with an accompanying ascending figure of disputable relation to the chord itself – and the interrupted statement of the principal theme. The melodic "development," more like an iteration, is then interrupted with an extended middle section of a contrasting *agitato* character, with the opening melody reprised in a third section. This theme, a descending figure, is constantly interrupted only to begin again in some novel guise. Serge Gut has called the piece "a kind of mono-thematic fantasy-sonata," which is to say it defies generic categorization.[117] Other critics have resorted to programmatic descriptions, calling it a form of "romantic landscape painting," "literary," or "a spiritual journey."[118] The florid variety of these descriptions adds up to the truth of the matter: the *Années* are essentially idiosyncratic, unplaceable. They are only moderately difficult, pianistically speaking, but are wholly modern and virtuosic from a conceptual point of view, wherein "difficulty and complexity," in Jim Samson's formulation, represent "an accumulation of 'excessive' surface detail added to a relatively simple 'given' structure."[119] The absence of thematic structure both brings into focus and belies the conventional definition of accompaniment texture. The tremolos, arpeggiation, octave ostinato patterns, trills, chromatic octave runs, variations in chordal spacing, and dramatic contrasts in dynamics (i.e. loud–soft) define the character of the musical experience itself.

Rosen has called Liszt "the most radical musician of his generation" because he substituted chordal texture and tone color for the traditional musical properties of pitch, rhythm, and thematic development, a protomodernist whose presiding objective was "the transformation of sound into gesture."[120] These gestures, in turn, suggested an intrinsic Romanticism: the continual interruption and return of thematic material, with its changing settings, represented a complex psychology of desire, a Byronic

Sehnsucht, the poetry of wandering itself musically realized. Between the first editions in 1839–40 and their final consolidation as the two-volume *Années de pèlerinage* in 1855, Liszt simplified his Byronic pieces in various ways, suppressing many of the virtuosic keyboard effects and reducing the technical difficulty of key passages. But even the first versions of the pieces are not "virtuosic" in the sense of his concert showpieces, such as the *Grand galop chromatique*. The pianistic effects are not for display but are gestural elements for the purpose of "expression" as Liszt understood it. *Glissandi*, for example, a staple of his virtuoso concerts, are wholly absent from the *Années*. Liszt, like Berlioz, was drawn to Byron not to perform virtuosity but to defend it as Beethoven did, to redefine an essentially performative aesthetic as serious music, as avant-garde sound. The *Années de pèlerinage* thus represents a deeply gestural, material understanding of the keyboard that runs deeper than mere bravura technique. The effect, as Leon Botstein has argued, is profoundly literary. Liszt's attention to "rhetorical gesture and direct symbolic analogues between sound and language" means that the relationship of the *Années* pieces to their Byronic epigraphs is not merely suggestive, but illustrative. The fluid relation between thematic material and a musical context characterized by repetition and digression creates a distinctly Byronic "voice" and an elasticity of narrative time that recalls both *Childe Harold* and *Don Juan*. Listening to Liszt becomes a musical analogue of reading Byron.[121]

How, finally, to connect this proposition to our actual reading of Byron? When Berlioz was welcomed as the Byron of music in 1828, the name "Byron" did not signify simply a persona or set of cultural citations – as Byronism would later be reduced to – but was a code-word for the new. So too in 1841, the critic François Fétis nominated Liszt's Byronic *Années de pèlerinage* as "the future ... of the art." Fétis, in self-congratulatory fashion, saw this new music as the natural working-out of a metaphysical harmonic order he himself had suggested to the young pianist. He heard in Liszt's music the coming of what he had foreseen in the early 1830s as the new *ordre omnitonique*, where "the greatest possible number of tones and modes would be put into relation with each other." He may have prophesied modernism, even the twelve-tone row, but Fétis's worldview, like Liszt's, was Romantic, albeit in the sense of an avant-garde. The *ordre omnitonique* was to be underwritten by the metaphysical guarantee of "tonality," whereby the most remote dissonances might be traced to a set of "universal chords" prescribed by nature.[122]

"Tonality," like any other metaphysical first term, was both chimerical and immensely productive. The alternative to sonata form, according to

Fétis, was not chaos (as some British critics called Liszt's music in 1840) but only a more complex order. Exciting for Liszt to hear, at Fetis's 1832 lectures, was his repudiation of functional harmonic orthodoxy and the implicit legitimation, from France's most influential critic, of a liberating new aesthetic, a "revolution." This new "science" of music was not mathematical – the analysis of harmonic argument – but based in "the sounds of music themselves, as psychological phenomena."[123] As a theory of sound, Fétisian tonality was to be interpreted by Liszt in a performative rather than metaphysical sense, as a figure for his own overweening presence at the keyboard, for his desire for an "increase of the piano's power," for his material treatment of the keyboard – whether in concert or the pages of a Liszt score – as a sonic machine.[124]

In short, "tonality" in Liszt functioned as a metaphysical guarantee for an otherwise discontinuous, fragmented musical phenomenon. In analogous fashion, readers of Byron have traditionally relied on metaphysical categories such as "personality" and "voice" to describe what they find in *Childe Harold's Pilgrimage* and *Don Juan*.[125] The French Romantic composers of the 1830s, like the French poets, were attracted to the persona of nomadic disaffection labeled Childe Harold, but more materially applicable to their own medium were Byron's formal innovations: specifically, his eschewing conventional narrative development in favor of a new poetics of personality described by a set of rhetorical gestures. Jerome McGann has called it Byronic irony or "style":

> [Byron] always has a theoretical stylistic norm to which he can return as to a point of open possibility. Mostly in *Don Juan* we do not see this "pure," theoretically normative style, for Byron's method is to play variations upon it. Nonetheless, it is always present and can be invoked as a medium for amazing transition, or as a narrative last resort.[126]

Similar to the assurance of tonality in the radically gestural, fragmented music of Berlioz and Liszt, Byron's "irony," "voice," "personality," and "style" are names given to our readerly intuition of a single authorial sensibility presiding over the heterogeneous Byronic text.

French Romantic music of the 1830s likewise can illuminate our understanding of Byronic digression which, even more than "personality" or "style," has come to serve as an essential description of Byron's technique, particularly in *Don Juan*. Fétis saw that tonality in music might be understood horizontally as the unfolding musical character of a work, rather than simply as the serial accumulation of vertical harmonic instants. The listener's impression of tonality – as a quasi-metaphysical idea of sound – was best gained in the form of the extended episode and in the absence of thematic (melodic) development. At a Liszt concert, the suppression of melody – for instance, in the pianistic evocation of a storm he featured on his British tour – enabled the virtuosic technique, the Lisztian "voice" or "style," to be heard most distinctly, and the virtuosic "personality" to be brought into being as the object of wonder, astonishment, and exhilaration, even to the point of sexual arousal. Analogously, Byron's digressive style puts on display the independence of the Byronic voice from its narrative materials, just as Byronic irony exhibits that independence through playful dissonances of tone and content, as in the notorious cannibalism episode in canto II of *Don Juan*.

The usefulness of the form–content binary, however, remains local. Style in *Harold* and *Don Juan* can be endlessly exemplified, but remains so difficult to define because it points to what can never be fully exposed in a single analysis, namely the machinery of the words themselves, how the authorial personality – not as a metaphysical presence but a working guarantee of idiomatic integrity – unfolds in the course of reading according to a self-justifying but otherwise impalpable logic we can only call Byronic. Jerome Christensen has called it Byron's "ethos of invention," how *Don Juan*, for example, in M. K. Joseph's words, "bounds and impersonalises itself by insisting on its own nature."[127] Berlioz and Liszt looked to Byron because they perceived in *Childe Harold's Pilgrimage* an advanced ironic form of art self-consciously absorbed in its own rhetorical materials at the expense of almost all other binding structure. In the Romantic reception of Wordsworth or Beethoven, the aesthetic medium was conceived *expressively* – a "truth" of poetic voice mediated through "common language" or sonata form. In a Byron poem, by contrast, the truth of personality lay, phantasmatically, in the production of a patented, reiterable vocabulary, and set of rhetorical gestures. Fétis perceived Liszt's dramatic new direction in *Années de pèlerinage* in analogous terms. Liszt's published music in the 1830s had subordinated the piano as a transcriptive medium for symphonic and operatic music, so that the piano score served, epiphenomenally, as a translation or approximation of an orchestral text. The *Années de pèlerinage*, by contrast, displayed Liszt's new "Byronic" interest in idiomatically pianistic effects, in the sonorities of the instrument itself.

Canto III of *Childe Harold's Pilgrimage* exemplifies the virtuosic, gestural poetics Liszt later employed as the basis of his pianistic art. The second stanza, which Liszt famously paraphrased in *La Revue et Gazette Musicale*, casts us immediately into a pseudo-fictive drama – exile on the sea – which threatens to collapse the distinction (formally given up in canto IV) between the Byronic narrator and his fictional hero: "Once more upon the waters! yet once more!" Collapsed, too, as Liszt readily saw, was the scene of "action" with the scene of writing. The vehicles of exilic motion – the waters and steed – are literal descriptions of the narrator/Harold's journey to and across the continent, but also metaphors for the activity of Byron's verse-making, for the motion of the pen across the page. The exclamation "once more!" applies, with a virtuosic flourish, to the resumption of writing, to the act of picking up that pen.

One of the signatures of Byron's style in *Childe Harold* is that he continually returns us to the dramatic present of composition. In doing so, he encourages the reader to focus less on the narrated material than on the wonder of his own making of it. He thematizes this ironic method in the celebrated sixth stanza:

> 'Tis to create, and in creating live
> A being more intense, that we endow
> With form our fancy, gaining as we give
> The life we imagine, even as I do now.

Poetry itself is the referent here, as the exemplary creation of "A being more intense," but the relation between poetry and life, as that between poetry and the "waters" in stanza two, is held in a kind of suspension – like a cadence never fully resolved – somewhere between emblem, metaphor, and literal identification. The addended phrase, "even as I do now," directs us not to read the foregoing reflection epigrammatically as a routine piece of wisdom, but dramatically as an act of "creating," a gesture of art happening before our very eyes. What follows in the stanza is not an elaboration of the prior thought – a thematic movement – but a new dramatic gesture suggested by a single material element of the preceding line, namely "I":

> What am I? Nothing; but not so art thou,
> Soul of my thought! with whom I traverse earth,
> Invisible but gazing, as I glow
> Mix'd with thy spirit, blended with thy birth,
> And feeling still with thee in my crush'd feelings' dearth.

In his suffocating identification with his hero, the Byronic narrator provides the psychological model for cultural Byronism. His self-abnegation – "What am I? Nothing" – in order to follow and feel for his idol anticipates the Byronic reader's overweening desire to fantasize and emulate the life of the celebrity poet. Like Liszt's memory of his desire for the Haroldian figure in his dream, the narrator imagines himself "glow[ing]/Mix'd with thy spirit, blended with thy birth,/And feeling still with thee." In then asking the question – What am I? – the narrator makes the apparent change of subject an emblematic act of Byronic sensibility that is both the medium and matter of the poem. The answer – "Nothing" – cannot be believed except as the opening to an elaborate rhetorical joke. "Not so" is both the rejection of nothing and its repetition, and "Soul of my thought" an image of Childe Harold abstracted to vanishing point. The referential tenuousness of these two lines is hardly relieved by the subsequent description of the narrator as "Invisible but gazing," and his "feeling still" in "feelings' dearth." While the meaning of the passage approximates zero, its significance, as a rendering of the irresistible Byronic idiom of "soul," "earth," "spirit," and "feeling," is definitive, the very matter of reading *Childe Harold's Pilgrimage*. The reader *hears* the tonality of the poem, which is the only structure it bears.

Seriality, a key theme of McGann's seminal *Don Juan in Context* (1976), has been extended by Jerome Christensen to an understanding of Byronism as a commercial form of "speculative grammar," whereby, for example, *Childe Harold* III "announces itself as a poem constituted out of the resources of *Childe Harold* I and II."[128] Thus might stanza six of canto III of *Childe Harold* stand in for any other stanza, or for all of them, as a representative iteration in a series within a single Byronic tonality. Byron's technique in canto III is thus not a classical theme-and-variation structure, nor is his "theme" developed beyond its opening statement and placed in dialectical relation to others, as in sonata form. It is, rather, a virtuosic form of *serial iteration*. "Feelings' dearth" in the narrator is subsequently reharmonized in canto III as Harold's "desolation" (12: 8), after which the original images of sea and steed are reprised and given full orchestral treatment in the world-historical form of Napoleon, whose "breath is agitation, and life/A storm whereon they ride, to sink at last" (44: 1–2). We then return, abruptly and *sotto voce*, to Harold whose "days/Of passion had consumed themselves to dust" (53: 1–2), before modulating to an Alpine reverie and the last of the Byronic iterations of the canto, called "wild Rousseau/The apostle of affliction" (77: 1–2).

Seriality is likewise essential to an understanding of musical Byronism. In *Années de pèlerinage*, Liszt serialized a small amount of often banal or borrowed thematic material through a series of textural restatements, deeply ironic and virtuosic in conception (if not always in their technical demands). The fourth piece of the *Années*, "Au bord d'une source," follows this Byronic structure closely. Anticipating Debussy in its liquid evocations, "Au bord d'une source" consists of five versions of a single theme, the original or definitive form of which remains elusive. The brief coda constitutes the only mark of difference within the music and does not perform closure so much as define structure itself ironically. The distinction between composition and paraphrase in Liszt becomes impossible to define.[129] Like Byron, Liszt essentially cites and transcribes himself, as he transcribed Beethoven and Berlioz. His artistic precedent was not musical but literary, the self-plagiarizing Byron of *Childe Harold's Pilgrimage*.[130]

This Byronic aesthetic, which the French Romantics considered quintessentially modern and critical, was inseparable from a new ontology. "I live not in my self," says the poet of *Childe Harold* III, "but I become/ Portion of that around me." In that canto authorial identity is portioned out, by turns, into Byron the father of Ada, Harold, Napoleon, a disguised Haroldian Byron in love with his half-sister Augusta, and Rousseau, all of them bound by a single idiom or tonality of "affliction," identifiably Byronic. Liszt chose these lines as the epigraph for the original version of "Les Cloches de Genève" (titled "Les Cloches de G*****"), his other long piece in the first edition of the *Années de pèlerinage*. Like "Vallée," the original "Cloches," inspired by the birth of his daughter Blandine, is elaborated from a negligible amount of thematic material. Principally devoted to the sonic evocation of the eponymous bells interrupted by virtuosic reprises of the theme, "Les Cloches de G*****" is an exquisite example of extended serial iteration with no larger meaning beyond the pianistic soundscape and its poetic engagement with an imagined Geneva. Those who "do not live in themselves," Liszt seems to suggest in "Les Cloches," live virtuosically as exteriorized beings absorbed in performance, in their medium of expression.

It is significant that Liszt, after retiring from the concert stage, deleted the Byronic epigraph from his revision of "Les Cloches de Genève," as if he wished to retreat from the radical implications of Byron's modernity and re-romanticize himself. Or perhaps it was because Byron's modernity was no longer apparent. Sales of Byron dropped dramatically in France in the late 1840s. By 1853 Byron was no longer a byword for the future but the past – Byronism was a "dead body." To this extent Liszt's long career embodied the dialectic of virtue and virtuosity in its fullest description. The young Byronist of the 1840 letters – as their recipient, Marie d'Agoult, predicted – had passed into respectability, even to the extent of taking orders. "Les Cloches" was accordingly the most heavily revised of the 1853 *Années* – cut in half, stripped of its virtuosic runs and sonoristic effects, given a conventional operatic melody and contrasting

B section, and pushed from the heart of the suite to the end – where it has served, in the Liszt canon, as a modest valediction to virtuosity, a gentle fade-to-black for the Byron of the piano.[131]

With Liszt's virtuous revisions of the *Années de pèlerinage*, and conventional Romantic seclusion at Weimar, certain historical limits of virtuosity and its critique come into view. In the decade 1830–40 to perceive a new paradigm of personality in Byron or Liszt was a matter of idiomatic recognition or rejection. The Byron poem or Liszt concert either appeared the most powerful possible medium of Romantic heroic expression, representative of a brave new subjectivity, or it appeared insincere and mechanical, even chaotic. This explains the radical differences of opinion regarding Liszt's pianism during his tours of Britain in 1840–1, how Chorley could perceive profound emotion in Liszt's playing where Davison lamented precisely the absence of that emotion. It explains also how a reader of Byron such as Carlyle might condemn his own former Byronist infatuations, and discover as "theatrical" in Byron what he had so recently taken for deep truth.

By contrast with the audiences and readers of 1840, the enjoyment of Liszt or Byron, for us, is a matter of taste not virtue. We feel smug and anxious by turns when we perceive only sentimental showmanship in *Childe Harold* where its contemporary readers saw their full-life poeticized selves. We scoff at accounts of bacchanalian rapture at the concerts of Liszt then worry that we have missed out. Byron and Liszt were palimpsests of early nineteenth-century European culture and compulsive plagiarists, principally of themselves. But with virtuosic style conceived as serial iteration, the distinction blurs between composition and paraphrase, Byron and Byronism, artist and franchise. The oddness of Byron, as Richard Jeffrey observed, was that he was both utterly original and "most deeply indebted to [his] predecessors."[132] This effect applies to the larger phenomenon of the *Childe Harold* project. The post-war canto III, as Christensen has recognized, was "rendered readable by its similarity as part to the Byronic system as whole."[133] Tonality, in Byron's poetry, describes not simply a style but Byronism's commodity potential after 1812, the total permeability of Byron and Byronism commercially conceived. Popular virtuosity thus turns upon a paradox. The virtuoso's *unique* gifts, his *signature* performances mask a dependent relationship to "others," be it an artistic tradition, the consumer masses, or the iterative logic of his own virtuosic style. With the decline of the virtuosi in the mid-nineteenth century, that mask of crowd-pleasing egotism came to obscure from historical view the raw modernity of European Byronism and its extraordinary incarnation in Liszt. If *we* now find it hard to see anything like "individuality" or "the modern" sincerely realized in Byron or Liszt's art, this is not because their art is not modern or sincere, but because we live on the far side of virtuosity's historical decline and do not inhabit the living dialectic by which these artists met the astonished judgment of their contemporaries. The Romantic reforms that defined the mature Liszt remain in the ascendant. Virtuosity may be forever in bad taste but, even as a species of vulgar greatness, it is rarely now taken for an aesthetic future, let alone a revolutionary mode of being.

Coda: the mechanical nightingale

Hans Christian Andersen's "The Nightingale" (1843) opens with an account of the bird's legend in poetry. The Chinese emperor first becomes aware of the marvelous songster's residence in his own garden on reading "long odes" to the nightingale by foreign poets, published in the accounts of "world travelers" who have toured his kingdom.[1] The nightingale's exotic Asian residence in Andersen's fairytale – "in the forest, on the shores of the deep blue sea" – recalls the "perilous seas, in faery lands forlorn" (70) imagined by Keats's mental traveler in his 1819 ode, while the voice of both nightingales is heard "In ancient days by emperor and clown" (64). Inspired by the same melopoetic tradition as Keats – in which a duel, implicit or explicit, is staged between the poet/singer and the nightingale – Andersen's own "deceiving" fancy was to think of a dazzling mechanical rival to the songbird in the forest. The subsequent musical showdown is rich in historical and literary precedents – from Apollo and Marsyas, to Mozart and Clementi, to Emma Woodhouse and Jane Fairfax – though Andersen's story defers the predictable outcome. At first, the nightingale finds itself supplanted in the emperor's favor by the jeweled newcomer and flees the court. Years pass, the mechanical bird breaks down and with it the emperor's health. Only at the last does the true nightingale return to charm death itself from the emperor's bedside and claim its victory.

Musical inspiration for Andersen's story lay with Swedish soprano sensation Jenny Lind, for whom he nurtured a worshipful regard. The so-called "Swedish Nightingale's" impact on the opera world in the early 1840s, according to Andersen in his autobiography, had been to restore the "truth and nature" of national folk song tradition to an international *bel canto* style long corrupted by virtuosic excess.[2] An opera star in his thoughts, Andersen thus employs the classical nightingale topos to compose an anti-virtuosic fable of nature's triumph over technique and artifice. His fairytale thus stands upon the twin pillars of virtuosophobia as I have described them in this book: a contempt for aristocratic luxury, embodied in the jeweled bird, and fear of the dehumanizing impact of modern machine technology, evidenced by its wondrous replication of a nightingale's song.

Presumably because of its appeal to deep-set virtuosophobic instincts, Andersen's "The Nightingale" has attracted generations of sympathetic readers. But Igor Stravinsky – in his musical adaptation of the story – rejected both its folkish simplicity and the Romantic fairytale ending. "I prefer a music box to a nightingale," Stravinsky confessed, and in his *Song of the Nightingale* score – a ballet written for Diaghilev in the mid-1910s – he makes no clear distinction between the songs of the real and artificial birds, and delights throughout in a virtuosic orchestral palette rich in mechanical motifs, in a "music full of cadenzas, vocalises, and melismata of all kinds."[3] Instead of championing the rights of nature over technology – the nightingale's virtuous simplicity over his rival's shallow virtuosity – Stravinsky's ballet score raucously celebrates the necessary distance between nature and all art. His music, no less than Andersen's story – Stravinsky seems to say – stands closer to the workings of a mechanical bird than an actual nightingale's song. As Daniel Albright puts it, Stravinsky's *Nightingale* "erects a theatre of automata in order to show how smeared and faded the old operatic expressivity of the bird sounds by contrast."[4] Stravinsky historicizes his nightingale and so de-naturalizes it. The mechanical bird's parts wear out, while the "real" one warbles on in a worn-out aesthetic: both are creatures of artifice. In a modernist symphonic poem of the early twentieth century, then, we observe a conscious deconstruction of virtue and virtuosity both as the working binary of Andersen's fable and, more largely, as a founding opposition of Romantic aesthetics.

The classical figure of the nightingale enjoyed a florid revival in the early modern period and into the eigheenth century. Well-known examples in Spenser, Shakespeare, and Milton were followed by a rash of neoclassical and Romantic meditations. An incomplete list of purveyors in the tradition, in the century before Keats's ode, would include Anne Finch, Anne Radcliffe, William Cowper, Mary Hays, Charlotte Smith, Mary Robinson, John Clare, Coleridge, and Wordsworth. The Georgian precedents for Keats's poem are matched, in sheer volume, by the musical tradition into which Stravinsky inserted himself in the 1910s. Indeed, the nightingale, since Ovid, has been the supreme figure of melopoesis, the putative natural union of music and poetry. But while Keats's ode refers us to an eighteenth-century poetic tradition replete with well-known names, the nightingale's musical history opens a wholly different vista – a veritable "magic casement" – on to a fairytale world of forgotten popular songs. In Georgian music culture the nightingale was a ubiquitous inspiration and commercial tag. Between 1738 and 1791 more than a dozen separate collections of popular songs published in London – ranging in size from 8 to 400 pages – entered the cultural marketplace as "The Nightingale," many to be reissued numerous times. Individual songs also bore the title. The prolific songwriter John Moulds published his "Nightingale" in 1785, an amateur named "Miss Bonwick" hers in 1792, while in 1810, the piano teacher to the children of the Prince of Wales, T. [Jean] Latour, published "The Nightingale: A favourite military rondo, with twelve variations for the pianoforte."[5] The Ovidian nightingale has always been susceptible to metamorphosis, and Latour's "military" bird suggests a creature snared midflight between its native forest and the mechanic's workshop.

The songs of Moulds and Bonwick make for interesting comparison and together distill the structural essence of virtuoso aesthetics. Moulds was a well-known composer for the English opera, whose hits at the Theatre Royal included *The Phisiognomist* (1789), *The Sultan* (1792), and *The Deserted Village* (1795). He published over thirty individual songs in the decade and a half before 1800, and "The Nightingale" handles a simple tune with the harmonic elegance and dash of *galant* chromaticism one would expect from a professional songsmith of his water.[6] The title page, which proclaims it "A Favourite Song, Sung by Mrs. Botarelli at Ranelagh," shows Moulds operating within a sophisticated commercial network by which popular songs debuted on the stage, were revived at the pleasure gardens and, if successful, found their way into the music collections of thousands of young female pianists for rendition in the home. By contrast, the effort by his amateur counterpart, Miss Bonwick, bears no such popular imprimatur, being "Printed and Sold for the Author." In addition to there being no reference to public performance, its juvenile musical content marks it as a vanity piece, the work of an overestimated child whose parental patrons published her prize exercise at their own expense.

Differences in quality are immaterial, however, to the identical compositional structures of the two "nightingale" songs, which are exemplary in their adherence to the binary aesthetic that has been the presiding theme of this book. In each case, a simple, balladic melody is concluded – or interrupted – by an extravagant cadenza. Neither Moulds nor Bonwick makes serious technical demands on the performer; in fact, both songs are clearly marketed to amateur players of decidedly modest accomplishment. Nevertheless, both offer an approximation or simulacrum of operatic virtuosity in the extended cadenza section. Why is this? Why would the structural illusion of virtuosity be so integral, so carefully managed, and so universally legible? The answer to this question crystallizes the importance of virtuosity – and its discontents – as a master-metaphor of Georgian aesthetic discourse. The theatrical ritual of virtuosity in both songs stages a definitive Romantic-era morality tale: one in which the simple virtues of lyric self-expression succumb to the temptations of mechanical brilliance and self-display. It is a story with which both Moulds and Bonwick – for all their differences in musical competence and professional stature – are fully acquainted and equally equipped to tell.

The same uneasy but compulsive accommodation between virtue and virtuosity can be seen in Keats's "Ode to a Nightingale." The virtuosophobic strain of the poem is evident in its exoticization of the nightingale as a baroque object of wonder removed from the bodily, mundane realities of the poet: "What thou among the leaves hast never known/ The weariness, the fever, and the fret" (22–3). In his elusive nightingale, Keats finds the objective correlative of his own lyric virtuosity – publicly condemned on the publication of *Endymion* – which he both repudiates and desires. "I will fly to thee," he proclaims at the beginning of stanza four, only to bid a resentful "Adieu" to the bird in stanza eight. Just as the "Nightingale" songs of Moulds and Bonwick baldly juxtaposed a simple lyric voice with its melismatic opposite, virtuosophobia manifests itself in Keats's poem in a self-reflexive economy of lure and threat, wonder and disgust, figured in the mercurial flight of the bird and the poet's halting pursuit. This economy becomes more visible if we read the subject of the ode, retrospectively through Andersen's 1843 story, as a mechanical bird, a wind-up toy, a figure for unnatural powers that are not mythic and transcendent but technologically engineered. By concluding thus with the image of a musical-mechanical ornament, we come full circle to 1770s London, to the Jaquet-Droz robots and James Cox's musical-mechanical wonders in *Evelina* where this book began. Somewhere between Cox's bejeweled "Jem cracks" bound for the Chinese court and Andersen's fable that tells the story of just such a luxury Asiatic toy, lies Keats's famous ode, surrounded on all sides by a melopoetic discourse of the nightingale that compulsively policed an imagined divide between nature and the material lures of artifice and display.

The "full-throated ease" (10) that concludes the first stanza of Keats's nightingale ode superbly captures the paradox of virtuosic performance. Vocal technique marks the disciplinary character of virtuosity, the bodily self-control that, ironically, makes "full-throated ease" possible. Technique, not "truth," is the rational, empirical shell from which the irrational exuberances of virtuoso exhibition – bravura, erotic, carnivalesque – can be released. Virtuosity, founded on superlative technique, is thus a rationality that performs its own limits or negation, combining absolute mechanical command with the vertiginous affect of improvisation and a dazzling spontaneity. From the first to the second stanza, Keats's somatic focus stays with the vocal organ, though instead of the nightingale's throat it is his own as a conduit of liquid narcotics – "hemlock," "opiate," "a draught of vintage" – thereby establishing a tropic connection between virtuosity, intoxication, and death that shapes the remainder of the poem. For the "darkling" listener of stanza six, the bravura mode of the bird is an "ecstasy" and a "Death." The poet is "half in love," but also, implicitly, half despising. The "full-throated ease" of the nightingale now returns to double and blend with the poet's imagined "easeful Death" as the dark reward for a lyric facility – namely Keats's – fatally enraptured by its own power of sound. Hence the wondrous "immortal Bird" is also a "deceiving elf" (74), a dangerously talented charlatan like the stupendous Catalani, who aurally "enchained" her London audiences in the 1810s. Through self-glorifying exhibitions of sonic virtuosity on the stage of the King's Theatre, La Catalani cast spells of vocal art that the politically active members of Keats's circle, including Leigh Hunt, recognized as an aesthetic of tyranny, and sought to break through the modern skeptical power of review journalism.

The anxieties of Keats's poem, expressed as the ritual pursuit and disguised abjection of a (mechanical) bird of song, thus belong to a time-worn British skepticism toward virtuosic display divorced from the sentimentalized body, from "heart," "feeling," etc. The poet's valedictory exclamation, however – "Fled is that music" (80) – evokes the more specific historical moment of Keats's ode. By 1819 the London pleasure gardens in which, a generation before, popular songs like John Moulds's "The Nightingale" found fame, were in terminal decline. The age of outdoor polite entertainment, attracting a mixed and mostly unregulated metropolitan audience, had passed, and with it our image of an Italian soprano (Mrs. Bottarelli) singing a musical ode to a nightingale before a colorful urban crowd of the type memorialized by Burney's early novels.[7] Abandoning the pseudo-rural, sociable spaces of Ranelagh and Vauxhall Gardens – and a necessarily theatrical identity – Keats's post-Waterloo nightingale alights in the interior, private landscape of high Romantic lyric, where it enacts both its own historical passing as a baroque object of wonder as well as the crime – namely virtuosity – for which it has earned its banishment. Keats's ode, like Wordsworth's Preface to *Lyrical Ballads*, thus performs a quintessential Romantic *rite de passage*: the relegation of the "gaudiness and inane phraseology" of the virtuoso mode, and all its "plaintive anthem[s]," to a discredited past.

I conclude not with Keats, but with another baroque object he is said to have surpassed – his friend and mentor Leigh Hunt. In a moving passage from his 1850 autobiography, Hunt recounts coming across two old Vauxhall songs at a music stall in Wardour Street, whereupon he reflects on the accelerated obsolescence of popular songs within a modern commercial music culture driven by fashion rather than folk tradition: "how had they not been thumbed and thrown aside by all the pianoforte young ladies – our mother and grandmothers – fifty years ago, never to be brought forth again, except by an explorer of old stalls, and to meet, perhaps, with no sympathy but in his single imagination." One of the songs, "Dans votre lit" – about a lady-lily on a flower bed – Hunt remembers as the favorite of his sister, who imagined the song referred to her little brother by name. This book has mostly told the story of the rise and sometimes triumph of late Georgian music culture. But amid its "rage for music," the Romantic period also produced a quickening sense of vanishing musics, of ephemeral songs and styles, and traditions fading with the nightingale – an emerging historical consciousness of music evident in the scholarship of Burney and Hawkins and the antiquarian collections of Ritson, Scott, and Burns. "Mary died not long after," Hunt recalls, and his only memory of his sister, revived by his late chance encounter at the music stall, is "her custom of leading me by the hand to some stool or seat on the staircase, and making me sing the song with her favourite burden."[8] Here is no Romantic critique of the commercialization of music, or of fashion-driven modernity, but rather Hunt's gentle reckoning with the losses of his own past. According to this personal equation, rapid changes in musical taste are as inevitable as time and death. The forgotten music of his childhood is naturalized in the figure of his beloved sister's early passing.

Hunt's unanguished account of music and modernity is evident also in a poem from his own heyday, published in *The Examiner* in 1816.[9] "On Hearing a Little Music Box" takes delight in the mechanical wonders of its subject, the "epithet-exhausting toy":

> O full of sweetness, crispness, ease,
> Compound of lovely smallnesses,
> Accomplished trifle,—tell us what
> To call thee, and disgrace thee not.   (19–22)

In his 1843 story of the nightingale, Andersen narrativized the standard virtuosophobic questions: what if the natural voice of the nightingale is replaced by a machine – and, by extension, humanity itself degraded by the corrupting luxuries of technology? Hunt, by contrast – like Stravinsky a century later – insisted on an affinity between the nightingale's song and mechanical reproduction. Music boxes, he fancies, are "Nightingales endued with art,/Caught in listening to Mozart." In his poem, the toy nightingale has made a seamless crossing from nature into art(ifice), whereby Hunt inverts Andersen's anti-virtuosic formulation: if a mechanical nightingale can be mistaken for the real thing, must there not already be something machine-like about the "true" nightingale's song? In Andersen's fairytale, the bird is first adored, subsequently replaced by a toy, then returned at last as a proper replacement for its rival. For Stravinsky, the rapid sequence of subsitutions in the story suggested not the ultimate triumph of nature but the interchangeability of the two nightingales – that music, in its Ovidian essence, is in perpetual metamorphosis in the contrived space between performer and the listening audience, where "nature" is only one useful fiction among many. In a similar way, Hunt's poem lights on the mechanical power of repetition as the singular charm of his music box: "Hark! it scarcely ends the strain,/But it gives it o'er again,/Lovely thing!" (9–10). Sidestepping the stale virtuosophobic rhetoric of a century past, Hunt looks ahead to the union of the musical arts with the technology of reproduction. The hidden parts of his toy represent not mere machinery but "great springs/Of divine and human things" (51–2). In the pretty gimcrack in Leigh Hunt's lap sits the welcome genie of virtuosity, demystified.

Select bibliography

PRIMARY SOURCES

Addison, Joseph and Richard Steele. *The Spectator, with Illustrative Notes. To which are Prefixed the Lives of the Authors.* 8 vols. Ed. Robert Bisset. London, 1799.
Avison, Charles. *Essay on Musical Expression.* London, 1752.
Baker, H. Barton. *The London Stage: Its History and Traditions, 1576–1888.* London, 1889.
Baretti, Giuseppe. *A Dissertation upon the Italian Poetry.* London, 1753.
Bayley, Anselm. *A Practical Treatise on Singing and Playing with Just Expression and Real Elegance.* London, 1771.
  The Alliance of Musick, Poetry, and Oratory. London, 1789.
Brown, John. *An Estimate of the Manners and Principles of the Times.* London, 1757.
Burgh, Allatson. *Anecdotes of Music.* 3 vols. London, 1814.
Burney, Charles. *The Present State of Music in Germany, the Netherlands, and United Provinces.* London, 1775.
  An Account of the Musical Performances in Westminster Abbey. London, 1785.
  Memoirs of the Life and Writings of the Abaté Metastasio. 3 vols. London, 1796.
  A General History of Music [1776–89]. 2 vols. Ed. Frank Mercer. New York: Dover, 1935.
  Memoirs of Dr. Charles Burney, 1726–1769. Ed. Slava Klima, Garry Bowers, and Kerry S. Grant. Lincoln: University of Nebraska Press, 1988.
  The Letters of Dr. Charles Burney. Ed. Alvaro Ribeiro. Oxford: Clarendon Press, 1991.
Burney, Frances. *Journals and Letters of Fanny Burney.* Ed. Joyce Hemlow. Oxford: Clarendon Press, 1972–.
  The Early Journals and Letters. 4 vols. Ed. Lars E. Troide, Betty Rizzo, Stewart J. Cooke. Montreal: McGill–Queen's University Press, 1988–.
  Complete Plays. 2 vols. Ed. Peter Sabor. London: William Pickering, 1995.
  Journals and Letters. Ed. Peter Sabor and Lars E. Troide. London, Penguin, 2001.
Burney, Frances [Madame D'Arblay] (ed.), *Memoirs of Doctor Burney.* 3 vols. London, 1832.
Chorley, Henry. *Music and Manners in France and Germany.* 3 vols. London, 1844.

Cowden Clarke, Mary and Charles. *Recollections of Writers.* London, 1876.
Cowper, William. *The Task, a Poem in Six Books.* London, 1785.
   Letters and Prose Writings. 5 vols. Ed. James King and Charles Ryskamp. Oxford: Clarendon Press, 1979–86.
Crotch, William. *Substance of Several Courses of Lectures on Music.* London, 1831.
D'Agoult, Marie (Comtesse). *Mémoires, Souvenirs et Journaux.* 2 vols. Paris: Mercure de France, 1990.
Dennis, John. *Critical Works.* 2 vols. Ed. Edward Niles Hooker. Baltimore, MD: Johns Hopkins University Press, 1985.
Dibdin, Charles. *A Letter on Musical Education.* London, 1791.
Diehl, Alice Mangold. *Musical Memories.* London, 1897.
Edgeworth, Maria and Richard Lovell Edgeworth. *Practical Education.* 2 vols. London, 1798.
Euterpe: or, Remarks on the Use and Abuse of Music, as a Part of Modern Education. Bath, 1778.
Fordyce, James. *Sermons to Young Women.* 12th edn. 2 vols. London, 1800.
Gardiner, William. *Music and Friends, or, Pleasant Recollections of a Dilettante.* London, 1838.
Hawkins, John. *A General History of the Science and Practice of Music* [1776]. 2 vols. New York: Dover, 1963.
Hazlitt, William. *Complete Works.* 21 vols. Ed. P. P. Howe. London: Dent, 1934.
Hill, Aaron and William Popple. *The Prompter, 1734–6.* Ed. William W. Appleton and Kalman A. Burnim. New York: Benjamin Blom, 1996.
Hogarth, George. *Memoirs of the Musical Drama.* 2 vols. London, 1838.
Hoole, John. *Dramas and Other Poems of the Abbé Pietro Metastasio.* 3 vols. London, 1800.
Hueffer, Francis. *Half a Century of Music in England, 1847–1887.* London, 1889.
Hunt, Leigh. *Autobiography* [1850]. Ed. Edmund Blunden. Oxford University Press, 1928.
   Musical Evenings; or, Selections, Vocal and Instrumental. Ed. David R. Cheney. Columbia: University of Missouri Press, 1964.
   Selected Writings. Ed. Michael Eberle-Sinatra and Robert Morrison. 6 vols. London: Pickering and Chatto, 2003.
Isola, Augustine. *Pieces Selected from the Italian* London, 1783.
Johnson, Samuel. *Complete Works.* 18 vols. Ed. W. J. Bate and Albrecht B. Strauss. New Haven: Yale University Press, 1958–.
Jones, William. *A Treatise on the Art of Music.* Colchester, 1784.
Kassler, Jamie Croy (ed.). *The Science of Music in Britain: A Catalogue of Writings, Lectures, and Inventions.* New York: Garland, 1979.
Lamb, Charles. *Complete Works and Letters.* New York: Modern Library, 1935.
Liszt, Franz. *Correspondance de Liszt et de Madame d'Agoult.* 2 vols. Ed. Daniel Ollivier. Paris: Grasset, 1933–4.
   An Artist's Journey: Lettres d'un bachelier es musique, 1835–41. Trans and ed. Charles Suttoni. University of Chicago Press, 1989.
Macaulay, Catherine. *Letter on Education.* London, 1790.

[Maddison, Robert]. *An Examination of the Oratorios which have been Performed this Season at Covent-Garden Theatre.* London, 1763.
Mainwaring, John. *Memoirs of the Life of the Late George Frederic Handel.* London, 1760.
Marx, A. B. *Musical Form in the Age of Beethoven: Selected Writings on Theory and Method.* Ed. Scott Burnham. Cambridge: Cambridge University Press, 1997.
Miller, [Lady] Anna Riggs (ed.). *Poetical Amusements at a Villa Near Bath.* 2nd edn. 4 vols. Bath, 1776–81.
More, Hannah. *Strictures on the Modern System of Female Education.* 2 vols. London, 1799.
Mount-Edgcumbe, Richard (Earl of). *Musical Reminiscences: Containing an Account of the Italian Opera in England from 1773.* London, 1834.
Piozzi, Hester Thrale. *Thraliana: The Diary of Mrs. Hester Lynch Thrale Piozzi, 1776–1809.* 2 vols. Ed. Katherine C. Balderstone. Oxford: Clarendon Press, 1942.
Seward, Anna. *Louisa: A Poetical Novel in Four Epistles.* London, 1784.
 Poetical Works. 3 vols. Ed. Walter Scott. Edinburgh, 1810.
 Letters. 6 vols. Edinburgh, 1811.
[Sterland, John]. "Chronicles of the Italian Opera in England." *Harmonicon* 8–11 (1830–3).
Wollstonecraft, Mary. *Thoughts on the Education of Daughters.* London, 1787.
 A Vindication of the Rights of Men, with A Vindication of the Rights of Woman, and Hints. Ed. Sylvana Tomaselli. Cambridge University Press, 1995.
Wordsworth, William. *Lyrical Ballads, and Other Poems, 1797–1800.* Ed. James Butler and Karen Green. Ithaca: Cornell University Press, 1983.
 Poems in Two Volumes, and Other Poems, 1800–1807. Ed. Jared Curtis. Ithaca: Cornell University Press, 1983.
Zenobia: A Musical Drama in Two Acts Represented at the King's Theatre in the Haymarket the 22nd of May, 1800, for the Benefit of Madame Banti. London, 1800.

SECONDARY SOURCES

LITERARY CRITICISM AND HISTORY

Angletti, Gioia. "Women Re-writing Men: The Examples of Anna Seward and Lady Caroline Lamb." *Romantic Women Poets: Genre and Gender.* Ed. Lilla Maria Crisafulli and Cecilia Pietropoli. New York: Rodopi, 2007.
Armstrong, Nancy. *Desire and Domestic Fiction.* Oxford University Press, 1987.
Ashmun, Margaret. *Singing Swan: An Account of Anna Seward and Her Acquaintance with Dr. Johnson, Boswell and Others of Their Time.* New Haven: Yale University Press, 1931.
Backscheider, Paula. *Eighteenth-Century Women Poets and their Poetry: Inventing Agency, Inventing Genre.* Baltimore, MD: Johns Hopkins University Press, 2005.

Bainbridge, Simon. "'Men Are We': Wordsworth's 'Manly' Poetic Nation." *Romanticism* 5.2 (1999): 216–31.
Barker-Benfield, G. J. *The Culture of Sensibility*. Chicago: University of Chicago Press, 1992.
Barnard, Teresa. *Anna Seward: A Constructed Life*. Aldershot: Ashgate, 2009.
Bermingham, Ann. "The Aesthetics of Ignorance: The Accomplished Woman in the Culture of Connoisseurship." *Oxford Art Journal* 16.2 (1993): 3–20.
Bermingham, Ann and John Brewer (eds.). *The Consumption of Culture, 1600–1800: Image, Object, Text*. London: Routledge, 1995.
Bernstein, Susan. *Virtuosity of the Nineteenth Century: Performing Music in Heine, Liszt and Baudelaire*. Stanford University Press, 1998.
Blunden, Edmund. *Leigh Hunt and His Circle*. London: Harper & Bros., 1930.
Brewer, John. *The Pleasures of the Imagination: English Culture in the Eighteenth Century*. New York: Farrar, Straus, Giroux, 1997.
Burgan, Mary. "Heroines at the Piano: Women and Music in Nineteenth-Century Fiction." *The Lost Chord: Essays on Victorian Music*. Ed. Nicholas Temperley. Indianapolis: Indiana University Press, 1989.
Buzard, James. *The Beaten Track: European Tourism, Literature, and the Ways to Culture, 1800–1918*. Oxford: Clarendon Press, 1993.
Cardwell, Richard A. (ed.). *The Reception of Byron in Europe*. 2 vols. London: Thoemmes Continuum, 2004.
Carter, Philip. *Men and the Emergence of Polite Society, Britain 1660–1800*. Harlow: Longman, 2001.
Castle, Terry. *Masquerade and Civilization*. Stanford: Stanford University Press, 1986.
Chew, Samuel. *Byron in England: His Fame and After-Fame*. New York: Scribner's Sons, 1924.
Christensen, Jerome. *Lord Byron's Strength*. Baltimore, MD: Johns Hopkins University Press, 1993.
Clarke, Norma. "Anna Seward: Swan, Duckling, or Goose?" *British Women Writers in the Long Eighteenth Century: Authorship, Politics and History*. Ed. Jennie Batchelor and Cora Kaplan. New York: Palgrave, 2005.
Clery, E. J. *The Feminization Debate in Eighteenth-Century England: Literature, Commerce, and Luxury*. London: Palgrave Macmillan, 2004.
Clery, E. J., Caroline Franklin, and Peter Garside (eds.). *Authorship, Commerce and the Public: Scenes of Writing, 1750–1850*. New York: Palgrave, 2002.
Cohen, Michèle. *Fashioning Masculinity: National Identity and Language in the Eighteenth Century*. London: Routledge, 1996.
Cohen, Michèle and Tim Hitchcock (eds.). *English Masculinites, 1660–1800*. New York: Longman, 1999.
Corfield, Penelope. *Power and the Professions in Britain, 1700–1850*. London: Routledge, 1995.
Cox, Jeffrey. *Poetry and Politics in the Cockney School: Keats, Shelley, Hunt and Their Circle*. Cambridge University Press, 1998.

Cutting-Gray, Joanne. *Woman as "Nobody" and the Novels of Fanny Burney*. Miami: University of Florida Press, 1992.

Davidson, Jenny. "Professional Education and Female Accomplishments: Gender and Education in Maria Edgeworth's Patronage." *Eighteenth-Century Women* 4 (2006): 259–85.

Doody, Margaret Anne. *Frances Burney: The Life in the Works*. New Brunswick: Rutgers University Press, 1988.

Elfenbein, Andrew. *Byron and the Victorians*. Cambridge: Cambridge University Press, 1995.

Estève, Edmond. *Byron et le romanticisme français*. Paris: Librairie Hachette, 1907.

Foucault, Michel. *Discipline and Punish*. Trans. Alan Sheridan. New York: Vintage Books, 1979.

Fulford, Tim. *Romanticism and Masculinity*. New York: St. Martin's Press, 1999.

Gallagher, Catherine. *Nobody's Story: The Vanishing Acts of Women Writers in the Marketplace, 1670–1820*. Los Angeles: University of California Press, 1994.

Guest, Harriet. *Small Change: Women, Learning, Patriotism, 1750–1810*. University of Chicago Press, 2000.

Hart, Miriam. "Hardly an Innocent Diversion: Music in the Life and Works of Jane Austen." Ph.D. dissertation, University of Ohio, 1999.

Hemlow, Joyce. *The History of Fanny Burney*. Oxford: Oxford University Press, 1958.

Hesselgrave, Ruth Avaline. *Lady Miller and the Batheaston Literary Circle*. New Haven: Yale University Press, 1927.

Johnson, Claudia. *Equivocal Beings: Politics, Gender, and Sentimentality in the 1790s*. Chicago: University of Chicago Press, 1995.

Jones, David L. "Hazlitt and Hunt at the Opera House." *Symposium* 16 (1962): 5–16.

Kelly, Gary. *Women, Writing, and Revolution, 1790–1827*. Oxford: Clarendon Press, 1993.

Klancher, Jon. *The Making of English Reading Audiences, 1790–1832*. Madison: University of Wisconsin Press, 1987.

Kowalski-Wallace, Beth. "A Night at the Opera: The Body, Class, and Art in *Evelina* and Frances Burney's *Early Diaries*." *History, Gender, and Eighteenth-Century Literature*. Ed. Beth Fawkes Tobin. Athens, GA: University of Georgia Press, 1994.

Landau, Leya. "'The Middle State': Italian Opera in Frances Burney's *Cecilia*." *Eighteenth-Century Fiction* 17.4 (2005): 649–82.

Langford, Paul. *A Polite and Commercial People: England 1721–83*. Oxford: Oxford University Press, 1989.

Le Corbeiller, Clare. "James Cox and His Curious Toys." *The Metropolitan Museum of Art Bulletin* 18.10 (1960): 318–24.

Levy, Michelle. *Family Authorship and Romantic Print Culture*. New York: Palgrave Macmillan, 2008.

Lipking, Lawrence. *The Ordering of the Arts in Eighteenth-Century England*. Princeton: Princeton University Press, 1970.

Lynch, Deidre. *Economy of Character: Novels, Market Culture, and the Business of Inner Meaning*. Chicago: University of Chicago Press, 1998.

Marshall, Roderick. *Italy in English Literature: Origin of the Romantic Interest in Italy.* New York: Columbia University Press, 1934.
McCue, Kirsteen. "'An individual flowering on a common stem': Melody, Performance, and National Song." *Romanticism and Popular Culture in Britain and Ireland.* Ed. Philip Connell and Nigel Leask. Cambridge: Cambridge University Press, 2009, 88–106.
McGann, Jerome. *Don Juan in Context.* Baltimore, MD: Johns Hopkins University Press, 1976.
  Byron and Romanticism. Cambridge University Press, 2002.
Myers, Robert Manson. *Anna Seward: An Eighteenth-Century Handelian.* Williamsburg: Manson Park Press, 1947.
Pagani, Catherine. *Eastern Magnificence and European Ingenuity.* Ann Arbor: University of Michigan Press, 2001.
Page, Judith. *Wordsworth and the Cultivation of Women.* Berkeley: University of California Press, 1994.
Park, Julie. "Pain and Pleasures of the Automaton: Frances Burney's Mechanics of Coming Out." *Eighteenth-Century Studies* 40.1 (2006): 23–49.
Parker, Mark. *Literary Magazines and British Romanticism.* Cambridge: Cambridge University Press, 2000.
Piggott, Patrick. *The Innocent Diversion: A Study of Music in the Life and Writings of Jane Austen.* London: Clover Hill, 1979.
Pinch, Adela. "Female Chatter: Meter, Masochism, and the Lyrical Ballads." *English Literary History* 55.4 (1988): 835–52.
Robinson, Daniel. "Forging the Poetical Novel: The Elision of Form in Anna Seward's *Louisa.*" *The Wordsworth Circle* 27.1 (1996): 25–9.
Robinson, Jeffrey. *Unfettering Poetry: Fancy in British Romanticism.* New York: Palgrave, 2006.
Roe, Nicholas (ed.). *Leigh Hunt: Life, Poetics, Politics.* London: Routledge, 2003.
Sabor, Peter (ed.). *The Cambridge Companion to Frances Burney.* Cambridge: Cambridge University Press, 2007.
Schellenberg, Betty. *The Professionalization of Women Writers in Eighteenth-Century Britain.* Cambridge: Cambridge University Press, 2005.
Shapiro, Susan C. "'Yon Plumed Dandebrat': Male 'Effeminacy' in English Satire and Criticism." *Review of English Studies* 39 (1988): 400–12.
Tadmor, Naomi. "Women, Reading, and Household Life." *The Practice and Representation of Reading in England.* Ed. James Raven, Helen Small, and Naomi Tadmor. Cambridge University Press, 1996.
Todd, Janet. "Jane Austen and the Professional Wife." *Repossessing the Romantic Past.* Ed. Heather Glen and Paul Hamilton. Cambridge: Cambridge University Press, 2006.
Tuite, Clara. *Romantic Austen.* Cambridge: Cambridge University Press, 2002.
Tuite, Clara and Gillian Russell (eds.). *Romantic Sociability: Social Networks and Literary Culture in Britain, 1770–1840.* Cambridge: Cambridge University Press, 2002.
Turner, Cheryl. *Living by the Pen: Women Writers in the Eighteenth Century.* New York: Routledge, 1992.

Wallace, Robert K. *Jane Austen and Mozart.* Athens, GA: University of Georgia Press, 1983.
Wheatley, Kim (ed.). *Romantic Periodicals and Print Culture.* London: Frank Cass, 2003.
Wickham, D. E. "Thomas Massa Alsager: An Elian Shade Illuminated." *Charles Lamb Bulletin* 35 (1981): 45–62.
Wilson, Frances (ed.) *Byromania: Portraits of the Artist in Nineteenth and Twentieth-Century Culture.* London: Macmillan, 1999.
Wilson, Kathleen. *The Sense of the People: Politics, Culture, and Imperialism in England, 1715–85.* Cambridge: Cambridge University Press, 1995.
Wells, Juliette. "Accomplished Women: Gender, Artistry, and Authorship in Nineteenth-Century England." Ph.D. dissertation, Yale University, 2003.
  "'In Music She Had Always Used to Feel Alone in the World': Jane Austen, Solitude and the Artistic Woman." *Persuasions: The Jane Austen Journal* 26 (2004): 98–110.
Wolfson, Susan. "*Lyrical Ballads* and the Language of (Men) Feeling: Wordsworth Writing Women's Voices." *Men Writing the Feminine: Literature, Theory, and the Question of Genders.* Ed. Thais E. Morgan. Binghamton: State University of New York Press, 1994.
Woolf, Virginia. *The Common Reader.* London: Hogarth Press, 1948.

MUSICOLOGY

Adorno, Theodor. *Beethoven: The Philosophy of Music.* Ed. Rolf Tiedemann. Oxford: Polity Press, 1998.
  Sound Figures. Trans. Rodney Livingstone. Stanford University Press, 1999.
André, Naomi. *Voicing Gender: Castrati, Travesti, and the Second Woman in Early Nineteenth-Century Opera.* Indianapolis: Indiana University Press, 2006.
Arnold, Ben (ed.). *The Liszt Companion.* Westport, CT: Greenwood Press, 2002.
Bashford, Christina and Leanne Langley (eds.). *Music and British Culture, 1785–1914.* Oxford: Oxford University Press, 2000.
Bloom, Peter (ed.). *Music in Paris in the 1830s.* Stuyvesant, NY: Pendragon Press, 1987.
Botstein, Leon. "A Mirror to the Nineteenth Century: Reflections on Franz Liszt." *Franz Liszt and His World.* Ed. Christopher H. Gibbs and Dana Gooley. Princeton: Princeton University Press, 2006.
Burrows, Donald and Rosemary Dunhill. *Music and Theatre in Handel's World: The Family Papers of James Harris, 1732–1780.* Oxford: Oxford University Press, 2002.
Burden, Michael. "Metastasio on the London Stage: Adaptations and Permutations." *Studies in Music from the University of Western Ontario* 16 (1997): 111–34.
Burnham, Scott. *Beethoven Hero.* Princeton: Princeton University Press, 1995.
  "The Four Ages of Beethoven: Critical Reception and the Canonic Composer." *The Cambridge Companion to Beethoven.* Ed. Gerald Stanley. Cambridge: Cambridge University Press, 2000.

Christensen, Thomas. "Public Music in Private Spaces: Piano-Vocal Scores and the Domestication of Opera." *Music and the Cultures of Print.* Ed. Kate van Orden. New York: Garland Publishing, 2000.

Cole, Michael. *The Pianoforte in the Classical Era.* Oxford: Clarendon Press, 1998.

Cowgill, Rachel. "'Wise Men from the East': Mozart's Operas and their Advocates in Early Nineteenth-Century London." *Music and British Culture, 1785–1914.* Ed. Christina Bashford and Leanne Langley. Oxford: Oxford University Press, 2000.

"Mozart Productions and the Emergence of *Werktreue* at London's Italian Opera House, 1780–1830." *Operatic Migrations: Transforming Works and Crossing Boundaries.* Ed. Roberta Montemorra Marvin and Downing A. Thomas. Aldershot: Ashgate, 2006.

Dahlhaus, Carl. *Nineteenth-Century Music.* Trans. J. Bradford Robinson. Berkeley: University of California Press, 1989.

Ludwig van Beethoven. Trans. Mary Whittall. Oxford: Clarendon Press, 1991.

Dean, Winton. *Handel's Dramatic Oratorio and Masques.* London: Oxford University Press, 1959.

Deaville, James. "Liszt's Virtuosity and His Audience: Gender, Class and Power in the Concert Hall of the Early 19th Century." *Das Andere. Eine Spurensuche in der Musikgeschichte.* Ed. Annette Kreutzige-Herr. Frankfurt: Peter Lang, 1988.

DeNora, Tia. *Beethoven and the Construction of Genius: Musical Politics in Vienna, 1792–1803.* Berkeley: University of California Press, 1995.

After Adorno: Rethinking Music Sociology. Cambridge: Cambridge University Press, 2003.

Deutsch, Otto Erich. *Handel: A Documentary Biography.* New York: Norton, 1955.

Ehrlich, Cyril. *The Music Profession in Britain since the Eighteenth Century.* Oxford: Clarendon Press, 1985.

First Philharmonic. Oxford: Clarendon Press, 1995.

Ellis, Katherine. *Music Criticism in Nineteenth-Century France.* Cambridge: Cambridge University Press, 1995.

Feldman, Martha. "Magic Mirrors and the *Seria* Stage: Thoughts toward a Ritual View." *Journal of the American Musicological Society* 48.3 (1995): 423–84.

Fenner, Theodore. *Leigh Hunt and Opera Criticism: The "Examiner" Years, 1808–21.* Lawrence: University of Kansas Press, 1972.

Opera in London: Views of the Press, 1785–1830. Carbondale: Southern Illinois University Press, 1994.

Fiske, Roger and H. Diack Johnstone (eds.). *Music in Britain: The Eighteenth Century.* Oxford: Blackwell, 1990.

Gammie, Ian and Derek McCulloch (eds.). *Jane Austen's Music.* St. Albans: Corda Music, 1996.

Gilman, Todd S. "The Italian (Castrato) in London." *The Work of Opera: Genre, Nationhood, and Sexual Difference.* Ed. Richard Dellamora and Daniel Fischlin. New York: Columbia University Press, 1997.

Gramit, David. *Cultivating Music: The Aspirations, Interests and Limits of German Musical Culture, 1770–1848.* Berkeley: University of California Press, 2002.

"Unremarkable Musical Lives: Autobiographical Narratives, Music, and the Shaping of the Self." *Musical Biography: Towards New Paradigms.* Ed. Jolanta T. Pekacz. Aldershot: Ashgate, 2006.

Grant, Kerry S. *Dr. Burney as Critic and Historian of Music.* Ann Arbor: UMI Research Press, 1983.

Goehr, Lydia. *The Imaginary Museum of Musical Works: An Essay in the Philosophy of Music.* Oxford: Clarendon Press, 1992.

Golby, David. *Instrumental Teaching in Nineteenth-Century Britain.* Aldershot: Ashgate, 2004.

Gooley, Dana. *The Virtuoso Liszt.* Cambridge: Cambridge University Press, 2004.

"The Virtuoso as Strategist." *The Musician as Entrepreneur, 1700–1914.* Ed. William Weber. Indianapolis: Indiana University Press, 2004.

"The Battle against Instrumental Virtuosity in the Early Nineteenth Century." *Franz Liszt and His World.* Ed. Christopher H. Gibbs and Dana Gooley. Princeton: Princeton University Press, 2006.

Hadley, David Warren. "Beethoven and the Philharmonic Society of London: A Reappraisal." *The Musical Quarterly* 59.3 (1973): 449–61.

Hall-Witt, Jennifer. *Fashionable Acts: Opera and Elite Culture in London, 1780–1880.* Durham: University of New Hampshire Press, 2007.

Hamilton, Kenneth. "The Virtuoso Tradition." *The Cambridge Companion to the Pianoforte.* Ed. David Rowland. Cambridge University Press, 1998.

Hatch, Christopher. "The 'Cockney' Writers and Mozart's Operas." *Opera Quarterly* 3.2 (1985): 45–58.

Heartz, Daniel. *Music in European Capitals: The Galant Style, 1720–1780.* New York: Norton, 2003.

From Garrick to Gluck: Essays on Opera in the Age of Enlightenment. Hillsdale, NY: Pendragon Press, 2004.

Hunter, Mary. "'To Play as if from the Soul of the Composer': The Idea of the Performer in Early Romantic Aesthetics." *Journal of the American Musicological Society* 58.2 (2005): 357–98.

Irving, Howard. *Ancients and Moderns: William Crotch and the Development of Classical Music.* Aldershot: Ashgate, 1999.

Jones, David Wynn (ed.). *Music in Eighteenth-Century Britain.* Aldershot: Ashgate, 2000.

Kassler, Michael (ed.). *Music Entries at Stationers' Hall, 1710–1818.* Aldershot: Ashgate, 2004.

King, Alec Hyatt. *Musical Pursuits: Selected Essays.* London: British Library, 1987.

Kramer, Lawrence. *Music as Cultural Practice, 1800–1900.* Berkeley: University of California Press, 1990.

Musical Meaning: Toward a Critical History. Berkeley: University of California Press, 2002.

Langley, Leanne. "The English Musical Journal in the Early Nineteenth Century." Ph.D. dissertation, University of North Carolina, 1983.

Larsson, Roger. "The Beautiful, the Sublime and the Picturesque in Eighteenth-Century Musical Thought in Britain." Ph.D. dissertation, State University of New York at Buffalo, 1980.

Leppert, Richard D. "Music Teachers of Upper-Class Amateur Musicians in Eighteenth-Century England." *Music in the Classic Period*. Ed. Allan Atlas. New York: Pendragon Press, 1985.

  The Sight of Sound: Music, Representation, and the History of the Body. Berkeley: University of California Press, 1993.

Lindenberger, Herbert. *Opera: The Extravagant Art*. Ithaca: Cornell University Press, 1984.

Loesser, Arthur. *Men, Women and Pianos: A Social History*. London: Victor Gollancz, 1955.

Lonsdale, Roger. *Dr. Charles Burney: A Literary Biography*. Oxford: Clarendon Press, 1965.

McVeigh, Simon. *Concert Life in London from Mozart to Haydn*. Cambridge: Cambridge University Press, 2001.

McVeigh, Simon and Susan Wollenberg (eds.). *Concert Life in Eighteenth-Century Britain*. Aldershot: Ashgate, 2004.

Metzner, Paul. *Crescendo of the Virtuoso*. Berkeley: University of California Press, 1998.

Parakilas, James and Gretchen A. Wheelock (eds.). *Piano Roles: Three Hundred Years of Life with the Piano*. New Haven: Yale University Press, 1999.

Petty, Frederick C. *Italian Opera in London, 1760–1800*. Ann Arbor: UMI Research Press, 1980.

Price, Curtis, Judith Milhous and Robert D. Hume. *Italian Opera in Late Eighteenth-Century London*. Oxford: Clarendon Press, 1995.

Richards, Annette. "Automatic Genius: Mozart and the Mechanical Sublime." *Music and Letters* 80.3 (1999): 366–89.

Ritchie, Leslie. *Women Writing Music in Late Eighteenth-Century England*. Aldershot: Ashgate, 2007.

Rohr, Deborah. *The Careers of British Musicians: A Profession of Artisans*. Cambridge: Cambridge University Press, 2001.

Rosen, Charles. *The Romantic Generation*. Cambridge, MA: Harvard University Press, 1995.

  The Classical Style: Haydn, Mozart, Beethoven. 2nd edn. New York: Norton, 1997.

Rowland, David (ed.). *Cambridge Companion to the Pianoforte*. Cambridge: Cambridge University Press, 1998.

Rumbold, Valerie. "Music Aspires to Letters: Charles Burney, Queeney Thrale, and the Streatham Circle." *Music and Letters* 74.1 (1993): 24–38.

Samson, Jim. *The Cambridge History of Nineteenth-Century Music*. Cambridge: Cambridge University Press, 2001.

  (ed.). *Virtuosity and the Musical Work: The Transcendental Etudes of Liszt*. Cambridge: Cambridge University Press, 2003.

Senici, Emanuele. "'Adapted to the Modern Stage': *La Clemenza di Tito* in London." *Cambridge Opera Journal* 7.1 (1995): 1–22.

Sheldon, David. "The Galant Style Revisited and Re-evaluated." *Acta Musicologica* 47 (1975): 240–70.
"The Concept Galant in the Eighteenth Century." *Musicological Research* 9 (1989): 89–108.
Smith, Ruth. *Handel's Oratorios and Eighteenth-Century Thought.* Cambridge: Cambridge University Press, 1995.
Steinberg, Michael P. *Listening to Reason: Culture, Subjectivity, and Nineteenth-Century Music.* Princeton: Princeton University Press, 2004.
Subotnik, Rose Rosengard. *Developing Variations: Style and Ideology in Western Music.* Minneapolis: University of Minnesota Press, 1991.
Temperley, Nicholas (ed.). *The Romantic Age, 1800–1914.* London: Athlone Press, 1981.
Todd, Larry (ed.). *Nineteenth-Century Piano Music.* New York: Routledge, 2004.
Walker, Alan. *Franz Liszt: The Virtuoso Years, 1811–1847.* Ithaca: Cornell University Press, 1983.
Weber, William. *Music and the Middle Class: The Social Structure of Concert Life in London, Paris and Vienna.* New York: Holmes and Meier, 1975.
The Rise of Musical Classics in Eighteenth-Century England: A Study in Canon, Ritual, and Ideology. Oxford: Clarendon Press, 1992.
"Did People Listen in the Eighteenth Century?" *Early Music* 25 (1997): 678–91.
The Great Transformation of Musical Taste: Concert Programming from Haydn to Brahms. Cambridge: Cambridge University Press, 2008.
Weber, William. (ed.) *The Musician as Entrepreneur, 1700–1914.* Indianapolis: Indiana University Press, 2004.
Wollenberg, Susan and Therese Ellsworth (eds.). *The Piano in Nineteenth-Century British Culture.* Aldershot: Ashgate, 2007.
Woodfield, Ian. *Salomon and the Burneys: Private Patronage and a Public Career.* Aldershot: Ashgate, 2003.
Zon, Bennett (ed.). *Nineteenth-Century British Music Studies.* Aldershot: Ashgate, 1999.

Notes

INTRODUCTION

1 *A Descriptive Catalogue of Several Superb and Magnificent Pieces of Mechanism and Jewellery, exhibited in Mr. Cox's Museum at Spring Gardens, Charing Cross* (1772) (unpaginated). See Clare Le Corbeiller, "James Cox and His Curious Toys," *The Metropolitan Museum of Art Bulletin* 18.10 (June 1960): 318–24, and Richard Altick, *The Shows of London* (Cambridge, MA: Belknap Press, 1978), 69–76. For critical histories of the exhibition, and Cox's career, see Catherine Pagani, *Eastern Magnificence and European Ingenuity* (Ann Arbor: University of Michigan Press, 2001), 99–112, and Simon During, *Modern Enchantments: The Cultural Power of Secular Magic* (Cambridge, MA: Harvard University Press, 2002), 234–46.
2 Frances Burney, *Evelina*, ed. Edward A. Bloom (Oxford: Oxford University Press, 2002), 78.
3 Annette Richards, "Automatic Genius: Mozart and the Mechanical Sublime," *Music and Letters* 80.3 (1999): 384.
4 *The Wanderer*, ed. Margaret Anne Doody, Robert L. Mack, and Peter Sabor (Oxford: Oxford University Press, 2001). In his *Dictionnaire de Musique* (1703) Sebastien de Brossard defined the Italian word *virtuoso* as an "excellent musician," with the indication that it was not yet in French usage.
5 *A Further Justification of the Present War against the United Netherlands* (London, 1673), 82.
6 *Rambler* 85 (January 1, 1751); Mary Astell, *An Essay in Defence of the Female Sex* [1696] (New York: Source Book Press, 1970), 90.
7 *The Virtuoso*, ed. Marjorie Hope Nicholson and David Stuart Rodes (London: Edward Arnold, 1966), v. iii. 75–8.
8 *Memoires for my Grand-son*, ed. Geoffrey Keynes (London: Nonesuch Press, 1926), 78.
9 "In the second half of the eighteenth century, the status of natural history was in no sense secure … If not exactly antithetical, curiosity and virtue were far from readily reconciled; curiosity, collecting, curiosities, and licentiousness were uncomfortably connected." Nicholas Thomas, "Licensed Curiosity: Cook's Pacific Voyages," *The Cultures of Collecting*, ed. John Elsner and Roger Cardinal (Cambridge, MA: Harvard University Press,

1994), 116–18. See also Michael Hunter, *Establishing the New Science* (Suffolk: Boydell, 1989), 123–55.
10 *Characteristicks, of Men, Manners, Opinions, Times* (London, 1733), vol. III: 157. See also Addison: "There is no study more becoming a rational creature than that of natural philosophy; but, as several of our modern virtuosi manage it, their speculations do not so much tend to open and enlarge the mind, as to contract and fix it upon trifles." *Tatler* 236 (October 12, 1710).
11 Pagani, *Eastern Magnificence*, 101.
12 Altick, *The Shows of London*, 76.
13 Kenneth Hamilton, "The Virtuoso Tradition," *The Cambridge Companion to the Pianoforte*, ed. David Rowland (Cambridge: Cambridge University Press, 1998), 57.
14 *Revue et Gazette Musicale* 6 (1838): 58.
15 John Hawkins, *A General History of the Science and Practice of Music* [1776] (New York: Dover, 1963), vol. II: 919.
16 *The Works of Tobias Smollett, with Memoirs of his Life; to which is Prefixed A View of the Commencement and Progress of Romance, by John Moore* (London, 1797), vol. I: xcii.
17 Ann H. Jones, *Ideas and Innovations: Best Sellers of Jane Austen's Age* (New York: AMS Press, 1987), 2; Frances Burney, *Journals and Letters*, ed. Peter Sabor and Lars E. Troide (London: Penguin, 2001), 202.
18 Burney, *The Wanderer*, 7.
19 *Concert Life in Eighteenth-Century Britain*, ed. Susan Wollenberg and Simon McVeigh (Aldershot: Ashgate, 2004), 12.
20 Frances Burney, *Cecilia*, ed. Peter Sabor and Margaret Ann Doody (Oxford: Oxford University Press, 1988), 62.
21 *The Early Journals and Letters of Fanny Burney*, vol. III, ed. Lars E. Troide and Stewart J. Cooke (Montreal: McGill-Queen's University Press, 1994), 93.
22 Quoted in Joyce Hemlow, *The History of Fanny Burney* (Oxford: Oxford University Press, 1958), 164. Debate over Burney's putative connection to the automaton motif continues. In her influential critical biography (1988) Margaret Anne Doody rejects routine characterization of Burney, inaugurated by Thrale, as "a mere impersonal machine ... a tape recorder," while Julie Park, in a recent essay, discovers once more in Burney's writerly practice, and the Cox Museum episode in particular, "a compulsive identification with the automaton." Margaret Anne Doody, *Frances Burney: The Life in the Works* (New Brunswick: Rutgers University Press, 1988), 34; Julie Park, "Pains and Pleasures of the Automaton: Frances Burney's Mechanics of Coming Out," *Eighteenth-Century Studies* 40.1 (2006): 23, 35–9.
23 Thomas Love Peacock, *Works*, ed. H. F. B. Brett-Smith and C. E. Jones (London: Constable & Co., 1934), vol. VIII: 12.
24 William Weber, *The Great Transformation of Musical Taste: Concert Programming from Haydn to Brahms* (Cambridge: Cambridge University Press, 2008), 20.

25 Richard Leppert, "The Musician of the Imagination," *The Musician as Entrepreneur, 1700–1914*, ed. William Weber (Indianapolis: Indiana University Press, 2004), 26.
26 Anna Seward, *Louisa: A Poetical Novel in Four Epistles* (London, 1784). (Citations from this work are page numbers.)
27 *Musical World* (October 28, 1841): 276.
28 Joseph Addison, Prologue to Edmund Smith, *Phaedra and Hippolitus, a Tragedy* (London, 1707).
29 *Musical World* (February 6, 1858): 88–9.
30 See Penelope J. Corfield, *Power and the Professions in Britain, 1700–1850* (London: Routledge, 1995), 18–26.
31 *Byron: Interviews and Recollections*, ed. Norman Page (London: Macmillan, 1985), 58.
32 Various nineteenth-century sources do suggest, however, that British music critics felt the lack of a major native composer to stand with Beethoven or Wagner. London's very success as the most vibrant cosmopolitan music capital in Europe, and magnet for foreign musicians, was lamented as a principal cause of the suppression of local talent. See Nicholas Temperley, "The Land Without Music," *Musical Times* 116 (July 1975): 625.
33 Peter Holman, "Eighteenth-Century English Music: Past, Present, Future," *Music in Eighteenth-Century Britain*, ed. David Wynn Jones (Aldershot: Ashgate, 2000), 3.
34 *Musical World* (May 17, 1838): 47.
35 The phrase "rage for music" was a journalistic commonplace of the 1780s and early 1790s. "Music is so much the rage," wrote composer William Jackson, "to use a fashionable term." *Observations on the Present State of Music in London* (London, 1791), 1. See Simon McVeigh, *Concert Life in London from Mozart to Haydn* (Cambridge: Cambridge University Press, 1993), 1, 252.
36 Introduction, *The Cambridge History of Nineteenth-Century Music*, ed. Jim Samson (Cambridge: Cambridge University Press, 2001), 6.
37 *Cultivating Music: The Aspirations, Interests and Limits of German Musical Culture, 1770–1848* (Berkeley: University of California Press, 2002), 165.
38 The Romantic period, in conventional literary-historical periodization, embraces both the "Classical" and early "Romantic" periods of academic music history. Aside from chapters 5 and 6, on Beethoven and Liszt respectively, the music-historical focus of this book is not on Romantic music but the eighteenth-century music, later formalized into baroque, *galant*, and Classical categories, which constituted the dominant repertoire in British polite music culture for the period 1770–1840. Anachronisms are an ever-present danger in music historiography. For example, in the 1830s, the term "classical" referred to "serious" music – to a body of complex instrumental works distinct from the opera and opera-derived repertoire – not a specific period or style. See Weber, *The Great Transformation*, 122.
39 William Wordsworth, "On the Power of Sound," *Last Poems, 1821–50*, ed. Jored Curtis (Ithaca: Cornell University Press, 1999), ll. 187–90.

40 *The Notebooks of Samuel Taylor Coleridge*, ed. Kathleen Coburn (Princeton: Princeton University Press, 1957), vol. II: 2035.
41 Tia DeNora, *After Adorno: Rethinking Music Sociology* (Cambridge: Cambridge University Press, 2003), 10.
42 David Gramit, "Unremarkable Musical Lives: Autobiographical Narratives, Music, and the Shaping of the Self," *Musical Biography: Towards New Paradigms*, ed. Jolanta T. Pekacz (Aldershot: Ashgate, 2006), 160.
43 *Letters of John Keats*, ed. Hyder Edward Rollins (Cambridge, MA: Harvard University Press, 1958), vol. I: 170.
44 *Quarterly Review* (September 1818), reprinted in *Keats: The Critical Heritage*, ed. G. M. Matthews (London: Routledge & Kegan Paul, 1971), 112.
45 *British Critic* (June 1818), reprinted in *Keats: The Critical Heritage*, 94.
46 For a book-length study of the English opera in the early Romantic period, see Jane Girdham, *English Opera in Late Eighteenth-Century London: Stephen Storace at Drury Lane* (Oxford: Clarendon Press, 1997).
47 Susan Stewart, *Crimes of Writing: Problems in the Containment of Representation* (New York: Oxford University Press, 1991), 102–31.
48 "'An individual flowering on a common stem': Melody, Performance, and National Song," *Romanticism and Popular Culture in Britain and Ireland*, ed. Philip Connell and Nigel Leask (Cambridge: Cambridge University Press, 2009), 90.
49 For analysis of the centrality of Scotland in the discursive formation of folk music, and hence Romantic musical nationalism, see Mark Gelbart, *The Invention of Folk Music and Art Music: Emerging Categories from Ossian to Wagner* (Cambridge: Cambridge University Press, 2007).
50 Leigh Hunt, *Autobiography*, ed. Edmund Blunden (Oxford: Oxford University Press, 1928), 61.
51 "The Limits of Cosmopolitanism and the Case for Translation," *European Romantic Review* 16.2 (April 2005): 141.
52 Nicholas Temperley, "Xenophilia in British Musical History," *Nineteenth-Century British Music Studies*, ed. Bennett Zon (Aldershot: Ashgate, 1999), vol. I: 3–19.
53 Two recent studies seek to redress the largely metropolitan focus of British musicology with accounts of independent practices in provincial centers. See Jenny Birchall, *Polite or Commercial Concerts? Concert Management and Orchestral Repertoire in Edinburgh, Bath, Oxford, Manchester, and Newcastle, 1730–1799* (London: Garland Publishing, 1996), and Roz Souther, *Music-Making in North-East England during the Eighteenth Century* (Aldershot: Ashgate, 2006).
54 *The Musical Quarterly* 70.2 (1984): 175–94.
55 Jeffrey Robinson, *Unfettering Poetry: Fancy in British Romanticism* (New York: Palgrave, 2006), ch. 3. See also Jeffrey Cox's seminal volume on Romantic sociability and the Cockney School, *Poetry and Politics in the Cockney School: Keats, Shelley, Hunt and Their Circle* (Cambridge: Cambridge University Press, 1998).

56 I borrow the phrase from Derek Carew, *The Mechanical Muse: The Piano, Pianism, and Piano Music, c. 1760–1850* (Aldershot: Ashgate, 2007).
57 Bennett, Zon (general editor's preface), *The Piano in Nineteenth-Century British Culture*, ed. Therese Ellsworth and Susan Wollenberg (Aldershot: Ashgate, 2007).

1 SEWARD'S HANDELOMANIA

1 *An Account of the Musical Performances in Westminster Abbey* (London, 1785), 40.
2 Thomas Twining, *Critical Review* 59 (February 1785): 131; *The Torrington Diaries*, ed. C. Bruyn Andrews (London: Eyre and Spottiswoode, 1935), vol. II: 26. For a detailed analysis of the politics of the Commemoration, see William Weber, *The Rise of Musical Classics in Eighteenth-Century England: A Study in Canon, Ritual, and Ideology* (Oxford: Clarendon Press, 1992), 222–42.
3 Edmund Burke, *Reflections on the Revolution in France* [1790], ed. J. G. A. Pocock (Indianapolis: Hackett Publishing, 1987), 63.
4 *The Gazetteer and New Daily Advertiser* (May 31, 1784).
5 May 1784, "Supplement."
6 William Wordsworth, *Lyrical Ballads, and Other Poems, 1797–1800*, ed. James Butler and Karen Green (Ithaca: Cornell University Press, 1983), 750 (1802 Preface, l. 55).
7 *The Poetical Works of Anna Seward*, ed. Walter Scott (Edinburgh, 1810), vol. II: 224, 221, 219.
8 Preface to *Fugitive Verses* (London, 1840), x.
9 In her recent critical biography of Seward, Teresa Barnard exposes Scott's destructive editorial impact on the letters, in which much of the anecdotal and local color was excised, thus impoverishing their biographic and literary character. Also suppressed were many of Seward's pointed criticisms of the publishing industry with which Scott was so closely involved. *Anna Seward: A Constructed Life* (Aldershot: Ashgate Press, 2009), 5–9, 207.
10 Robert Manson Myers, *Anna Seward: An Eighteenth-Century Handelian* (Williamsburg, VA: Manson Park Press, 1947), 6.
11 *The Task, A Poem in Six Books* (London, 1785), vol. VI: 632–7.
12 *Letters and Prose Writings of William Cowper*, ed. James King and Charles Ryskamp (Oxford: Clarendon Press, 1981), vol. II: 254.
13 Seward, *Poetical Works*, III: 5.
14 *Ibid.*, 14.
15 *Letters of Anna Seward*, ed. Walter Scott (Edinburgh, 1811), vol. I: 183–4.
16 *Romantic Sociability: Social Networks and Literary Culture in Britain, 1770–1840*, ed. Clara Tuite and Gillian Russell (Cambridge: Cambridge University Press, 2002), 5.
17 *Letters*, II: 5.
18 *Louisa*, 6.

19 *Letters*, I: 106.
20 Naomi Tadmor, "Women, Reading, and Household Life," *The Practice and Representation of Reading in England*, ed. James Raven, Helen Small, and Naomi Tadmor (Cambridge: Cambridge University Press, 1996), 165.
21 Weber, *The Great Transformation*, 16.
22 "L'Origine de la mélodie," *Oeuvres Complètes*, ed. Bernard Gagnebin and Marcel Raymond (Paris: Gallimard, 1995), vol. V: 337.
23 Charles Avison, *Essay on Musical Expression* (London, 1752), 4. In his "Essay on Poetry and Music, as they Affect the Mind," James Beattie restates the neoclassical consensus on music's social benefits within the new Avisonian framework of "affect" and "expression": "Does not a most judicious author [Polybius] ascribe the humanity of the Arcadians to the influence of this art, and barbarity of their neighbours the Cynethias to their neglect of it?" *Essays* (London, 1776), 462. See Leslie Ritchie, *Women Writing Music in Late Eighteenth-Century England* (Aldershot: Ashgate, 2007), 1–11.
24 This poem, with two others on the same subject, appears in Lady Miller's *Poetical Amusements at a Villa Near Bath*, vol. III (London, 1777). Hester Thrale also submitted a poem on the theme to the "Vase," but it was not published. For Thrale's description of Miller and the Batheaston vase, see *Thraliana: The Diary of Mrs. Hester Lynch Thrale Piozzi, 1776–1809*, ed. Katherine C. Balderstone (Oxford: Clarendon Press, 1942), vol. I: 229–31.
25 "An Ode to Mr. Handel, on his Playing on the Organ" (London, 1722). This poem was reprinted in 1781 and 1791 at the height of Handelomania. See Otto Erich Deutsch, *Handel: A Documentary Biography* (New York: Norton, 1955), 144.
26 *Gentleman's Magazine* 3 (February, 1733): 94.
27 *Handel's Oratorios and Eighteenth-Century Thought* (Cambridge: Cambridge University Press, 1995); see especially ch. 9.
28 *The Surest Grounds for Hopes of Success in War. A Sermon . . .* (London, 1740), 18. As Smith argues, however, the politics of individual oratorio texts and settings were more complex than their patriotic staging would often admit. For an example of the multiple, sometimes dissonant nationalisms available in specific productions of the oratorios, see Daniel O'Quinn's account of *Judas Maccabbaeus* in India in 1792: "Projection, Patriotism, Surrogation: Handel in Calcutta," *Romanticism and Patriotism: Nation, Empire, Bodies, Rhetoric*, ed. Orrin Wang, *Romantic Circles Praxis Series* (online journal) (May 2006).
29 The lessons of *Judas Maccabaeus*, like *Saul*, *Solomon*, and the other Old Testament oratorios, are thus practical and moral rather than theological, and are aimed at the social virtues: justice, courage, obedience, and peaceful government. The ultimate triumph of the Anglo-Israelite "nation" over their enemies – in the case of *Judas*, the Samaritans and Syrians – is determined not by the eternal guarantees of Providence, but by a right-minded corporate will through which the virtuous endeavors of the people have earned divine intercession in the current historical moment. Morell, in

both his sermons and his oratorio libretti, translates the familiar stories of the Old Testament into the language of eighteenth-century Whig nationalism. As the chorus sings in *Judas Maccabaeus*, "If to fall/For laws, Religion, Liberty, we fall." *Judas Maccabaeus. A Sacred Drama. As it is Perform'd at the Theatre-Royal in Covent-Garden. The Musick by Mr. Handel* (Dublin, 1748), 14.
30 Eliza Haywood, *Epistle for Ladies* (London, 1749), vol. I: 71–2.
31 *Georgiana: Extracts from the Correspondence of Georgiana, Duchess of Devonshire*, ed. Earl of Bessborough (London: J. Murray, 1955), 97.
32 Acceptance of Handel as a national composer was by no means universal, nor was resentment confined to principled dissenters like Cowper. Charles Dibdin, in 1790, condemned the king for patronage of Handel at the expense of native composers such as himself. *The Bystander* (London, 1790), 399 (see Weber, *The Great Transformation*, 72).
33 Quoted in Ruth Avaline Hesselgrave, *Lady Miller and the Batheaston Literary Circle* (New Haven: Yale University Press, 1927), 7.
34 *New Prose Bath Guide* (London, 1778), 85.
35 *Poetical Works*, I: xi.
36 *Poetical Amusements*, II: vi.
37 *The Prompter* 42 (April 4, 1735), reprinted in *The Prompter, 1734–6*, ed. William W. Appleton and Kalman A. Burnim (New York: Benjamin Blom, 1966), 47.
38 *Letters*, II: 311.
39 *Poetical Amusements*, I: v–vi.
40 *Letters*, I: 136.
41 *Epistle to Dr. Arbuthnot* (London, 1735), ll. 283–4.
42 *Poem to the Memory of Lady Miller* (London, 1782), ll. 6–7.
43 Horace Walpole, though known to Lady Miller, mocks the proceedings of the "Vase" in letters to Lady Ossory in January 1775. He calls the Batheaston circle a "puppet-show Parnassus" and the first volume of *Poetical Amusements*, sent to him by Lady Miller herself, a "bouquet of artificial flowers ... ten degrees duller than a magazine." *Horace Walpole's Correspondence*, ed. W. S. Lewis (New Haven: Yale University Press, 1963), vol. XXXII: 221, 225.
44 Frances Burney, *Early Journals and Letters*, vol. IV, ed. Betty Rizzo (Montreal: McGill-Queen's University Press, 2003), 127.
45 *Boswell's Life of Johnson*, ed. George Birbeck Hill (Oxford: Clarendon Press, 1934), vol. II: 336–7.
46 *Morning Post and Daily Advertiser*, May 6, 1778.
47 *Poetical Amusements*, I: IV.
48 Margaret Ashmun, *The Singing Swan* (New Haven: Yale University Press, 1931), 163–4.
49 Judith Pascoe, *Romantic Theatricality: Gender, Poetry, and Spectatorship* (Ithaca: Cornell University Press, 1997).
50 Anselm Bayly, *Alliance of Musick, Poetry, and Oratory* (London, 1789), 3.
51 *A Practical Treatise on Singing and Playing with Just Expression and Real Elegance* (London, 1771), 15, 62. For historical discussion of the method of

instructing singers in the performance of Handel's oratorios in particular, see Robert Toft, *Heart to Heart: Expressive Singing in England, 1780–1850* (Oxford: Oxford University Press, 2000), 161.
52 *Memoirs of the Life of the Late George Frederic Handel* (London, 1760), 193.
53 *Letters*, I: 132–3.
54 See note 9.
55 *Works of Samuel Johnson*, ed. W. J. Bate and Albrecht B. Strauss (New Haven: Yale University Press, 1969), vol. IV: 133–4.
56 Frank Donoghue, "Colonizing Readers: Review Criticism and the Formation of a Reading Public," *The Consumption of Culture, 1600–1800*, ed. Ann Bermingham and John Brewer (London: Routledge, 1995), 58–9.
57 *Works*, IV: 70.
58 William Blake, *Complete Writings*, ed. Geoffrey Keynes (Oxford: Oxford University Press, 1966), 847. See Martin Aske, "Critical Disfigurings: The 'Jealous Leer Malign' in Romantic Criticism," *Questioning Romanticism*, ed. John Beer (Baltimore, MD: Johns Hopkins University Press, 1995), 49–70.
59 Samuel Taylor Coleridge, *Collected Works*, ed. James Engell and W. Jackson Bate (Princeton, NJ: Princeton University Press, 1983), vol. VII 1: 57. An example pertinent to this study is Charles Burney's journalistic conspiracy against his rival John Hawkins's *General History of Music*. Burney enlisted his friend William Bewley to mock Hawkins's book in a series of essays for the *Monthly Review* (February 1777), which "shattered its growing reputation," and proportionally enhanced his own. Roger Lonsdale, *Dr. Charles Burney: A Literary Biography* (Oxford: Clarendon Press, 1965), 209.
60 "Literary Police" was the title of a regular column in the *London Magazine* (founded 1820) that reviewed literature in the parodic form of a police report. The existence of such a column suggests that the criminalization of authorship was a popular trope, readily understood. "Nearly all periodicals in the 1820s," writes Mark Parker, "traded in 'personality' or rancorous personal attack." *Literary Magazines and British Romanticism* (Cambridge: Cambridge University Press, 2000), 4. Jon Klancher first challenged the Habermasian model of a benign periodical culture in his indispensable study, *The Making of English Reading Audiences, 1790–1832* (Madison, WI: University of Wisconsin Press, 1987).
61 *Complete Works of William Hazlitt*, ed. P. P. Howe (London: Dent, 1934), vol. XVI: 220, 230–1, 238–9.
62 Donoghue, "Colonizing Readers," 63.
63 John Brewer, *The Pleasures of the Imagination: English Culture in the Eighteenth Century* (New York: Farrar, Straus, Giroux, 1997), 589. Brewer's long chapter on Seward and her Lichfield circle was a seminal contribution to her current critical revival.
64 *Boswell: The English Experiment, 1785–89*, ed. Irma S. Lustig and Frederick A. Pottle (New York: McGraw-Hill, 1986), 67, 252. See Barnard, *Anna Seward*, 198–206.
65 *Letters*, I: 62–3.

66 Seward's first letters on Johnson are from the February and April 1786 issues of the *Gentleman's Magazine*. Her letter published in October 1793 was answered by Boswell in the November issue, and the back-and-forth continued over the next two issues. For another account of the Seward–Boswell exchange, see Norma Clarke, "Anna Seward: Swan, Duckling, or Goose?" *British Women Writers in the Long Eighteenth Century: Authorship, Politics and History*, ed. Jennie Batchelor and Cora Kaplan (New York: Palgrave, 2005), 34–41.

67 See Gretchen Foster, *Pope Versus Dryden: A Controversy in Letters to the* Gentleman's Magazine, *1789–91* (Victoria, BC: Victoria University Press, 1989).

68 *Elegy on Captain Cook, to which is added An Ode to the Sun* (London, 1780), l. 222.

69 *Monody on Major Andrè* (London, 1781), l. 2.

70 Thomas Park, "To Miss Seward," *Sonnets and Other Small Poems* (London, 1797), unpaginated. See Harriet Guest, *Small Change: Women, Learning, Patriotism, 1750–1810* (Chicago, IL: University of Chicago Press, 2000), 253. The *Monody on Major Andrè* is most remembered for its attack on George Washington, whom Seward blamed for Andrè's execution as a spy: "Remorseless Washington! The day shall come/Of deep repentance for this barbarous doom!" (25). It is a measure of Seward's status as a national poet that, after the war, Washington sent a personal emissary to Lichfield to clear his name.

71 Karen O'Brien, "Imperial Georgic, 1660–1789," *The Country and City Revisited*, ed. Donna Landry, Gerald MacLean, and Joseph P. Ward (Cambridge: Cambridge University Press, 1999), 160–79. See also Gioia Angletti's comments on colonialism in *Louisa* in "Women Re-writing Men: The Examples of Anna Seward and Lady Caroline Lamb," *Romantic Women Poets: Genre and Gender*, ed. Lilla Maria Crisafulli and Cecilia Pietropoli (New York: Rodopi, 2007), 248–50.

72 Adriana Craciun, "Mary Robinson, the *Monthly Magazine*, and the Free Press," *Romantic Periodicals and Print Culture*, ed. Kim Wheatley (London: Frank Cass, 2003), 28. Seward's jaundiced view of London and its booming print culture became the standard historical view, and Robinson's not, because it was echoed by canonized writers such as Wordsworth and Coleridge. A more positive, Robinsonian account of a greatly enlarged and diversified public sphere in the Romantic period, centered in London, is only now finding currency. See, for example, James Chandler and Kevin Gilmartin's introduction to *Romantic Metropolis* (Cambridge: Cambridge University Press, 2005), 1–41.

73 Klancher, *The Making of English Reading Audiences*, 24.

74 "It gratifies my literary ambition not slightly," Seward wrote to William Hayley, "that you liked me so much in my doublet and hose in the letters on Johnson's character." *Letters*, 1: 256.

75 Deutsch, *Handel*, 622.

76 *Letters*, I: 152–3.
77 *Letters*, V: 361–2.
78 *Dionysus on the Sublime*, trans. William Smith (London, 1751), 47.
79 Roger Larsson, "The Beautiful, the Sublime and the Picturesque in Eighteenth-Century Musical Thought in Britain" (Ph.D. dissertation, State University of New York at Buffalo, 1980), 84.
80 *Letters*, II: 427. Starting with the 1784 Commemoration, the discourse of the Romantic sublime began to have a deformative effect on the reception of Handel. The language of sublimity originally invoked by Handelians to describe, promote, and legitimate Handel in his lifetime came to own his posthumous legacy, and transform not only his reception but performance of the music itself, culminating in the vast Victorian festival chorus later derided by George Bernard Shaw. This phenomenon shows the mutually generative relation of art and criticism. The sublime – originally a descriptive language – became prescriptive: it produced the nineteenth-century Handel as much as it might be said to have produced the cataclysmic canvases of Martin and Turner, or the vertiginous imagery of a thousand landscape poems and prose set pieces of the Romantic period.
81 *London Daily Post*, April 18, 1739.
82 Collier concedes the power of music, but sees it of no great advantage to the soul that "our Passions lie at the Mercy of a little Minstrelsy; to be fiddled out of our Reason and Sobriety; to have our Courage depend upon a Drum or our Devotions on an Organ." Handel's oratorios, in many respects a creation of the Puritan moment in British history, accord closely with Collier's prescription that church music should "Transport us with the Beauty of holiness; to raise us above the Satisfactions of Life, and make us Ambitious of the Glories of Heaven." *Essays upon Several Moral Subjects* (London, 1702), 24–5. See also Arthur Bedford, *The Great Abuse of Music* (London, 1711).
83 [Robert Maddison], *An Examination of the Oratorios which have been Performed this Season at Covent-Garden Theatre* (London, 1763), 4.
84 *Letters*, I: 76, 89.
85 *Letters*, I: 76, II: 135.
86 Myers, *Anna Seward*, 6.
87 *An Essay on the Writings and Genius of Pope* (London, 1756), vol. I: 40.
88 *Poetical Works*, I: cvi–cx.
89 "Literary Journal," *The European Magazine* (August, 1784), 107–8 (emphases original).
90 Ritchie, *Women Writing Music*, 133.
91 John Sitter, *Literary Loneliness in Mid-Eighteenth-Century England* (Ithaca: Cornell University Press, 1982), 9.
92 In his reading of *Louisa* Daniel Robinson places the same emphasis on narrative deferral – as Seward's means "to elevate the poetic over novelistic convention" – but comes to precisely the opposite conclusion I argue here. He equates the poetics of delay with virtue and "chastity" rather than

sensuality and sexual teasing. "Forging the Poetical Novel: The Elision of Form in Anna Seward's *Louisa*," *The Wordsworth Circle* 27.1 (1996): 25–9.
93 James Boswell, *Letters*, ed. Chauncey Brewster Tinker (Oxford: Clarendon Press, 1924), vol. II: 349.
94 *Public Advertiser*, June 3, 1784.
95 *Boswell: The Applause of the Jury, 1782–85*, ed. Irma S. Lustig and Frederick A. Pottle (New York: McGraw-Hill, 1981), 256–7.
96 James Harris, *Three Treatises: the First Concerning Art, the Second Concerning Music, Painting & Poetry, the Third Concerning Happiness* (London, 1744); Donald Burrows and Rosemary Dunhill, *Music and Theatre in Handel's World: The Family Papers of James Harris, 1732–1780* (Oxford: Oxford University Press, 2002), 845. Louisa Harris was "a much-sought-after singer in private concerts" (xx).
97 Paula Backsheider, *Eighteenth-Century Women Poets and Their Poetry: Inventing Agency, Inventing Genre* (Baltimore, MD: Johns Hopkins University Press, 2005), 267.
98 *Letters*, V: 320.
99 *Letters*, V: 343, I: 255, I: 121, VI: 60.
100 *Letters*, I: 64 (my emphasis).
101 *Poetical Works*, I: cx.
102 Critics have conventionally viewed their own task in reading Cowper's poem as first to acknowledge its oddity as "a rambling, disunified piece," then to combat that perception with a unifying theme or rubric, be it theological, cultural, or literary-historical. See, for example, W. Gerald Marshall, "The Presence of 'the Word' in Cowper's *The Task*," *Studies in English Literature* 27 (1987): 475–87, and Dustin Griffin, "Redefining Georgic: Cowper's *Task*," *English Literary History* 57 (1990): 865–79.
103 *Letters*, I: 112.
104 "An Essay on Fashionable Literature," Thomas Love Peacock, *Works*, ed. H. F. B. Brett-Smith and C. E. Jones (London: Constable & Co., 1924–34), vol. VIII: 267.
105 *Works*, V: 146.
106 *Letters of Sir Walter Scott*, ed. H. J. C. Grierson (London: Constable & Co., 1932), vol. II: 315.
107 *Selections from the Letters of Robert Southey*, ed. John Wood Warter (London, 1856), vol. IV: 336.

2 THE BURNEY BAROQUE

1 *The Early Journals and Letters of Fanny Burney*, vol. 1, ed. Lars E. Troide (Montreal: McGill-Queen's University Press, 1988), 229, 236.
2 Cyril Ehrlich, *The Music Profession in Britain since the Eighteenth Century* (Oxford: Clarendon Press, 1985), 47–8.
3 Quoted in Howard Irving, *Ancient and Moderns: William Crotch and the Development of Classical Music* (Aldershot: Ashgate, 1999), 152.

4 *Memoirs of Dr. Charles Burney, 1726–1769*, ed. Slava Klima, Garry Bowers, and Kerry S. Grant (Lincoln: University of Nebraska Press, 1988), 136.
5 *Early Journals and Letters*, I: 237.
6 Deborah Rohr, *The Careers of British Musicians: A Profession of Artisans* (Cambridge: Cambridge University Press, 2001), 37.
7 Quoted in James T. Lightwood, *Samuel Wesley, Musician* (London: Epworth Press, 1937), 113.
8 Frances Burney [Madame D'Arblay] (ed.), *Memoirs of Doctor Burney* (1832), vol. I: 81.
9 *The Letters of Dr. Charles Burney*, ed. Alvaro Ribeiro (Oxford: Clarendon Press, 1991), vol. I: 180.
10 Richard D. Leppert, "Music Teachers of Upper-Class Amateur Musicians in Eighteenth-Century England," *Music in the Classic Period*, ed. Allan Atlas (New York: Pendragon Press, 1985), 156–7.
11 *Letters of Charles Burney*, I: 318.
12 *Memoirs* [D'Arblay], III: 369.
13 Julia Epstein, *Eighteenth-Century Fiction* 3.4 (1991): 277.
14 In the introduction to her critical biography, Doody defends herself against the charge that Charles Burney will appear "the villain of the piece." She explains how, in researching Burney, she became "almost unwillingly, increasingly impressed by the vital importance to her – both in her life and her writings – of her relationship with her father." *Frances Burney*, 5, 10.
15 Conversely, recent scholarship on the Italian opera in Burney's novels largely ignores Charles Burney. See Leya Landau, "'The Middle State': Italian Opera in Frances Burney's *Cecilia*," *Eighteenth-Century Fiction* 17.4 (2005): 649–82, and Beth Kowalski-Wallace, "A Night at the Opera: The Body, Class, and Art in *Evelina* and Frances Burney's *Early Diaries*," *History, Gender, and Eighteenth-Century Literature*, ed. Beth Fawkes Tobin (Athens, GA: University of Georgia Press, 1994), 141–58.
16 Virginia Woolf, *The Common Reader* (London: Hogarth Press, 1948), 109.
17 *Edinburgh Review* 76 (1842–3): 566, 564.
18 Lorna Clark, "The Afterlife and Further Reading," *The Cambridge Companion to Frances Burney*, ed. Peter Sabor (Cambridge: Cambridge University Press, 2007), 172.
19 Terry Castle, *Masquerade and Civilization* (Stanford: Stanford University Press, 1986), 284.
20 *Frances Burney*, 383.
21 Frances Burney, *Camilla*, ed. Edward and Lillian Bloom (Oxford: Oxford University Press, 1972), 147, 913.
22 Michelle Levy, *Family Authorship and Romantic Print Culture* (New York: Palgrave Macmillan, 2008).
23 *Thraliana*, I: 399.
24 *Memoirs* [D'Arblay], III: 363.
25 Vanessa Agnew nominates Burney's European *Tours* the origin of a "socially and anthropologically inflected study of music." *Enlightenment Orpheus:*

The Power of Music in Other Worlds (Oxford: Oxford University Press, 2008), 170.
26 Ian Woodfield, *Salomon and the Burneys: Private Patronage and a Public Career* (Aldershot: Ashgate, 2003), 1.
27 Quoted in Lonsdale, *Dr. Charles Burney*, 272.
28 Mary Astell, *Essay in Defense of the Female Sex*, 91.
29 *Letters of Charles Burney*, 1: 196.
30 Walter E. Houghton, "The English Virtuoso in the Seventeenth Century," *Journal of the History of Ideas* 3 (1942): 65.
31 Charles Burney, *A General History of Music* [1776–1789], ed. Frank Mercer (New York: Dover, 1935), vol. 1: 222–3 (cited hereafter in text).
32 *Letters of Charles Burney*, 1: 428.
33 McVeigh, *Concert Life*, 157.
34 Valerie Rumbold reproduces the contents of the music book in "Music Aspires to Letters: Charles Burney, Queeney Thrale, and the Streatham Circle," *Music and Letters* 74.1 (1993): 24–38. In Rumbold's words, the J. C. Bach arrangements "exemplify the graceful, sociable aspirations of the galant style, using brief melodic ideas lightly accompanied" (26).
35 *Thraliana*, 1: 137.
36 Arthur Young, *Autobiography*, ed. M. Betham-Edwards (London, 1898), 10, quoted in Lonsdale, *Dr. Charles Burney*, 272.
37 *Journals and Letters of Fanny Burney*, ed. Joyce Hemlow (Oxford: Clarendon Press, 1972–), vol. VI: 58–9.
38 Leonard G. Ratner, *Classic Music: Expression, Form, and Style* (New York: Schirmer Books, 1980), 23.
39 *Letters of Charles Burney*, 1: 145.
40 Daniel Heartz, *Music in European Capitals: The Galant Style, 1720–1780* (New York: Norton, 2003), 19.
41 "The Galant Style Revisited and Re-evaluated," *Acta Musicologica* 47 (1975): 261, 245. See also Sheldon's later article, "The Concept *Galant* in the 18th Century," *Musicological Research* 9 (1989): 89–108.
42 *Letters of Charles Burney*, 1: 261, 1: 323.
43 *Thraliana*, 1: 458, 1: 136.
44 McVeigh, *Concert Life*, 4.
45 See Kerry S. Grant, *Dr. Burney as Critic and Historian of Music* (Ann Arbor: UMI Research Press, 1983), 248.
46 William Jones, *A Treatise on the Art of Music* (Colchester, 1784), iv. It is less easy for the modern reader to imagine what music might fit this description than to be reminded of the strange language idioms – the "wildness of Air, effeminacy, tautology" – of the fops who populate Frances Burney's novels, from Mr. Lovel in *Evelina* to Captain Aresby in *Cecilia* to Sedley Clarendel in *Camilla*. The same critique of luxury served music, language, and manners, be it in a treatise on music or a satirical novel.
47 Hannah More, *Strictures on the Modern System of Female Education* (London, 1799), vol. 1: 72–3.

48 *Euterpe; or, Remarks on the Use and Abuse of Music, as a Part of Modern Education* (Bath, 1778), 20.
49 William Crotch, *Substance of Several Courses of Lectures on Music* (London, 1831), 149.
50 Hawkins, *General History*, I: xxiii.
51 Burney might have won the battle but Hawkins won the war, at least for a century. The bourgeois-nationalist biases of early twentieth-century German and German-American musicology elevated Viennese classicism above the cosmopolitan, aristocratic culture of Italian opera, and aesthetic judgment above historical description. Revision of conventional scholarly categories of eighteenth-century music was first suggested by Carl Dahlhaus in *Nineteenth-Century Music*, trans. J. Bradford Robinson (Berkeley, University of California Press, 1989), in which he noted the imbalanced attention given to the music of the early and late decades with the long interim, 1720–80, granted only negative descriptions, as a period either of "decline" or merely "pre-classical." The impact of this revisionism on British musicology has been to challenge the consensus surrounding Handel's dominance of Georgian music culture (see Jones [ed.], *Music in Eighteenth-Century Britain*). Despite the now general acknowledgment that "virtually every eighteenth-century critic points to opera as the dominant force in musical life," the long-standing academic contempt for the mid-century *galant* style is still evident (Grant, *Dr. Burney as Critic*, 305). In Blackwell's *Music in Britain* series, for example, the *galant* is described as "a trivialization of music," marking a "decline in the levels of taste." *Music in Britain: The Eighteenth Century*, ed. H. Diack Johnstone and Roger Fiske (Oxford: Blackwell, 1990), 205, 314.
52 *Letters of Charles Burney*, I: 328.
53 Grant, *Dr. Burney as Critic*, 289; *Letters*, I: 340.
54 Charles Burney, *The Present State of Music in Germany, the Netherlands, and United Provinces* (London, 1775), 239. Rousseau called the fugue "a residue of barbarism and bad taste, which exists, like the buttresses of our Gothic churches, only to the shame of those who have taken the trouble to construct them." *Oeuvres Complètes*, V: 305, 308. See Downing A. Thomas, *Music and the Origins of Language: Theories from the French Enlightenment* (Cambridge: Cambridge University Press, 1995), 82–142.
55 *Cyclopedia, or Universal Dictionary of Arts, Sciences, and Literature* (London, 1819), vol. VII.
56 Weber, *The Rise of Musical Classics*, 218.
57 Hawkins, *General History*, I: xxxix.
58 *Letters of Charles Burney*, I: 126.
59 *The Monthly Review* (1790): 277. This is a commonplace of Burney criticism from Hazlitt – who called him more a "courtier" than a historian or musician – to Lawrence Lipking who, like Mrs. Thrale, anthropomorphizes his prose in the language of the *galant*: "Its most obvious virtues are grace, charm, energy, and good humor. It delights us with a liveliness of personality, and coaxes us into friendship." Hazlitt, *Works*, VIII: 209; *The Ordering of the*

Arts in Eighteenth-Century England (Princeton: Princeton University Press, 1970), 270.
60 Rohr, *Careers*, 9.
61 *The Monthly Review* (1786): 177.
62 Weber, *The Rise of Musical Classics*, 221.
63 Giuseppe Baretti, *La Frusta Letteraria*, ed. Massimo Bontanpelli (Milan: La Santa, 1929), vol. I: 100–10. Baretti describes Metastasio as "inimitable" despite his legions of imitators, and the "perfect" exponent of "simplicity, variety, energy, tenderness, sublimity, and thoughtful taste" in poetry. Baretti's language is indistinguishable from Burney's descriptions of the *galant* music adapted to Metastasian verse throughout the eighteenth century. In his *Dictionnaire de musique* (Paris, 1768), Rousseau advised young composers to find inspiration not in music but in Metastasio (*Œuvres Complètes*, V: 837–8).
64 Charles Burney, *Memoirs of the Life and Writings of the Abaté Metastasio* (London 1796), vol. I: 10.
65 *Early Journals and Letters*, I: 235, I: 161.
66 *The Early Journals and Letters of Frances Burney*, vol. II, ed. Lars E. Troide (Montreal: McGill-Queen's University Press, 1990), 32–3, 14.
67 *Thraliana*, I: 368.
68 *Thraliana*, I: 368, 372, 400.
69 *The Complete Plays of Frances Burney*, ed. Peter Sabor (London: William Pickering, 1995), vol. I: 101.
70 "Burney and Society," *Cambridge Companion to Frances Burney*, 146.
71 *Early Journals and Letters*, III: 81.
72 Terry Lovell, "Subjective Powers? Consumption, the Reading Public, and Domestic Woman in Early Eighteenth-Century England," *The Consumption of Culture*, 33.
73 *Authorship, Commerce and the Public: Scenes of Writing, 1750–1850*, ed. E. J. Clery, Caroline Franklin, and Peter Garside (New York: Palgrave, 2002), 5.
74 Betty Schellenberg, *The Professionalization of Women Writers in Eighteenth-Century Britain* (Cambridge: Cambridge University Press, 2005), 1. In a related article devoted to Burney, Schellenberg revises the central premise of Mary Poovey's influential *The Proper Lady and the Woman Writer* (Chicago: University of Chicago Press, 1984): "the 1770s and early 1780s were not predominantly hostile to women's literary and dramatic activity" ("From Propensity to Profession: Female Authorship and the Early Career of Frances Burney," *Eighteenth-Century Fiction* 14.3–4 [2002]: 349). The shift away from the "proper lady" thesis was already evident a decade earlier, when Cheryl Turner could argue from abundant historical evidence that "women novelists were among the most commercially successful authors of their day," for whom "literary professionalism was clearly an established employment option for women from the middle and upper classes." *Living by the Pen: Women Writers in the Eighteenth Century* (New York: Routledge, 1992), 78.

75 See Catherine Gallagher, *Nobody's Story: The Vanishing Acts of Women Writers in the Marketplace, 1670–1820* (Los Angeles: University of California Press, 1994), 46.
76 *Early Journals and Letters*, III: 187, 116, 436, 249, 291. On the first publication of her *Diary and Letters* (London, 1842), edited by her niece, critics viewed Burney's apparent bashfulness even more severely, as a screen for the author's insatiable vanity: "there is nothing so intrinsically coxcombical and self-centred as this excessive modesty, this 'pride which apes humility.'" *The Athenaeum* (April 23, 1842): 355.
77 *Journals and Letters* (ed. Sabor and Troide), 233.
78 Gallagher, *Nobody's Story*, 225; Schellenberg, "From Propensity to Profession," 370. Though Johnson famously told Boswell that "we have done with patronage," such recent scholarship suggests a far more mixed picture (*Boswell's Life of Johnson*, ed. George Birbeck Hill [Oxford: Clarendon Press, 1934], vol. V: 59). For example, Burney's sale of *Camilla* by subscription was itself "a modification of the patronage system." Clery *et al.* (ed.), *Authorship*, 13.
79 George Justice has identified a surrogate for Burney's authorial struggle for independence in the hapless Belfield in *Cecilia*. "Burney and the Literary Marketplace," *Cambridge Companion to Frances Burney*, 148.
80 *Thraliana*, II: 695.
81 William Makepeace Thackeray, *Contributions to the Morning Chronicle*, ed. Gordon N. Ray (Urbana, IL: University of Illinois Press, 1955), 185.
82 *Journals and Letters* (ed. Sabor and Troide), 398.
83 *Early Journals and Letters*, III: 39, 215.
84 *Memoirs* [D'Arblay], II: 146.
85 *Early Journals and Letters*, IV: 246; also III: 104, 168, 394, 400.
86 *Ibid.*, I: 92.
87 *Complete Plays*, II: 65.
88 *Ibid.*, III: 347.
89 *Edinburgh Review* (1842–3): 564.
90 In an addended essay to the 1991 Burney issue of *Eighteenth-Century Fiction*, Doody complains of the volume's disproportional interest in the novel as a "fable of identity," and laments a "lack of interest in Burney's comic effects," which had been the basis of the novel's continuing popularity over two centuries (364). In the ensuing two decades, the worm appears to have turned again toward *Evelina* as broad theatrical comedy and sociological document of High Georgian London. For important examples of this shift, see Timothy Dykstal, "*Evelina* and the Culture Industry" (*Criticism* 37.4 [fall 1995]: 559–81), and Vivien Jones's introduction to a recent Penguin edition of the novel (2003), in which she focusses not on the thematics of female identity but on the "linguistic richness and exuberance" of the novel, the differing social strata these idiolects represent, and Burney's comedic techniques (x).
91 Deidre Lynch, "Counter Publics: Shopping and Women's Sociability," *Romantic Sociability*, 215.

92 "Justness of Thought and Stile, Refinement in Manners, good Breeding, and Politeness of every kind, can come only from the Trial and Experience of what is best. Let but the Search go freely on, and the right Measure of everything will soon be found." *Characteristicks of Men, Manners, Opinions*, ed. Philip Ayres (Oxford: Clarendon Press 1999), I: 10. See Philip Carter, *Men and the Emergence of Polite Society, Britain 1660–1800* (Harlow: Longman, 2001).
93 James Fordyce, *Addresses to Young Men* (London, 1777), 186; David Fordyce, *Dialogues Concerning Education* (London 1745), vol. I: 43–5.
94 *Thraliana*, I: 368.
95 Erin Mackie, *Market à la Mode: Fashion, Commodity, and Gender in the* Tatler *and the* Spectator (Baltimore, MD: Johns Hopkins University Press, 1997), 15, 20.
96 As Claudia Johnson observes, "Working by complicating accretion rather than progression, the narrative flow of *Camilla* ... is fitful, impeded, constantly breaking down." *Equivocal Beings: Politics, Gender, and Sentimentality in the 1790s* (Chicago, IL: University of Chicago Press, 1995), 146.
97 Castle, *Masquerade and Civilization*, 276.
98 Joanne Cutting-Gray, *Woman as "Nobody" and the Novels of Fanny Burney* (Miami: University Press of Florida, 1992), 52.
99 Patricia Meyer Spacks, *Imagining a Self: Autobiography and the Novel in Eighteenth-Century England* (Cambridge, MA: Harvard University Press, 1976), 192.
100 This, for example, from the opening of the second essay (March 24, 1750):

> That the mind of man is never satisfied with the objects immediately before it, but is always breaking away from the present moment, and losing itself in schemes of future felicity; and that we forget the proper use of the time now in our power, to provide for the enjoyment of that which, perhaps, may never be granted us, has been frequently remarked; and as this practice is a commodious subject of raillery to the gay, and of declamation to the serious, it has been ridiculed with all the pleasantry of wit, and exaggerated with all the amplifications of rhetoric.

In the *Memoirs*, Burney praises the *Rambler* as the best of "the sublime author ... because emanating from original genius," thus giving Romantic shape to the lately unfashionable Johnson (II: 181).
101 Woolf, *Common Reader*, 111.
102 *Memoirs* (Klima *et al.*), xxxiv–xxxv.
103 Lonsdale, *Dr. Charles Burney*, 449.
104 *Memoirs* [D'Arblay], I: 188.
105 *Memoirs* [D'Arblay], I: 188, I: 90, II: 10, II: 215.
106 *Early Journals and Letters*, II: 149.
107 Burney did preserve, however, an account of the contest between the celebrated sopranos Agujari and Gabrielli for the public's favor in the 1775 season. It was customary for opera divas to perform a few songs at the houses of the nobility for enormous fees. But one extraordinary night in

early June, Agujari sang for five hours in the small Burney music-room on St. Martin's Street for nothing but the assurance of Charles Burney's gratitude. "She sung in 20 different styles," the young Frances recorded in a letter, "The greatest was son Regina & son[o] amante from Didone. Good God! What a song! & how sung! Then she gave us 2 or 3 *Cantabiles*, sung divinely, then she chanted some *Church Music*, in a style so nobly simple & unadorned, that it stole into one's very soul!" (*Early Journals and Letters*, II: 155). The concert survives in the Burney manuscript as a record of the author's budding sensibility, much like the heroines' responses to the opera in *Evelina* and *Cecilia*, but also of her own intimate knowledge, elsewhere suppressed, of the fashionable musical repertoire of the 1770s. The issue of her father's power to command such a performance is not entered into. Music itself is idealized as an advertisement of sensibility, but the operations of the music industry are sunk beneath the horizon of literary respectability.

108 *Early Journals and Letters*, I: 199–200.
109 See Stephen A. Willier, "Gasparo Pacchierotti in London: The 1779–80 Season in Susanna Burney's 'Letter-Journal'" (*Studi Musicali* 29.2 [2000]: 251–91), and Woodfield's *Salomon and the Burneys* (Aldershot: Ashgate, 2003) for generous extracts from those journals. A more comprehensive selection, edited by Philip Olleson, is forthcoming.
110 *Memoirs* [D'Arblay], III: 283.
111 *Quarterly Review* 49 (1833): 98; *Edinburgh Review* (1842–3): 524.
112 Doody, *Frances Burney*, 10.
113 *Memoirs*, II: 75.
114 Lonsdale, *Dr. Charles Burney*, 447.
115 *Memoirs* [D'Arblay], II: 200, 252–3.
116 *Ibid.*, I: 222.
117 In the *General History*, Pacchierotti is invoked as a modern virtuosic ideal within the immediate living memory of Burney's readers: "there was a perfection so exquisite in tone, taste, knowledge, sensibility, and expression, that my conceptions in the art could not imagine it possible to be surpassed." Burney also uses this passage on Pacchierotti to argue that anti-virtuosic criticism represents a failure of taste on the part of "envious professors" who have "poisoned" public opinion against the singer. For Burney, virtuosity enables the glamorous union of repetition and novelty:

> many hearers lament his condescending to rival the lark, or ever ... quitting simplicity in order to change or embellish a passage in the most new, artful, or ingenious manner possible. But to lovers and judges of Music who constantly attend the opera, it seems desirable that the performers ... should have the power of stimulating attention to an air often repeated, by a variety of new graces and ornaments, which, in some measure, renovate a song every time it is performed. (II: 888).

118 *Edinburgh Review* (1842–3): 526.
119 "I am afraid of seeing my Father," Burney wrote to Susan in the winter of 1781, having been sent to Chessington to complete *Cecilia:* "O that I could

defer the publication, & relieve my mind from this vile solicitude which does but shackle it, & disturbs my rest so abominably, that I cannot sleep half the Night for planning what to write next Day – and then next Day I am half dead for want of rest!" *Early Journals and Letters*, IV: 265.
120 *Early Journals and Letters*, III: 353, 350.

3 WORDSWORTH CASTRATO

1 Daniel Heartz, "Farinelli and Metastasio: Rival Twins of Public Favour," *Early Music* 12.3 (August 1984): 361–2.
2 "[D]as schlappe Kastraten-Jahrhundert." Friedrich Schiller, *Die Räuber* (1781), 1.ii; *Sämtliche Werke* ed. Albert Meier (Munich: Carl Hanser Verlag, 2004), 1: 503; Adela Pinch, "Female Chatter: Meter, Masochism, and the *Lyrical Ballads*," *English Literary History* 55.4 (1988): 848.
3 Adam Smith, *Theory of Moral Sentiments*, ed. D. D. Raphael and A. L. Mackie (Oxford: Clarendon Press, 1976), 46.
4 *Lyrical Ballads, and Other Poems 1797–1800*, ed. James Butler and Karen Green (Ithaca: Cornell University Press, 1983), 751, 1802 edition, l. 296. I distinguish the Preface of 1800, and its expanded 1802 version, from the brief "Advertisement" of the 1798 *Lyrical Ballads*. I will refer to them in my text inclusively as "the Preface," but will hereafter distinguish specific quotes with *P*, with reference to the edition in which they first appear and the line numbering of the Cornell edition. Quotations from the "Appendix on Poetic Diction" of the 1802 edition will be specified separately as "Appendix," and cited likewise according to the Cornell edition.
5 See Marlon Ross, *The Contours of Masculine Desire: Romanticism and the Rise of Women's Poetry* (Oxford: Oxford University Press, 1989), and Roger Lonsdale's introduction to his volume *Eighteenth-Century Women Poets* (Oxford: Oxford University Press, 1990).
6 Hazlitt, "On Effeminacy of Character," *Works*, VIII: 254–5; "Mr. Wordsworth," *Works*, XI: 87–8.
7 David Hume, "On the Rise and Progress of the Arts and Sciences," *Essays and Treatises on Several Subjects* (London 1753), I: 186. In her "Effeminacy in the Army Censured," Haywood mocks those officers who "find it an insuperable Difficulty to bring themselves to that Hardiness and Neglect of personal Ornaments, which suits the Life of a Soldier" (*The Female Spectator, 1744–46*, ed. Gabrielle M. Firmager [Bristol: Bristol Classical Press, 1993], 30). More famously, Wollstonecraft derided Burke's "ornamental feelings" for the French royal family. *A Vindications of the Rights of Men, with A Vindication of the Rights of Woman, and Hints*, ed. Sylvana Tomaselli (Cambridge: Cambridge University Press, 1995), 6.
8 According to biographical accounts, Wordsworth reinforced this distinction by an unimpeachable manliness of personal conduct and affect. Hazlitt remarked on the "great depth and manliness and a rugged harmony, in the tones of his voice," while Coleridge went further, declaring that "Of all

the men I ever knew, Wordsworth has the least femininity in his mind. He is all man." Hazlitt, *Works*, XI: 91; *Letters, Conversations, Recollections of Samuel Taylor Coleridge*, ed. Thomas Allsop (London, 1836), II: 228, quoted in Susan Wolfson, "*Lyrical Ballads* and the Language of (Men) Feeling: Wordsworth Writing Women's Voices," *Men Writing the Feminine: Literature, Theory, and the Question of Genders*, ed. Thais E. Morgan (Binghamton: State University of New York Press, 1994), 47.

9 Charles Burney, *Monthly Review* 29 (1799): 209. Wordsworth quotes Gray's "Sonnet on the Death of West" in full in order, he says, to demonstrate the superiority of those lines that "in no respect differ from that of good prose" (*P* 1800: 221). Wordsworth offers no proof or analysis of the supposed distinction between plain and ornamental diction in Gray's poem beyond rhetorical assurances that the distinction is a clear one: "it will easily be perceived," "it is equally obvious that" (*P* 1800: 245–6). Coleridge, in ch. 18 of the *Biographia Literaria*, was the first of many readers to point out the vagueness of the case. According to the masculinist logic of the Preface, however, what is important is not the clarity of the argument against Gray's diction, but what Gray himself signifies. Linda Zionkowski has shown how Gray's poetic career was clouded by charges of effeminate dilettantism, and Peter Manning how, in the sonnet Wordsworth selects, Gray adopts the conventions of Petrarchan heterosexual love poetry for an elegiac address to a male friend ("Gray, the Marketplace, and the Masculine Poet," *Criticism* 35.4 [1993]: 589–608; "Wordsworth and Gray's Sonnet on the Death of West," *Studies in English Literature* 22.3 [1983]: 504–18). Simon Bainbridge in turn has argued for the significance of Wordsworth's placement of Gray immediately after an encomium to Milton, "as if Wordsworth is drawing an implicit distinction between the 'manly' Milton and the 'unmanly' Gray" ("'Men Are We': Wordsworth's 'Manly' Poetic Nation," *Romanticism* 5.2 [1999]: 224). The obscurity of Wordsworth's actual critique of Gray on poetic grounds only brings into bolder relief his symbolic function as the effeminate poet against which Wordsworth's own "manly" style will be set.

10 *Le Beau Monde* 2 (1807): 138; Francis Jeffrey, *Edinburgh Review* 11 (1807): 231.
11 Judith Page, *Wordsworth and the Cultivation of Women* (Berkeley: University of California Press, 1994), 2.
12 Ross, *The Contours of Masculine Desire*, 38, 35.
13 "Romanticism and the Colonization of the Feminine," *Romanticism and Feminism*, ed. Anne K. Mellor (Bloomington: Indiana University Press, 1988), 13. Diane Hoeveler comes to a similar conclusion regarding Wordsworth's female speakers in *Lyrical Ballads* who, she claims, "cannot be understood apart from this radical metaphoric tradition of literary absorption/cannibalization." *Romantic Androgyny* (University Park: Pennsylvania State University Press, 1990), xiv.
14 Wolfson, "*Lyrical Ballads* and the Language of (Men) Feeling," 31.
15 Page, *Wordsworth and the Cultivation of Women*, 12.
16 Pinch, "Female Chatter," 846.

17 Tim Fulford, *Romanticism and Masculinity* (New York: St. Martin's Press, 1999), 187, 17.
18 Edmund Burke, "The New Morality," *The Anti-Jacobin* (1798), I. 116, quoted in Fulford, *Romanticism*, 10.
19 A gendered understanding of meter may have been suggested to Wordsworth by his reading of Quintilian, who was sufficiently influential for Wordsworth to include a quotation from *Institutio oratoria* as a motto for volume I of the 1802 *Lyrical Ballads*. In his *Oratory* Quintilian speaks of the current fashions for "effeminate" verse in a tone strikingly similar to that which Wordsworth employs so many centuries later to chide his own peers. He prescribes, as Wordsworth implicitly does, a masculinization of meter: "I should prefer my rhythm to be harsh and violent rather than nerveless and effeminate [*compositionem . . . effeminatam et enervem*], as it is in so many writers, more especially in our own day, when it trips along in wanton measures that suggest the accompaniment of castanets." *Institutio oratoria*, trans. H. E. Butler, 4 vols. (Cambridge, MA: Harvard University Press, 1943), vol. III: 587.
20 Herbert Lindenberger, *Opera: The Extravagant Art* (Ithaca: Cornell University Press, 1984), 76.
21 Linda Phyllis Austern, "'Alluring the Auditorie to Effeminace': Music and the Idea of the Feminine in Early Modern England," *Music and Letters* 74.3 (1993): 343–54.
22 See, for example, Cicero: "The two things which we must above all avoid are effeminate and unmanly [*effeminatum aut molle*] conduct on the one hand, and boorish and uncouth behaviour on the other." *On Obligations (De officiis)*, trans. P. G. Walsh (Oxford: Oxford University Press, 2000), 44.
23 Hazlitt, *Works* VIII: 248–55. Susan S. Shapiro, in a discussion of effeminacy that ranges from the sixteenth century to the Victorian period, concludes that "until approximately 1870, the most common associations with male 'effeminacy' were uxoriousness, foppery, libertinism, *omni*sexuality, and paradoxically, *a*sexuality, but only very rarely exclusive *homo*sexuality." "'Yon Plumed Dandebrat': Male 'Effeminacy' in English Satire and Criticism," *Review of English Studies* 39 (1988): 401. See also G. J. Barker-Benfield's chapter on effeminacy in *The Culture of Sensibility* (Chicago: Chicago University Press, 1992), 104–53.
24 Linda Dowling, *Hellenism and Homosexuality in Victorian Oxford* (Ithaca: Cornell University Press, 1994), 9, quoted in Kathleen Wilson, *The Sense of the People: Politics, Culture, and Imperialism in England, 1715–85* (Cambridge University Press, 1995), 195; John Brown, *An Estimate of the Manners and Principles of the Times* (London, 1757), 29.
25 Paul Langford, *A Polite and Commercial People: England 1721–1783* (Oxford: Oxford University Press, 1989), 3.
26 John Tosh, "The Old Adam and the New Man: Emerging Themes in the History of English Masculinities, 1750–1850," *English Masculinities, 1660–1800*, ed. Tim Hitchcock and Michèle Cohen (New York: Longman, 1999), 220.

27 Michèle Cohen, *Fashioning Masculinity: National Identity and Language in the Eighteenth Century* (London: Routledge, 1996).
28 Henry Carey, *Poems on Several Occasions*, 3rd edn. (London, 1729), 30. For an analysis of the castrati's discursive link with "unnatural" male sexualities, and their relation to a nascent British national ideology, see Todd S. Gilman, "The Italian (Castrato) in London," *The Work of Opera: Genre, Nationhood, and Sexual Difference*, ed. Richard Dellamora and Daniel Fischlin (New York: Columbia University Press, 1997), 49–70. For Gilman, the cultural potency of the castrato lies in his multiple gender significations, as *effeminatus*, stage hero, and virile lover. Thus Gilman, like Shapiro, finds in the effeminate sodomite of legend only a partial account of the castrato's impact, identifying instead "a more general fear … that the castrato's excessive, uncontainable gender exposed the contingent nature of gender and sexuality" (58).
29 John Dennis, "Essay on the Operas," *Critical Works*, ed. Edward Niles Hooker (Baltimore, MD: Johns Hopkins University Press, 1985), II: 389; Jonathan Swift, *The Intelligencer* 3 (1728): 8; Aaron Hill, *The Plain Dealer* 94 (February 12, 1725), 310–11; *Satan's Harvest Home* (London, 1749), 56.
30 Roland Barthes, *S/Z*, trans. Richard Miller (New York: Hill and Wang, 1974), 110.
31 Brown, *Estimate*, 47. See Suzanne Aspden, "'An Infinity of Factions': Opera in Eighteenth-Century Britain and the Undoing of Society," *Cambridge Opera Journal* 9.1 (1997): 14.
32 Giuseppe Baretti, *A Dissertation upon the Italian Poetry* (London, 1753), 50.
33 Giuseppe Baretti, *Italian Library* (London, 1757), xxvii; *Quarterly Review* 24 (1820): 82.
34 Christopher Wordsworth, *Memoirs of William Wordsworth* (London, 1851), I: 14. In 1784 Isola, an Italian emigré, published a new edition of translations by his students from the Italian poets, including Petrarch, Ariosto, Tasso, and Metastasio. Wordsworth owned a copy of this volume, entitled *Pieces Selected from the Italian*, and it was in its margins that he later drafted the translations from Metastasio that would appear in the *Morning Post* in 1803.
35 In her journal entry for January 11, 1803, Dorothy Wordsworth records that "Mary has been down stairs copying out Italian poems for [Daniel] Stuart," the owner and editor of the *Morning Post*. Jared Curtis places the composition date for Wordsworth's Metastasio translations "perhaps between around November 1802 and early January 1803" (*Poems, in Two Volumes, and Other Poems, 1800–1807*, ed. Jared Curtis [Ithaca: Cornell University Press]: 589). Robert Woof suggests "the end of 1802." "Wordsworth's Poetry and Stuart's Newspapers: 1797–1803," *Studies in Bibliography* 15 (1962): 186.
36 Daniel Heartz, *From Garrick to Gluck: Essays on Opera in the Age of Enlightenment* (Hillsdale, NY: Pendragon Press, 2004), 102–3.
37 Oliver Goldsmith, *Works*, ed. Peter Cunningham (New York: Harper & Bros., 1900), v: 142.

38 On Metastasio's reputation and popularity in England, see C. P. Brand, *Italy and the English Romantics* (Cambridge: Cambridge University Press, 1957), 36–45, 174–84, and Roderick Marshall, *Italy in English Literature, 1755–1815: Origin of the Romantic Interest in Italy* (New York: Columbia University Press, 1934), 62–7, 323–5.
39 A. W. Schlegel, *Course of Lectures on Dramatic Art and Literature*, trans. John Black (New York: AMS Press, 1965), 219.
40 Hazlitt, *Works*, v: 156.
41 I quote two of Wordsworth's translations and their original Italian texts as they appear in the Cornell edition (*Poems 1800–1807*, 589–93, 679). A sixth poem included in the Cornell edition, "Saro qual madre amante," which Wordsworth translated in the margins of the Isola volume but chose not to include in the *Morning Post* series, is sung by the eponymous hero of the oratorio *Giuseppe Riconosciutto* (1733). The aria expressed a form of gender license characteristic of Metastasian opera (and *Lyrical Ballads*). In it, the male hero likens his patriotic feelings to those of a "fond mother" restrained by love from beating her child.
42 Thomas Moore, *Journal*, ed. Wilfred S. Dowden (Newark: University of Delaware Press, 1984), iv: 1660.
43 *Spectator*, 135 (August 4, 1711), reprinted in *The Spectator, with Illustrative Notes. To Which are Prefixed the Lives of the Authors*, ed. Robert Bisset (1799), iii: 64.
44 [Alexander Jardine], *Letters from Barbary, France, Spain, Portugal, &c. By an English Officer* (1788), i: 360–1.
45 Dryden, *Works*, ed. Walter Scott (London, 1808), vii: 220–1.
46 *The Prompter*, 1734–6, 10.
47 John Hoole, *Dramas and Other Poems of the Abbé Pietro Metastasio* (1800), i: ix (my emphasis).
48 *A Comparative Sketch of England and Italy* (London, 1793), 11.
49 *Zenobia: A Musical Drama in Two Acts Represented at the King's Theatre in the Haymarket the 22nd of May, 1800, for the Benefit of Madame Banti* (London, 1800). Michael Burden has traced the cavalier adaptations of Metastasian texts on the London stage in two articles: "Metastasio's 'London Pasties': Curate's Egg or Pudding's Proof?" *Pietro Metastasio. Uomo universale*, ed. Andrea Sommer-Mathis and Elisabeth Theresia Hilscher (Vienna: Verlag der Österreichischen Akademie der Wissenschaften, 2000): 293–309; and "Metastasio on the London Stage: Adaptations and Permutations," *Studies in Music from the University of Western Ontario* 16 (1997): 111–34. For more general studies on the reception and legacy of Metastasio, see Raymond Monelle, "The Rehabilitation of Metastasio," *Music and Letters* 57.3 (1976): 268–91, and the 1998 special issue of *Early Music* (26.4).
50 The English Metastasians found it necessary to defend not only the manhood of Metastasio's texts but his personal reputation as well. In the 1730s, the Grand Tour diarist and Oxford Poetry Professor Joseph Spence had

recorded as common knowledge a salacious anecdote concerning the relationship between the young Metastasio and his mentor Gian Gravina, who had discovered the poet as a boy improvising songs on the streets of Rome. Gravina was a well-known pederast, according to Spence's story, and Metastasio a not unwilling ephebe (*Observations, Anecdotes, and Characters of Books and Men*, ed. James M. Osborn, 2 vols. [Oxford: Clarendon Press, 1966], vol. II: 556). Given the existence of such stories, when Charles Burney came to write his *Memoirs of Metastasio* (1796) he found himself under a dual obligation. In addition to crafting a distinctly *literary* reputation for Metastasio as a gift to "the lovers of Italian Poetry," it was necessary for him to rewrite the relationship between Gravina and Metastasio as an innocent paternal interest, and to make a strong claim for Metastasio's "innoxious life and moral character." As an argument for his publication of a selection of Metastasio's letters, Burney deliberately sets the themes of poetry and virtue (with an emphasis on *vir*) side by side: "a POET of refined taste and sentiments, and a MAN possessed of every moral and social virtue that embellishes human nature, his conduct and opinions deserve display, as much as his literary abilities admiration" (iii–iv). Burney's equation of poetry and manly virtue is intended to suppress the opposite conjunction more associated with Metastasio, namely opera and effeminacy.

51 For an account of Hoole's career see Marshall, *Italy in English Literature*, 52–70.
52 See Duncan Wu, *Wordsworth's Reading, 1770–1799* (Cambridge: Cambridge University Press, 1993), 134–5.
53 Walter Scott, *Journal, 1825–32* (Edinburgh, 1891), 204; Thomas Macaulay (unsigned review), *Edinburgh Review* 78 (July 1843): 201.
54 *Ezio* ran for eight performances in a King's Theatre production of 1770, and was revived in 1781 as a virtuoso vehicle for the great castrato Pacchierotti. Curtis Price, Judith Milhous, and Robert D. Hume, *Italian Opera in Late Eighteenth-Century London* (Oxford: Clarendon Press, 1995), vol. I: 268.
55 Hoole, *Dramas*, II: 320.
56 *Spectator* 135 (August 4, 1711).
57 Martha Feldman, "Magic Mirrors and the *Seria* Stage: Thoughts toward a Ritual View," *Journal of the American Musicological Society* 48.3 (1995): 459, 461.
58 *Musical Reminiscences: Containing an Account of the Italian Opera in England from 1773* (London, 1834), 81–2.
59 Naomi André has described how in the transition period, 1800–30, the banished castrato voice continued to "haunt" opera culture in the form of the vocal expectations of *bel canto*, and the predominance of heroic roles given to women *en travesti*. In that period women rather than men "became the primary site of cross-sexual casting" and continued the baroque "stylization of sound and image" until the full impact of Romantic reform was felt in the advent of those heroic *female* roles – Norma, Lucia – that are the staples of the modern opera repertoire (*Voicing Gender: Castrati, Travesti, and the Second*

Woman in Early Nineteenth-Century Opera [Indianapolis: Indiana University Press, 2006], 36, 44). The year 1800 did not mark the final appearance of a castrato on the Italian stage, however. Giovanni Velluti visited London twice in the 1820s, but met with outrage and disgust from the press and audiences. Leigh Hunt came to the singer's defense in his remarkable poem, "Vellutti [sic] to his Revilers," in which the aging castrato takes the shape of Mary Shelley's sympathetic monster, a "solitary" lovelorn man-child left "wand'ring in aching space." *The Examiner* (August 7, 1825): 495–7.

60 *The Letters of Mary Wordsworth, 1800–55*, ed. Mary E. Burton (Westport, CT: Greenwood Press, 1979), xxv.

4 COCKNEY MOZART

1 Charles and Mary Cowden Clarke, *Recollections of Writers* (London, 1878), 196.
2 H. Barton Baker, *The London Stage: Its History and Traditions, 1576–1888* (London, 1889), 255.
3 *British Stage and Literary Gazette*, September 1817.
4 *British Stage and Literary Gazette*, June 1817.
5 Charles Lamb, *Complete Works and Letters* (New York: Modern Library, 1935), 205.
6 *Memoirs of Shelley, and Other Essays and Reviews*, ed. Howard Mills (New York: New York University Press, 1970), 45.
7 Lamb, *Complete Works*, 35.
8 *Literary Gazette*, April 19, 1817.
9 "Mozart Productions and the Emergence of *Werktreue* at London's Italian Opera House, 1780–1830," *Operatic Migrations*, ed. Roberta Montemorra Marvin and Downing A. Thomas (Aldershot: Ashgate, 2006), 165.
10 The distinction between "event" and "work" is elucidated by Carl Dahlhaus in *Nineteenth-Century Music*, trans. J. Bradford Robinson (Berkeley: University of California, 1989), 11–15, and forms the basis of Lydia Goehr's influential study, *The Imaginary Museum of Musical Works: An Essay in the Philosophy of Music* (Oxford: Clarendon Press, 1992).
11 In "A Chapter on Ears," Lamb describes a musical evening at the Novellos with a mix of exaggerated Catholic and pagan imagery, designed to evoke its cultish, heterodox, subcultural character. *Elia* (London, 1823), 92–4.
12 Selections from Mozart's operas circulated in England in printed anthologies through the 1790s, though usually with varying English texts. Full vocal scores began to appear the following decade. In the years 1809–17, Robert Birchall, Monzani and Hill, and Falkner all published scores of *Don Giovanni*. Alec Hyatt King, "Vignettes in Early Nineteenth-Century London Editions of Mozart's Operas," *British Library Journal* 6 (1980): 25.
13 Leigh Hunt, *Musical Evenings, or Selections, Vocal and Instrumental*, ed. David R. Cheney (Columbia: University of Missouri Press, 1964), 17.
14 *The Athenaeum* (July 7, 1832), 439, I. 5–8.

15 "Music in the Home II," *Music in Britain: The Eighteenth Century*, 315.
16 Hunt had written the first chapter of "Musical Evenings" before deciding that the project was "much too far in advance of the then existing public taste for music" (Cowden Clarke and Cowden Clarke, *Recollections*, 202). Hunt's misreading of his public in this venture is revealing in itself: it shows that the Hunt circle's musical tastes stood parallel with its politics, "in advance" of the putative mainstream.
17 "Harry Brown's Letters to His Friends. Letter III. To W. H., Esq." *The Examiner* (July 14, 1816), 441. Republished in *Foliage* (London, 1818) as "To William Hazlitt."
18 John Barnard, "Hunt and Charles Cowden Clarke, 1812–18," *Leigh Hunt: Life, Poetics, Politics*, ed. Nicholas Roe (London: Routledge, 2003), 40–1.
19 Richard Altick, *The Cowden Clarkes* (Oxford: Oxford University Press, 1948), 193; Mary Cowden Clarke, *My Long Life* (New York: Dodd, Mead & Co., 1896), 26.
20 Weber, *The Great Transformation*, 144.
21 "Public Music in Private Spaces: Piano-Vocal Scores and the Domestication of Opera," *Music and the Cultures of Print*, ed. Kate van Orden (New York: Garland Publishing, 2000), 84–5.
22 Thornton Hunt, "Proserpine," in Edmund Blunden, *Leigh Hunt and His Circle* (London: Harper & Bros., 1930), 361.
23 The Cockney cult of Mozart finally proved too much for Keats. His falling out with Hunt in late 1818 was synonymous, in Keats's mind, with alienation from Mozart: "The night we went to Novello's there was a complete set to of Mozart and punning – I was so completely tired of it that if I were to follow my own inclination I should never meet any one of that set again, not even Hunt. . . . Through him I am indifferent to Mozart." *Letters*, II: 11.
24 Cowden Clarke, *My Long Life*, 15, 25.
25 Hunt "had intermittently composed and published songs for the pianoforte from the late 1800s onwards," two of which were set by John Whitaker in 1809. *Selected Writings of Leigh Hunt*, vol. VI, ed. John Strachan (London: Pickering and Chatto, 2003), 73.
26 Robinson, *Unfettering Poetry*, 88–101.
27 Cox, *Poetry and Politics in the Cockney School*, 87.
28 Leigh Hunt, *Poetical Works*, ed. H. S. Milford (Oxford: Oxford University Press, 1923), 254.
29 "Hunt and the Poetics and Politics of Fancy," *Leigh Hunt: Life, Poetics, Politics*, 156.
30 Leigh Hunt, *The Descent of Liberty: A Mask* (London, 1815), 1. 76–8.
31 "Preface to *Foliage*, Including Cursory Observations on Poetry and Cheerfulness," *Leigh Hunt's Literary Criticism*, ed. Lawrence H. Houtchens and Carolyn W. Houtchens (New York: Columbia University Press, 1956), 133.
32 Blunden, *Leigh Hunt*, 193–4.
33 *Blackwood's Edinburgh Magazine* (October, 1817).

34 For the English Mozartians, Mozart's operas represented an historic solution to the deep German-Italian divide in European music, where the Italian school was identified with melodic *bel canto* and the German baroque with a taste for intricate counterpoint and dense orchestration (see chapter 2). The Italians themselves, of course, saw no such thing in Mozart, whom they considered "German," while in Germany itself, Mozart was performed in vernacular translation. It is in England therefore, as Emanuele Senici states, that "Mozart's Italian operas entered the repertory as 'Italian operas.'" "'Adapted to the Modern Stage': *La Clemenza di Tito* in London," *Cambridge Opera Journal* 7.1 (1995): 2.
35 Blunden, *Leigh Hunt*, 200–1.
36 Marilyn Butler, *Romantics, Rebels and Reactionaries* (Oxford: Oxford University Press, 1981), 121.
37 Lorenzo Da Ponte, *Memoirs*, trans. Elisabeth Abbot (New York: Dover, 1929), 251.
38 See, for example, John Sterland [S.D.] "Chronicles of the Italian Opera in England," *Harmonicon* 8 (1830): 246, and Baker, *The London Stage*, 255. I follow Alec Hyatt King in his suggestion that John Sterland, a City amateur and member of the Philharmonic Society, authored those articles for the *Harmonicon* between 1830 and 1833 signed "S.D." *Musical Pursuits: Selected Essays* (London: British Library, 1987), 126–35.
39 Vincent and Mary Novello, *A Mozart Pilgrimage: Being the Travel Diaries of Vincent and Mary Novello in 1829*, ed. Rosemary Hughes (London: Novello & Co., 1955), 256–7.
40 *Examiner*, April 18, 1824.
41 Cowden Clarke and Cowden Clarke, *Recollections*, 34.
42 George Hogarth, *Memoirs of the Musical Drama* (London, 1838), vol. II: 373.
43 Frederick C. Petty, *Italian Opera in London, 1760–1800* (Ann Arbor: UMI Research Press, 1980), 38.
44 When Queen Charlotte attended a production of *Don Giovanni* at the King's Theatre in 1821, she found "a splendidly bound copy of the opera" on her cushion (*The Times*, 25 May). For an opera score to be bound, let alone thought worthy as a royal gift, was unthinkable before Mozart.
45 *Literary Gazette*, April 19, 1817.
46 Mount-Edgcumbe, *Musical Reminiscences*, 100.
47 Sterland, "Chronicles," 73. Catalani was once paid £1700 for seventeen songs by the Marquis of Buckingham, more than US$100,000 today, for a weekend parlor-room concert (Rees Gronow, *The Reminiscences and Recollections of Captain Gronow, 1810–60* [New York: Scribner & Welford, 1889], vol. I: 35). The fashion for such exclusive concerts as an alternative to the increasingly deregulated social order of the King's Theatre enraged middle-class critics. Richard Mackenzie Bacon, who founded England's first musical journal and was the most significant music critic outside the Hunt circle, deplored these private concerts for Catalani as "a means of excluding all but those whom these titled managers may choose should breathe the same air

with themselves – a mode of keeping out *improper people*, as they would phrase it." Bacon's tone rises to an almost jacobinical pitch: "If the Aristocracy entertain a serious intention of bringing themselves (the few) into a dangerous degree of contempt with the nation (the many), they cannot adopt a readier mode; and such a division, they need scarcely be told, will go dreadfully against the powers that be" (*London Magazine*, June 1824). The politicization of opera in the Regency period is here graphically demonstrated.

48 Thomas Tegg, *The Rise, Progress, and Termination of the O. P. War in Poetic Epistles* (London, 1810), 3.
49 Mount-Edgcumbe, *Musical Reminiscences*, 98.
50 *The Times*, April 16, 1817.
51 Mary Shelley, *The Last Man*, ed. Hugh J. Lake (Lincoln: University of Nebraska Press, 1965), 99.
52 Allatson Burgh, *Anecdotes of Music* (London, 1814), vol. III: 361.
53 *Ibid.*; *Harmonicon* 10 (1832): 400.
54 Hogarth, *Memoirs of the Musical Drama*, II: 368.
55 As Martha Feldman has argued, the courtly formality of *opera seria* was also overlaid by a more "slippery semantics of Carnival, masquerade and transvestism." The opera as a scene of fantasy and free play was musically enacted in the virtuoso aria, which juxtaposed stock compositional structures with "the unfixed elements" of ornament and the "extraordinary sensory effects" of virtuosic vocal improvisation. "Magic Mirrors," 478, 470.
56 Quoted in Richard Somerset-Ward, *Angels and Monsters: Male and Female Sopranos in the Story of Opera* (New Haven: Yale University Press, 2004), 116.
57 *Harmonicon* 6 (1828): 172.
58 John Dennis, "Essay on the Opera," *Critical Works*, vol. II: 389–90.
59 Sterland, "Chronicles," 72. Burgh called Catalani the "Semiramis of those regions of fiction," namely the King's Theatre. Burgh, *Anecdotes*, III: 361.
60 *The Times*, June 1, 1818.
61 Mount-Edgcumbe, *Musical Reminiscences*, 125.
62 Sterland, "Chronicles," 10.
63 *Harmonicon* 2 (April, 1824): 78.
64 Alsager's relationship to the Hunt–Lamb circle is detailed in D. E. Wickham, "Thomas Massa Alsager: An Elian Shade Illuminated," *Charles Lamb Bulletin* 35 (July, 1981): 45–62. Leanne Langley provides the most thorough description of both Alsager's and Ayrton's contribution to English music journalism in "The English Musical Journal in the Early Nineteenth Century" (Ph.D. dissertation, University of North Carolina, 1983).
65 Leigh Hunt, *Autobiography*, ed. Edmund Blunden (Oxford: Oxford University Press, 1928), 297.
66 Ayrton's dogmatic personality is showcased in his role as doltish foil to Lamb's wit in Hazlitt's essay, "Of Persons One Would Wish to Have Seen," *Works*, XVII: 122–34.
67 *The Times*, January 12, 1818.

68 Sterland, "Chronicles," 246.
69 *The Times*, May 28, 1817.
70 *Examiner*, March 22, 1812.
71 Hunt, *Poetical Works*, 238.
72 Precisely the same language was employed to describe Ayrton to the Sheriff's Court: "He was a gentleman – a scholar – acquainted with foreign languages; understood not only what belonged to the science of music, but to the business of the world" (*The Times*, January 12, 1818). These epithets define the new bourgeois man as an educated, cultured, worldly professional, in implicit contrast to the "semi-barbarous" narrowness, in both education and experience, of his aristocratic counterpart.
73 Alsager later became an important promoter of Beethoven in London, hosting the English premiere of the *Missa Solemnis* in 1832, and establishing the Beethoven String Quartet in 1845. David B. Levy, "Thomas Massa Alsager, Esq.: A Beethoven Advocate in London," *Nineteenth-Century Music* 9.2 (fall 1985): 119–27.
74 I am indebted, both for her original research and for her analysis of the class politics of Mozart, to Rachel Cowgill, "'Wise Men from the East': Mozart's Operas and Their Advocates in Early Nineteenth-Century London," in *Music and British Culture, 1785–1914*, ed. Christina Bashford and Leanne Langley (Oxford: Oxford University Press, 2000), 39–64.
75 *Harmonicon*, 9 (1831), 135–6.
76 Pamela Willetts, "The Ayrton Papers: Music in London, 1786–1858," *British Library Journal*, 6 (1980): 12.
77 March 6, 1711.
78 *Works*, II: 388.
79 Jennifer Hall-Witt, *Fashionable Acts: Opera and Elite Culture in London, 1780–1880* (Durham: University of New Hampshire Press, 2007), 100–1.
80 William Gardiner, *Music and Friends, or Pleasant Recollections of a Dilettante* (1838), I: 154–5.
81 It is important in making this argument not to mistake the rise of middle-class participation at the opera house as the simple cause of the aristocracy's declining interest, or of such symptoms of class change as the reform of listening. As Hall-Witt argues, the rapid enlargement of the titled ranks diluted the subscriber base of the opera house to the point where it became a less effective venue for elite socializing and the operations of patronage and social gatekeeping. This dilution also meant that one's visit to the King's Theatre in the 1820s entailed mixing with strangers to a significantly greater degree than in the 1790s. This would certainly have encouraged silent listening, quite independently of the moralized urgings of middle-class music critics. Hall-Witt, *Fashionable Acts*, 8.
82 For other comparative analyses of Hunt and Hazlitt's opera criticism, see Christopher Hatch, "The 'Cockney' Writers and Mozart's Operas," *Opera Quarterly* 3.2 (1985): 45–58, and David L. Jones, "Hazlitt and Hunt at the Opera House," *Symposium*, 16 (1962): 5–16.

83 *Leigh Hunt's Literary Criticism*, 129. For analysis of the preface see Jeffrey Cox, "Leigh Hunt's *Foliage*: A Cockney Manifesto," *Leigh Hunt: Life, Poetics, Politics*, 58–77, and Robinson, *Unfettered Poetry*, 83–108.
84 *Leigh Hunt's Literary Criticism*, 129.
85 *Autobiography*, 160.
86 Robinson, "Hunt and the Poetics and Politics of Fancy," *Leigh Hunt*, 165.
87 Cowgill, "Mozart Productions," 176.

5 AUSTEN'S ACCOMPLISHMENT

1 *A Description of Several Pieces of Mechanism, Invented by the Sieur Jacquet Droz* (London, 1775). See Paul Metzner, *Crescendo of the Virtuoso* (Berkeley: University of California Press, 1998), 150–4. Henri-Louis Jaquet-Droz ran the London branch of the family firm from 1774–84, a business principally devoted, like James Cox's, to the manufacture of luxury items for the Chinese market. In fact, the Jaquet-Droz firm at times worked in close partnership with Cox in both manufacture and trade. Pagani, *Eastern Magnificence*, 101.
2 See Otto Mayr, *Authority, Liberty and Automatic Machinery in Early Modern Europe* (Baltimore, MD: Johns Hopkins University Press, 1986).
3 Michael P. Steinberg, *Listening to Reason: Culture, Subjectivity, and Nineteenth-Century Music* (Princeton University Press, 2004), 9. See also Mark Evan Bonds, *Music as Thought: Listening to the Symphony in the Age of Beethoven* (Princeton: Princeton University Press, 2006).
4 "Aunt Jane began her day with music." Caroline Austen-Leigh, *My Aunt Jane Austen: A Memoir* (London: Jane Austen Society, 1952), 6.
5 *Letters*, ed. Deirdre Le Faye (Oxford: Oxford University Press, 1995), 7.
6 Patrick Piggott, "Jane Austen's Southampton Piano," *Jane Austen Society Reports* (1980): 6–9.
7 Tadmor, "Women, Reading, and Household Life," 167–8.
8 Ian Gammie and Derek McCulloch, *Jane Austen's Music* (St. Albans: Corda Music, 1996), 4.
9 The most musically informative assessment of Austen's repertoire is Robert K. Wallace's *Jane Austen and Mozart* (Athens, GA: University of Georgia Press, 1983), 249–63.
10 Dibdin, *A Letter on Musical Education*, 21.
11 It is likewise the "first question" Mary Crawford must ask regarding the rival Miss Owens in *Mansfield Park* (1814): "It is a regular thing. Two play on the pianoforte, and one on the harp – and all sing." Ed. James Kinsley (Oxford: Oxford University Press, 1998), 261.
12 "The Piano and the Nineteenth Century," *Nineteenth-Century Piano Music*, ed. Larry Todd (New York: Routledge, 2004), 3.
13 Ritchie, *Women Writing Music*, 221.
14 The two book-length treatments of Austen and music are Patrick Piggott's largely biographical study, *The Innocent Diversion: A Study of Music in the*

Life and Writings of Jane Austen (London: Clover Hill, 1979) and Wallace's *Jane Austen and Mozart*. Wallace joins a long tradition of Austen critics (Trilling, Litz, etc.) who have equated Austen's supposed Augustan decorum with Mozartian "balance." His theorization of the connection, however, does not go beyond imagined thematic connections between literature and music, e.g. "Individual and Society," "Life and Death." Wallace's analysis is ahistorical and never ventures, in the formal terms it sets itself, beyond impressionistic description. For example, *Pride and Prejudice* and Mozart's G minor Symphony are said to have in common "the balance of the parts, the clarity of articulation, and the elegance of the surface" (16). Without specific technical examples, such a vocabulary is of little use in illuminating either Austen or the Viennese composers of her age, let alone their relationship.

15 "Vanity... makes them value accomplishments more than virtues." Wollstonecraft, *Vindication*, 262.
16 More, *Strictures*, 1: 62–3. The "two Miss Beauforts were just such young Ladies as may be met with, in at least one family out of three, throughout the Kingdom ... they were very accomplished and very Ignorant... ." *Northanger Abbey, Lady Susan, The Watsons, and Sanditon*, ed. John Davie (Oxford: Oxford University Press, 1990), 373.
17 Wollstonecraft, *Vindication*, 95.
18 Jenny Davidson, "Professional Education and Female Accomplishments," *Eighteenth-Century Women* 4 (2006): 274.
19 Richard Leppert, *The Sight of Sound: Music, Representation, and the History of the Body* (Berkeley: University of California Press, 1993), 68–9. Leppert builds his reading of a sexist music culture principally on the basis of portrait painting, in which he observes a lack of enjoyment in the women subjects seated at their harpsichords, etc. It is a dubious point on which to dwell, however, since it defies the logic of Leppert's own argument that the status interests of the male commissioner of the painting (husband, father) would be served by having the women's supposed unhappiness as musicians be made explicit (74).
20 Kelly, "Education and Accomplishments," *Jane Austen in Context*, ed. Janet Todd (Cambridge: Cambridge University Press, 2005), 257; Mary Poovey, *The Proper Lady and the Woman Writer* (Chicago: University of Chicago Press, 1984), 29.
21 *Enquiries into the Duties of the Female Sex* (1799), 84.
22 Burgh, *Anecdotes*, 1: vii–viii.
23 *Persuasion*, ed. John Davie (Oxford: Oxford University Press, 1990), 48. Exceptions are worth noting. Leslie Ritchie has called for "a more complex understanding of musical practice as an activity that afforded [women] self-defining intellectual and sensual pleasures ... sometimes subversive of moral discipline and the social purposes that musical practice was thought to serve." *Women Writing Music*, 31. The historical data that Ritchie assembles suggest that many women defied the "narrow domestic and devotional

boundaries" of musical accomplishment to which the conduct-book literature sought to confine them (79). Two other significant critiques of the anti-accomplishment consensus remain unpublished. Juliette Wells, in her dissertation on the 1790s' education debate, argues that even those critics "committed to unearthing traces of women authors' struggle with feminine ideology, have dismissed accomplishments as trivial," and that "the influence of the contemporary controversy regarding accomplishments upon [Austen's] novels has received scarcely any attention" ("Accomplished Women: Gender, Artistry, and Authorship in Nineteenth-Century England" [Ph.D. dissertation, Yale University, 2003], 52). Interdisciplinarian Miriam Hart makes similar points in her dissertation, pointing out, as I do here, that Austen herself exemplifies that "music was an integral part of most middle-class women's lives and was capable of signifying far more than a mere female accomplishment." "Hardly an Innocent Diversion: Music in the Life and Works of Jane Austen" (Ph.D. dissertation, University of Ohio, 1999), 3.

24 Burgh, *Anecdotes*, I: v–vi. In Frances Burney's *The Wanderer* (1814), the heroine gives piano instruction to a grocer's daughter "with a very large fortune," in addition to the more conventionally genteel young women of Brightelmstone (222; see my chapter 2).

25 Arthur Loesser, *Men, Women and Pianos: A Social History* (London: Victor Gollancz, 1955), 252.

26 Nicholas Temperley, "Foreword," *The Piano in Nineteenth-Century British Culture*, xvi.

27 *Emma*, ed. James Kinsley (Oxford: Oxford University Press, 1995).

28 Edgeworth, *Practical Education* (1798), II: 529.

29 Nicholas Temperley, "Ballroom and Drawing-Room Music," *The Romantic Age, 1800–1914*, ed. Nicholas Temperley (Oxford: Blackwell, 1981), 118–19.

30 Mary Burgan, "Heroines at the Piano: Women and Music in Nineteenth-Century Fiction," *The Lost Chord: Essays on Victorian Music*, ed. Nicholas Temperley (Indianapolis: Indiana University Press, 1989), 43.

31 See Juliette Wells, "In Music She Had Always Used to Feel Alone in the World: Jane Austen, Solitude, and the Artistic Woman," *Persuasions: The Jane Austen Journal* 26 (2004): 103.

32 Mary Hunter, "'To Play as if from the Soul of the Composer': The Idea of the Performer in Early Romantic Aesthetics," *Journal of the American Musicological Society* 58.2 (2005): 373.

33 Janet Todd, "Jane Austen and the Professional Wife," *Repossessing the Romantic Past*, ed. Heather Glen and Paul Hamilton (Cambridge: Cambridge University Press, 2006), 207.

34 The term is Adolph Marx's, in a periodical essay on Beethoven's symphonies from 1824 (*The Critical Reception of Beethoven's Compositions by His German Contemporaries*, ed. Wayne M. Senner, Robin Wallace, and William Meredith [Lincoln: University of Nebraska Press, 1999], 67). As Ann Bermingham has argued, musical "accomplishment is directly tied to [a] new construction of the domestic space as the space of authentic subjectivity" ("The Aesthetics

of Ignorance: The Accomplished Woman in the Culture of Connoisseurship," *Oxford Art Journal* 16.2 [1993]: 4). As her title suggests, however, Bermingham considers the idea of feminine subjectivity as bankrupt as any other claims made for Georgian music-making. Her position is as indiscriminately negative, and as prejudiced against music, as Leppert's.
35 See chapter 3. For a useful survey of the early Georgian context, see E. J. Clery, *The Feminization Debate in Eighteenth-Century England: Literature, Commerce, and Luxury* (London: Palgrave Macmillan, 2004).
36 Ritchie, *Women Writing Music*, 5.
37 More, *Strictures*, I: 62.
38 Edgeworth, *Practical Education*, II: 531 (my emphasis); *Essays on Various Subjects* (London, 1785), 130.
39 Nancy Armstrong, *Desire and Domestic Fiction* (Oxford: Oxford University Press, 1987), 134. Gary Kelly's reading of Romantic literary culture under the rubric of professionalism has also been influential to my argument in this chapter. See *Women, Writing, and Revolution, 1790–1827* (Oxford: Clarendon Press, 1993), 1–5.
40 Edgeworth, *Practical Education* II: 521.
41 Dibdin, *Letter on Musical Education*, 10; John Burton, *Lectures on Female Education and Manners* (London, 1793), vol. I: 136. Dibdin was the first public performer on the pianoforte in England, and a songwriter for Garrick, Ranelagh Gardens, and the government in need of patriotic airs during the Napoleonic Wars.
42 Edgeworth, *Practical Education*, II: 537; James Fordyce, *Sermons to Young Women*, 12th edn. (London, 1800), vol. I: 200. Fordyce's language closely echoes Johnson's critique of the virtuoso collector in the *Rambler*, who "los[es] in petty speculations, those hours by which if he had spent them in nobler studies, he might have given new light to the intellectual world." The critique of virtuosity fixes its moral targets – luxury, effeminacy, uselessness – without special regard for the medium. Be it amateur collecting or women's piano-playing, virtuosity ranks as a "secondary class of learning." *Complete Works*, IV: 74–5.
43 Edmund Burke, *A Philosophical Enquiry into the Origin of our Ideas of the Sublime and Beautiful*, 9th edn. (London, 1782), 226. It is a point Catharine Macaulay returns to on several occasions in her *Letter on Education* (London, 1790): "Gracefulness is an idea of beauty belonging to posture and motion; in both of which, to be graceful, says Mr. Burke, it is requisite that there be no appearance of difficulty" (58).
44 See Deidre Lynch's discussion of the automaton figure in Burney in *The Economy of Character: Novels, Market Culture, and the Business of Inner Meaning* (Chicago: University of Chicago Press, 1998), 192–9.
45 *Bach in Berlin: Nation and Culture in Mendelssohn's Revival of the St. Matthew Passion* (Ithaca: Cornell University Press, 2005), 156. The pamphlet war over Logier's system was sustained and extensive. See *The Science of Music in Britain: A Catalogue of Writings, Lectures and*

Inventions, ed. Jamie Croy Kassler (New York: Garland, 1979). See also Loesser, *Men, Women and Pianos* (295–301), and Bernarr Rainbow, "Johann Bernhard Logier and the Chiroplast Controversy," *The Musical Times* 131 (April, 1990): 193–6. David Golby's maverick opinion that "Logier was effectively vindicated by widespread application" is neither logically sound nor supported by considered examination of the controversy. *Instrumental Teaching in Nineteenth-Century Britain* (Aldershot: Ashgate, 2004), 72.

46 Michel Foucault, *Discipline and Punish*, trans. Alan Sheridan (New York: Vintage Books, 1979), 135–69.

47 A. F. C. Kollmann, *Remarks on what Mr. J. B. Logier Calls his New System of Musical Education* (London, 1824), 45.

48 Logier denied "the slanderous charge, eagerly circulated, and malignantly dwelt upon, that my object was insidiously to dispossess worthy and industrious professors engaged in schools of their livelihood." *An Authentic Account of the Examination of Pupil Instruction in the New System of Musical Education by Certain Members of the Philharmonic Society* (London, 1818), 7.

49 Kollmann, *Remarks*, iv; *An Exposition of the Musical System of Mr. Logier, with Strictures on his Chiroplast* (London, 1818), 6–7.

50 Other responses shared a fascinated contempt for the mechanization of music but were less dignified in tone, taking advantage of the obvious comic possibilities presented by the Logier "system." One satirist, assuming the Logierian character of "Dr. Minim," exults in conducting class "with seven pianofortes, and surrounded by my appoggiatorical automarini, viz. Misses Kitty Chromatic, Diana Diesis, Tabitha Tonic, Sally Dominant, Dolly Redundant, Peggy Majore, and Constantia Boggleini, who were playing on their respective instruments all at the same time." *The Musical Tour of Dr. Minim with a Description of a New Invented Instrument, a New Mode of Teaching Music by Machinery, and an Account of the Gullabaic System in General* (London, 1818), 22–3.

51 *General Observations upon Music, and Remarks on Mr. Logier's System* (Edinburgh, 1817), 48.

52 See Golby's "Chronology of Principal British Instrumental Treatises, 1780–1900," *Instrumental Teaching*, 277–304.

53 James Parakilas and Gretchen A. Wheelock have detailed Clementi's central role in the cultural revolution of early nineteenth-century music, casting him as a "Father of the Entertainment Industry," when entertainment meant the family piano. *Piano Roles: Three Hundred Years of Life with the Piano*, ed. James Parakilas (New Haven: Yale University Press, 1999), 77–93.

54 There are many contemporary satirical portraits of music masters, but none better than Austen's Lady Catherine in *Pride and Prejudice*, who browbeats Elizabeth on the subjects of taste, practice and even correct fingering, without herself being able to play a note.

55 *General Observations*, 37.

56 F. H. Shera, *The Amateur in Music* (Oxford: Oxford University Press, 1939), 26.

57 *Discipline and Punish*, 154. E. P. Thompson nominates the 1790s as the period when the status of timepieces shifted from luxury to necessity: "a general diffusion of clocks and watches is occurring (as one would expect) at the exact moment when the industrial revolution demanded a greater synchronization of labor." *Customs in Common* (New York: The New Press, 1991), 368.
58 *The Letters of Mozart and His Family*, ed. Emily Anderson (London: Macmillan, 1985), 793. In his autobiography, the composer Carl von Dittersdorf, who was in the audience, records the emperor's identical judgment that "Clementi's playing was execution, pure and simple, while Mozart's combined execution and taste." Katalin Komlos, "Mozart and Clementi," *Historical Performance* 2.1 (spring 1989): 7, translation modified.
59 *Beethoven: Impressions of Contemporaries*, ed. O. G. Sonneck (New York: Schirmer, 1926), 13. See also Tia DeNora's analysis of the 1799 "duel" between Beethoven and Joseph Wölffl, accounts of which adhered to the same binary logic. *Beethoven and the Construction of Genius: Musical Politics in Vienna, 1792–1803* (Berkeley: University of California Press, 1995), 147–69.
60 Kathryn Shanks makes the connection between Jane and Emma's performances and the Mozart–Clementi duel, but in describing Jane Fairfax as "an illustration of the ancient equation of virtuosity with virtue," she elides the complexities shaping the eighteenth-century discourse of virtuosity. "Music, Character, and Social Standing in Jane Austen's *Emma*," *Persuasions: Journal of the Jane Austen Society* 22 (2000): 27, 16.
61 Fordyce, *Sermons to Young Women*, 1: 202.
62 Wollstonecraft, *Thoughts on the Education of Daughters* (London, 1787), 43–4.
63 David Wainwright, *Broadwood, by Appointment* (London: Quiller Press, 1982), 122. The top of the range Broadwood square piano was also expensive, costing about £26, which Patrick Piggott has estimated as about a quarter of Mrs. Bates's annual pension. Piggott, *The Innocent Diversion*, 86.
64 Michael Cole, *The Pianoforte in the Classical Era* (Oxford: Clarendon Press, 1998), 309.
65 DeNora, *Beethoven and the Construction of Genius*, 170–1. Debate continues among music historians as to Beethoven's preference among his pianos, but majority opinion coincides with the judgment of his contemporary biographer, and well-known London-based virtuoso, Ignaz Moscheles, who reported that "of all his pianos, Beethoven preferred the Broadwood," even taking it with him on holidays (Wainwright, *Broadwood*, 118–19). The Broadwood is the piano featured, lid open and littered with music, in a sketch taken of Beethoven's apartment days after his death.
66 *A Room with a View* (London: Edward Arnold, 1977), 31. Forster emphasizes Lucy's artistic self-absorption at the piano, her obliviousness to the praise of her audience or any other social rewards of accomplishment: "Like every other *true* performer, she was intoxicated by the mere feel of the notes" (30, my emphasis).

67 See William Kinderman, *Beethoven's Diabelli Variations* (Oxford: Clarendon Press, 1987), 114–15.
68 Knightley, in these terms, is a "late-style" hero: a prototype of the modern, practical professional male erected on Austen's own discursive memory of the chivalric past or, at least, its Burkean revival in the 1790s. "It is the work of *Emma*," as Claudia Johnson has observed, "to make Mr. Knightley seem traditional" (Johnson, *Equivocal Beings*, 201). Knightley represents Austen's unassimilable desires both to restore the hero's *droits de seigneur* while at the same time allowing her heroine's bourgeois ambitions to be satisfied in the assumption of his name and property, which he gallantly volunteers to "leave" on the last page.
69 Rose Rosengard Subotnik, *Developing Variations: Style and Ideology in Western Music* (Minneapolis: University of Minnesota Press, 1991), 29.
70 Parakilas and Wheelock, *Piano Roles*, 120.
71 Austen herself could not have intended the pun, but her placing "Cramer" on Jane Fairfax's Broadwood in *Emma* was a choice made within months of the Broadwood manufacturer's literal inscription of Cramer's name on an embossed plate alongside other elite English admirers on its piano for Beethoven.
72 Cramer was a valued member of the Novello circle, and therefore a strong supporter of Mozart's operas (see chapter 4). The Cowden Clarkes describe him as a continental musician of the old school, "polished in manner as a frequenter of Courts, as much an adept in subtly elegant flattery as a veteran courtier." Cowden Clarke and Cowden Clarke, *Recollections of Writers*, 65.
73 The *Studio per il Piano Forte* (1804–10) were the first of their genre, and "occupy a position of great historical importance" in the nineteenth-century piano repertoire. Temperley, "Piano Music: 1800–1870," *The Romantic Age*, 403.
74 For example, the technical challenge represented by combining a trill and separate melody in the same hand, rarely explored until Cramer's study no. 11, is a feature of Beethoven's late piano music; also Beethoven openly borrowed from Cramer's F minor study (no. 16) for the last movement of the "Appassionata" sonata; and Beethoven's student Carl Czerny reported that Cramer's studies were the inspiration for his teacher's sonata no. 26.
75 David Rowland, "Pianos and Pianists, c.1770–c.1825," *The Cambridge Companion to the Pianoforte*, ed. David Rowland (Cambridge University Press, 1998), 37. The first-hand account is given by Ernst Pauer, as quoted by Derek Melville in "Beethoven's Pianos," *The Beethoven Companion*, ed. Denis Arnold and Nigel Fortune (London: Faber and Faber, 1971), 48.
76 Jean-Jacques Eigeldinger, *Chopin: Pianist and Teacher*, ed. Ray Howat (Cambridge: Cambridge University Press, 1986), 59.
77 *Allgemeine Musikalische Zeitung* 12 (December 20, 1809): 175 (my emphasis).
78 Nicholas Salwey, "Women Pianists in Late Eighteenth-Century London," *Concert Life in Eighteenth-Century Britain*, 286. For the years 1800–22, Therese Ellsworth puts the figure of concert performances by women at

35 per cent. One female pianist alone, Lucy Anderson, "was responsible for over one-third of the presentations of the 'Emperor' Concerto ... in the first half of the nineteenth century ("Women Soloists and the Piano Concerto in Nineteenth-Century London," *Ad Parnassum* 2.1 [2003]: 24, 29). In light of these facts, Salwey declares "the myth of the female amateur" difficult to sustain (286).
79 See Stuart Sherman, *Telling Time: Clock Diaries and English Diurnal Form, 1660–1785* (Chicago, University of Chicago Press, 1996), 21.
80 In *Beethoven and the Construction of Genius*, Tia DeNora warns against the overeager subscription of Beethoven into the cause of the middle-class cultural revolution, arguing that the promotion of Beethoven occurred mostly in the private world of the aristocratic salons. The class-based arguments of Adorno are more applicable, however, to Beethoven's reception in the commercial music market of Britain, and his championing by the professional Philharmonic Society.
81 David Rowland, "The Music of the Early Pianists (to c.1830)," *Cambridge Companion to the Pianoforte*, 137. Austen's reference to "Robin Adair" is a pianistic in-joke typical of *Emma*. While the tune existed in simple, popular forms, Austen herself almost certainly possessed in her repertoire, and intended Jane Fairfax to play, a virtuosic set of variations published by G. Kiallmark in 1813.
82 See Weber, *The Great Transformation*, 13–18.
83 Gramit, *Cultivating Music*, 130, 145.
84 Jim Samson (ed.), *Virtuosity and the Musical Work: The Transcendental Etudes of Liszt* (Cambridge: Cambridge University Press, 2003), 102.
85 David Warren Hadley, "Beethoven and the Philharmonic Society of London: A Reappraisal," *The Musical Quarterly* 59.3 (1973): 450.
86 Dana Gooley, "The Battle against Instrumental Virtuosity in the Early Nineteenth Century," *Franz Liszt and His World*, ed. Christopher H. Gibbs and Dana Gooley (Princeton, Princeton University Press, 2006), 78–9.
87 From the Society charter, quoted in Myles Birket Foster, *History of the Philharmonic Society of London, 1813–1912* (London: John Lane, 1912), 5; Cyril Ehrlich, *First Philharmonic* (Oxford: Clarendon Press, 1995), 9.
88 *Quarterly Magazine and Musical Review* 4 (1822): 433, quoted in Ehrlich, 17.
89 Simon McVeigh, "Clementi, Viotti, and the London Philharmonic Society," *Muzio Clementi: Studies and Prospects*, ed. Roberto Illian, Luca Sala, and Massimiliano Sala (Bologna: Orpheus, 2002), 68; "'An Audience for High-Class Music': Concert Promoters and Entrepreneurs in Late-Nineteenth-Century London," Weber (ed.), *Musician as Entrepreneur*, 165.
90 The recent flurry of interest in the history of listening, across a broad spectrum of disciplines, has been illuminatingly summarized by William Weber ("Did People Listen in the Eighteenth Century?" *Early Music* 25 [1997]: 678–91). Weber argues that the analyses of James Johnson, Peter Gay, Lydia Goehr, and others are marred by Romantic prejudices: they

denigrate the listening practices of the eighteenth century as frivolous and merely "sociable," while the ideology of "absorbed" nineteenth-century listening goes unchallenged. The prejudice Weber identifies is central to this book: that is, recent criticism on listening rehearses the Georgian antagonism between literary (and academic) culture and the sociable practices of music, between Romantic, middle-class "virtues" and aristocratic virtuosity.

91 Weber, "Did People Listen," 689.
92 Andrew Elfenbein, *Byron and the Victorians* (Cambridge: Cambridge University Press, 1995), 53.
93 Gramit, *Cultivating Music*, 138.
94 Scott Burnham, "The Four Ages of Beethoven: Critical Reception and the Canonic Composer," *The Cambridge Companion to Beethoven*, ed. Gerald Stanley (Cambridge: Cambridge University Press, 2000), 279.
95 Dahlhaus, *Nineteenth-Century Music*, 9.
96 "The aesthetic integration of the symphonic structure is at the same time the pattern of a social integration." *Beethoven: The Philosophy of Music*, ed. Rolf Tiedemann (Oxford: Polity Press, 1998), 119. Gramit, in his study of the origins of "serious" music culture in Germany, has described Adorno as a late embodiment of that project: Adorno's "insistence on the supreme and unique achievement of Beethoven" is inseparable from his "anguished awareness that that music was also inevitably the cultural property of a limited, privileged group" (*Cultivating Music*, 163).
97 Subotnik, *Developing Variations*, 20.
98 Charles Rosen, *The Classical Style: Haydn, Mozart, Beethoven*, 2nd edn. (New York: Norton, 1997), 395.
99 Lawrence Kramer, *Music as Cultural Practice, 1800–1900* (Berkeley: University of California Press, 1990), 23.
100 Golby, *Instrumental Teaching*, 15. The *Allgemeine Musikalische Zeitung*, the first forum for serious music criticism in Europe, was founded in Leipzig in 1798.
101 Arthur Schopenhauer, *The World as Will and Representation*, trans. E. F. J. Payne (New York: Dover, 1969), vol. I: 262.
102 G. W. F. Hegel, *Aesthetics: Lectures on Fine Art*, trans. T. M. Knox (Oxford: Clarendon Press, 1975), vol. II: 891. Friedrich Schleiermacher used similar language in his Berlin lectures beginning in 1819, collected in the *Vorlesungen über die Ästhetik* (1842). See Andrew Bowie, "Music and the Rise of Aesthetics," *The Cambridge History of Nineteenth-Century Music*, 46–8.
103 A. B. Marx, *Musical Form in the Age of Beethoven: Selected Writings on Theory and Method*, ed. Scott Burnham (Cambridge University Press, 1997), 175.
104 Scott Burnham, *Beethoven Hero* (Princeton, Princeton University Press, 1995), xiii.
105 Rosen, *The Classical Style*, 445.
106 See Carl Dahlhaus, *Ludwig van Beethoven*, trans. Mary Whittall (Oxford: Clarendon Press, 1991), 81.

107 Bowie, "Music and the Rise of Aesthetics," 41–2.
108 *E. T. A. Hoffmann's Musical Writings*, ed. David Charlton (Cambridge: Cambridge University Press, 1989), 96.
109 Hegel, *Aesthetics*, II: 908.
110 The epigraph to *On Liberty* is taken from Alexander von Humboldt's *Sphere and Duties of Government* (trans. 1854); it places at the heart of liberal political philosophy "the absolute and essential importance of human development [*Bildung*] in its richest diversity."
111 David B. Greene, *Temporal Processes in Beethoven's Music* (New York: Gordon and Breach, 1982), 24, 18, 58.
112 The principal English-language contribution to the new discourse of sonata form in the 1790s is A. F. C. Kollmann's *An Essay on Practical Musical Composition* (London, 1799). By the mid-nineteenth century, sonata form was established as the basis of academic theory of music even as contemporary composers – Berlioz, Mendelssohn, Liszt – had abandoned it (see chapter 6).
113 Burnham, *Beethoven Hero*, 142, 146.
114 Marilyn Butler, *Jane Austen and the War of Ideas* (Oxford: Clarendon Press, 1975), 273. It is a sign of the increasing fragmentation (or diversity) of Austen studies that interest in epistemological issues, independent of historical context, has recently revived even in the face of three decades of rhetorical and historicist criticism. See recent articles by Susan C. Greenfield in *Eighteenth-Century Studies* 39.3 (2006): 337–50, Felicia Bonaparte in *Studies in the Novel* 37.2 (2005): 141–61, and William Nelles in *Narrative* 14.2 (2006): 118–31.
115 Scott borrows from the language of art theory to praise Austen who, like the Dutch realists, has learned the "art of copying from nature as she really exists." *Quarterly Review* (March 1816), reprinted in *Jane Austen: The Critical Heritage*, ed. B. C. Southam (London: Routledge & Kegan Paul, 1968), 63.
116 Jon Klancher has identified an equivalent contemporary articulation of the new bourgeois subject in the editorial voice of *Blackwood's Magazine*, founded in 1817, specifically "its tireless promotion of intellect ... the structure and workings of the human mind, as they are exhibited in its reasoning powers, in its imagination and invention, in its taste, as well as modes of expressing them." Austen's free indirect discourse and *Blackwood's* "subjective" style arrive together on the English scene and to the same purpose: the representation of bourgeois subjectivity as both a rhetorical practice and object of knowledge, in its full heroic potential. Klancher, *The Making of English Reading Audiences*, 52.
117 Dahlhaus, *Ludwig van Beethoven*, 92, 175.
118 For A. Walton Litz, Austen's "combination of absolute naturalness and absolute self-consciousness has been the foundation of [her] reputation." The question remains, of course, how these literary effects were achieved, and whether "naturalness" and "self-consciousness" are Austen's gifts or her creations. "'A Development of Self': Character and Personality in Jane

119 Kelly, *Women, Writing, and Revolution*, 183.
120 Adorno, *Beethoven*, 63.
121 See Lynch, *Economy of Character*, 207–49.
122 "'The Tittle-Tattle of Highbury": Gossip and Free Indirect Style in *Emma*," *Representations* 31 (1990): 11.
123 Steinberg, *Listening to Reason*, 7.
124 Clifford Siskin, *The Historicity of Romantic Discourse* (Oxford: Oxford University Press, 1988), 126, 146. See also Clara Tuite, who describes the product of free indirect discourse as "a new kind of intelligent female subjectivity," and the "strategy by which Austen recommends bourgeois femininity to a paternal aristocratic culture, which is then reformed and refitted by the bourgeois heroine." *Romantic Austen* (Cambridge: Cambridge University Press, 2002), 75, 94.
125 Adorno, *Beethoven*, 173; Hegel, *Aesthetics*, II: 902.
126 See D. A. Miller, *Jane Austen, or, The Secret of Style* (Princeton: Princeton University Press, 2003), 67.
127 *Jane Austen* (ed. Southam), 127.
128 Bermingham, "Aesthetics of Ignorance," 12.

6 THE BYRON OF THE PIANO

1 Francis Hueffer, *Half a Century of Music in England, 1837–1887* (London, 1889), 150; Alan Walker, *Franz Liszt: The Virtuoso Years, 1811–1847* (Ithaca: Cornell University Press, 1983), 354.
2 David Allsobrook, *Liszt: My Travelling Circus Life* (Carbondale: Southern Illinois University Press, 1991), 27; *Correspondance de Liszt et de Madame d'Agoult*, ed. Daniel Ollivier (Paris: Grasset, 1934), vol. II: 11, I: 444.
3 *Liszt Society Journal* 7 (1982): 19. For reprints of reviews from Liszt's British tour and the tour diary of the singer John Orlando Parry, see *The Liszt Society Journal* 6–12 (1981–7). See also Ben Arnold and Michael Saffle, "Liszt in Ireland (and Belgium): Reports from a Concert Tour," *American Liszt Society Journal* 26 (1989): 3–11.
4 *Correspondance*, II: 15, 21, 54, 90, 101.
5 Hueffer, *Half a Century*, 126.
6 *Correspondance*, II: 106, 104, 147.
7 *The Athenaeum*, May 16, 1840; *Musical World*, May 14, 1840. Chorley and Davison's often divergent aesthetic judgments carried over into strong personal dislike. Chorley "hated Davison and ignored the rest" of the critics, while Davison referred to Chorley's journal as the "Asinaeum" (Joseph Bennett, *Forty Years of Music, 1865–1905* [London: Methuen, 1908], 307). When Liszt had retired from the concert stage to establish himself as a composer, Davison called his music "hateful fungi which choke up and poison the fertile plains of harmony" (*Musical World*, June 30, 1855).

See Charles Reid's hostile biography of Davison, *The Music Monster* (London: Quartet Books, 1984) and Richard Kitson's more even-handed assessment in *Nineteenth-Century British Music Studies*, 303–10.
8 *Musical World* (June 11, 1840): 362–3.
9 *Blackwood's Edinburgh Magazine* 170 (September 1901): 314.
10 Susan Bernstein, *Virtuosity of the Nineteenth Century: Performing Music and Language in Heine, Liszt, and Baudelaire* (Stanford: Stanford University Press, 1998), 112. Richard Leppert and Stephen Zank refer likewise to the "broad range of paradoxical, often contradictory meanings" embodied in Liszt in "The Concert and the Virtuoso," *Piano Roles*, 281.
11 *Letters*, II: 167.
12 Quoted in Joanne Wilkes, "'Infernal Magnetism': Byron and the Nineteenth-Century French Reader," Richard A. Cardwell (ed.), *The Reception of Byron in Europe* (London: Thoemmes Continuum, 2004), vol. I: 18.
13 *Lord Byron: The Complete Poetical Works*, ed. Jerome J. McGann, vol. V (Oxford: Clarendon Press, 1986).
14 Leigh Hunt, *Lord Byron and Some of His Contemporaries*, (London, 1828), 42.
15 Moore, *Byron: Interviews and Recollections*, 58. On his visit to Venice in 1819, Moore was struck by the unfamiliar sight of a bearded Byron, the whiskers grown, so he learned, to disguise his flabby "faccia di musico."
16 *Liszt Society Journal* 11 (1986): 50.
17 *Liszt Society Journal* 8 (1983): 12.
18 *Liszt Society Journal* 11 (1986): 47.
19 See Dana Gooley, *The Virtuoso Liszt* (Cambridge: Cambridge University Press, 2004), 13–14. A characteristic diatribe from the early 1840s describes the baneful effects of a virtuoso concert on the educated music lover: "the man who has his entire life venerated art is baffled, unnerved, but still applauds, swept up by the avalanche, mechanically. But later, when he has sobered up, there is nothing left but a headache and dizziness, with no lingering, beatific echo." Carl Gollmick, "Das heutige Virtuosenwesen," *Neue Zeitschrift für Musik*, December 2, 1842.
20 See Robert Wangermée, "Conscience et Inconscience du Virtuose Romantique. A Propos des Années Parisiennes de Franz Liszt," *Music in Paris in the 1830s*, ed. Peter Bloom (Stuyvesant, NY: Pendragon Press, 1987), 553–73.
21 Hamilton, "The Virtuoso Tradition," 62–3.
22 Gooley, *Virtuoso Liszt*, 7.
23 Katherine Ellis, *Music Criticism in Nineteenth-Century France* (Cambridge: Cambridge University Press, 1995), 143.
24 *Gazette D'Augsbourg*, March 20, 1843, reprinted in *Musical World* 36 (August 7, 1858), 500–1.
25 However influential the critics of the music journals, the non-specialist daily press was arguably more important in providing publicity to pianists such as Liszt, who could weather the criticisms of highbrow commentators provided they did not affect the greater machinery of his popular celebrity. See James Deaville, "Liszt's Virtuosity and his Audience: Gender, Class and Power in

the Concert Hall of the Early 19th Century," *Das Andere. Eine Spurensuche in der Musikgeschichte*, ed. Annette Kreutzige-Herr (Frankfurt: Peter Lang, 1998), 291.

26 Charles Rosen, *The Romantic Generation* (Cambridge, MA: Harvard University Press, 1995), 474.

27 "Concert de MM. Berlioz et Liszt," *Revue et Gazette Musicale*, December 25, 1836.

28 Franz Liszt, *Gesammelte Schriften* (Leipzig, 1880–3), vol. III: 129. For an account of the history of this distinction between "true" and "false" virtuosity, see Gooley, "The Battle against Instrumental Virtuosity," 82. The "interpretive" defense of virtuosity remains the founding premise of conservatory instruction. As Liszt's future son-in-law, Richard Wagner, wrote in *La Revue et Gazette Musicale* while Liszt was in England,

> The greatest merit of the virtuoso consists in perfect understanding of the musical idea underlying the piece he is playing, without introducing any modification of his own … [he is] endowed both with a creative faculty and a technique supple enough to assimilate the thoughts of another in whatever manner required. (October 18, 1840)

Chorley himself chose Liszt's subordination of performative flair to the composer's genius as his strongest case for the pianist: "he illuminates every composition he undertakes, with a living but lightening fire, and imparts to it a soul of passion, or a dazzling vivacity, the interpretation never contradicting the author's intention, but more poignant, more intense, more glowing than ever the author dreamed of" (*Music and Manners in France and Germany* [London, 1844], vol. I: 275). For its defenders, the dazzle of virtuosity "illuminates" rather than blinds.

29 Charlotte Moscheles, *Life of Moscheles*, trans. A. Coleridge (London: Hurst and Blackett, 1873), I: 53.

30 Dahlhaus, *Nineteenth-Century Music*, 11–12.

31 Hector Berlioz, *Revue et Gazette Musicale*, June 12, 1836.

32 Deaville, "Liszt's Virtuosity," 295.

33 Heinrich Adami, *Wiener Theaterzeitung* (November 30, 1839): 1175.

34 *Musical World* (October 28, 1841): 276.

35 See Samson, *Virtuosity and the Musical Work*, 69.

36 Lawrence Kramer, *Musical Meaning: Toward a Critical History* (Berkeley: University of California Press, 1990), 70. See also Leppert and Zank, *Piano Roles*, ch. 6. Susan McClary nominates Liszt as the nineteenth-century model for rock-star sexuality and phallic exhibitionism in *Feminine Endings: Music, Gender, and Sexuality* (Minneapolis: Minnesota University Press, 1991), a connection made explicit in the Ken Russell film *Lisztomania* (1975), which starred Roger Daltrey, lead singer of The Who, as Liszt.

37 For a survey of Lisztian caricature, see Ernst Burger, *Franz Liszt: A Chronicle of his Life in Pictures and Documents*, trans. Stewart Spencer (Princeton: Princeton University Press, 1989).

38 Gooley, *Virtuoso Liszt*, 2.
39 During the Rhine Crisis of the early 1840s, the Paris music journal *Le Ménestrel* called Liszt's performance in Germany of several anti-French songs "a truly disgraceful act" and published a letter signed by 400 fellow pianists deploring it (June 26, July 24, 1842). See Gooley's chapter on Liszt's strategic participation in early German nationalism in *Virtuoso Liszt*, 156–200.
40 Not extra-musical, but of the same ilk, was Liszt's appropriation of Beethoven as a musical father. He transcribed his symphonies for the piano, performed "séances" of Beethoven to select Parisian audiences, and later expended a small fortune and incredible effort to organize the erection of a Beethoven statue to honor the centenary of his birth (widely reported in the press). His public devotion to Beethoven during the 1830s, both strategic and sincere, arguably did more than anything else (his actual genius aside) to legitimize Liszt's self-ordination as a "priest of art" in the eyes of his public. See Gooley, "The Virtuoso as Strategist," Weber (ed.), *Musician as Entrepreneur*, 145–61.
41 Gooley, "The Battle against Instrumental Virtuosity," 91.
42 Burger, *Franz Liszt*, 120, 336; *Thalia*, November 21, 1840.
43 Quoted in Adrian Williams, *Portrait of Liszt: By Himself and His Contemporaries* (Oxford: Clarendon Press, 1990), 183.
44 It is nevertheless difficult to judge the exact degree of self-parody involved in the famous account of Liszt and George Sand's entries in the Alpine hotel registers. For birthplace, Liszt nominated "Parnassus" and his destination "Truth," while Sand listed "Nature" as her residence, having arrived from "God." Adolphe Pictet, *Une Course à Chamounix* (Geneva, 1872), 28.
45 *Revue et Gazette Musicale*, March 25, 1838, reprinted in *An Artist's Journey: Lettres d'un bachelier ès musique, 1835–41*, ed. and trans. Charles Suttoni (Chicago: University of Chicago Press, 1989), 61.
46 *Mémoires, Souvenirs et Journaux de la Comtesse d'Agoult* (Paris: Mercure de France, 1990), vol. II: 101 (my translation).
47 As an adolescent, Marie set herself to learn English expressly for the purpose of reading Byron. *Mémoires*, I: 195.
48 *Revue et Gazette Musicale*, July 16, 1837.
49 *Complete Poetical Works*, vol. II (Oxford, Clarendon Press, 1980), I: 841–2, 869–70.
50 Peter Cochran, "From Pichot to Stendahl to Musset: Byron's Progress through Early Nineteenth-Century French Literature," *The Reception of Byron in Europe*, vol. I: 32.
51 *Selected Letters*, 96–7.
52 This Byronic image recalls a Romantic nationalism of a specific kind, namely that felt by the early nineteenth-century cosmopolite for indigenous liberation movements across Europe. During the course of Liszt's composition of this letter, he received news of the disastrous floods in Pest and experienced "feelings that revealed the meaning of the 'homeland' to me" (*L'Artiste*, August 11, 1839). His subsequent dash to Vienna to give charity

concerts for flood relief is one of the principal episodes of the Liszt legend, as is his grateful reception in Hungary in 1840 where he received the famous saber. Liszt, following Byron, exchanged his Childe Harold costume of affectless exile for Romantic revolutionary garb (the Magyar hero Kossuth was later said to resemble Liszt, as Liszt did Napoleon). Liszt, though of Hungarian parentage, could not speak the language. The image he called to mind in Venice of Byron learning the language of an East European people with nationalist yearnings is narratively inseparable from Liszt's reported inspiration to become involved in Hungarian flood relief. It was a Byronic act, the next best thing to martyring oneself at Missolonghi.

53. *Selected Letters*, 96–7, 105, 127, 133.
54. See James Buzard's rich analysis of the semiotics of Byronic tourism in *The Beaten Track: European Tourism, Literature, and the Ways to Culture, 1800–1918* (Oxford: Clarendon Press, 1993), 114–30.
55. *Correspondance générale*, ed. Pierre Citron (Paris: Flammarion, 1972), vol. I: 478.
56. Gooley, *Virtuoso Liszt*, 61.
57. *Byron: The Critical Heritage*, ed. Andrew Rutherford (London: Routledge & Kegan Paul, 1970), 458. With a title borrowed from Arnold, Jerome Christensen has identified the origins of Byronism in a conspiracy between Byron's publishers and the literary reviews to exploit "the residual affective charge that still clung to the paraphernalia of aristocracy in order to reproduce it in commodities that could be vended to a reading public avid for glamour" (*Lord Byron's Strength* [Baltimore, MD: Johns Hopkins University Press, 1993], xvi). Ghislaine McDayter has figured this relationship between Byron and the market in vampiric terms, in which the best-selling celebrity author manipulates the expectations of his audience, and is then in turn consumed by his public. Like the Byronic body on its return to England, "Byron" is altered beyond recognition by the machinery of literary commodification. "Conjuring Byron: Byromania, Literary Commodification and the Birth of Celebrity," *Byromania: Portraits of the Artist in Nineteenth- and Twentieth-Century Culture*, ed. Frances Wilson (London: Macmillan, 1999), 43–62.
58. Henri Blaze du Bury, "Lord Byron et Le Byronisme," *Revue des Deux Mondes* (October 1, 1872): 549; W. E. McCann, "Byronism," *Galaxy Miscellany* (June 1868): 779.
59. *Revue et Gazette Musicale*, July 8, 1838, reprinted in Suttoni, *An Artist's Journey*, 101. Mutual admiration subsisted between Liszt and Heine, whom the pianist dubbed "the most spiritual, and most Parisian, of Germans." *Revue et Gazette Musicale*, July 26, 1835.
60. *Revue et Gazette Musicale*, February 11, 1838, reprinted in Suttoni, *An Artist's Journey*, 44.
61. *Ibid.*, 45.
62. *Correspondance*, II: 198.

63 In Kramer's words, a "paradoxical element" of the virtuoso concert is that "a dimension of the self is produced … by the sacrificial lack of any pretension to inwardness." Kramer, *Musical Meaning*, 75.
64 Christensen, *Lord Byron's Strength*, 156. See also Andrew Elfenbein: "Byron's work displays for its readers the pleasures of a subjectivity that is perpetually at risk, whose depths are so precious that they need to be protected from depletion" (*Byron and the Victorians*, 28).
65 James Soderholm, "Byronic Confession," *Byromania*, 184. Lady Byron, of course, turned the trope of the unspeakable secret back on Byron to devastating effect.
66 See Michelle Biget-Mainfroy, "La Virtuosité au Piano: Pour Quoi Faire?" *Défense et Illustration de la Virtuosité*, ed. Anne Penesco (Lyons: Presses Universitaire, 1997), 155.
67 "Properly speaking, all virtuosos are famous" (176). See also Vladimir Jankélévitch, *Liszt. Rhapsodie et Improvisation* (Paris: Flammarion, 1998), 90–8.
68 *Correspondance*, II: 321.
69 *Revue et Gazette Musicale*, September 2, 1838, reprinted in Suttoni, *An Artist's Journey*, 95. For analysis of this passage, see Anna Harwell Celenza, "Liszt, Italy, and the Republic of the Imagination," *Franz Liszt and His World*, 14–17.
70 *Correspondance*, II: 28–9.
71 *Revue et Gazette Musicale*, September 2, 1838, reprinted in Suttoni, *An Artist's Journey*, 85.
72 This could lead to acts of extraordinary rhetorical bravado, such as the occasion in the *Revue* – in whose pages he consistently invited recognition as the true inheritor of Byronic fame – when Liszt denounced that very "mania of hyperbole … that rage to BYRONIZE." *Revue et Gazette Musicale*, February 12, 1837, reprinted in Suttoni, *An Artist's Journey*, 20.
73 *Correspondance*, I: 432.
74 *Ibid*., I: 428.
75 *Musical World*, November 14, 1839.
76 *Correspondance*, I: 432.
77 The actor William Macready's journal entry of May 31, 1840 reads: "Went to Lady Blessington's, where I saw the Fonblanques, Lords Normanby and Canterbury, Milnes, Chorley … and Liszt, the most marvellous pianist I ever heard. I do not know when I have been so excited" (*The Diaries of William Macready*, ed. William Toynbee [New York: Putnam's, 1912], vol. II: 63–4). It was Liszt's custom to perform casually in these settings without expectation of a fee, unlike at a more formal salon appearance. "Our musical parties were very brilliant," remembered the editor of the *Edinburgh Review*, Henry Reeve, who had attended Liszt performances in Paris: "We had Liszt, the Battas, Ole Bull, Moscheles … Liszt and Batta played the great Beethoven Sonata *en doublant les passages*" (*Memoirs of the Life and Correspondence of Henry Reeve*, ed. John Knox Laughton

[London, 1898], vol. I: 116–17). It was Reeve, not a person of the Comtesse's social rank, whom Liszt asked to accompany Marie to his Hanover Square Rooms recital on June 9. This must have been from necessity, not choice.

78 *Correspondance*, I: 438. Liszt was also under commission from the piano manufacturer Erard for the tour.

79 Weber, *Music and the Middle Class*, 38.

80 Here I develop the position suggested by Allsobrook (23–5), *contra* Walker and the more recent historians of Liszt's British tour, David and Peter Gordon, who beg the question of Liszt's success with their misleading equation of Lady Blessington and "society." *Musical Visitors to Britain* (London: Routledge, 2005), 163.

81 Diehl, *Musical Memories* (London, 1897), 240.

82 It is a central element of the Liszt myth that women formed an almost religious-styled cult around him – souveniring hair, fashioning keepsakes from his discarded cigar butts, etc. The full spectrum of female "hysteria," from swooning to public flirtations with insanity, was also a signature of "Lisztomanie." Apochryphal or not, the following news item from 1842 is characteristic: "A lady was recently arrested in the street, calling Mr. Liszt the most intimate names at the top of her voice. She was visited by doctors and led like a madwoman to the Charity hospital to be treated." *France Musicale*, March 20, 1842, quoted in Gooley, *Virtuoso Liszt*, 212.

83 R. R. Madden, *The Literary Life and Correspondence of the Countess of Blessington* (London 1855), vol. III: 477. See also Robert Terrell Bledsoe's account of the Blessington salon in *Henry Fothergill Chorley: Victorian Journalist* (Aldershot: Ashgate, 1998).

84 Quoted in Iris Origo, *The Last Attachment* (New York: Scribner's, 1949), 298.

85 *Correspondance*, I: 443, 447.

86 Jerome McGann, *Byron and Romanticism* (Cambridge: Cambridge University Press, 2002), 142; Pons's poem is reprinted in *La Couronne Poétique de Byron*, ed. George Roth (Paris: Les Presses françaises, 1924), 93–5. Extending the proposition further, Christensen has called Byronism "a para-Napoleonic phenomenon, an empire based on the sale of books rather than on the conquest of nations" (*Lord Byron's Strength*, 147). Marie, meanwhile, was clearly jealous of Liszt's intimacy with Lady Blessington. She fought back by advertising her flirtation with Henry Bulwer-Lytton (brother of the novelist), who reported to her, and through her to Liszt, that Lady Blessington was a woman "wholly without *esprit*, but who through force of money and impudence had thumbed her nose at everybody and even the Court" (*Correspondance*, I: 436). This is likely to have been a common view in mainstream fashionable society.

87 The other French celebrity in Lady Blessington's circle that season was the exiled Prince Louis-Napoleon, for whom Liszt had a lifelong admiration. The Comte d'Orsay was subsequently accused in the press of collusion with the Prince's failed attempt to reclaim the throne in August (Michael Sadleir, *Blessington-D'Orsay: A Masquerade* [London: Constable & Co., 1933],

270–4). This note of political intrigue surrounding Gore House, presents Liszt in a very different light from the radicalized "subaltern" he promoted in Paris. The Napoleonic (and, by association, Byronic) aura worked only to sharpen Liszt's imperious image while in England, which could not have endeared him to his more progressive middle-class constituency. John Parry remembered Liszt as being "touchy" on the subject of Napoleon. *Liszt Society Journal* 6 (1981): 9.

88 *Correspondance*, I: 445, 437; Sacheverell Sitwell, *Liszt* [1934] (New York: Dover Press, 1995), 97. Sand's account of her Alpine tour with Liszt and Marie contains a devastating satire on the English tourist, whose greatest object was to return home without having displaced a single hair, and looked upon her bohemian tribe as "savages" and "Cossacks" (*Lettres d'un Voyageur* [Paris, 1837], no. 10).

89 *Correspondance*, II: 26–7.

90 *Correspondance*, I: 438–9.

91 *Liszt Society Journal* 6 (1981): 6–7; 7 (1982): 18.

92 Sitwell, *Liszt*, 100.

93 *Correspondance*, II: 18, 53–5, 76, 59.

94 Chorley, *The Authors of England* (London, 1838), 17.

95 Rutherford, *The Critical Heritage*, 183.

96 *The Englishman in Paris* (1753), 40. At the conclusion of the first act, the audience is called upon to "refuse a Gallic reign,/Nor let their Arts win that their Arms could never gain" (24).

97 Hazlitt, *Works*, XI: 72, 75, 70. In Liszt's case, the operatic aria or popular tune served this purpose. Rosen has succinctly described Liszt's modernist, virtuosic practice: "Beautifully sensitive to the character of his musical material, and deeply indifferent to its quality, all Liszt's genius was directed toward the realization in sound ... one suspects that as he developed new effects of realization, he created material to fit and show them." Rosen, *The Romantic Generation*, 507.

98 *Edinburgh Review* (December 1828), reprinted in Rutherford, *The Critical Heritage*, 290; letter to Macvey Napier (April 28, 1832) reprinted *ibid.*, 291. "The middle classes," suggests Samuel Chew, "were essentially anti-Byronic," and excluded him from the Victorian compromise (*Byron in England: His Fame and After-Fame* [New York: Scribner's Sons, 1924], 259). For an important critique of Chew's long-standard study, see Elfenbein, *Byron and the Victorians*, 47–89. Elfenbein challenges the simple narrative of Byron's "decline" after 1830, arguing that his reception was increasingly diverse in terms of readership and criticism, but united in implicit recognition of Byron's unique significance as "a cultural phenomenon available to all" (74). This analysis is supported by William St. Clair's empirical study of Byron's readership in "The Impact of Byron's Writings," *Byron: Augustan and Romantic*, ed. Andrew Rutherford (London: Macmillan, 1990), 1–25.

99 *Edinburgh Review* (June 1831), reprinted in Rutherford, *The Critical Heritage*, 316; *Life, Letters, and Friendships of Richard Monckton Milnes*, ed.

T. Wemyss Reid (1890), I: 72–4; Augustus and Julius Hare, *Guesses at Truth* (London, 1829; reprinted 1851), 404. Julius Hare, in league with Arthur Hallam and Richard Monckton Milnes as leaders of the "Cambridge Apostles," had discovered Shelley, and debated their confreres at Oxford for his superiority to Byron.

100 John Henry Newman, "Poetry, with reference to Aristotle's Poetics," *The London Review*, January 1829 (reprinted in *Essays Critical and Historical* [London: Longmans, Green & Co., 1901], vol. I: 17–18); Henry Taylor, *Philip Van Artevelde* (London, 1834), vol. I: xvi, reprinted in Rutherford, *The Critical Heritage*, 329.

101 William Thackeray, *Works* (New York: Collier, 1912), vol. XVI: 321; *The Autobiography of Henry Taylor* (New York: Harper & Bros., 1855), vol. I: 154.

102 Elfenbein, *Byron and the Victorians*, 88–9.

103 Rutherford, *The Critical Heritage*, 343.

104 Salaman, *Blackwood's*, 315.

105 *Manchester Chronicle*, May 19, 1840, *Liszt Society Journal* 12 (1987): 23; Hazlitt, *Works*, XI: 70–2. "Virtuosity presents rather than represents," Jim Samson has written, "It encourages us to wonder at the act, rather than to commune with the work." *Virtuosity and the Musical Work*, 84.

106 Edmond Estève, *Byron et le Romanticisme français* (Paris, 1907), 257.

107 Cochran, "From Pichot to Stendhal," 32. Flaubert, in his posthumously published memoir, *Mémoires d'un fou*, described how, as a youth, he had set himself adrift on "the waves of the sea in Byron's works. Often, I retained entire fragments of my reading, and repeated them to myself like a charming song whose melody pursues you eternally. How many times did I recite the opening of *The Giaour* ... or *Childe Harold*." *Revue Blanche* (December–January 1900–1).

108 Herbert von Pückler-Muskau, *Puckler's Progress: The Adventures of Prince Pückler-Muskau in England, Wales and Ireland as Told in Letters to his Former Wife, 1826–9* (London: Collins, 1987), 17, modern edition of *Tour in England, Ireland, and France* (1832).

109 *Morning Chronicle*, September 1839, reprinted in Rutherford, *The Critical Heritage*, 340.

110 Alice Mangold Diehl, *Musical Memories* (London, 1897), 239.

111 *Correspondance Générale*, I: 199.

112 Hugh MacDonald, *Berlioz* (Oxford: Oxford University Press, 1982), 81.

113 *The Memoirs of Hector Berlioz*, trans. David Cairns (New York: Knopf, 2002), 214, 241.

114 "The absence of melody ... encourages the listener to make the *performer* the site of hermeneutic entry" (Gooley, *Virtuoso Liszt*, 244). As Adorno observes, the same principle was historically transferred to composers such as Berlioz, who employed a virtuosic approach to orchestration: "Since Berlioz musical performance has been virtually surrendered to the composer." "Music and Technique," *Sound Figures*, trans. Rodney Livingstone (Stanford: Stanford University Press, 1999), 199.

115 Jean-Pierre Bartoli, "Liszt and French Exoticism in Music," *Liszt and the Birth of Modern Europe*, ed. Michael Saffle and Rossana Delmonte (Hillsdale, NY: Pendragon Press, 2003), 200.
116 For a thorough harmonic analysis of the *Années*, see Karen Sue Wilson, "A Historical Study and Stylistic Analysis of Franz Liszt's *Années de Pèlerinage*" (Ph.D dissertation, University of North Carolina, 1977).
117 Serge Gut, *Liszt* (Paris: Fallois, 1989), 312.
118 Humphrey Searle, *The Music of Liszt* (New York: Dover, 1966), 29; Dolores Pesce, "Expressive Resonance in Liszt's Piano Music," *Nineteenth-Century Piano Music*, 361.
119 Samson, *Virtuosity and the Musical Work*, 93–5.
120 Rosen, *The Romantic Generation*, 507, 541.
121 "A Mirror to the Nineteenth Century: Reflections on Franz Liszt," *Franz Liszt and His World*, 531, 552.
122 "Sur L'Harmonie," *Revue et Gazette Musicale*, August 28, 1836. For a detailed discussion of Fétis's philosophy of music in the context of his career as editor of the *Revue*, see Ellis, *Music Criticism*, ch. 2.
123 *Revue et Gazette Musicale*, May 9, 1841; Robert S. Nichols, "Fétis' Theories of *Tonalité* and the Aesthetics of Music," *Revue Belge de Musicologie* 26–7 (1972–3): 116.
124 Implicit here is an argument against the current of recent criticism, which has emphasized the Lisztian body at the expense of his "omnitonic" sound. Though Liszt discovered a powerful symbiosis between virtuosic music and his gesturing body, it did not amount to the imposition of a legible, conventional narrative on a new music otherwise incomprehensible to his audience.
125 "The poem is a triumph of personality," W. W. Robson, "Byron as Improviser," *Byron*, ed. Paul West (Englewood Cliffs, NJ: Prentice Hall, 1963), 89; "the poem defines the nature of personality," Jerome McGann, *Fiery Dust* (Chicago: University of Chicago Press, 1968), 288. See also M. K. Joseph, *Byron the Poet* (London: Victor Gallancz, 1966), 203.
126 *Don Juan in Context* (Baltimore, MD: Johns Hopkins University Press, 1976), 98.
127 Christensen, *Lord Byron's Strength*, xviii; *Byron the Poet*, 195.
128 *Lord Byron's Strength*, 154.
129 Rosen, *The Romantic Generation*, 502–3.
130 On a thematic rather than formal level, the extended passages of war tourism in canto III likewise look forward to French Romantic music, specifically to the martial elements favored by Berlioz and Liszt. Heraldic trumpets are a feature of the overture to *Les Francs-juges*, and Liszt's performance of the third movement of Weber's *Konzertstück* reminded listeners of Napoleon on his horse advancing with his terrible legions. See Gooley, *Virtuoso Liszt*, ch. 2.
131 See Ben Arnold's discussion of the revisions to "Les Cloches" in his edited volume, *The Liszt Companion* (Westport, CT: Greenwood Press, 2002), 83; also Jean-Pierre Bartoli, "Des *Cloches de G****** aux *Cloches de Genève* et les deux versions de la *Vallée d'Obermann* de Franz Liszt. Une étude

comparative," *Liszt 2000*, ed. Klara Hamburger (Budapest: Hungarian Liszt Society, 2000), 135–56.
132 *Edinburgh Review* 27 (December, 1816): 278.
133 Christensen, *Lord Byron's Strength*, 154.

CODA

1 *The Complete Fairy Tales and Stories*, trans. Erik Christian Haugaard (New York: Doubleday, 1974), 203–4. Given's Keats's posthumous obscurity, no argument can be made for his direct influence on Andersen's fable.
2 *The Fairy Tale of My Life* [1871] (New York: Cooper Square Press, 2000), 208. That said, Andersen's bird is overdetermined. The story represents the artist, be it writer or singer, as a bearer of folk truths. Andersen's early works were disdained by cosmopolitan critics and, in his fairytale imagination, the author-nightingale returns to the literary marketplace in triumph.
3 "J'aime mieux une boîte a musique qu'un rossignol." Igor Stravinsky and Robert Craft, *Dialogues and a Diary* (London: Faber and Faber, 1961), 69; *Igor Stravinsky: An Autobiography* (New York: Norton, 1962), 84.
4 *Stravinsky: The Music Box and the Nightingale* (New York: Gordon and Breach, 1989), 21. After the ballet's premiere performance in Geneva in December 1919, the music journal *La Suisse Musicale* ran a cartoon that pictured Stravinsky, brandishing a heavy tome titled "Harmonie," about to crush a little nightingale at his feet.
5 For an analysis of the Bonwick piece, and a survey of the nightingale theme in eighteenth-century poetry and popular song, see Ritchie, 143–6. Latour's career bears many hallmarks of the shape-shifting virtuoso mode. His *Imitations of Many of the Most Eminent Professors on the Favorite Gavot in* Achille et Deidamie (London, 1810?), by honoring pianists, singers (Catalani, Billington, etc.) and composers alike with the title of "professor," resisted the Romantic distinction between composer and performer, and work and event. His employment in the music market was likewise multi-dimensional, a hybrid of the royal patronage he enjoyed at Carlton House and speculations in commercial publishing as a co-founder of Chappell & Co. His being French, and embedded in cosmopolitan musical circles, likewise did not prevent him from contributing to the national-musical war effort: his 1813 *Variations on Rule Britannia* served as a patriotic concert showpiece well into the nineteenth century.
6 See *Music Entries at Stationers' Hall, 1710–1818*, ed. Michael Kassler (Aldershot: Ashgate, 2004).
7 Programming of musical concerts at the London pleasure gardens preserved the eighteenth-century virtuosic principle of miscellany, mixing songs from current English operas and popular ballads with symphonies and concerti by continental composers. Weber, *The Great Transformation*, 60.
8 *Autobiography*, 64–5.
9 Hunt, *Selected Writings*, v: 133–4.

Index

Academy of Ancient Music (London) 30
Addison, Joseph 8
   on English language 101, 104
   on Italian opera 143
Adorno, Theodor 172, 174
   on Beethoven 177
   on Romanticism 12–13
aesthetic discourse, eighteenth-century 1–2
Albright, Daniel 216
Alsager, Thomas 122, 138, 140–1
   on applause 144
   and Hunt 141
   on Mozart 137, 141–2
   as opera critic 142
amateurs
   aristocratic tradition of 6
Ambrogetti, Giuseppe 140
Amigoni, Jacopo
   Singer Farinelli and Friends 89
Ancients and Moderns, quarrel between 66
Andersen, Hans Christian 218
   autobiography of 215
   "Nightingale" 215–16, 220
André, Major
   Seward's elegy on 36
Annual Register for 1777, 32
Applegate, Celia 161
Armstrong, Nancy 159
Arnold, Matthew 191
Astell, Mary 61
Attwood, Thomas 123
Austen, Jane
   Cowper's influence on 22
   development in 178
   Emma 152, 161, 163, 167, 169, 172, 175–8, 178–9
   on female musical accomplishment 7, 18, 178
   on female professionals 163
   free indirect discourse of 13, 14, 151, 152, 174–5, 177, 178
   interiority in 158, 160, 174
   irony in 167, 179
   and Johnson 9
   late style of 167
   musical community of 15
   parlor-room culture in 167
   piano studies of 152, 153–5, 174, 178
   politeness in 158
   Pride and Prejudice 17, 152, 164, 171
   realism of 176
   in Regency music culture 10, 178
   Sanditon 156
   Sense and Sensibility 157, 163
   social displacement in 166
   subjectivity in 177
automata 2, 7
   of Jaquet-Droz family 151, 160, 161, 218
   musical 1, 53
   performers as 65, 185
   Stravinsky's 216
Avison, Charles 44
   Essay on Musical Expression 27–8
Ayrton, William 138–40
   championing of Mozart 139
   and *Don Giovanni* 120
   management of King's Theatre 139–40
   and Philharmonic Society 170
   on singers' salaries 135

Bach, J. C. 62
Bacon, Richard Mackenzie 120
Baillie, Joanna 22, 51
Baretti, Giuseppe 68
   promotion of Italian literature 97–8
Barnard, Teresa 34
Barnes, Thomas 118
Barthes, Roland 97
Batheaston salon 30–3, 41, 52
   obscurity of 50
   urban periodicals on 32
Bayly, Anselm 33, 41
Beau Monde (journal) 92

Beaumarchais Pierre
  Follies of the Day 137
Beethoven, Ludwig van
  Broadwood piano of 165–6
  Diabelli Variations 166, 167
  and *Emma* 152, 169, 177, 178, 179
  Eroica Symphony 173, 174, 176
  Fifth Symphony 152, 172
  heroic style of 173–4
  importance for middle class 172, 174
  introduction to Britain 7
  late style of 166, 167
  Liszt's playing of 186
  middle period of 169, 176
  and modern liberalism 174
  Ninth Symphony 172
  Philharmonic Society's
    championing of 172, 173
  reception of 173, 209
  rivalry with Vogler 164
  role in middle-class revolution 12
  as Romantic genius 9
  serious repertoire of 16
  sonata form of 172–3, 176, 178
  temporality in 173
  use of metronome 161
Berlioz, Hector 186, 191
  Les Francs-juges 204
  Harold en Italie 190, 204, 205, 209
  rhythmic gestures of 205
  Symphonie fantastique 204
Bildung in sonata form 175
Blackwood, William 34
Blake, William, on literary culture 34
Blessington, Lady 180
  Conversations with Lord Byron 196
  Liszt and 196–7
Bonwick, Miss 217, 218
book trade
  Georgian 2
  mass-market 171
Boswell, James 20, 32
  gender-based attitudes of 36
  on *Louisa* 45–6, 51
  relationship with Seward 35–6, 37, 45
Bowen, Peter 177
Britain
  Christian culture in 28
  musical stereotype of 11
  Protestant nationalism in 29
Brontë, Charlotte 179
Brown, John 97
Bulwer-Lytton, Edward 201
Burgh, Allatson 133, 156
Burke, Edmund 20, 94, 161

Burney, Charles
  on baroque music 65
  celebrity status of 60
  on *chiarezza* 66
  continental tour of 83
  and Frances's authorship 18, 71, 73, 86
  in Frances's fiction 59–60
  galant style of 53, 59, 62, 63, 68, 79, 83, 84
  General History of Music 60, 61, 62–3, 64, 82, 86
  on Handel 66
  on Handel Commemoration 20
  influence of 55, 81
  and Johnson 60, 80
  at King's Theatre 81
  Life and Writings of Metastasio 99
  and literary marketplace 72
  literary style of 61, 77
  in luxury economy 61
  on *Lyrical Ballads* 92, 95, 116
  Memoirs 80–1, 82–4, 86
  Memoirs of Metastasio 68, 86
  and Merlin 53, 81
  music instruction by 53, 57, 80
  music parties of 60
  opera attendance 81
  popular idiom of 67
  relationship with Thrales 60, 63, 81
  scholarship of 61
  social status of 3, 60, 67
  Tory politics of 66
  Tours 60, 61, 82
  and virtuosity 7
  wages of 57
Burney, Edward Francesco
  Handel Commemoration, 1784 21
Burney, Esther 53, 65, 69, 82
  virtuosity of 55
Burney, Frances
  anonymity of 71–2
  attendance at operas 81
  attitude to music 56
  baroque style of 79, 85, 86
  at Batheaston salon 30, 32
  Camilla 59, 71, 76, 78
  Cecilia 4, 5, 55, 76, 86
  correspondence with sister 59
  and Cox's Museum 1, 3
  Croker on 82
  decline in reputation 14
  dialect writing of 74–6
  editing of father's memoirs 80–1, 82–4, 86
  Evelina 1–2, 3, 4, 53, 70, 72, 73–6,
    79, 85
  fame of 72–3
  on fashion 77, 86

as father's amanuensis 69, 85
financial independence of 72
and *galant* style 68, 75, 76, 77, 79
heroines of 70, 72
Johnson and 9, 71, 82
Johnson's influence on 58, 73, 85
knowledge of Georgian music culture 82
and literary marketplace 72
literary style of 77
in London music culture 10
marriage of 84
memoirs of 81–2
modesty of 70
in Paris 84
piano-playing by 53
professionalism of 70–2, 86
readers of 5
recording of conversation 69
relationship with father 53, 55, 58, 59–60, 71, 86–7
on Romantic virtue 7
style of 58–9, 82–4
and Thrale, Hester 69–70, 82
Wanderer 2, 3, 4–5, 56–7, 79
Witlings 70, 73, 86
Burney, Susan 59, 82
Burnham, Scott 12
Burns, Robert 16
Butler, Marilyn 126, 176
Byron, Lord
  authorial identity in 212
  celebrity of 210
  Childe Harold's Pilgrimage 192–5, 205, 209, 210–11; canto III, 184
  continental reputation of 202
  Corsair 194
  Don Juan 183, 208, 209
  dualities of 182–3
  English reputation of 200–2, 203, 204
  feelings of persecution 198
  insincerity of 201, 213, 214
  interiority of 193
  irony of 10, 29, 147, 166, 176, 178, 193, 208, 209, 210, 211
  Manfred 194
  modernity of 184, 212
  and Napoleon 211
  originality of 213
  plays of 40
  self-plagiarism of 213
  simulating of intimacy 171
  virtuosity of 8, 10–11, 182, 200
  virtuosophobia concerning 183
Byronism 18, 52
  commodity potential of 213
  cultural 210

  as cultural phenomenon 191
  English rejection of 200–2
  European 213
  French 190, 197, 198, 202, 208, 212
  Liszt's 183–4, 188–9, 190–1, 191–2, 194, 198–9, 203–4, 206–7
  musical 211
  virtuosity in 202

canon formation 66, 169
Carey, Henry, "Satyr on the Luxury and Effeminacy of the Age" 96
Carlyle, Thomas 213
  on Byron 201
Castellini (soprano) 88
Castle, Terry 58
castrati
  effect on manliness 97
  end of era of 115
  improvisations by 64
  at King's Theatre 13, 115
  mutilation imagery concerning 101
Catalani, Angelica 127, 219
  attitude to Mozart 128
  at King's Theatre 129–31, 132–3, 135
  London debut of 136
  ornamentation by 129
  repertoire of 128
  return to London stage 138
  salary of 130–1, 139
  as symbol of Regency power 133, 135–6
Charlotte, Princess 140
chiarezza
  Charles Burney on 66
  Metastasio's 68
Ch'ien Lung (emperor of China) 3
chiroplast 161–2
Chopin, Frédéric 168
Chorley, Henry 188, 197, 203, 213
  on Byron 200
Christensen, Jerome 209, 211, 213
Christensen, Thomas 122
Clark, Lorna 58
class conflict, at King's Theatre 133
class distinction, in *Evelina* 76
Clementi, Muzio 161
  duel with Mozart 164
  Introduction to the Art of Playing on the Piano Forte 162
Cockney intellectuals
  cultural reform by 142
  democratic ideals of 138
  depravity charges against 125
  love for Mozart 120–4, 125–6, 149
  meter of 123

Cockney intellectuals (cont.)
  sociability of 127
  sublime of 123
  style of 124
  Tory critics on 124, 125
Cohen, Michèle 96
Coleridge, Samuel Taylor
  Cowper's influence on 22
  on music 12
  on periodicals 34
Collier, Jeremy 40
Cook, James, Seward's elegy on 36
Corelli, Arcangelo 67
Cowden Clarke, Charles 122, 123
Cowgill, Rachel 120
Cowper, William
  dispute with Seward 18, 23, 24–5,
    33, 47–50
  factionalism of 25–6
  and Milton 41
  Milton's influence on 47
  on Handel Commemoration 6, 20, 23–5, 47, 50
  Romanticism of 50
  Task 22, 23, 24, 25, 40, 47–50, 51
  use of satire 48, 49
Cox, James 1
  Descriptive Catalogue 3
  and Merlin 53
Cox, Jeffrey 147
Cox's Museum 1, 2, 5, 218
  in *Evelina* 76
  role in commercial culture 3
  virtuosity of 3
Cramer, Johann Baptist 161
  84 Études 168–9
  Instructions for the Piano Forte 163
  and Liszt 184
  relationship with Broadwood company 168
Crisp, Samuel 57
  on Charles Burney 60
  and Frances Burney 71, 78, 86
Critical Review 34
Croker, John Wilson 13
  on Frances Burney 82
Crotch, William 65
culture, British; *see also* music culture, British
  commercial versus high 2
  embourgeoisement of 18
  feminization of 18, 159
  Handelian model of 48
  Philharmonic Society's importance to 170
  professionalization of 9
  regressive image of 13
Cumberland, Duke of 29
Cutting-Gray, Joanne 78

D'Agoult, Marie 181, 189, 196, 212
  on Byron 195
  on Liszt's costume 199
  and Liszt's English tour 198
Dahlhaus, Carl 12, 185
Danhauser, Josef, *Franz Liszt am Flügel* 188
"Dans votre lit" (song) 220
Da Ponte, Lorenzo 126
D'Arblay, Madame *see* Burney, Frances
Davison, John 8
  on Liszt 181–2, 185, 193, 203, 213
Delaney, Mary 4
Demosthenes 33
Dennis, John 8, 96, 135
  objections to opera 143
DeNora, Tia 13, 165
Devonshire, Duchess of 30
dialects, in *Evelina* 74–6
Dibdin, Charles 153, 160
Dickens, Charles, *Pickwick Papers* 50
Diehl, Alice Mangold 197
Doody, Margaret Anne 58, 59, 82
D'Orsay, Comte 196
Dowling, Linda 96
Dryden, John, on gender in language, 101

Edgeworth, Maria 185
  on female accomplishment 157, 159
  on piano-playing 160
  Patronage 155
  Practical Education 160
effeminacy 159
  charges against Wordsworth 91, 92–4
  in English literature 90–1
  extravagance as 92
  Georgian 96, 116
  Italian opera and 96–7
  music and 94
  Regency 95
  and virtuosity 7, 91, 115
  Wordsworth's defense against 91
Elfenbein, Andrew 171, 201
English language, masculinity of 101
Epstein, Julia 58
eroticism, in *Louisa* 43, 46
European Magazine
  on Handel Commemoration 20
  on *Louisa* 43, 45, 49
Evelyn, John 2
Examiner
  attack on Prince Regent 136, 148
  on Hunt's imprisonment 119
  influence in music 132
  opera reviews of 127, 149

political program of 10, 138
pro-Mozart campaign of 7, 18, 137, 142

Farinelli (castrato) 64
    Amigoni portrait of 88
    relationship to Metastasio 88
fashion
    Frances Burney on 77, 86
    Hazlitt on 144, 146
    Hunt on 146
Federici, Vincenzo 127
female accomplishment
    Austen on 7, 18, 178
    debate over 155–7
    as mytheme 179
    in Romanticism 18
    vanity in 158
Fétis, François 185, 207
    on Liszt 209
    on tonality 207–8
Fischer, J. C. 81
Foote, Samuel, *Englishman in Paris*, 200
Fordyce, James 74, 160, 164
Forster, E. M., *Room with a View* 166
Foucault, Michel 161, 163
Fulford, Tim 93

Gainsborough, Thomas
    Johann Christian Fischer 54
galant style 53, 62–3; *see also* Burney, Charles:, *galant* style of
    critics of 64–5
    decline of 68
    era, 59–70
    in *Evelina* 75
    Frances Burney's view of 76, 77, 79
    Metastasio's 68
    in music 68
    social leveling in 85
Gallagher, Catherine 72
Gardiner, William 145
gender
    in Georgian culture 18
    in Wordsworth's *Lyrical Ballads* 89
Gentleman's Magazine 32, 34–5
    Seward in 35–6
George (Prince Regent) 119
    and Charles Burney 81
    Examiner's attack on 136, 148
    Hunt's satire on 136–7
George III (king of England)
    at Handel Commemoration 20
    madness of 84
    political allegiance under 50
Gisborne, Thomas 156

Glorious Revolution 22
Goethe, Johann Wolfgang von 202
Goldsmith, Oliver 99
Gooley, Dana 6, 12, 185
    on Liszt 187, 191
Gramit, David 11, 172
Graves, Richard 30
Guiccioli, Teresa 198
Gut, Serge 206

Hall-Witt, Jennifer 144
Handel, Georg Friedrich; *see also* Seward, Anna, Handelianism of
    Athalia 43
    Charles Burney on 66
    Corelli and 67
    effect on factionalism 28–30, 50
    in *Louisa* 44
    mechanical performances of 2
    Messiah 23–4, 38
    nationalism in music of 20–2, 23, 26
    operas 38, 63
    oratorios 20, 23, 27, 29–30, 38, 50
    setting of Metastasio 98
    settings of Milton 41–2
    sublime in 38–40
    xenophilia concerning 15
Handel Commemoration (1784) 6, 12, 20–2, 139
    audience of 27
    Cowper on 20, 23–5, 47, 50
    templates for 23
    Tory elite and 66
    women at 26
Harmonicon (journal) 138, 141
Harris, James 47
Harris, Louisa 47
Hawkins, John 4, 65, 67
Hayley, William 23, 35
    obscurity of 50
Hayward, Thomas 141
Haywood, Eliza 92
    Epistle for Ladies 29–30
Hazlitt, William 34
    on Byron, 200, 201
    on effeminacy 92, 95
    "On Effeminacy of Character" 91
    on factionalism 34
    on Italian opera 142–3
    on literary masculinity 91–2
    lectures at Surrey Institution 140
    on *Lyrical Ballads* 92
    "Mr. Wordsworth" 91
    opera reviews of 143–4
    on Seward 50
Heartz, Daniel 98

288   Index

Hegel, Georg Wilhelm Friedrich 174
  on modern music 173
Heine, Heinrich 191
  on virtuosity 185, 194
Hill, Aaron 28, 30
  on factionalism 31
  on luxury 96
Hoffmann, E. T. A. 174
Hogarth, George 128, 134
Holcroft, Thomas 137
Holmes, Edward 122
Hoole, John 95
  on castrati 101
  Dramas and Other Poems of Pietro Metastasio 99
  effeminate style of 103
  translations of 102–4, 106
Hueffer, Francis 180
Hume, David 92
Hunt, Leigh
  on aristocratic patrons 7
  attack on Prince Regent 148
  Autobiography 138
  on bourgeois aspiration 146
  on Byron 200
  circle of 120–4
  Cockney politics of 18
  Descent of Liberty 125
  Don Giovanni reviews 118, 145–6
  imprisonment of 119, 140, 148
  in Italy 126
  on Keats 13
  on listening 124
  love for Mozart 10, 13, 126, 147
  "Lover of Music to the Pianoforte" 121
  meaning of music for 123, 124–5
  on mechanical music 221
  musical advice by 122
  musical gatherings of 122
  opera criticism of 15, 146–7, 149
  on popular song 220
  "Regent's First Levee" 136–7
  on sociability 146–7
  "Thought on Music" 124
  Tory critics of 147, 148
Hunter, Mary 158
hysteria
  concerning Byron 204
  over celebrities 180

interiority
  Austen's 158, 160, 174
  bourgeois 172
  Byron's 193
  and civic discourse 177
  Romantic 7, 158, 219
  of sonata form 174
  virtuosity and 193
Italian language, effeminacy of 105
Italian literature 97–8
  emasculation of 102

Jacobinism 50
Jaquet-Droz family, automata of 151, 160, 161, 218
Jeffrey, Francis 92
Jeffrey, Richard 213
Jennens, Charles 38
Johnson, James, *Scots Musical Museum* 16
Johnson, Samuel
  and Charles Burney 60
  on *Evelina* 75
  and Frances Burney 58, 71, 82
  at *Gentleman's Magazine* 35
  influence of 9
  on literary sociability 32
  on professional literature 34
  Seward on 35–6
  on virtuosity 2
Joseph, M. K. 209

Kant, Immanuel 174
Keats, John
  on Byron 200
  Endymion 13, 45, 218
  friendship with Hunt 34
  at musical gatherings 123
  "Ode to a Nightingale" 215, 218–20
  Tory critique of 13–14
Kelly, Gary 156, 177
King's Theatre (London)
  anti-Mozart cabal at 118
  aristocratic management of 127
  aristocratic patrons of 8, 119, 138, 144
  audience of 133, 143–4, 144–5
  Ayrton's management 139–40
  bad taste at 136
  baroque *pasticcio* at 128
  castrati at 13, 115
  Catalani at 127, 129–31, 132–3, 135
  Charles Burney at 81
  class issues at 133, 149–50
  diva culture at 128, 130, 140
  Don Giovanni at 118, 138, 140
  eighteenth-century repertoire of 128
  financial problems of 139
  Italian cabal at 139, 140, 149
  Metastasio at 98, 102
  middle class at 118, 120, 133, 144, 150
  Mozartian constituency at 145
  Philharmonic Society and 170

Index

Kramer, Lawrence 6, 172
 on Liszt 186

Lamartine, Alphonse de 190
Lamb, Charles, and *Don Giovanni* 120
Langford, Paul 96
Latour, Jean 217
Lavenu, Louis 181
Leppert, Richard 6, 156
Levy, Michelle 59
Lind, Jenny 215
Lindenberger, Herbert 94
listening
 silent 171–2
 subject in 173
Liszt, Franz, 6
 Années de pèlerinage 193, 195, 204, 206, 207, 209, 211–12
 aristocratic aspects of, 7–8
 audiences of 181, 185, 187
 and Blessington, Lady 196–7
 British strategy of 199
 Byronic costume of 199
 Byronism of 183–4, 188–9, 190–1, 191–2, 194, 198–9, 203–4, 206–7
 celebrity of 181, 187
 Childe Harold and 184, 190, 192–5, 199
 "Cloches de Genève" 212
 correspondence of 191
 cultural threat of 182
 European sojourn of 189–90, 190–1
 gestural poetics of 209
 Grand Galop Chromatique 181
 humanitarianism of 187
 Impressions et Poésies 193
 insincerity of 182, 203
 Italian influence on 10
 key identification in 206
 musical Byronism of 211–12
 at Newstead Abbey 180, 199
 performative aesthetic of 207
 personae of 187–9, 195
 piano compositions of 193
 piano transcriptions of 185, 190, 204, 212
 on piano virtuosity 4
 playing of Beethoven 186
 proto-modernism of 13
 public image of 185
 in public sphere 187
 reception in Britain 181–2, 183, 184, 186, 197–8, 199–200
 self-plagiarism of 213
 sincerity of 203
 tonality in 208
 tour of Britain 18, 180–2, 213
 on tourism 189
 tour repertoire of 181
 "Vallée d'Obermann" 193, 206
 virtuosity of 17, 183, 186–7, 195, 202, 203, 204, 209
 virtuosophobia concerning 184, 185, 189, 193, 203
 at Weimar, 213
literary culture, British
 amateur 33
 and music culture ix, 5, 6, 10, 11–12
 music-making in 26–7
 Regency 16
 Romantic 9
 separate spheres of 70
 sociability in 35
literary culture, provincial, sociability and 25, 26
literature
 antagonism with opera 95
 professionalization of 18
Lockhart, John Gibson 125, 148
 on Byron 200
Logier, Johann 162, 170
 chiroplast of 161–2
London
 dialects 74
 European music in 15
 music market of 11
 pleasure gardens of 219
 public concerts in 169
Longinus 33, 38
Lonsdale, Roger 80
Lovell, Terry 70
luxury
 and effeminacy, 96
 eighteenth-century trade in, 3
 Georgian 53
 and labor 4
 and utility, 1
 virtuosity and 131
Lynch, Deidre 73

Macaulay, Catharine 156
Macaulay, Thomas Babington
 on Burney, Frances 73, 82, 83, 85
 on Byron 201
 on Hoole, 102
Mainwaring, John 33
Mälzel, Johann 161
manuscript practices, women-centered 59
Marx, Adolph 173, 174
masculinity, Georgian 91
masculinity, Wordsworthian 89–94, 101, 112, 116, 117
 of *Lyrical Ballads* 105, 115
Mazzini, Guiseppe 202

McGann, Jerome 208
    Don Juan in Context 211
McVeigh, Simon 12, 64
mechanization; *see also* automata
    dehumanizing 216
    industrialization and 161–2
    in piano pedagogy 160, 161–2
    in public music culture 3, 152
Merlin, Joseph 53
    Charles Burney and 81
    musical notation of 69
Metastasio, Pietro, 68; *see also* Wordsworth, William:, translations of Metastasio
    Amigoni portrait of 88
    chiarezza of 68
    decline in popularity 99
    "Ecco quel fiero istante" 88
    effeminacy and 97
    fame of 98–9
    galant style of 68
    Hoole's translations of 103
    literary translations of 101
    relationship to Farinelli 88
    Zenobia 115
meter
    of Cockney poets 123
    Wordsworth on 94
metronome, Beethoven's use of 161
middle class, British
    Beethoven's importance for 172
    consumption of sonatas 174
    control of musical life 9
    domestic music culture of 27, 157–8, 159
    in *Emma* 172
    at King's Theatre 118, 120, 133, 144, 150
    in *Pride and Prejudice* 171
Mill, John Stuart 174
Miller, Anna
    Batheaston salon of 28, 30–3
    obscurity of 50
    Poetical Amusements 32, 33
    sociability of 31
    Tuscan vase of 30, 32
Millico (castrato) 53, 55, 69
Milton, John 42
    Allegro 42
    Handel's settings of 41–2
    influence on Cowper 47
    Penseroso 42, 49, 51
    Seward on 41–2
    Wordsworth on 93
modernity
    Byron's 184, 212
    fashion-driven 220

music business in 157
of piano 166
sublime and 6
Monthly Review 34
Moore, John 4
Moore, Thomas 100, 183
    on Byron 10
More, Hannah 65, 155, 159
More, John,
    "Ancient and Modern Music Compared" 28
Morell, Thomas 29
Moulds, John 217, 218
    "Nightingale" 217
Mount-Edgcumbe, Richard 115, 138
Mozart, Constanze 127
Mozart, Wolfgang Amadeus
    anti-diva music of 137
    aristocratic resistance to 132
    audience demand for 119
    Clemenza di Tito 141
    Cockney poets, love of 125–6
    Cosi fan Tutte 131–2
    dissemination of operas 122
    Don Giovanni concert performance 141
    Don Giovanni debut 118, 119, 138, 140, 145–6
    duel with Clementi 164
    Hunt circle and 120–4
    introduction to Britain 7
    Italian qualities of 126
    role in middle-class reform 12, 13, 137–8
    Romanticism of 132
    serious repertoire of 16
    singers' difficulties with 127
    Zauberflöte 131
Murphy, Arthur 71
music
    affective power of 27
    baroque versus modern, 30
    commercialization of 220
    equality with poetry 121–2
    erotic power of 43
    galant style in 68
    historical consciousness of 220
    as imitative art 27
    and leisure 44
    literary community 124
    Ovidian essence of 221
    as psychological phenomenon 208
    sociability in 16, 27
    and social harmony 27–8
    and subjectivity 13
    sublime in 38–40
    union with poetry 42, 216
    Viennese piano 153

music business
  in Burney's *Wanderer* 57
  commercial character of 5
  Georgian 55
  modernity in 157
music culture, British
  bourgeois 145
  commercial aspects of 11, 158
  Frances Burney and 56, 82
  Handel in 20
  and literary culture ix, 5, 6, 10, 11–12
  literary performance in 49
  literary reform of 7
  mechanization in 3
  metropolitan 6
  nationalism in 15–16
  nightingales in 217–18
  novelty in 64
  and poetry production 25
  private concerts in 163
  Regency 121
  sentimental expression in 27
  sociability in 24, 25, 48
  taste-makers in 119
  transnational character of 14
  women's influence in 159
music culture, domestic 153, 157–8, 159
  concerts in, 44
  decline in, 170
  virtuosity in 163
musical machines, ornamental 1;
  see also automata
musicians, British
  church careers of 67
  status of 56
  use of publicity 60
musicology
  "new" 11
  Romanticism and ix

Napoleon, Byron and 211
Napoleonic Wars, effect on Georgian music 7
national defense, masculine responsibility for 90
nationalism
  Handelianism in 20
  Romantic 66
  Whig 48
nature
  and artifice, 216, 218
  triumph over technique 215
Newman, John Henry 201
Newstead Abbey, Liszt at 180, 199
nightingales
  automata and 8
  classical figure of 216
  duels with singers 215
  in Georgian music culture 217–18
  melopoetic discourse of 218
  odes to 215
  Ovidian 217
  real versus mechanical 215–16, 221
Novello, Mary 122, 123, 126
Novello, Vincent 118, 121
  Mozart pilgrimage of 127
novels
  bourgeois 120
  commercial value of 5
  virtue in 5
novelty
  in music culture 64

Old Price riots (1809), 127
"On Hearing a Little Music Box"
  (poem) 220
opera, Italian; *see also* castrati; King's Theatre
  (London)
  antagonism with literature 8
  arias in 88
  aristocratic patronage of 170
  British rage for 16
  and British Romanticism 88
  cross-gender casting in 100
  effeminacy and 96
  galant idiom of 62
  Lyrical Ballads and 90
  moderns' patronage of 66
  novelty in 64
  pasticcio aesthetic of 149
  poetry and 121
  Romantics on 99
  social injustice and 135
  virtuosity in 71
oratorios, moral ideas in, 40; *see also* Handel,
  Georg Friedrich: oratorios

Pacchierotti (castrato) 64, 84
Paganini, Niccolo 205
Pascoe, Judith 33
patronage
  aristocratic 7, 38, 57, 119, 127, 130, 132, 135, 138,
    139, 144, 149, 170, 171
  Augustan 72
  in *Evelina* 73
Peacock, Thomas Love 5, 50, 120
periodicals
  commercial 33–5
  expansion of 37
  on piano music industry 185
  political affiliations of 34, 50
  rise of 18

periodicals (cont.)
  Seward on 37, 48
  skeptical power of 219
Philharmonic Society (London), 9, 152, 169–70
  championing of Beethoven 172, 173
  governance of 170
  importance for bourgeoisie 170–1
  King's Theatre and 170
  and mechanization 162
  unpopularity with aristocracy 196
piano
  in Austen's fiction 154–5, 159
  Broadwood's 152, 165–6
  in *Emma* 152, 161, 165
  eroticization of 121
  female aspiration and 152
  improvements in manufacture of 4
  modern 16
  modernity of 166
  in *Pride and Prejudice* 154
piano music
  in Austen's fiction 160
  availability of 122, 157
  commercialization of 184
  in Viennese repertoire 159
  for women 17
piano pedagogy
  in *Emma* 163
  mechanization in 160, 161–2
  in Romanticism 158
piano playing, automatism in 160–1
Pinch, Adela 89, 93
Plantinga, Leon 154
poetics, and historicism 12
poetry
  Italian opera and 143
  and life 210
  of sensibility 91
  union with music 42, 121–2, 216
politeness
  of audiences 171–2
  in Austen 158
  in *Camilla* 78
  in *Evelina* 75, 79
  middle-class 167
  Shaftesburian 73, 74
Pons, Gaspard de 197
Poovey, Mary 156
Popple, William 101
  on castrati 115
popular songs, British 16
  Hunt on 220
  nightingales in 217
  pastoral 43–4
  performance venues for 17

press, London
  on *Don Giovanni* 120
  radical bourgeois 119
professionalism
  bourgeois 168
  in culture 159
  gendered 177
  literary 18, 48
  post-Waterloo 9
  virtuosity and 9, 84
  women's 163, 179
Prynne, William 94

Ramann, Lina 180
Rees, Abraham, *Cyclopedia* 66
Rellstab, Ludwig 188
retreat, pastoral trope of 49
Reynolds, Joshua 20
Richardson, Alan 93
Ritchie, Leslie 12, 43
Ritson, Joseph, *Select Collection of English Songs* 16
Rizzo, Betty 70
Robertson, Henry 123, 127–8
  on Catalani 129–30, 133
  Mozart reviews of 131–2
Robinson, Jeffrey 16, 123, 124
Robinson, Mary 37
Roe, Nicholas 147
Romanticism
  anti-theatricality of 18
  and baroque opera 89
  Cowper's 50
  of *Childe Harold* 194
  cultural production in 171
  European 12
  female accomplishment in 17
  feminist studies of 92
  in French music 204, 208
  interiority in 12, 219
  Liszt's 206–7
  man of feeling in 90
  Mozart's 132
  music revolution in 155
  and musical sociability 6
  and musicology ix
  nationalism in 66
  piano pedagogy in 158
  and professionalism 9
  sincerity in 51
  sociability in 25, 123
  solitude in 71
  subject in 177
  and the sublime, 16
  virtuosity and 6, 152

Index

and virtuoso culture, 7
virtuosophobia in 9–10, 182
Rory Tories 30
Roselli (castrato) 115
Rosen, Charles 173
　on Liszt 185, 206
Rossini, Gioachino 190
Rousseau, Jean-Jacques 212
　Lettre sur la musique française 66
　on melody 16
　on music 27
Royal Society (London) 3
　scientific values of 2
Russell, Gillian 26

Sacchini, Antonio 69
Sadie, Stanley 122
Salaman, Charles 182
Samson, Jim 11, 170, 206
Sand, George
　Byronism of 190, 192
　on the English 198
　Liszt's correspondence with 190
Saville, John 23, 40
Schellenberg, Betty 70
Schlegel, A. W. 99
　on Metastasio 114
Schopenhauer, Arthur 173
Schumann, Robert 168, 185
Scott, Walter 31, 176
　on Hoole 102
　Minstrelsy of the Scottish Border 16
　on Seward 33, 51
sensibility
　feminine 93
　poetry of 91
seriality 213
　in *Childe Harold* 211
　in musical Byronism 211
Seward, Anna 26
　at Batheaston salon 31, 41
　decline in reputation 14, 37
　defenders of 49
　dispute with Cowper 18, 23, 24–5, 33, 47–50
　elegy to Lady Miller 32
　fame of 23
　in *Gentleman's Magazine* 35–6
　Handelianism of 10, 13, 20, 23, 38, 50
　influence of 50
　on Johnson 35–6
　Lichfield salon of 33, 42–3, 51, 123
　Louisa 6, 22–3, 28, 35, 36, 41–3, 44–7, 47–50, 51
　on Milton 41–2

musical community of 15, 26–7
nationalism of 36
on operatic culture 40
on periodicals 48
poetics of retirement 47
public role of 37
relationship with Boswell 35–6, 37, 45
"Remonstrance" 50
sociability of 25, 30, 33, 48, 51
theatricality of 47
view of periodicals 37
virtuosity of 47
sexuality, Wordsworthian 94
　in *Lyrical Ballads* 89
Shadwell, Thomas, *Virtuoso* 2
Shaftesbury, Earl of 2, 3
　modernism of 67
Shakespeare, William, *Macbeth* 90
Sheldon, David 63
Shelley, Mary 123, 125
　Last Man 132
Shelley, Percy Bysshe 12, 120
Simpson, David 15
sincerity
　as British virtue 200
　in Romanticism 6, 51
　virtuosity and 194
　of virtuosi 182
　Wordsworth's 10
singing
　and civic strength 97
　relationship to oratory 33
　virtuosity in 64
Sitter, John 44
Sitwell, Sacheverell 198, 199
Smart, John,
　Misses Elizabeth and Harriet Binney 154
Smith, Adam 90
Smith, Charles Loraine, *A Sunday Concert* 61
Smith, Ruth 12, 29
Smith, William 38
sociability
　Cockney poets' 125, 127
　Georgian 25, 50
　Hunt on 146–7
　in literary culture 35
　in music culture 16, 24, 25, 48
　rhetoric of 18
　Romantic 123
　and Romanticism, 16, 25
　Seward's 48, 51
sonata form 172
　alternatives to 207
　Beethoven's 172–3, 176, 178
　interiority of 13, 174

sonatas, piano
    middle-class consumption of 174
    popularity of 121
Southey, Robert, at Lichfield 51
Sterland, John 135, 140
Stravinsky, Igor 221
    Song of the Nightingale 216
Stubbe, Henry, on virtuosity 2
Stubbes, Phillip 94
style, politics of 13, 148
subjectivity
    in Georgian culture 18
    Romantic 213
sublime, the
    aesthetics of 6
    Cockney poets on 123
    in Handel, 38–40
    Hunt on, 146
    masculine metaphorics of 93
    in music 38–40
    in Romanticism 6, 16
Swift, Jonathan
    on effeminacy 96
    Polite Conversation 63
symphonic music
    democratic process and 170
    Romantic 186

Taylor, Henry 201
Taylor, William 127
tears
    and femininity 90
    in *Lyrical Ballads* 109, 110, 112
Temple, William 45
Thackeray, William Makepeace
    on Byron 201
    on Frances Burney 72, 87
Thicknesse, Philip 30
Thrale, Hester 5, 59
    at Batheaston salon 30
    and Burney, Charles 62, 63
    and Burney, Frances 69–70, 71, 72, 82
    on Burney children 59
    salon of 60
Thrale, Queeney 62
time, in *Emma* 175, 176, 177
Todd, Janet 158
ton, London
    in *Camilla* 76
    language of 74
tonality
    in Byron's poetry 211, 213
    in Liszt 208
tourism, European 189
Trelawney, Edward 197

Tuite, Clara 26
Twiss, Richard 69

Vallon, Annette 91
Viganoni (tenor) 115
virtue
    Frances Burney's rhetoric of 73, 78
    in novels 5
    poetic 115
    and virtuosity 1, 6, 17, 164, 212
virtuosi 6
    fear of 19
    sincerity of 182
    technical accomplishments of 3
virtuosity
    amateur 50
    Byron's 8, 10–11, 182, 200
    in Byronism 202
    in *Cecilia* 85
    disciplinary character of 218
    domestication of 163
    effeminacy in 7, 115
    in eighteenth-century discourse 2, 4
    in *Emma* 160
    in *Evelina* 84, 85
    Georgian 4, 53, 55
    historical limits of 213, 214
    improvisation in 64
    as intellectual prostitution 143
    interiority and 193
    in Italian opera 67
    Johnson on 2
    late eighteenth-century 84
    and literary culture 6
    and literary idealism 8
    Liszt's 183, 186–7, 195, 202, 203, 209
    and luxury 131
    marginalization of 170
    mechanical 151
    and mechanization 9
    modern connotations of 2
    in nightingale songs 217
    the other and 213
    in poetry 108
    and professionalism 84
    public fascination with i
    and Romanticism 4, 6, 9, 152
    ridicule of ix
    Seward's 47
    and sex 186
    sincerity and 194
    in singing 64
    and technical efficiency 9
    as triviality 178

and utility 2
virtue and 1, 6, 17, 164, 212
virtuosophobia 8, 65
   concerning Byron 183
   in *Emma* 169
   Georgian 14
   concerning Liszt 184, 185, 189, 193, 203
   mechanization in, 162
   in nightingale fable 215
   in "Ode to a Nightingale" 218
   and ornamentation, 92
   in Romanticism 5, 9–10, 18, 182
   and xenophobia 8

Walker, Alan 180
Warton, Joseph 42
Weber, William 12, 16, 27, 197
   Rise of Musical Classics in Eighteenth-Century England 66
Wesley, Samuel 56
Whalley, Thomas 49
Wolfson, Susan 93
Wollstonecraft, Mary 92, 155, 164
women writers
   in Georgian society 70
   professionalization and 18
Wood, Gillen D'Arcy, *The Shock of the Real: Romanticism and Visual Culture 1760–1860*, 9
Woolf, Virginia 58
Wordsworth, William
   appropriation of feminine language 93
   attack on women poets 91
   "Brothers" 89–91, 92, 94, 109, 116
   "Childless Father" 109, 110
   "Complaint of the Forsaken Indian Woman" 111, 112–13
   Cowper's influence on 22
   effeminacy charges against 91, 92–4
   "Female Vagrant" 111–12
   feminine speakers of 14, 93, 111, 112, 113
   Italian language and 10, 100–1
   and Italian literature 98
   "Last of the Flock" 93, 110–11
   "Lines left upon a Seat in a Yew-Tree" 108–9, 112
   linguistic localism of 10
   literary masculinity of 89–94, 101, 112, 116, 117
   Lyrical Ballads 47, 89, 92–4, 105, 115–17
      see also specific poems
   Lyrical Ballads, Preface 7, 22, 91, 107, 114, 116
   "Mad Mother" 111
   on meter 94, 106, 117
   on music 12
   on periodicals 37
   "Pet Lamb" 113–14
   poetic restraint of 108, 111
   Prelude 91
   return to England 91
   Romantic reception of 209
   sincerity of 10
   translations of Metastasio 7, 88, 95, 98, 99–100, 101, 104–6, 107, 115–16
Wynne, William Watkins 30

xenophobia, Georgian 8

Young, Arthur 62

CAMBRIDGE STUDIES IN ROMANTICISM

General Editor
James Chandler, *University of Chicago*

1. Romantic Correspondence: Women, Politics and the Fiction of Letters
   MARY A. FAVRET
2. British Romantic Writers and the East: Anxieties of Empire
   NIGEL LEASK
3. Poetry as an Occupation and an Art in Britain, 1760–1830
   PETER MURPHY
4. Edmund Burke's Aesthetic Ideology: Language, Gender and Political Economy in Revolution
   TOM FURNISS
5. In the Theatre of Romanticism: Coleridge, Nationalism, Women
   JULIE A. CARLSON
6. Keats, Narrative and Audience
   ANDREW BENNETT
7. Romance and Revolution: Shelley and the Politics of a Genre
   DAVID DUFF
8. Literature, Education, and Romanticism: Reading as Social Practice, 1780–1832
   ALAN RICHARDSON
9. Women Writing about Money: Women's Fiction in England, 1790–1820
   EDWARD COPELAND
10. Shelley and the Revolution in Taste: The Body and the Natural World
    TIMOTHY MORTON
11. William Cobbett: The Politics of Style
    LEONORA NATTRASS
12. The Rise of Supernatural Fiction, 1762–1800
    E. J. CLERY
13. Women Travel Writers and the Language of Aesthetics, 1716–1818
    ELIZABETH A. BOHLS
14. Napoleon and English Romanticism
    SIMON BAINBRIDGE

15. Romantic Vagrancy: Wordsworth and the Simulation of Freedom
    CELESTE LANGAN

16. Wordsworth and the Geologists
    JOHN WYATT

17. Wordsworth's Pope: A Study in Literary Historiography
    ROBERT J. GRIFFIN

18. The Politics of Sensibility: Race, Gender and Commerce in the Sentimental Novel
    MARKMAN ELLIS

19. Reading Daughters' Fictions, 1709–1834: Novels and Society from Manley to Edgeworth
    CAROLINE GONDA

20. Romantic Identities: Varieties of Subjectivity, 1774–1830
    ANDREA K. HENDERSON

21. Print Politics: The Press and Radical Opposition in Early Nineteenth-Century England
    KEVIN GILMARTIN

22. Reinventing Allegory
    THERESA M. KELLEY

23. British Satire and the Politics of Style, 1789–1832
    GARY DYER

24. The Romantic Reformation: Religious Politics in English Literature, 1789–1824
    ROBERT M. RYAN

25. De Quincey's Romanticism: Canonical Minority and the Forms of Transmission
    MARGARET RUSSETT

26. Coleridge on Dreaming: Romanticism, Dreams and the Medical Imagination
    JENNIFER FORD

27. Romantic Imperialism: Universal Empire and the Culture of Modernity
    SAREE MAKDISI

28. Ideology and Utopia in the Poetry of William Blake
    NICHOLAS M. WILLIAMS

29. Sexual Politics and the Romantic Author
    SONIA HOFKOSH

30. Lyric and Labour in the Romantic Tradition
    ANNE JANOWITZ

31. Poetry and Politics in the Cockney School: Keats, Shelley, Hunt and their Circle
   JEFFREY N. COX

32. Rousseau, Robespierre and English Romanticism
   GREGORY DART

33. Contesting the Gothic: Fiction, Genre and Cultural Conflict, 1764–1832
   JAMES WATT

34. Romanticism, Aesthetics, and Nationalism
   DAVID ARAM KAISER

35. Romantic Poets and the Culture of Posterity
   ANDREW BENNETT

36. The Crisis of Literature in the 1790s: Print Culture and the Public Sphere
   PAUL KEEN

37. Romantic Atheism: Poetry and Freethought, 1780–1830
   MARTIN PRIESTMAN

38. Romanticism and Slave Narratives: Transatlantic Testimonies
   HELEN THOMAS

39. Imagination Under Pressure, 1789–1832: Aesthetics, Politics, and Utility
   JOHN WHALE

40. Romanticism and the Gothic: Genre, Reception, and Canon Formation, 1790–1820
   MICHAEL GAMER

41. Romanticism and the Human Sciences: Poetry, Population, and the Discourse of the Species
   MAUREEN N. MCLANE

42. The Poetics of Spice: Romantic Consumerism and the Exotic
   TIMOTHY MORTON

43. British Fiction and the Production of Social Order, 1740–1830
   MIRANDA J. BURGESS

44. Women Writers and the English Nation in the 1790s
   ANGELA KEANE

45. Literary Magazines and British Romanticism
   MARK PARKER

46. Women, Nationalism and the Romantic Stage: Theatre and Politics in Britain, 1780–1800
   BETSY BOLTON

47. British Romanticism and the Science of the Mind
   ALAN RICHARDSON

48. The Anti-Jacobin Novel: British Conservatism and the French Revolution
    M. O. GRENBY

49. Romantic Austen: Sexual Politics and the Literary Canon
    CLARA TUITE

50. Byron and Romanticism
    JEROME MCGANN AND JAMES SODERHOLM

51. The Romantic National Tale and the Question of Ireland
    INA FERRIS

52. Byron, Poetics and History
    JANE STABLER

53. Religion, Toleration, and British Writing, 1790–1830
    MARK CANUEL

54. Fatal Women of Romanticism
    ADRIANA CRACIUN

55. Knowledge and Indifference in English Romantic Prose
    TIM MILNES

56. Mary Wollstonecraft and the Feminist Imagination
    BARBARA TAYLOR

57. Romanticism, Maternity and the Body Politic
    JULIE KIPP

58. Romanticism and Animal Rights
    DAVID PERKINS

59. Georgic Modernity and British Romanticism: Poetry and the Mediation of History
    KEVIS GOODMAN

60. Literature, Science and Exploration in the Romantic Era: Bodies of Knowledge
    TIMOTHY FULFORD, DEBBIE LEE AND PETER J. KITSON

61. Romantic Colonization and British Anti-Slavery
    DEIRDRE COLEMAN

62. Anger, Revolution, and Romanticism
    ANDREW M. STAUFFER

63. Shelley and the Revolutionary Sublime
    CIAN DUFFY

64. Fictions and Fakes: Forging Romantic Authenticity, 1760–1845
    MARGARET RUSSETT

65. Early Romanticism and Religious Dissent
    DANIEL E. WHITE

66. The Invention of Evening: Perception and Time in Romantic Poetry
   CHRISTOPHER R. MILLER

67. Wordsworth's Philosophic Song
   SIMON JARVIS

68. Romanticism and the Rise of the Mass Public
   ANDREW FRANTA

69. Writing against Revolution: Literary Conservatism in Britain, 1790–1832
   KEVIN GILMARTIN

70. Women, Sociability and Theatre in Georgian London
   GILLIAN RUSSELL

71. The Lake Poets and Professional Identity
   BRIAN GOLDBERG

72. Wordsworth Writing
   ANDREW BENNETT

73. Science and Sensation in Romantic Poetry
   NOEL JACKSON

74. Advertising and Satirical Culture in the Romantic Period
   JOHN STRACHAN

75. Romanticism and the Painful Pleasures of Modern Life
   ANDREA K. HENDERSON

76. Balladeering, Minstrelsy, and the Making of British Romantic Poetry
   MAUREEN N. MCLANE

77. Romanticism and Improvisation, 1750–1850
   ANGELA ESTERHAMMER

78. Scotland and the Fictions of Geography: North Britain, 1760–1830
   PENNY FIELDING

79. Wordsworth, Commodification and Social Concern: The Poetics of Modernity
   DAVID SIMPSON

80. Sentimental Masculinity and the Rise of History, 1790–1890
   MIKE GOODE

81. Fracture and Fragmentation in British Romanticism
   ALEXANDER REGIER

82. Romanticism and Music Culture in Britain, 1770–1840: Virtue and Virtuosity
   GILLEN D'ARCY WOOD